PAS

MW00473858

GALATIANS

and

EPHESIANS
(In The Heavenlies)

GALATIANS

and

EPHESIANS

(In The Heavenlies)

by H. A. IRONSIDE

LOIZEAUX BROTHERS

Neptune, New Jersey

FIRST EDITION, GALATIANS 1941
FIRST EDITION, EPHESIANS 1937

COMBINED EDITION 1981
THIRD PRINTING, NOVEMBER 1985

PUBLISHED BY LOIZEAUX BROTHERS, INC.
*A Nonprofit Organization, Devoted to the
Lord's Work and to the Spread of His Truth*

ISBN 0-87213-397-4
PRINTED IN THE UNITED STATES OF AMERICA

PREFATORY NOTE

The messages that follow were given in the Moody Church, Chicago, as a series, and are now published in the hope that they may prove helpful to some who have been confused regarding law and grace.

They are not intended for the learned, or for theologians, but for the common people, who value plain unfoldings of the Word of God.

H. A. Ironside.

CONTENTS

GALATIANS

CONTENTS

EPHESIANS

CONTENTS

CHAPTER ONE

INTRODUCTION

(Gal. 1: 1-5)

"Paul, an apostle (not of men, neither by man, but by Jesus Christ, and God the Father, who raised Him from the dead;) and all the brethren which are with me, unto the churches of Galatia: Grace be to you and peace from God the Father, and from our Lord Jesus Christ, who gave Himself for our sins, that He might deliver us from this present evil world, according to the will of God and our Father: to whom be glory for ever and ever. Amen."

THE epistle to the Galatians links very intimately with that to the Romans. There seem to be good reasons for believing that both of these letters were written at about the same time, probably from Corinth while Paul was ministering in that great city. In Romans we have the fullest, the most complete opening up of the gospel of the grace of God that we get anywhere in the New Testament. In the letter to the Galatians we have that glorious gospel message defended against those who were seeking to substitute legality for grace. There are many expressions in the two letters that are very similar. Both, as also the epistle to the Hebrews, are based

9

upon one Old Testament text found in chapter 2 of the book of Habakkuk: "The just shall live by faith." May I repeat what I have mentioned in my Lectures on Romans and also my Notes on Hebrews? In the epistle to the Romans the emphasis is put upon the first two words. How shall men be just with God? The answer is, *"The just* shall live by faith." But if one has been justified by faith how is he maintained in that place before God? The answer is given in the epistle to the Galatians, and here the emphasis is upon the next two words, "The just *shall live* by faith." But what is that power by which men are made just and by which they live? The epistle to the Hebrews answers that by putting the emphasis upon the last two words of the same text, "The just shall live *by faith.*" So we may see that these three letters really constitute a very remarkable trio, and in spite of all that many scholars have written to the contrary, personally I am absolutely convinced that the three are from the same human hand, that of the apostle Paul. I have given my reasons for this view in my book on the Hebrews, so need not go into that here.

Now something of the reasons for the writing of this letter. Paul had labored in Galatia on two distinct occasions. A third time he was minded to go there, but the Spirit of God plainly indicated that it was not His will and led him elsewhere, eventually over to Europe. In chapters 13 and 14 of Acts we read of Paul's ministry in Antioch of Pisidia, in Iconium, in Lystra, and Derbe. While Antioch is said to be in Pisidia and these other three cities are located in Lycaonia, according to the best records we have, both the provinces of Pisidia and Lycaonia were united to Galatia at this time, so that these were really the cities of Galatia where Paul labored and where God wrought so mightily. The inhabitants of Galatia are the same people racially as the ancient inhabitants of Ireland, Wales, and the Highlands of Scotland, also of France and northern Spain, the Gauls. Galatia is really the country of the Gauls, and those deep emotional feelings that characterize the races I have mentioned, the mystical Scots, the warm-hearted Welsh, the volatile French, and the brilliant, energetic Irish, were manifested in these Gauls of old. They spread from Galatia over into western Europe and settled France and northern Spain, and then came over to the British Isles. As many of us are somewhat linked with these different groups which we have mentioned, we should have a special interest in the epistle to the Galatians, which, by the way, is the death-blow to so-called British-Israelism. The Gauls were Gentiles, not Israelites.

When Paul first went in among them they were

all idolators, but through the ministry of the Word he was used to bring many of them to a saving knowledge of the Lord Jesus Christ, and they became deeply devoted to the man who had led them to know the Lord Jesus Christ as their Saviour. It was a wonderful thing to them to be brought out of the darkness of heathenism into the glorious light and liberty of the gospel. But sometimes when people accept the gospel message with great delight and enthusiasm, they have to go through very severe testings afterward, and so it proved in the case of the Galatians. After Paul had left them there came down from Judea certain men claiming to be sent out by James and the apostolic band at Jerusalem, who told the Galatians that unless they kept the law of Moses, observed the covenant of circumcision, and the different holy days of the Jewish economy and the appointed seasons, they could not be saved. This so stirred the apostle Paul when he learned of it that he sought on a second visit to deliver these people from that legality. But some way or another there is something about error when once it grips the minds of people that makes it assume an importance in their minds that the truth itself never had. That is a singular thing. One may be going on with the truth of God in a calm, easy way, and then he gets hold of something erroneous, and he pushes that thing to the very limit. We have often seen this demonstrated.

I refer here only to false teaching. I do not know the names of the men who came into Galatia to seek to turn the Galatians away from the truth of the gospel as set forth by the apostle Paul, but I do know what their teaching was. They were substituting law for grace, they were turning the hearts and minds of these earnest Christians away from their glorious liberty in Christ, and bringing them into bondage to legal rites and ceremonies. In order to do this it was necessary for them to try to shake the confidence of the people in their great teacher who had led them to Christ, the apostle Paul himself, and so they called in question his authority. Their attack was directed against his apostleship, nor did they hesitate to impugn his integrity.

They wormed their way into the confidence of the believers by undermining their faith in the man who had led them to Christ, hoping thereby that they would break down their reliance upon the gospel of the grace of God and substitute legal observances in its place.

When Paul heard this he was deeply grieved. With him, doctrine was not simply a matter of views. It was not a question of maintaining his own position at all costs. He realized that men are sanctified by the truth of God, and that on

the other hand they are demoralized by error, and
so to him it was a matter of extreme importance
that his converts should cling to that truth which
edifies and leads on in the ways that be in Christ.
When this news of their defection came to him
he sat down and wrote this letter. He did not do
what he generally did. We have no other instance
in the New Testament, so far as I know, of Paul
writing a letter with his own hand. Ordinarily
he dictated his letters to a secretary who wrote
for him. They had a form of shorthand in those
days, and copies have come down to us, so that
we may see how they worked. And then these
letters were properly prepared and sent out by
his different amanuenses. But on this occasion
he was so stirred, so deeply moved, that apparently he could not wait for an amanuensis. Instead, he called for parchment, pen, and ink, and
sat down and with nervous hand wrote this entire letter. He says at the close of it, "You see
with what large characters I have written you
with mine own hand." That is the correct translation of his words. Paul evidently had something the matter with his eyes, and so could not
see very well, and like a partially blind person he
took his pen and with large, nervous characters
filled up the parchment, and it looked like a long
letter. He then hurried it off to Galatia, hoping
it would be used of God to recover these people

from the errors into which they had fallen. In some respects it is the most interesting of all his letters, for it is so self-revealing. It is as though he opens a window into his own heart, that we may look into the very soul of the man and see the motives that dominated and controlled him.

The letter itself is simple in structure. Instead of breaking it up into a great many small sections, I look at it as having three great divisions.

Chapters 1 and 2—Personal
       ,,   3 and 4—Doctrinal
       ,,   5 and 6—Practical

If we once have these firmly fixed in our minds we shall never forget them. The subject of the letter is "Law and Grace." The way the apostle unfolds it is this: Chapters 1 and 2 are personal. In these chapters he is largely dealing with his own personal experiences. He shows how he, at one time a rigid, legalistic Jew, had been brought into the knowledge of the grace of God, and how he had had to defend that position against legalists. Chapters 3 and 4 are doctrinal. In these chapters, the very heart of the letter, he opens up, as in the epistle to the Romans, the great truth of salvation by grace alone. Chapters 5 and 6 are practical. They show us the moral and ethical considerations that result from a knowledge of salvation by free grace. These divisions are very simple.

We turn now to consider the introduction to the letter in the personal portion. The first three verses constitute the apostolic salutation: "Paul, an apostle." Go over the other letters, and you will find that he never refers to himself as "apostle" unless writing to some people where his apostleship has been called in question, or where he has some great doctrine to unfold that people are not likely to accept unless they realize that he had a definite commission to make it known. He evidently prefers to speak of himself as "the servant of Jesus Christ," and that word "servant" means a bondman, one bought and paid for. Paul loved to think of that. He had been bought and paid for by the precious blood of Christ, and so he was Christ's bondman. But on this occasion he saw the necessity of emphasizing his apostleship because great truths were in question, and they were so intimately linked with his personal commission from God that it was necessary to stress the fact that he was a definitely appointed messenger. The word "apostle," after all, really means "messenger," or "minister," but is used in a professional sense in connection with the twelve who were the apostles particularly to the Jews, though also to the Gentiles, and then of Paul himself, who was pre-eminently the apostle to the Gentiles, and yet always went first to the Jews in every place where he labored.

Paul was an apostle, "not of men, neither by man." I think he had special reason for writing like this. His detractors said, "Where did he get his apostleship? Where did he get his commission? Not from Peter, not from John. Where did he get his authority?" Oh, he says, I glory in the fact that I did not get anything from man. What I have received I received directly from heaven. I am not an apostle of men nor by means of man. It was not men originally having authority who conferred authority upon me, it was not a school, or a bishop, or a board of bishops, at Jerusalem, that conferred this authority on me. "Not *of* men, neither *by* man." Even though God appointed me my authority was not conferred of man. St. Jerome says, "Really there are four classes of ministry in the professing Christian Church. First, there are those sent neither from men, nor through men, but directly from God." And then he points out that this was true of the prophets of the Old Testament dispensation. They were not commissioned by men, neither authorized by men, but they were commissioned directly from God, and of course this is true of the apostle Paul. "Then secondly," Jerome says, "there are those who get their commissions from God and through man, as for instance a man feels distinctly called of God to preach, and he is examined by his brethren and they are satisfied that he is called to preach, and so commend him to the work, perhaps by the laying on of hands. And so he is a servant of God, a minister of God, from God and through man. Then in the third class there are those who have their commissions from man, but not from God. These are the men who have chosen the Christian ministry as a profession; perhaps they never have been born again, but having chosen the ministry as a profession they apply to the bishop, or presbytery, or church, to ordain them." But as Spurgeon said, "Ordination can do nothing for a man who has not received his call from God. It is simply a matter of laying empty hands on an empty head." The man goes out heralded as a minister, but he is not God's minister. And then Jerome says, "There is a fourth class. There are men who pose as Christ's ministers, and have received their authority neither from God nor from man, but they are simply free-lances. You have to take their own word for it that they are definitely appointed. Nobody else has been able to recognize any evidence of it." Paul was in the first class. He had received his commission directly from God, and no man had anything to do with even confirming it. But what about the saints at Antioch laying hands on him when he and

Barnabas were to preach to the Gentiles? you may ask. That was not a human confirmation of his apostleship because he went there as an apostle of the Lord.

How did Paul get his commission? He tells us in chapter 26 of the book of Acts. When he fell stricken on the Damascus road the risen Christ appeared to him, and said to him, "I am Jesus whom thou persecutest. But rise, and stand upon thy feet: for I have appeared unto thee for this purpose, to make thee a minister and a witness both of these things which thou hast seen, and of those things in the which I will appear unto thee; delivering thee from the people, and from the Gentiles, unto whom now I send thee, to open their eyes, and to turn them from darkness to light, and from the power of Satan unto God, that they may receive forgiveness of sins, and inheritance among them which are sanctified by faith that is in Me" (vers. 15-18). Paul says that is where he got his commission. "Whereupon, O King Agrippa, I was not disobedient unto the heavenly vision" (ver. 19), but in accord with his divinely-given instructions he went forth to teach at "Damascus and at Jerusalem, and throughout all the coasts of Judea, and then to the Gentiles, that they should repent and turn to God, and do works meet for repentance" (ver. 20). So Paul was an apostle "not of men, neither by man, but by Jesus Christ, and God the Father, who raised Him from the dead."

I think he had special reason for emphasizing the resurrection. There were those who said, "Paul cannot be an apostle, because he never saw the Lord Jesus. He was not one of the twelve, he was not instructed by Christ. How then can he rightly appropriate to himself the name of an apostle?" He says, "Have not I seen Jesus Christ? I saw Him as none of the rest did. I saw Him in the glory as the risen One, and heard His voice from heaven, and received my commission from His lips." That is why in one place he calls his message the "glorious gospel of the blessed God." That might be translated, "The gospel of the glory of the happy God." God is so happy now that the sin question has been settled and He can send the message of His grace into all the world, and it is "the gospel of the glory of the happy God" because it is from the glory.

And then Paul links others with himself. He was not alone but was always glad to recognize his fellow-workers, and so says, "All the brethren which are with me, unto the churches of Galatia: Grace be to you and peace from God the Father, and from our Lord Jesus Christ." "Grace" was the Greek greeting; "Peace" was the Hebrew greeting. Paul glories in the fact that the middle wall of partition between Jew and Gentile has been broken down in the new creation, and so brings these two greetings together. How beautifully they fit with the Christian revelation. It is not the grace that saves, but the grace that keeps. It is not peace *with* God, which was made by the blood of His cross and which was their's already, but the peace *of* God which they were so liable to forfeit if they got out of communion with Him.

Then in verses 4 and 5 he goes on to emphasize the work of our Lord Jesus. Let us consider these words very thoughtfully, very tenderly, very meditatively. "Our Lord Jesus Christ, who gave Himself for our sins." Oh, that we might never forget what Christ has suffered for our sakes! "Who gave Himself." To whom does the pronoun refer? The One who was the Eternal Son of the Father, who was with the Father before all worlds, and yet who stooped in infinite grace to become Man. As Man He did not cease to be God; He was God and Man in one glorious Person, and therefore abounding in merit so that He could pay the mighty debt that we owed to God. He settled the sin question for us as no one else could. The little hymn says:

> "No angel could our place have taken,
> Highest of the high though he;
> The loved One, on the cross forsaken,
> Was one of the Godhead Three!"

Of all men it is written, "None of them can by any means redeem his brother, nor give to God a ransom for him: for the redemption of their soul is too costly; let it alone for ever" (Ps. 49: 7, 8). But here is One who became Man to redeem our soul: "The Son of Man came not to be ministered unto, but to minister, and to give His life a ransom for many" (Matt. 20: 28).

"Who gave Himself." Think of it! When we call to mind our own sinfulness, the corruption of our hearts, the wickedness of our lips, when we think of what our sins deserve and how utterly helpless we were to deliver ourselves from the justly deserved judgment, and then we think of Him, the Holy One, the Just One,

> "The Sovereign of the skies,
>   Who stooped to man's estate and dust
> That guilty worms might rise,"

how our hearts ought to go out to Him in love and worship. I think it was hard for Paul to keep the tears back when he wrote this, "Who gave Himself for our sins." We would like to forget those sins, and yet it is well sometimes that we should remember the hole of the pit from which we were digged, for our sins will be the black background that will display the glorious jewel of divine grace for all eternity. Not only that He might save us from eternal judgment, not only that we might never be lost in that dark,

dark pit of woe of which Scripture speaks so solemnly and seriously, but that even here we may be altogether for Himself, "that He might deliver us from this present evil world." Man has made it wicked by his sinfulness, his disloyalty to God, but we who are saved are to be delivered from it, that we might be set apart to God.

"According to the will of God and our Father." In these words he sums up the purpose of our Lord's coming into the world. He came to die for our sins that we might be delivered from the power of sin and be altogether for Himself. "To whom be glory for ever and ever. Amen." This forms the salutation, and the introduction follows.

CHAPTER TWO

NO OTHER GOSPEL

(Gal. 1: 6-9)

"I marvel that ye are so soon removed from Him that called you into the grace of Christ unto another gospel: which is not another; but there be some that trouble you, and would pervert the gospel of Christ. But though we, or an angel from heaven, preach any other gospel unto you than that which we have preached unto you, let him be accursed. As we said before, so say I now again, If any man preach any other gospel unto you than that ye have received, let him be accursed."

THOSE are very strong words, and I can quite understand that some people may have difficulty in reconciling them with the grace that is in Christ Jesus. Twice the apostle pronounces a curse upon those who preach any other gospel than that which he himself had proclaimed to these Galatians when they were poor sinners, and which had been used of God to lead them to the Lord Jesus Christ. Some might ask, Is this the attitude of the Christian minister, to go about cursing people who do not agree with him? No, and it certainly was not Paul's attitude. Why, then, does he use such strong language? It is not that he himself is invoking a curse upon anyone, but he is declaring, by the inspiration of the Holy Spirit of God, that divine judgment must fall upon any one who seeks to pervert the gospel of Christ or to turn people away from that gospel. In other words, the apostle Paul realizes the fact that the gospel is God's only message to lost man, and that to pervert that gospel, to offer people something else in place of it, for a man to attempt to foist upon them an imitation gospel is to put in jeopardy the souls of those who listen to him. Our Lord Jesus Christ emphasized this when He pointed out that those men who taught people to trust in their own efforts for salvation were blind leaders of the blind, and that eventually both leader and led would fall into the ditch. It is a very serious thing to mislead men along spiritual lines; it is a terrible thing to give wrong direction when souls are seeking the way to heaven.

I remember reading a story of a woman who with her little babe was on a train going up through one of the eastern states. It was a very wintry day. Outside a terrific storm was blowing, snow was falling, and sleet covered everything. The train made its way along slowly because of the ice on the tracks and the snow-plow went ahead to clear the way. The woman seemed very nervous. She was to get off at a small station where she would be met by some friends, and she said to the conductor, "You will be sure and let me know the right station; won't you?"

"Certainly," he said, "just remain here until I tell you the right station."

She sat rather nervously, and again spoke to the conductor, "You won't forget me?"

"No; just trust me. I will tell you when to get off."

A commercial man sat across the aisle, and he leaned over and said, "Pardon me, but I see you are rather nervous about getting off at your station. I know this road well. Your station is the first stop after such-and-such a city. These conductors are very forgetful, they have a great many things to attend to, and he may overlook your request, but I will see that you get off all right. I will help you with your baggage."

"Oh, thank you," she said. And she leaned back greatly relieved.

By-and-by the name of the city she mentioned was called, and he leaned over and said, "The next stop will be yours."

As they drew near to the station she looked around anxiously for the conductor, but he did not come. "You see," said the man, "he has forgotten you. I will get you off," and he helped her with her baggage, and as the conductor had not come to open the door, he opened it, and when the train stopped he stepped off, lifted her bag, helped her off, and in a moment the train moved on.

A few minutes later the conductor came and looking all about said, "Why, that is strange! There was a woman here who wanted to get off at this station. I wonder where she is."

The commercial man spoke up and said, "Yes, you forgot her, but I saw that she got off all right."

"Got off where?" the conductor asked.

"When the train stopped."

"But that was not a station! That was an emergency stop! I was looking after that woman. Why, man, you have put her off in a wild country district in the midst of all this storm where there will be nobody to meet her!"

There was only one thing to do, and although it was a rather dangerous thing, they had to reverse the engine and go back a number of miles, and then they went out to look for the woman. They searched and searched, and finally somebody stumbled upon her, and there she was frozen on the ground with her little dead babe in her arms. She was the victim of wrong information.

If it is such a serious thing to give people wrong information in regard to temporal things, what about the man who misleads men and women in regard to the great question of the salvation of their immortal souls? If men believe a false gospel, if they put their trust in something that is contrary to the Word of God, their loss will be not for time only but for eternity.

And that is why the apostle Paul, speaking by the inspiration of the Holy Ghost, uses such strong language in regard to the wickedness, the awfulness of misleading souls as to eternal things. These Galatians were living in their sins, they were living in idolatry, in the darkness of pagan superstition, when Paul came to them and preached the glorious gospel that tells how "Christ died for our sins . . . and that He was buried, and that He rose again the third day according to the Scriptures" (1 Cor. 15: 3, 4). They were saved, for you know the gospel of the grace of God works. It is wonderful when you see a man who has been living in all kinds of sin, and God by the Holy Spirit brings him to repentance and leads him to believe the gospel; everything changes, old habits fall off like withered leaves, a new life is his. He has power to overcome sin, he has hope of heaven, and he has assurance of salvation. That is what God's gospel gives.

These Galatians, after Paul had been used to bring them into the liberty of grace, were being misled by false teachers, men who had come down from Judea, who professed to be Christians but had never been delivered from legality. They said to these young Christians, "You have only a smattering of the gospel; you need to add to this message that you have received, the teaching of the law of Moses, 'Except ye be circumcised after the manner of Moses, ye cannot be saved' " (Acts 15: 1). Thus they threw them back on self-effort, turning their eyes away from Christ and fixing them upon themselves and their ability to keep the law. Paul says, "This thing will ruin men who depend upon their own self-efforts to get to heaven; they will miss the gates of pearl." No matter how earnest they are, if they depend upon their own works they will never be partakers of the inheritance of the saints in light. So far as these Galatians who were really born again were concerned, this false doctrine could not be the means of their eternal perdition, yet it would rob them of the joy and gladness that the Christian ought to have. How could any one have peace who believed that salvation depended on his own efforts? How could he be certain that he had paid enough attention to the demands of the law or ritual? It is the gospel of the grace of God which believed gives men full assurance. And so the apostle Paul was very indignant to find people bringing in something else instead of the gospel of the grace of God, and he is surprised that these Galatians who rejoiced in the liberty of Christ should be so ready to go back to the bondage of law.

"I marvel," he says, "that ye are so soon removed from Him that called you into the grace of Christ unto another gospel." He marvels that they should so soon be turned aside from the message of grace. What is grace? It is God's free, unmerited favor to those who have merited the very opposite. These Galatians, like ourselves, had merited eternal judgment, they deserved to be shut away from the presence of God forever, as you and I deserve to be, but through the preaching of grace they had been brought to see that God has a righteousness which He offers freely to unrighteous sinners who put their faith in His blessed Son. But now, occupied with legal ceremonies, laws, rules, and regulations they had lost the joy of grace and had become taken up with self-effort. Paul says, "I cannot understand it," and yet after all, it is very natural for these poor hearts of ours. How often you see people who seem to be wonderfully converted, and then they lose it all as they get occupied with all kinds of questions, rules, ceremonies and ritual. God would have each heart occupied with His blessed Son, "in whom dwelleth all the treasures of wisdom and knowledge."

"I marvel that ye are so soon removed from Him that called you into the grace of Christ unto another gospel." In our Authorized Version we read, "Another gospel," and then verse 7 continues, "Which is not another." That sounds like a contradiction, but there are two different Greek words used here. The first is the word *"heteron,"* something contrary to sound teaching, something different. The apostle says, "I marvel that ye are so soon removed from Him that called you into the grace of Christ to a *different* gospel." This mixture of law and grace is not God's gospel, not something to be added to what you have already received, not something to complete the gospel message; it is opposed to that, it is a heterodox message, one opposed to sound teaching. There is only one gospel.

Go through the Book from Genesis to Revelation and there is only one gospel—that first preached in the Garden of Eden when the message went forth that the Seed of the woman should bruise Satan's head. That was the gospel, salvation through the coming Christ, the Son of God born of a woman. It is the same gospel preached to Abraham. We read in this Book that the gospel was before preached to Abraham. God took him out one night and said, "Look at the stars; count them."

And Abraham said, "I cannot count them."

He said, "Look at the dust of the earth, and count the dust."

Abraham said, "I cannot count it."

"Well, think of the sand at the seashore; count the grains of sand."

And Abraham said, "I cannot count them."

And God answered, "In thy seed shall all the nations of the earth be blessed" (Gen. 22:18). "And I will make thy seed as the dust of the earth" (Gen. 13:16). Abraham might have said, "Impossible! My seed! I have no child, and I am already a man advanced in years, and my wife is an elderly woman. Impossible!" But God had given the word, "In thy Seed (which is Christ) shall all the nations of the earth be blessed." That was the gospel—all nations to be blessed through Christ, the Seed of Abraham. And "Abraham believed God, and it was counted unto him for righteousness" (Rom. 4:3). He was justified by faith because he believed the gospel. It is the same gospel that we find running through the book of Psalms. David, stained with sin, the twin sins of adultery and murder, cries, "Thou desirest not sacrifice; else would I give it: Thou delightest not in burnt-offering. The sacrifices of God are a broken spirit: a broken and a contrite heart, O God, Thou wilt not despise" (Ps. 51:16, 17). "Purge me with hyssop, and I shall be clean: wash me, and I shall be whiter than snow" (Ps. 51:7). And there is only one way a poor sinner can be purged, and that is by the precious blood of the Lord Jesus Christ. David looked on in faith to the Christ, the Son of God, and his hope was in this one gospel.

It is the gospel that Isaiah proclaimed when he

looked down through the ages and cried, "He was wounded for our transgressions, He was bruised for our iniquities: the chastisement of our peace was upon Him; and with His stripes we are healed" (Isa. 53:5). It was the gospel that Jeremiah preached when he said, "This is His name whereby He shall be called, the Lord our Righteousness" (Jer. 23:6). It was the gospel of Zechariah, "Awake, O sword, against My Shepherd, and against the Man that is My Fellow, saith the Lord of hosts: smite the Shepherd, and the sheep shall be scattered" (Zech. 13:7).

This was the gospel that John the Baptist preached. He came preaching the gospel of the kingdom, and as he pointed to Jesus he said, "Behold the Lamb of God, which taketh away the sin of the world" (John 1:29). And this was the gospel that Jesus Himself proclaimed when He said, "For God so loved the world, that He gave His only begotten Son, that whosoever believeth in Him should not perish, but have everlasting life" (John 3:16). This was Peter's gospel when he spoke of Jesus, saying, "To Him give all the prophets witness, that through His name whosoever believeth in Him shall receive remission of sins" (Acts 10:43). This was the gospel of the apostle John who said, "If we walk in the light, as He is in the light, we have fellowship one with another, and the blood of Jesus Christ His Son

cleanseth us from all sin" (1 John 1:7). This
was the gospel of the apostle James who said, "Of
His own will begat He us with the word of truth"
(Jas. 1:18). This is the gospel that they will
celebrate through all the ages to come as millions
and millions of redeemed sing their song of
praise, "Unto Him that loveth us, and loosed us
from our sins in His own blood" (Rev. 1:5).
And this was Paul's gospel when he declared,
"Through this Man is preached unto you the forgiveness of sins: and by Him all that believe are
justified from all things" (Acts 13:38, 39). One
gospel! And there is no other!

I have often felt sorry when I have heard some
of my brethren whom I have learned to love in
the truth, and with whom I hold a great deal in
common, try to explain some apparent differences
throughout the gospel centuries and talk as
though there are a number of different gospels.
Some say when Christ was on earth and in the
early part of the book of Acts, they preached the
gospel of the kingdom but did not know the grace
of God. I wonder whether they remember the
words of John 3:16 and John 1:29, and recollect
that it was the Lord who said, "Verily, verily, I
say unto you, He that heareth My word, and believeth on Him that sent Me, hath everlasting life,
and shall not come into condemnation; but is
passed from death unto life" (John 5:24). How

short our memories are sometimes, if we say that Jesus was not preaching grace when here on earth when Scripture says, "The law was given by Moses, but grace and truth came by Jesus Christ" (John 1: 17). Can we say that Peter and his fellow-apostles in the early part of Acts were not preaching grace when it was Peter who declared, "To Him give all the prophets witness, that through His name whosoever believeth in Him shall receive remission of sins" (Acts 10: 43). There is only one gospel!

They say there is one gospel of the kingdom, another gospel of the grace of God, then there is the gospel of the glory, and some day there will be the everlasting gospel, and that these are all different gospels. If such statements were true, these words of Paul would fall to the ground, "If any man preach any other gospel unto you than that ye have received, let him be accursed." Someone wrote me that she was surprised that a man who ought to know better should talk about there being only one gospel. "Why," she said, "even Dr. C. I. Scofield would teach you better, because in his Bible he shows that there are four gospels." I want to read you what Dr. Scofield says, in his notes on Revelation 14: 6:

"This great theme may be summarized as follows:

"1. In itself the word gospel means good news.

"2. Four *forms* of the gospel are to be distinguished:

"(1) The gospel of the kingdom. This is the good news that God purposes to set up on the earth, in fulfilment of the Davidic Covenant, a kingdom, political, spiritual, Israelitish, universal, over which God's Son, David's heir, shall be King, and which shall be, for one thousand years, the manifestation of the righteousness of God in human affairs.

"Two *preachings* of this gospel are mentioned, one past, beginning with the ministry of John the Baptist, continued by our Lord and His disciples, and ending with the Jewish rejection of the King. The other is yet future, during the great tribulation, and immediately preceding the coming of the King in glory.

"(2) The gospel of the grace of God. This is the good news that Jesus Christ, the rejected King, has died on the cross for the sins of the world, that He was raised from the dead for our justification, and that by Him all that believe are justified from all things. This form of the gospel is described in many ways. It is the gospel 'of God' because it originates in His love; 'of Christ' because it flows from His sacrifice, and because He is the alone Object of gospel faith; of 'the grace of God' because it saves those whom the law curses; of 'the glory' because it concerns

Him who is in the glory, and who is bringing the many sons to glory; of 'our salvation' because it is the 'power of God unto salvation to every one that believeth'; of 'the uncircumcision' because it saves wholly apart from forms and ordinances; of 'peace' because through Christ it makes peace between the sinner and God, and imparts inward peace.

"(3) The everlasting gospel. This is to be preached to the earth-dwellers at the very end of the great tribulation and immediately preceding the judgment of the nations. It is neither the gospel of the kingdom, nor of grace. Though its burden is judgment, not salvation, it is good news to Israel and to those who, during the tribulation, have been saved.

"(4) That which Paul calls, 'my gospel.' This is the gospel of the grace of God in its fullest development, but includes the revelation of the result of that gospel in the outcalling of the Church, her relationships, position, privileges, and responsibility. It is the distinctive truth of Ephesians and Colossians, but interpenetrates all of Paul's writings."

These words are very clear. There is only one gospel, and that is God's good news concerning His Son; but it takes on different aspects at different times according to the circumstances and conditions in which men are found. In Old Testament times they looked on to the coming of the Saviour, but they proclaimed salvation through His atoning death. In the days of John the Baptist stress was laid upon the coming kingdom, and the King was to lay down His life. In the days of the Lord's ministry on earth He presented Himself as King, but was rejected and went to the cross, for He Himself declared that He "came not to be ministered unto, but to minister, and to give His life a ransom for many" (Matt. 20:28). During the early chapters of the book of Acts we find this gospel proclaimed to Jews and Gentiles alike, offering free salvation to all who turn to God in repentance, but when God raised up the apostle Paul, He gave him a clearer vision of the gospel than any one had yet had. He showed that not only are men forgiven through faith in our Lord Jesus Christ, but that they are justified from all things, and stand in Christ before God as part of a new creation. This is a fuller revelation of the good tidings, but the same gospel.

By-and-by, during the days of the great tribulation, the everlasting gospel will be proclaimed, telling men that the once-rejected Christ shall come again to set up His glorious kingdom, but even in that day men will be taught that salvation is through His precious blood, for as the result of that preaching a great multitude will be brought out of all kindreds and tongues who have "washed their robes, and made them white in the blood of the Lamb" (Rev. 7: 14).

Yes, there is only one gospel and if any one comes preaching any other gospel, telling you there is any other way of salvation save through the atoning work of the Lord Jesus, it is a heterodox gospel. Some such had come to Galatia and perverted the gospel of Christ, and it is this that led Paul in the intensity of his zeal for that gospel to exclaim, as guided by the Holy Spirit who inspired him, "Though we, or an angel from heaven, preach any other gospel unto you than that which we have preached unto you, let him be Anathema" (let him be devoted to judgment), if he is substituting anything for the precious gospel of the grace of God. Notice, if the angel who proclaims the everlasting gospel in the days of the great tribulation preaches any other gospel than that of salvation through faith in Christ alone, that angel comes under the curse, for Paul says, "Though an angel from heaven preach any other gospel unto you than that which we have preached unto you, let him be accursed."

Out West I often met disciples of Joseph Smith, and when I got them in a corner with the Word of God and they could not wiggle out, they would say, "Well, we have what you do not have. An angel came to Joseph Smith and gave him the book of Mormon." And so they reasoned that the

Bible is not enough, because an angel had revealed something different. I do not believe in the prophet Joseph Smith, and I do not believe that an angel ever appeared to him, unless it was in a nightmare. But if he did, then that angel was from the pit and he is under the curse, because, "Though an angel from heaven preach any other gospel unto you than that which we have preached unto you, let him be accursed." People may say, "But Paul, you are all worked up, you are losing your temper." You know, if you become very fervent for the truth, folks say you are losing your temper. If you say strong things in defense of the truth, they will declare you are unkind; but men will use very fervent language about politics and other things, and yet no one questions their loss of temper, but they think we should be very calm when people tear the Bible to pieces! If anything calls for fervent and intense feelings it is the defence of the gospel against false teaching.

Lest any one should say, "Well, Paul, you would not have written that if you had been calmer; you would not have used such strong language," Paul repeats himself in verse 9, and says, "As we said before, so say I now again, If any man preach any other gospel unto you than that ye have received, let him be Anathema." That is cool enough. He is not speaking now as one wrought up. He has had time to think it over, and has weighed his words carefully. Yes, on sober, second thought he again insists on what he declared before, that the divine judgment hangs over any man who seeks to mislead lost humanity by telling them of any other way of salvation save through the precious atoning blood of the Lord Jesus Christ.

In closing I put the question to you: On what are *you* resting your hope for eternity? Are you resting on the Lord Jesus Christ? Are you trusting the gospel of the grace of God? "By grace are ye saved through faith; and that not of yourselves: it is the gift of God" (Eph. 2:8).

CHAPTER THREE

PAUL'S CONVERSION AND APOSTLESHIP

(Gal. 1: 10-24)

"For do I now persuade men, or God? or do I seek to please men? For if I yet pleased men, I should not be the servant of Christ. But I certify you, brethren, that the gospel which was preached of me is not after man. For I neither received it of man, neither was I taught it, but by the revelation of Jesus Christ. For ye have heard of my conversation in time past in the Jews' religion, how that beyond measure I persecuted the church of God, and wasted it: and profited in the Jews' religion above many my equals in mine own nation, being more exceedingly zealous of the traditions of my fathers. But when it pleased God, who separated me from my mother's womb, and called me by His grace, to reveal His Son in me, that I might preach Him among the heathen; immediately I conferred not with flesh and blood: neither went I up to Jerusalem to them which were apostles before me; but I went into Arabia, and returned again unto Damascus. Then after three years I went up to Jerusalem to see Peter, and abode with him fifteen days. But other of the apostles saw I none, save James the Lord's brother. Now the things which I write unto you, behold, before God, I lie not. Afterwards I came into the regions of Syria and Cilicia; and was unknown by face unto the churches of Judea which were in Christ: but they had heard only, That he which persecuted us in times past now preacheth the faith which once he destroyed. And they glorified God in me."

THE apostle Paul in this section is obliged to defend his apostleship. There is something pitiable about that. He had come to these Galatians when they were heathen, when they were idolaters, and had been God's messenger to them. Through him they had been brought

to the Lord Jesus Christ. But they had fallen
under the influence of false teachers, and now
looked down upon the man who had led them to
Christ; they despised his ministry and felt they
were far better informed than he. This is not
the only time in the history of the Church that
such things have happened. Often we see young
converts happy and radiant in the knowledge of
sins forgiven, until under the influence of false
teachers they look with contempt upon those who
presented the gospel to them.

In the first place, Paul undertakes to show how
he became the apostle to the Gentiles. In verse
10 he says, "For do I now persuade men, or
God?" What does he mean by that? Do I seek
the approval of men or of God? Manifestly, of
God. The apostle Paul was not a time-server,
he was not seeking simply to please men who in a
little while would have to stand before God in
judgment, if they died in their sins. His express
purpose was to do the will of the One who had
saved him and commissioned him to preach the
gospel of His grace. So he says, "I am not
attempting to seek the approval of men, but of
God. I do not seek to please men," that is, I am
not trying to get their approbation. It is true
that in another scripture he says, "Let every one
of us please his neighbor for his good to edification" (Rom. 15: 2), but there is no contradiction

there. It is right and proper to seek in every way I can to please and help my friend, my neighbor, my brother; but on the other hand, when I attempt to preach the Word of God, I am to do it "not as pleasing men, but God, which trieth our hearts" (1 Thess. 2:4). The preacher who speaks with man's approval as his object is untrue to the commission given to him. "If I yet pleased men, I should not be the servant of Christ." He would simply be making himself the servant of men.

"But I certify you, brethren, that the gospel which was preached of me is not after man. For I neither received it of man, neither was I taught it, but by the revelation of Jesus Christ." The gospel differs from every human religious system. In some of our universities they study what is called, "The Science of Comparative Religions." The study of comparative religions is both very interesting and informative, if you consider, for instance, the great religions of the pagan world such as Buddhism, Brahmanism, Mohammedanism. They have much in common, and much in which they stand in contrast one to another. But when you take Christianity and put it in with these religions, you make a mistake; Christianity is not simply a religion, it is a divine revelation. Paul says, "I did not get my gospel from men. No man communicated it to me. I received it directly from heaven." Of course we do not all get it in this way, as a direct revelation, as Paul did, and yet, in every instance, if a man is brought to understand the truth of the gospel, it is because the Holy Spirit, who is the Spirit of wisdom and revelation in the knowledge of Christ, opens that man's heart and mind and understanding to comprehend the truth. Otherwise he would not receive it. "The natural man receiveth not the things of the Spirit of God: for they are foolishness unto him: neither can he know them, because they are spiritually discerned" (1 Cor. 2: 14), and of course the natural man is not pleased with this divine revelation. Men are pleased when the preacher glosses over their sins, when he makes excuses for their wrong-doings, when he panders to their weaknesses or flatters them as they attempt to work out a righteousness of their own. But when a man preaches the gospel of the grace of God and insists upon man's utterly lost and ruined condition, declares that he is unable to do one thing to save himself, but must be saved through the atoning death of the Lord Jesus Christ, there is nothing about that to please the natural man. It is divine grace that opens the heart to receive that revelation. That was the revelation that came to Paul.

There was a time when the apostle hated Chris-

tianity, when he did all in his power to destroy
the infant Church, and now he says to these Galatians, "Ye have heard of my conversation—that
is, my behavior—in time past in the Jews' religion, how that beyond measure I persecuted the
Church of God, and wasted it." Twice here (vers.
13, 14) he uses the expression, "The Jews' religion." The original word simply means Judaism, and is not to be confounded with the word
used in the epistle of James, "Pure religion and
undefiled before God and the Father is this, To
visit the fatherless and widows in their affliction,
and to keep himself unspotted from the world"
(James 1:27). There "religion" is used in a
proper sense, and we who are saved should be
characterized by that; but as the apostle uses the
word here it is something entirely different. The
two English words, "Jews' religion," are translated from the one Greek word which means
"Judaism." Paul hoped through that to save his
soul and gain favor with God, until through a
divine revelation he had an altogether different
conception of things. As long as he believed in
Judaism he "persecuted the Church of God, and
wasted it." One of the pitiable things that have
occurred since is that members of the professed
Church of God have turned around to persecute
the people of Judaism. Strange, this seems, when
Jesus says, "Do good to them that hate you, and

pray for them which despitefully use you, and
persecute you" (Matt. 5: 44).

Paul hated Christianity. He persecuted Christians and tried to root up Christianity from the
earth, and says that he "profited in the Jews'
religion above many my equals in mine own
nation, being more exceedingly zealous of the
traditions of my fathers." He could say, "After
the most straitest sect of our religion I lived a
Pharisee" (Acts 26: 5). Judaism was dearer than
life to him. He thought it was the only truth,
that all men, if they would know God at all, must
find Him through Judaism. He was exceedingly
zealous of the traditions of the fathers, not only
of what was written in the Bible, in the law of
Moses, what the prophets had declared, but added
to that the great body of such traditions as have
come down to the Jews of the present day in the
Talmud. He would have lived and died an advo-
cate of Judaism if it had not been for the miracle
of grace. How did it happen that this Jew who
could see nothing good in Christianity turned
about and became its greatest exponent? There
is no way of accounting for it except through the
matchless sovereign grace of God. Something
took place in that man's heart and life that
changed his entire view-point, that made him the
protagonist who devoted over thirty years of his
life to making Christ known to Jews and Gen-

tiles. He tells us what brought about the change:
"But when it pleased God, who separated me
from my mother's womb, and called me by His
grace, to reveal His Son in me, that I might
preach Him among the heathen; immediately I
conferred not with flesh and blood" (vers. 15,
16). When the appointed time came, when God
in sovereign grace said, as it were, "Arrest that
man," and stopped him on the Damascus turnpike, and when Christ in glory appeared to him,
Saul of Tarsus was brought to see that he had
been fighting against Israel's Messiah and God's
blessed Son. Then Christ was not only revealed
to him, but Christ was revealed *in* him.

We have both the objective and the subjective
sides of truth. When I as a poor sinner saw the
Lord Jesus suffering, bleeding, dying for me,
when I saw that He was "wounded for my transgressions, He was bruised for my iniquities,"
when I realized that He had been "delivered up
for my offences and raised again for my justification," when I put my heart's trust in Him,
when I believed that objective truth, then something took place within subjectively. Christ came
to dwell in my very heart. "Christ in you," says
the apostle, "the hope of glory." It pleased God
to reveal His Son not only to me but in me. I
was brought to know Him in a richer, fuller way
than I could know the dearest earthly friend. It

was no longer for Paul a matter of one religion against another. Now he had a divine commission to go forth and make known to other men the Christ who had become so real to him. So when this glorious event took place, when through God's sovereign grace he was brought to know the Lord Jesus Christ, he says, "I realized that this glorious understanding was not for me alone but that I might make Him known to others; it pleased God 'to reveal His Son in me, that I might preach Him among the heathen.'" When the Lord saved Paul He told him He had that in view.

In Acts 9, in the story of the apostle's conversion, we read that God spoke to Ananias and sent him to see Paul in the street called Straight in Damascus. He did not want to go at first, he was afraid he would be taking his life in his hands; but the Lord said unto him, "Go thy way: for he is a chosen vessel unto Me, to bear My name before the Gentiles, and kings, and the children of Israel: for I will show him how great things he must suffer for My name's sake" (Acts 9: 15, 16). So Ananias went in obedience to the vision and communicated the mind of God to him. The Lord had already said, "I have appeared unto thee for this purpose, to make thee a minister and a witness both of these things which thou hast seen, and of those things in the which

I will appear unto thee; delivering thee from the people, and from the Gentiles, unto whom now I send thee" (Acts 26: 16, 17). Pre-eminently he was the apostle to the Gentiles, but he also had a wonderful ministry for his own people, and all through his life his motto was, "To the Jew first, and also to the Greek" (Rom. 1: 16).   Into city after city he went hunting out the synagogues or finding individual Jews or groups, telling them of the great change that had come to him and pleading with them to submit to the same wonderful Saviour. When they rejected his message, he turned to the Gentiles and preached the gospel to them.

Some of these Galatians questioned whether he really was an apostle, for he never saw the Lord when He was here on earth; he did not get his commission from the twelve. He says, "No, I did not, and I glory in that I am an apostle, not of men, neither by man, but by Jesus Christ. I received my commission from heaven when I saw the risen Christ in glory and He came to make His abode in my heart. He commissioned me to go out and preach His message." "Immediately I conferred not with flesh and blood." They thought he should have gone to Jerusalem to sit down and talk the matter over with the other apostles, and find out whether they indorsed him and were prepared to ordain him to the Christian ministry, or something like that. But he says, "No, I did not seek anyone out, nor confer with any one. My commission was from heaven, to carry it out in dependence upon the living God." So he adds, "Neither went I up to Jerusalem to them which were apostles before me; but I went into Arabia, and returned again unto Damascus" (ver. 17). He did not go at the beginning to what they considered the headquarters of the Christian Church, Jerusalem, to get authorization. Instead of that he seems to have slipped away. In reading Acts we would not know this, but here he indicates that he went into Arabia Petra, and there in some quiet place, perhaps living in a cave, he spent some time waiting on God that he might have things cleared up in his own mind. He wanted time to think things out, time for God to speak to him, and in which he could speak to God. There the truth in all its fulness, its beauty, its glory, opened up to him. It was not there that he had the revelation of the Body of Christ. He received that on the Damascus turnpike when the Lord said to him, "Saul, Saul, why persecutest thou Me?" What a revelation was that of the Body that all believers on earth constitute! They are so intimately linked with their glorious Head in heaven that one member cannot be touched without affecting their Head.

There was a great deal he needed to understand, and so into the wilderness he went.

Have you ever noticed how many of God's beloved servants had their finishing courses in the university of the wilderness? When God wanted to fit Moses to be the leader of His people He sent him to the wilderness. He had gone through all the Egyptian schools, and thought he was ready to be the deliverer of God's people. When he left the university of Egypt he may have said, "Now I am ready to undertake my great life-work." But, immediately, he started killing Egyptians and hiding them in the sand, and God says, "You are not ready yet, Moses; you want a post-graduate course." He was forty years learning the wisdom of Egypt, and forty years forgetting it and learning the wisdom of God, and finally, when he received his post-graduate degree he was sent of God to deliver His people.

Elijah had his time in the wilderness. David had his time there. Oh, those years in the wilderness when hunted by King Saul like a partridge on the mountainside. They were used to help fit him for his great work. And then think of our blessed Lord Himself! He was baptized in the Jordan, presenting Himself there in accordance with the Word of God as the One who was to go to the cross to fulfil all righteousness on behalf of needy sinners, and the Holy Spirit like a dove descended upon Him. He then went into the wilderness for forty days, and prayed and fasted in view of the great ministry upon which He was to enter. Then He passed through that serious temptation of Satan, emerging triumphant, and went forth to preach the gospel of the kingdom. Now here is this man who hated His name, who detested Christianity, but after having had a sight of the risen Christ he goes off into the wilderness for a period· of meditation, prayer, and instruction before he commences his great work. Then he says he "returned again unto Damascus," and he preached Christ in the synagogues "that He is the Son of God." If you read carefully in the book of Acts you will see that it was not until after the conversion of Paul that any one preached Christ as the Son of God. I know the expression, "Thy holy Child Jesus," is used, but the better rendering is "Servant." Peter preached Jesus as the Messiah, the Servant, but Paul began the testimony that Jesus was in very truth the Son of God. When the Lord Jesus interrogated Peter, "Whom say ye that I am?" Peter answered, "Thou art the Christ, the Son of the living God" (Matt. 16: 15, 16). But it was not yet God's time to make that known, for the message was limited, in measure, to the people of Israel in the early part of Acts. But when Saul was converted, without fear of man he preached in those very synagogues that Jesus is the Son of God and he himself now was persecuted bitterly by those who once admired him as the leader in their religious practices.

Three years went by before this man went to Jerusalem. He went from place to place and finally did go there, but not in order to be ordained or recognized as an apostle. In verse 18 he tells us why he went up, "Then after three years I went up to Jerusalem to see Peter, and abode with him fifteen days." The word "see" in the original is very interesting. It is the Greek word from which we get our English word, "history," the telling of a story, talking things over, and so Paul says that after three years he went up to Jerusalem to relate his history to Peter, to talk things over with him, to tell him what the Lord had done. What a wonderful meeting that was! It would have been wonderful, unnoticed in a corner of the room, to have heard the conversation. Peter who had known the Lord, who had denied the Lord, who had been so wonderfully restored, who preached with such power on the day of Pentecost and was used so mightily to open the door to the Jews and then to the Gentiles, Peter told his story and Paul told his. And when they got through I imagine Peter would say, "Well, Paul, you have the same message I have, but I think the Lord has given you more than He has given to me, and I want to give you the right hand of fellowship. I rejoice in your ministry, and we can go on together proclaiming this glad, glorious gospel." Fifteen days of wonderful fellowship!

As to the rest of the apostles Paul says, "But other of the apostles saw I none, save James the Lord's brother." We are not certain which James he means. He may be the man referred to as James the son of Alphæus, the cousin of the Lord, who would be spoken of as His brother. My personal opinion is that he is the James who occupies so large a place in the book of Acts— James who was the brother of our Lord Jesus Christ, who did not believe while the Saviour was here on earth, but was brought to believe in Him in resurrection, and who led the Church of God in Jerusalem. Paul saw him, but from none of them did he get any special indorsement or authorization. He met them on common ground. They were apostles of the Lord Jesus Christ; so was he, by divine appointment.

"Now the things which I write unto you, behold, before God, I lie not." Strange that he should have to say this! Strange that these Galatians, his own converts, should think for a moment that he might be untruthful! But when one gets under the power of false teaching, as a rule he is ready to make all kinds of charges as to the integrity, the honesty of other people. And so it is here, and the apostle has to say, "The things that I am telling you are true. I am not lying."

After returning from Jerusalem he launched out on his great missionary program. "Afterwards I came into the regions of Syria and Cilicia; and was unknown by face unto the churches of Judea which were in Christ." He had been known among other assemblies in Judaism, Jewish assemblies knew him well, but Christians in Judea, believers who had separated from Judaism, had never seen him. "But they had heard only, That he which persecuted us in times past now preacheth the faith which once he destroyed." And what power there was in that! Here was the man who had gone to all lengths to turn a man away from Christ, even attempted to compel him to blaspheme, threatened him with death if he would not repudiate the gospel of the Lord Jesus Christ. Now this great change has come, and word is going through the churches, "The great persecutor has become an evangelist; he is no longer our enemy, but is preaching to others the same faith that means so much to us." "And they glorified God in me." Truly, Paul's conversion was a divine, sovereign work of grace, and praise and glory redounded to the One who had chosen, commissioned, and sent him forth.

The abundant resultant fruit was to His glory. Nothing gives such power to the ministry of Christ as genuine conversion. I do not understand how any man can presume to be a minister who does not know the reality of a personal conversion and the truth of the gospel.

That gospel has lost none of its power. It can work just as wonderful miracles today for men who will put their trust in the Lord Jesus Christ. Have you trusted Him? Have you believed in Him? Is He your Saviour? Do you know what it means to be converted? Can you say, "Thank God, my soul is saved; God has revealed His Son in me"?

CHAPTER FOUR

THE GOSPEL AS MINISTERED TO JEW AND GENTILE

(Gal. 2: 1-10)

"Then fourteen years after I went up again to Jerusalem, with Barnabas, and took Titus with me also. And I went up by revelation, and communicated unto them that gospel which I preach among the Gentiles, but privately to them which were of reputation, lest by any means I should run, or had run, in vain. But neither Titus, who was with me, being a Greek, was compelled to be circumcised: and that because of false brethren unawares brought in, who came in privily to spy out our liberty which we have in Christ Jesus, that they might bring us into bondage: to whom we gave place by subjection, no, not for an hour; that the truth of the gospel might continue with you. But of these who seemed to be somewhat, (whatsoever they were, it maketh no matter to me: God accepteth no man's person:) for they who seemed to be somewhat in conference added nothing to me: but contrariwise, when they saw that the gospel of the uncircumcision was committed unto me, as the gospel of the circumcision was unto Peter; (for He that wrought effectually in Peter to the apostleship of the circumcision, the same was mighty in me toward the Gentiles;) and when James, Cephas, and John, who seemed to be pillars, perceived the grace that was given unto me, they gave to me and Barnabas the right hands of fellowship; that we should go unto the heathen, and they unto the circumcision. Only they would that we should remember the poor; the same which I also was forward to do."

IN this second chapter Paul tells of another visit to Jerusalem, a very important one, referred to in Acts 15. "Fourteen years after I went up again to Jerusalem with Barnabas, and took Titus with me also." This was after certain persons came from James to Antioch, where the apostle was laboring, and insisted upon things that are mentioned in this letter—that the Gentile believers must be subjected to Jewish rites and ceremonies, that they must be circumcised, must keep the law of Moses, or they could not be saved. When Paul came in contact with them he waited until he had a definite revelation commanding him to go to Jerusalem. He says, "I went up by revelation." He did not go alone; he took Barnabas with him.

Barnabas had come from Jerusalem to find him in Tarsus, to persuade him to go to Antioch and assist in the ministry there. In the beginning it was Barnabas who was the leader, and Paul was the follower. But as time went on Barnabas took the lower place and Paul came to the front. With Barnabas it was a case of, "He must increase, but I must decrease." We read elsewhere of him, "He was a good man, and full of the Holy Ghost and of faith" (Acts 11: 24). Such a man can stand to see some one else honored and himself set to one side. So Barnabas stepped into the background and Paul came to the front. And then Paul says, "And took Titus with me also." Why did he mention that? Because this was a test case. These false brethren who had come down to Galatia had insisted that in Jerusalem and Judea no one would condone the idea that a

Gentile could be saved if he did not accept the sign of the Abrahamic covenant and were not circumcised. But Paul says, "I took Titus with me also," and he was a Gentile. He had never submitted to this rite, and Paul had never suggested that he should, and so he took him to Jerusalem, as it were to the headquarters of the legalists.

"And I went up by revelation, and communicated unto them that gospel which I preach among the Gentiles, but privately to them which were of reputation, lest by any means I should run, or had run, in vain." He gave them an outline of the glad tidings that he preached among the Gentiles, but he did this privately "to them that were of reputation." When we go back to Acts 15 we find that Paul called together the apostles who happened to be in Jerusalem, James, Cephas, and John, together with the elders of the Church there, and to them he told the story of his ministry, his activities. He outlined for them the contents of the gospel message which he carried to the Gentiles. As they listened they accepted him as one with themselves in the proclamation of the same gospel that they preached, even though that gospel was fuller, was richer, than that to which they had attained, for there were certain things made known to Paul that had not been revealed to them.

A few years before, God had been obliged to

give Peter a special revelation in order that he might enter into that wondrous mystery, namely, that Jew and Gentile when saved were now to be recognized as one Body in Christ. Peter never uses the term "the Body," but he does convey the same thought. Blessing for Jew and Gentile was on the ground of grace, and the Lord revealed that to him on the housetop in Joppa when he had a vision of a sheet descending unto him, "wherein were all manner of fourfooted beasts of the earth, and wild beasts, and creeping things, and fowls of the air." And a voice from heaven said, "Rise, Peter; kill, and eat." But Peter, like a good Jew, said, "Not so, Lord; for I have never eaten any thing that is common or unclean." And the Lord said to him, "What God hath cleansed, that call not thou common" (Acts 10: 12-15), thus indicating the sanctification of the Gentiles. That prepared Peter for the mission to the house of Cornelius, where he preached Christ and opened the door of the kingdom to the Gentiles, as some time before he had been used to open it to the Jews in Jerusalem. Paul and Barnabas talked with the brethren freely, declaring what God had done, and after much discussion, Peter related God's dealings in grace, and James appealed to Scripture to decide the matter as to the Gentiles. They were in happy agreement. Paul, as we have already noticed, had had a fuller,

clearer unfolding than was given to Peter, but it
was the same gospel basically, and in order to
show that there was no such thought in their
minds as to subjecting Gentiles to legal ceremonies, he says, "But neither Titus, who was
with me, being a Greek, was compelled to be circumcised." What a tremendous answer that was
to these Judaisers who were perverting these
Galatians and turning them away from the simplicity of the grace of God. They said, "A man
uncircumcised cannot be recognized as in the
family of God." Paul says, "I took Titus with
me, and talked the matter over with the elders at
Jerusalem, and they did not say one word about
making Titus submit to circumcision. He was
accepted as a fellow-Christian just as he was."
What an answer to those who were criticizing
him and misleading his converts!

"And that because of false brethren unawares
brought in, who came in privily to spy out our
liberty which we have in Christ Jesus, that they
might bring us into bondage: to whom we gave
place by subjection, no, not for an hour; that the
truth of the gospel might continue with you." To
whom does he refer? To these Judaisers who had
wormed their way privately into the assembly of
the Christians in Galatia. Paul says, "Not even
for peace sake did we submit to them, because we
would have been robbing you of your blood-

bought heritage in Christ. And so because of our love for you and our realization of the value of the grace of God, we refused even on the ground of Christian love to submit to these men. We never subjected ourselves to them."

And then in the next few verses (6-10) he tells us an interesting little story about an arrangement made while in Jerusalem as to a division of spheres of labor, an arrangement made in perfect Christian fellowship and happy harmony. "But of these who seemed to be somewhat, (whatsoever they were, it maketh no matter to me: God accepteth no man's person:) for they who seemed to be somewhat in conference added nothing to me." He could speak that way, you see, because he had received his revelation directly from heaven. It was the risen, glorified Christ who had appeared to him on the Damascus road, the same blessed Lord who had taught him during those months in Arabia, where he had retired that he might mull things over and get a clear understanding of the wonderful message he was to carry to the Gentile world. Therefore, even though he mingled with the apostles and elders who had been saved years before he knew Christ, he did not stand in awe of them. They might be recognized leaders, but God does not accept any man's person, and they were simply brothers in Christ. They had to be taught of God, and so did he. He does not ask them to confer any authority on him nor give him any special opening up of the truth that he was to proclaim to the Gentiles, though he was glad to sit down on common ground and talk things over in a brotherly way. And they said, "Why, certainly, we recognize the fact that God has raised you up for a special mission, and we have fellowship with you in that."

"But contrariwise, when they saw that the gospel of the uncircumcision was committed unto me, as the gospel of the circumcision was unto Peter;" notice the preposition rendered here "of." The Greek word may be rendered "for," and the point was this—they saw that God had given him a special revelation, a special understanding of the gospel for the Gentiles. God had fitted him by early training, and then by enlightenment after conversion, to do a work among the Gentiles which they did not feel they were fitted for. On the other hand, God had fitted Peter to do a special work among the Jews and had used him in a remarkable way on the day of Pentecost, and through the years since God had set His seal upon Peter's ministry to Israel. And so they talked things over, and they said, "It is very evident, Paul, that God has marked you out to carry the message to the Gentiles as Peter is carrying it to the Jews." He says, "For He that wrought effectually in Peter to the apostleship of the circumcision, the same was mighty in me toward the Gentiles."

"And when James, Cephas, and John, who seemed to be pillars (apparently they were the leaders), perceived the grace that was given unto me, they gave to me and Barnabas the right hands of fellowship; that we should go unto the heathen, and they unto the circumcision." Is it not a remarkable thing that men have read into these words the amazing idea that what the apostle Paul is saying here is that as they talked together they found out that there were two gospels?—that Peter and the other apostles chosen by the Lord had one gospel, the gospel of the circumcision, and that Paul and Barnabas had another, the gospel of the Gentiles. And so they were to go on preaching one gospel to the Jews, and Paul and Barnabas were to preach a different gospel altogether to the Gentiles! What amazing ignorance of the divine plan that would lead any one to draw any such conclusion! The apostle has already told us, "Though we, or an angel from heaven, preach any other gospel unto you than that which we have preached unto you, let him be accursed" (chap. 1: 8). Peter had been among the Galatians preaching to them the same gospel he preached everywhere else. Was he accursed? Angels will proclaim the everlasting gospel in the coming day. Will they be under the curse? Surely

not.   There is only the one gospel, though it takes
on different forms at different times.   Peter's
gospel was that of a full, free, and eternal salvation through the death, resurrection, and un-
changing life of our Lord Jesus Christ, and Paul's
gospel was exactly the same.   Let us go back and
see something as to Peter's gospel and then compare it with Paul's.

On the day of Pentecost we listen to Peter
preaching.   He says, speaking of our Lord Jesus
Christ, that David witnessed concerning Him,
"He seeing this before, spake of the resurrection
of Christ, that His soul was not left in hell,
neither His flesh did see corruption.   This Jesus
hath God raised up, whereof we all are witnesses.
Therefore being by the right hand of God exalted,
and having received of the Father the promise of
the Holy Ghost, He hath shed forth this, which
ye now see and hear . . . Therefore let all the
house of Israel know assuredly, that God hath
made that same Jesus, whom ye have crucified,
both Lord and Christ" (Acts 2: 31-33, 36).   Does
this sound as if there was any difference from
the gospel the apostle Paul preached?   Surely
not.   It is the same message of the crucified,
risen, and exalted Saviour.

What was the effect of this preaching?   Remember, this was the gospel that Peter preached.
The people cried out, "Men and brethren, what

shall we do?" They did not cry as the Philippian jailer, "Sirs, what must I do to be saved?" (Acts 16:30), but, "Men and brethren, what shall we do?" It was as though they said, "Peter, we have been waiting for years for the coming of the Messiah; we have believed that He was the One who should put away our sins and bring us into everlasting blessing, and now we realize from what you say that He has come and has been crucified and has gone up to God's right hand. Whatever are we to do? Are we hopeless? Are we helpless? We have rejected our Messiah; what shall we do?" And Peter said, "Repent, and be baptized, every one of you in the name of Jesus Christ for the remission of sins, and ye shall receive the gift of the Holy Ghost. For the promise is unto you, and to your children, and to all that are afar off, even as many as the Lord our God shall call" (Acts 2: 38, 39). Peter is saying, "If you believe the message that I have preached to you that there is remission of sins, there is salvation for you; you do not need to go into judgment when the nation goes into judgment. But you must repent." And what is it to repent? It is a complete change of attitude. In other words, change your mind, change your attitude, and be baptized, acknowledging that you receive the Saviour that the nation has rejected, and when you do, you stand on new ground altogether. What a fitting message for those Jewish believers! On that day three thousand of them took the step, and by their baptism cut themselves off from the nation that rejected Christ and went over to the side of Christ, and were known as among the children of God.

Let us listen to Peter again. "Repent ye therefore, and be converted, that your sins may be blotted out, when the times of refreshing shall come from the presence of the Lord; and He shall send Jesus Christ, which before was preached unto you: whom the heaven must receive until the times of restitution of all things, which God hath spoken by the mouth of all His holy prophets since the world began . . . Unto you first God, having raised up His Son Jesus, sent Him to bless you, in turning away every one of you from his iniquities" (Acts 3: 19-21, 26). What is Peter preaching here? The same gospel that Paul preached afterwards. He is telling them that the Jewish nation has rejected Christ and is therefore under judgment. And how dire the judgment that has fallen upon that nation! But, he says, if you would be delivered from that, repent, change your attitude, turn again, accept the Christ that the nation is rejecting, and you will be ready to welcome Him when He comes back again. Peter is not yet giving them the revelation of the Rapture, but he is telling them that when Christ appears they as individuals will be ready to welcome Him, even though the nation has to know the power of His judgment. "Be it known unto you all, and to all the people of Israel, that by the name of Jesus Christ of Nazareth, whom ye crucified, whom God raised from the dead, even by Him doth this man stand here before you whole (he had just healed a lame man). This is the stone which was set at nought of you builders, which is become the head of the corner. Neither is there salvation in any other: for there is none other name under heaven given among men, whereby we must be saved" (Acts 4:10-12). Is this different from Paul's gospel? It is exactly the same, but Peter is presenting it in a way that the Jewish people, who had all the centuries of instruction behind them, would thoroughly understand.

Now you hear the same man preaching in the house of Cornelius (Acts 10). He tells the story of the life and death and resurrection of Jesus. "God anointed Jesus of Nazareth with the Holy Ghost and with power: who went about doing good, and healing all that were oppressed of the devil; for God was with Him. And we are witnesses of all things which He did both in the land of the Jews, and in Jerusalem; whom they slew and hanged on a tree: Him God raised up the third day, and showed Him openly; not to all the people, but unto witnesses chosen before of God, even to us, who did eat and drink with Him after He rose from the dead. And He commanded us to preach unto the people, and to testify that it is He which was ordained of God to be the Judge of quick and dead. To Him give all the prophets witness, that through His name whosoever believeth in Him shall receive remission of sins" (vers. 38-43). Is this a different gospel from that which we should preach today? Is this a different gospel from that proclaimed by the apostle Paul? Surely not. It is the same gospel, the gospel of the grace of God, salvation alone through the finished work of our Lord Jesus.

But now turn to the epistle of Peter which is addressed to Jewish converts, the gospel for the circumcision. "Forasmuch as ye know that ye were not redeemed with corruptible things, as silver and gold, from your vain conversation received by tradition from your fathers; but with the precious blood of Christ, as of a lamb without blemish and without spot: who verily was foreordained before the foundation of the world, but was manifest in these last times for you" (1 Pet. 1:18-20). This is the gospel that Peter preached to the circumcision. Compare it with that gospel preached by Paul to Jew and Gentile. "And we declare unto you glad tidings, how that the promise which was made unto the fathers, God hath fulfilled the same unto us their children, in that He hath raised up Jesus again; as it is also written in the second Psalm, Thou art My Son, this day have I begotten Thee. And as concerning that He raised Him up from the dead, now no more to return to corruption, He said on this wise, I will give you the sure mercies of David. Wherefore He saith also in another psalm, Thou shalt not suffer Thine Holy One to see corruption. For David, after he had served his own generation by the will of God, fell on sleep, and was laid unto his fathers, and saw corruption: but He whom God raised again, saw no corruption. Be it known unto you therefore, men and brethren, that through this Man is preached unto you the forgiveness of sins: and by Him all that believe are justified from all things, from which ye could not be justified by the law of Moses" (Acts 13:32-39). Is there anything different here from that which Peter preached? Nothing different, but a fuller unfolding. Peter is never said to have preached justification, but forgiveness and remission. Paul added justification. When God forgives through the risen, glorified Jesus He not only forgives but He justifies. It is impossible for an earthly judge to both forgive and to justify a man. If a man is justified, he does not need to be forgiven. Imagine a man charged with a crime going into court, and after the evidence is all in he is pronounced not guilty, and the judge sets him free. Someone says as he leaves the building, "I want to congratulate you; it was very nice of the judge to forgive you."

"Forgive nothing! He did not forgive me; I am justified. There is nothing to forgive."

You cannot justify a man if he does a wicked thing, but you can forgive. But God not only forgives but justifies the ungodly, because He links the believer with Christ, and we are made "accepted in the Beloved" (Eph. 1: 6). We stand before God as clear of every charge as if we had never sinned. The two messages are one; but Paul's is a little fuller than that of Peter. One had the message peculiarly adapted to the Jews and the other to the Gentiles, and so they decided on distinct spheres of labor. We have something similar on the mission fields today. The heads of the boards get together, and one says, "Suppose that such-and-such a group of you work in this district, and another in this one." Do you say, "Oh dear, they have four or five different gospels?" Not at all; it is the same gospel. One goes to Nigeria, another to Uganda, another to Tanganyika, and others to other sections, but it is the same glorious message. And it is very simple, unless one is trying to read into it things of which the apostles never dreamed. Paul and

Peter never had the privilege of studying the modern systems of some of our ultra-dispensationalists, and so did not have the ideas that some people try to foist upon Christians today.

Verse 10 is interesting: "Only they would that we should remember the poor; the same which I also was forward to do." I wonder whether Paul did not smile as he heard that. They said, "You go to the Gentiles, Paul, but don't forget there are many poor saints here in Judea, and although you do not preach among us, send us a collection from time to time." He did, and thus showed that it was one Body and one Spirit, even as they are called in one hope of their calling.

CHAPTER FIVE

PETER'S DEFECTION AT ANTIOCH

(Gal. 2: 11-21)

"But when Peter was come to Antioch, I withstood him to the face, because he was to be blamed. For before that certain came from James, he did eat with the Gentiles: but when they were come, he withdrew and separated himself, fearing them which were of the circumcision. And the other Jews dissembled likewise with him; insomuch that Barnabas also was carried away with their dissimulation. But when I saw that they walked not uprightly according to the truth of the gospel, I said unto Peter before them all, If thou, being a Jew, livest after the manner of Gentiles, and not as do the Jews, why compellest thou the Gentiles to live as do the Jews? We who are Jews by nature, and not sinners of the Gentiles, knowing that a man is not justified by the works of the law, but by the faith of Jesus Christ, even we have believed in Jesus Christ, that we might be justified by the faith of Christ, and not by the works of the law: for by the works of the law shall no flesh be justified. But if, while we seek to be justified by Christ, we ourselves also are found sinners, is therefore Christ the minister of sin? God forbid. For if I build again the things which I destroyed, I make myself a transgressor. For I through the law am dead to the law, that I might live unto God. I am crucified with Christ: nevertheless I live; yet not I, but Christ liveth in me: and the life which I now live in the flesh I live by the faith of the Son of God, who loved me, and gave Himself for me. I do not frustrate the grace of God: for if righteousness come by the law, then Christ is dead in vain."

THIS passage suggests a number of interesting considerations. First of all, we are rather astonished perhaps to find Paul and Peter, both inspired men, both commissioned by the Lord Jesus Christ to go out into the world proclaiming His gospel, both apostles, now sharply differing one from the other. It would suggest certainly that the apostle Peter who is the one at fault is not the rock upon which the Church is built. What a wobbly kind of a rock it would be if he were, for here is the very man to whom the Father gave that wonderful revelation that Christ was the Son of the living God, actually behaving in such a way at Antioch as to bring discredit upon the gospel of the grace of God. If Peter was the first Pope he was a very fallible one, not an infallible. But he himself knew nothing of any such position, for he tells us in the fifth chapter of his first epistle that he was a fellow-elder with the rest of the elders in the Church of God, not one set in a position of authority over the presbytery, the elders, in God's Church. Then too the reading of the Scripture suggests to us the tremendous importance of ever being on the alert lest in some way or another we compromise in regard to God's precious truth.

We have already seen what an important thing that truth was in the eyes of the apostle Paul when he could call down condign judgment on the man, or even the angel, who preaches any other gospel than that divine revelation communicated to him. We know it was not simply because of ill-temper that he wrote in this way but because he realized how important it is to hold "the faith which was once (for all) delivered unto the saints" (Jude 3). That explains his attitude here in regard to Peter, a brother apostle. It had been agreed, as we have seen, at the great council in Jerusalem that Peter was to go to the Jews and Paul to the Gentiles, but as they compared their messages they found that one did not contradict the other, that both taught and believed salvation was through faith alone in the Lord Jesus Christ, and that both recognized the futility of works of law as providing a righteousness for sinful men.

To Antioch, a Gentile city in which there was a large church composed mainly of Gentile believers, where Paul and Barnabas had been laboring for a long time, Peter came for a visit. I suppose he was welcomed with open arms. It must have been a very joyous thing for the apostle Paul to welcome Peter, and to be his fellow-laborer in ministering the Word of God to these people of Antioch. At first they had a wonderfully happy time. Together they went in and out of the homes of the believers and sat down at the same tables with Gentile Christians. Peter was once so rigid a Jew that he could not even think of going into the house of a Gentile to have any fellowship whatsoever. What a happy thing it was to see these different believers, some at one time Jews, and others once Gentiles, now members of one Body, the Body of Christ, enjoying fellowship together, not only at the Lord's table, but also in their homes. For when Paul speaks of eating with Gentiles I take it that it was at their own tables where they could have the sweetest Christian fellowship talking together of the things of God while enjoying the good things that the Lord provides. But unhappily there came in something that hindered, that spoiled that hallowed communion.

Some brethren came from Jerusalem who were of the rigid Pharisaic type, and although they called themselves (and possibly were) Christians, they had never been delivered from legalism. Peter realized that his reputation was at stake. If they should find him eating with Gentile believers and go back to Jerusalem and report this, it might shut the door on him there, and so prudently, as he might have thought, he withdrew from them, he no longer ate with them. If he chose not to eat with the Gentiles, could any one find fault with him for that? If he regarded the prejudices of these brethren might he not be showing a certain amount of Christian courtesy? He felt free to do these things, but not if they distressed these others. But Paul saw deeper than that; he saw that our liberty in Christ actually hung upon the question of whether one would

sit down at the dinner-table or not with those
who had come out from the Gentiles unto the
name of our Lord Jesus, and so this controversy.

"When Peter was come to Antioch," Paul says,
"I withstood him to the face, because he was to
be blamed." There is no subserviency on Paul's
part here, no recognition of Peter as the head of
the Church. Paul realized that a divine authority was vested in him, and that he was free to
call in question the behavior of Peter himself
though he was one of the original twelve. "For
before that certain came from James"—James
was the leader at Jerusalem—"he did eat with
the Gentiles: but when they were come, he withdrew and separated himself, fearing them which
were of the circumcision." We read in the Old
Testament, "The fear of man bringeth a snare,"
and here we are rather surprised to find the
apostle Peter, some years after Pentecost, afraid
of the face of man. It has often been said that
Peter before Pentecost was a coward, but when
he received the Pentecostal baptism everything
was changed. He stood before the people in Jerusalem and drove the truth home to them, "Ye
killed the Prince of Life," and he who had denied
his Lord because of the fear of man now strikes
home the fact that they "denied the Holy One and
the Just, and desired a murderer to be granted
unto you" (Acts 3:14). The inference has been

drawn by some that if one receives the Pentecostal baptism he will never be a coward again, and also that all inbred sin has been then burned out by the refining fire of God. But we do not find anything like that in the Word of God. It is true that under the influence of that Pentecostal baptism Peter did not fear the face of man, but now he had begun to slip. The fact that one has received great spiritual blessing at any particular time gives no guarantee that he will never fear again.

We now find Peter troubled by that same old besetment that had brought him into difficulty before, afraid of what others will say of him, and when he saw these legalists he forgot all about Pentecost, all about the blessing that had come, all about the marvelous revelation that he had when the sheet was let down from heaven and the Lord said, "What God hath cleansed, that call not thou common" (Acts 10: 15). He forgot how he himself had stood in Cornelius' household and said, "It is an unlawful thing for a man that is a Jew to . . . come unto one of another nation; but God hath showed me that I should not call any man common or unclean" (Acts 10: 28). He forgot that at the council in Jerusalem it was he who stood before them all and after relating the incidents in connection with his visit to Cornelius, exclaimed, "We (we who are Jews by nature) be-

lieve that through the grace of the Lord Jesus
Christ *we* shall be saved, even as they" (Acts 15:
11). That was a wonderful declaration. We
might have expected him to say, "We believe that
through the grace of the Lord Jesus Christ *they*
shall be saved, even as we," that is, "these Gentiles may be saved by grace even as we Jews are
saved by grace." But no; he had had a wonderful revelation of the real meaning of Pentecost
and this glorious dispensation of the grace of
God. What made him forget all this? The scowl-
ing looks of these men from Jerusalem. They
had heard that he had been exercising a liberty
in which they did not believe, and they had come
to watch him. He thought, It will never do for
me to go into the houses of the Gentiles to eat
while these men are around. So without thinking how he would offend these simple Gentile
Christians who had known the Lord only a short
time, and in order to please these Jerusalem
legalists, he withdrew from the Gentiles as far as
intimate fellowship was concerned. He was not
alone in this for he was a man of influence and
others followed him. "And the other Jews dissembled likewise with him." It looked as though
there might be two churches in Antioch very
soon, one for the Jews and another for the Gentiles, as though the middle wall of partition had
not been broken down.

"The other Jews dissembled likewise with him." And what must have cut Paul to the quick, his own intimate companion, his fellow-worker, the man who had understood so well from the beginning the work that he should do, "Barnabas also was carried away with their dissimulation." How much he puts into those words! Barnabas who knew so much better, Barnabas who had seen how mightily God had wrought among the Gentiles, and who knew that all this old legalistic system had fallen never to be raised again, even Barnabas was carried away with their dissimulation.

"Dissimulation" is rather a fine-sounding word. I wonder why the translators did not translate the Greek word the same as they generally did in other places in the Bible. It may have been that they did not like to use the other word in connection with a man like Barnabas. It is just the ordinary word for hypocrisy. "The other Jews became hypocrites likewise with him; insomuch that Barnabas also was carried away with their hypocrisy." Peter might have said, "We are doing this to glorify God," but it was nothing of the kind; it was downright hypocrisy in the sight of God. Paul recognized it as what it was, and said, "But when I saw that they walked not uprightly according to the truth of the gospel, I said unto Peter before them all—." This was not a clandestine meeting, there was no backbiting. What he had to say he said openly, and he did not seem to spare Peter's feelings. We must ever remember the Word, "Thou shalt in any wise rebuke thy neighbor, and not suffer sin upon him" (Lev. 19: 17). Some years afterwards he wrote to Timothy, "Them that sin rebuke before all, that others also may fear" (1 Tim. 5: 20). There was too much at stake to pass over this lightly. It was too serious a matter to settle quietly with Peter in a corner, for it had been a public scandal, and it called in question the liberty of Gentiles in Christ and so must be settled in a public way. One can imagine the feelings of Peter, noble man of God that he was, and yet he had been carried away with this snare. At first he was startled as he looked at Paul, and then I fancy with bowed head, the blood mantling his face in shame, he realized how guilty he was of seeking to please these legalists who would rob the Church of the marvelous gospel of grace. "If thou, being a Jew, livest after the manner of Gentiles, and not as do the Jews, why compellest thou the Gentiles to live as do the Jews?" He has let the cat out of the bag. I think I see those Jewish men look up and say, "What is this? He has been living after the manner of Gentiles?" Yes, they should have known it, for he had a right to do it. God had given all men this liberty and Peter had been exercising it, but now he was bringing himself into bondage. Peter had said, "We Jews know that a man is not justified by the works of the law, but we have to be saved by grace even as the Gentiles, so why insist upon bringing these Gentiles under bondage to Jewish forms and ceremonies?"

Paul went on: " 'We who are Jews by nature and not sinners of the Gentiles, knowing that a man is not justified by the works of the law, but by the faith of Jesus Christ, even we have believed in Christ, that we might be justified by the faith of Christ, and not by the works of the law: for by the works of the law shall no flesh be justified.' We gave up all confidence in law-keeping as a means of salvation when we turned to Christ, and now, Peter, would you by your behavior say to the Gentile brethren, 'You should come under the bondage of law-keeping, from which we have been delivered in order to be truly justified?' " It was a solemn occasion, for there was an important question at stake, and Paul handled it like the courageous man that he was.

Are you, like so many others, trying to do the best you can in order to obtain God's salvation? Listen then to what He says, "By the works of the law shall no flesh be justified."

> "Could my tears forever flow,
> Could my zeal no languor know,
> These for sin could not atone;
> Thou must save, and Thou alone."

Some years ago, after listening to me preach on the street corner a man said to me, "I detest this idea that through the death and righteousness of Another I should be saved. I do not want to be indebted to anybody for my salvation. I am not coming to God as a mendicant, but I believe that if a man lives up to the Sermon on the Mount and keeps the Ten Commandments, God does not require any more of him."

I asked, "My friend, have you lived up to the Sermon on the Mount and have you kept the Ten Commandments?"

"Oh," he said, "perhaps not perfectly; but I am doing the best I can."

"But," I replied, "the Word of God says, 'Whosoever shall keep the whole law and yet offend in one point, he is guilty of all' (Jas. 2:10). And, 'It is written, Cursed is every one that continueth not in *all* things which are written in the book of the law to do them' (Gal. 3:10), and because you have not continued you are under the curse."

That is all the law can do for any poor sinner. It can only condemn, for it demands perfect righteousness from sinful men, a righteousness which no sinful man can ever give, and so when God has shown us in His Word that men are bereft of righteousness, He says, "I have a righteousness for guilty sinners, but they must receive it by faith," and He tells us the wondrous story of the death and resurrection of our Lord Jesus Christ—"He was delivered for our offences" (Rom. 4: 25). And having trusted Him shall we go back to works of the law?

"If," says Paul, "while we seek to be justified by Christ, we ourselves also are found sinners"— if we who have trusted in Jesus are still sinners seeking a way of salvation—"is therefore Christ the minister of sin?" Moses was the mediator of the law, and it was to be used by God to make sin become exceeding sinful. Is that all Christ is for? Is it simply that His glorious example is to show me how deep is my sin, how lost my condition, and then am I to save myself by my own efforts? Surely not. That would be but to make Christ a minister of sin, but Christ is a minister of righteousness to all who believe. I think verse 17, and possibly verse 18, concludes what Paul says to Peter. "If I build again the things which I destroyed, I make myself a transgressor." We do not have quotation marks in the ancient Greek text, so have no way of knowing exactly where Paul's words to Peter end, but probably he concluded his admonition to Peter with this word.

"For I through the law am dead to the law, that I might live unto God." What does he mean by that? He means that the law condemned me to death, but Christ took my place and became my Substitute. I died in Him. "I through the

law died to the law, that I might live unto God."
Now I belong to a new creation altogether. And
oh, the wonder of that new creation! The old
creation fell in its head, Adam, and the new one
stands eternally in its Head, the Lord Jesus
Christ. We are not trying to work for our salvation, we are saved through the work that He
Himself accomplished. We can look back to that
cross upon which He hung, the bleeding Victim,
in our stead, and we can say in faith, "I am crucified with Christ." It is as though my life had
been taken, He took my place; "I am crucified
with Christ: nevertheless I live." As I was identified with Him in His death on the cross now I
am linked with Him in resurrection life, for He
has given me to be a partaker of His own glorious
eternal life. "Nevertheless I live; yet not I." It
is not the old I come back to life again, "but
Christ liveth in me." He, the glorious One, is my
real life, and that "life which I now live in the
flesh," my experience down here as a Christian
man in the body, "I live"—not by putting myself
under rules and regulations and trying to keep
the law of the Ten Commandments but—"by the
faith of the Son of God, who loved me, and gave
Himself for me." As I am occupied with Him,
my life will be the kind of life which He approves.

"The Son of God, who loved me, and gave Himself for me." I wish each of us might say those

words over in his heart. Can you say it in your heart? It is not, "The Son of God, who loved *the world,* and gave Himself for *the world,*" but, "The Son of God, who loved *me,* and gave Himself for *me.*" Only those who trust Him can speak like that. Can you say it from your heart? If you have never said it before you can look up into His face today, and say it for the first time. And so Paul concludes this section, "I do not set aside the grace of God" (or, I will not set it aside), "for if righteousness come by the law, then Christ is dead in vain." But because righteousness could not be found through legality, through self-effort, Christ gave Himself in grace for needy sinners, and He is Himself the righteousness of all who put their trust in Him.

CHAPTER SIX

"WHO HATH BEWITCHED YOU?"

(Gal. 3: 1-9)

"O foolish Galatians, who hath bewitched you, that ye should not obey the truth, before whose eyes Jesus Christ hath been evidently set forth, crucified among you? This only would I learn of you, Received ye the Spirit by the works of the law, or by the hearing of faith? Are ye so foolish? Having begun in the Spirit, are ye now made perfect by the flesh? Have ye suffered so many things in vain? If it be yet in vain. He therefore that ministereth to you the Spirit, and worketh miracles among you, doeth he it by the works of the law, or by the hearing of faith? Even as Abraham believed God, and it was accounted to him for righteousness. Know ye therefore that they which are of faith, the same are the children of Abraham. And the Scripture, foreseeing that God would justify the heathen through faith, preached before the gospel unto Abraham, saying, In thee shall all nations be blessed. So then they which be of faith are blessed with faithful Abraham."

WE now enter upon the strictly doctrinal part of this epistle. In verse 1 of this chapter the apostle Paul uses very unusual language. What he really means is this, "How is it that you seem to have come under a sort of spell, so that you have lost your grasp of the truth and your hearts and minds have become clouded by error?" Error affects people in that way. It is quite possible for one to have been truly converted and to have begun with a clear,

definite knowledge of the saving grace of the
Lord Jesus, and then because of failure to follow
on to study the Word and to pray over it, to come
under the influence of some false system, some
unscriptural line of teaching. And so often when
people do come under some such influence you
find it almost impossible to deliver them. They
seem to be under a spell.

Of course the apostle is not saying that one
person has the power of bewitching another, but
he is using that as an illustration. He says,
"These men who have come down from Jerusalem, teaching that you cannot be saved unless
you are circumcised and keep the law of Moses,
have gotten such an influence over you that you
are like people bewitched, and under a spell; you
are not able to reason things out, or to detect
what is true and what is false." It was not exactly that they had been "given up to strong delusion." When God offers men the truth and they
deliberately turn away from it, they stand in
danger of being delivered over judicially to that
which is absolutely false, but here he has something else in mind. In all likelihood these people
were real Christians, but real Christians acting
like men under a spell.

"O foolish Galatians, who hath bewitched you,
that ye should not obey the truth, before whose
eyes Jesus Christ hath been evidently set forth,

crucified among you?" When once one has laid
hold of the blessed truth that the Lord Jesus has
been crucified on our behalf, that in itself ought
to be the means of delivering us forever from
such error as that into which these people had
fallen. If Christ has actually given Himself for
me it is because it was impossible for me to do
one thing to save myself. Because I could not
fit myself for the presence of God, because I could
not cleanse my heart from sin, because no work
of righteousness of mine could fit me for a place
with the Lord, He had to come from heaven and
give Himself for me on the cross. How then can
I think of turning back to the ground of human
merit as a means of securing salvation, or of
maintaining me in a condition of salvation before
God? I deserved to die, but Jesus Christ took my
place, and He has settled for me. He has met all
the claims of divine righteousness, and through
Him I am eternally saved. Shall I go back to
law to complete the work He has done? Surely
not.

The apostle now refers to the beginning of
their Christian lives and says, "This only would
I learn of you, Received ye the Spirit by the
works of the law, or by the hearing of faith?"
In the previous chapter he has shown how a man
is justified before God by faith alone, and has
declared that the law really is honored more in

the recognition of the fact that its penalty has
been met in the cross of our Lord Jesus, than by
any poor effort of man to keep it as a means of
salvation. Now he adds to justification by faith
the truth of the reception of the Holy Spirit. He
says, as it were, "Go back in your own Christian
experience. You received the Holy Spirit when
you believed in the Lord Jesus, when you accepted
the gospel message as I brought it to you (he is
referring to his own ministry among them). God
gave you the Holy Spirit, not on the ground of
any merit of your own, not because of any good
thing that you were able to do, certainly not because of law-keeping or ritualistic observances,
for you were uncircumcised Gentiles. Yet when
you believed in the Lord Jesus, God gave you the
Holy Spirit." Now he says, "Think it out; did
you receive the Spirit by works of the law? Surely not. How then? 'By the hearing of faith.'"

"Are ye so foolish? Having begun in the Spirit,
are ye now made perfect by the flesh?" In other
words, if the Holy Spirit came to dwell in you
in the condition you were when you came to
Christ, do you think you need to complete the
work by your own self-effort and by putting yourself under legal rules and regulations? You who
know the love of the Lord Jesus Christ have received the Holy Spirit. Some of you may say,
"I wish I were sure of that." But Scripture says

definitely, "Upon your believing, ye were sealed with that Holy Spirit of promise" (Eph. 1: 13), you were born of the Spirit. You ask, "Do you mean that when I was born again that was the reception of the Holy Spirit?" Scripture distinguishes between new birth by the Spirit and the reception of the Holy Spirit, but there need not necessarily be any interval between our new birth and the reception of the Holy Spirit. New birth is the work of the Spirit. The Spirit Himself is the One who does the work; He comes to dwell in the man who is born again. New birth is new creation, and the Holy Spirit is the Creator. New birth is the work of God, but the Holy Spirit is God. There is a difference between being born of God and being indwelt by the Spirit of God. In past dispensations men were born of God and yet not indwelt by His Spirit, but with the coming in of the dispensation of the grace of God, when people are born again, the Holy Spirit Himself comes to dwell in them. In the case of these Galatians, if He did not approve of the work that Paul had done, if He did not approve of the stand they had taken in receiving the Lord Jesus Christ, He never would have come to dwell in them as they were. If it were necessary to be subject to the Mosaic ritual He would have made that clear and said, "I cannot come and dwell in you until these things are settled, until you sub-

[handwritten margin note left-center:] This Refutes the idea of 2nd Baptism of the Spirit!

[handwritten margin note lower-left:] If it were necessary to speak in tongues, He would have said that.

mit yourselves to these regulations and rules,"
but He did nothing of the kind. They believed,
they took their places before God as lost sinners,
they turned to Him in repentance, they accepted
Christ by faith as their Saviour, and the Holy
Spirit says, as it were, "Now I can dwell in them,
they are washed from their sins in the precious
blood of Christ, and I will make their bodies My
temples." Do you not see what a clear argument
that was in meeting the teaching of these people?

"Having begun in the Spirit, are ye now made
perfect by the flesh?" He reminded them of
what they went through in those early days. It
meant much for people in their circumstances to
step out from heathenism and take a stand
against their friends and relatives, to accept the
Lord Jesus Christ as their Saviour, and to declare that the idols they had once worshipped
were dumb images and powerless to save. To
step out from all that in which they had participated for so many years meant a great deal, and
exposed them to suffering, bitter persecution, and
grave misunderstanding on the part of their fellow-men. Yet for Jesus' sake they gladly took
the step, for Jesus' sake they bore reproach, they
suffered, many of them, even unto death, and
those who were still living counted it all joy to
have part with Christ in His rejection. But they
were being brought under the power of an evil

system, teaching that they were not really saved until they submitted themselves to what these Jewish legalists had put before them.

"Have ye suffered so many things in vain?" All that they had gone through for Christ's sake —was it in vain? Was it simply a profession? If not, how is it that they seem to have lost their assurance? And then he adds, "If it be yet in vain." He cannot believe that it is in vain, for he looks back and remembers the exercises they went through, the joy that came to them when they professed to receive Christ, and the love that seemed to be welling up in their hearts one for another, and for him as a servant of God and for the Saviour Himself. He says, "I remember the afflictions you were ready to endure on behalf of the gospel; I cannot believe you were not converted, that it was not real. You have been misled, you have gotten into a fog, and if I can, I want by the grace of God to deliver you." He had no ill-will against them, and none against the men who came down from Jerusalem, but he detested the doctrine they brought. Some people find it difficult to distinguish between a hatred of false doctrine and a love for the people themselves who have come under the influence of it. When we stand up for the truth of God and warn people against false teaching, that does not imply for one moment that we have any unkind feeling

toward those taken up with that false teaching.
We love such a person as one for whom Christ
died, and pray that he may be delivered from his
error and brought into the light of the truth.

Then the apostle reminds them that when he
came among them to preach the gospel of the
grace of God, there were marvellous signs and
manifestations that followed. They themselves
had seen him and Barnabas work wondrous miracles and some among the number had similar
gifts granted to them. These miraculous evidences accompanied the testimony. "He therefore
that ministereth to you the Spirit, and worketh
miracles among you, doeth he it by the works of
the law, or by the hearing of faith?" I think he
intended them now to contrast the ministry of
these false teachers who had come among them
with that of his own and Barnabas when they
came in the simplicity and fulness of the gospel
of Christ. Are there any miraculous attestations
of these false teachers? Is their testimony ac-
credited by miraculous power? Not at all. But
when Paul went preaching Christ and Him crucified, God Himself put His seal of approval upon
that testimony by giving them the power to work
miracles. People say, "Why not the same today?"
Even today miraculous signs accompany the
preaching of the truth which are not found when

error is presented. When the gospel of the grace of God is preached, men and women believing it are delivered from their sins, the Holy Spirit works, creating a new life, a new nature, and sets them free. The drunkard listens to the gospel and believes it, and finds the chains of appetite are broken. The licentious man who revelled in his uncleanness like a swine in the mud, gets a sight of the Lord Jesus; his heart is stirred as he contemplates the holiness and purity of the Saviour, and he bows in repentance before God, abhorring himself and his sin, and becomes pure and clean and good. The liar who has not been able to speak honest words for years hears the gospel of the grace of God and falls in love with Him who is the truth, and learns henceforth to speak right words, true words. That bad-tempered man who was a terror to his family, so that his wife shrank from him, and his children were afraid when he entered the house, is subdued by divine grace and the lion becomes a lamb. These are miracles which have been wrought down through the centuries where the gospel of the grace of God was preached. Error does not produce these things. It gives men certain intellectual conceptions in which they glory, but it does not make unclean lives clean, nor deliver from impurity and iniquity. But it is the glory of the gospel that when men truly believe they actually become new creatures in Christ Jesus. There were no such signs and wonders accompanying this law-preaching.

And so he comes back to Abraham. These false teachers had said, "God called Abraham out from among the Gentiles and gave him the covenant of circumcision, and therefore unless these Gentiles do follow him in this they cannot be saved." Even as "Abraham believed God, and it was accounted to him for righteousness." Abraham was a Gentile just as these Galatians were, and God revealed His truth to him. In verse 8 we read, "God . . .preached before the gospel unto Abraham, saying, In thee shall all nations be blessed." And Abraham believed it, and God justified him by faith. When did God preach the gospel to him? He took him outside his tent one night and said, "Look now toward heaven, and tell the stars" (Gen. 15:5). And Abraham said, "I cannot count them, they are in number utterly beyond me." And then He told him to count the sand and the dust under his feet, and Abraham said, "I cannot do that." And God said, "So shall thy seed be. In thy Seed shall all the nations of the earth be blessed."

God gave Abraham the promise of a collective seed, as numberless as the stars of the heaven, as the sand of the sea, as the dust of the ground, and also the individual Seed, the Lord Jesus Christ Himself, the Son of Abraham, for in Him all the nations of the earth shall be blessed. Abraham was a childless old man, but "he staggered not at the promise of God through unbelief; but was strong in faith, giving glory to God; and being fully persuaded that what He had promised, He was able also to perform" (Rom. 4:20, 21). And when God saw this faith in Abraham He justified him. The covenant of circumcision had not yet been given to him, but he was justified by faith. What is the inference? If God can justify one Gentile by faith, can He not justify ten million by faith? If Abraham is the father of all the faithful in a spiritual sense, then we Gentiles need not fear to follow in his steps.

And so the next verse goes on, "Know ye therefore, that they which are of faith, the same are the children of Abraham." You see, Abraham has a spiritual seed as well as a natural seed. Those born of Abraham's lineage after the flesh are not really Abraham's sons unless born again; they must have the faith of Abraham to be his sons. But all over the world, wherever the message comes, wherever people, whether Jews or Gentiles, put their trust in that Seed of Abraham, our Lord Jesus Christ, and receive Him as Saviour and Lord, God says, "Write him down a son of Abraham." And so Abraham has a vast spiritual seed. Throughout all the centuries the millions and millions of people who have believed

God as he did, and trusted in the Saviour in whom he trusted will share his blessings, and will be with Abraham for all eternity.

"And the Scripture, foreseeing that God would justify the heathen through faith (not through faith and works, not through faith and ordinances, not through faith and sacramental observances), preached before the gospel unto Abraham, saying, In thee shall all nations be blessed." The gospel is God's good news concerning His Son. Abraham received that good news and believed it, and if you and I have received and believed it we are linked with him, we are children of Abraham.

"So then they which be of faith are blessed with believing Abraham." On what are you resting for your salvation? I have received letters from people who are indignant because I have said that salvation is through faith alone. It makes one start sometimes to find that after all our gospel preaching so many people who make a Christian profession have never yet learned that salvation is absolutely of grace through faith. We almost forget that there are hundreds of people who do not believe these things. And yet how can anyone profess to believe this Book and yet insist upon salvation by human effort? In Romans we read, "If by grace, then is it no more of works: otherwise grace is no more grace. But if it be

of works, then is it no more grace: otherwise
work is no more work" (Rom. 11: 6). Can you
not see how the Holy Spirit of God shuts us up to
this, that salvation is either altogether by grace
or it is altogether by works? It cannot be by a
combination of the two. Someone says, "But do you
not remember the old story about the two preachers who were in the rowboat, who were debating
as to whether salvation were by grace or by
works, by faith or by works? The boatman listened to them, and when they were unable to
come to a solution of the problem, one said to
him, 'You have heard our conversation; what do
you think of this?'

" 'Well,' he said, 'I have been thinking it is like
this—I have two oars. I will call this one Faith
and this one Works. If I pull only on this oar
the boat goes round and round and does not get
anywhere. If I pull on that one it goes round
and round and gets nowhere. But if I pull on
both I get across the river.' "

And people say that is a beautiful illustration
of the fact that salvation is by faith and works.
It would be if we were going to heaven in a rowboat, but we are not. We are going through in
the infinite grace of our Lord Jesus Christ, and
like that lost sheep that went astray and was
found by the shepherd, we are being carried by
the Saviour Home to Glory, and it is not a ques-

tion of working our way there. And so we come back to what Scripture says, "For by grace are ye saved through faith; and that not of yourselves: it is the gift of God: not of works, lest any man should boast" (Eph. 2: 8, 9). If I had to do as much as lift my little finger to save my soul I could strut up the golden streets saying, "Glory be to the Lord and to me, for by our combined efforts I am saved." No; it is no works of mine, no effort of mine, and so Jesus shall get all the glory.

> "Jesus paid it all,
>   All to Him I owe;
> Sin had left a crimson stain,
>   He washed it white as snow!"

Are you in perplexity and wanting the assurance of salvation? Possibly you have prayed and read your Bible, have gone to church, have been baptized and partaken of the sacrament, you have tried to do your religious duty; but you do not have peace and rest and you do not know whether your soul is saved. Turn from self and self-occupation, and fix your eyes upon the blessed Christ of God, put all your heart's trust in Him and be assured that, "Whosoever believeth in Him shall not perish, but have everlasting life" (John 3: 16).

CHAPTER SEVEN

REDEEMED FROM THE CURSE OF THE LAW

(Gal. 3: 10-18)

"For as many as are of the works of the law are under the curse: for it is written, Cursed is every one that continueth not in all things which are written in the book of the law to do them. But that no man is justified by the law in the sight of God, it is evident: for, The just shall live by faith. And the law is not of faith: but, The man that doeth them shall live in them. Christ hath redeemed us from the curse of the law, being made a curse for us: for it is written, Cursed is every one that hangeth on a tree: that the blessing of Abraham might come on the Gentiles through Jesus Christ; that we might receive the promise of the Spirit through faith. Brethren, I speak after the manner of men; Though it be but a man's covenant, yet if it be confirmed, no man disannulleth, or addeth thereto. Now to Abraham and his seed were the promises made. He saith not, And to seeds, as of many; but as of one, And to thy Seed, which is Christ. And this I say, that the covenant, that was confirmed before of God in Christ, the law, which was four hundred and thirty years after, cannot disannul, that it should make the promise of none effect. For if the inheritance be of the law, it is no more of promise: but God gave it to Abraham by promise."

NATURALLY one might ask, "What do we mean when we speak of the curse of the law?" Is it a curse to have good laws? Was it a curse for God to give to the people of Israel the Ten Commandments, the highest moral and ethical standard that any people had ever received and that ever had been given to mankind, until our Lord Jesus Christ proclaimed the Sermon on the Mount? Is this a curse? Surely not. It was a great blessing to Israel to have such instruction, showing them how to live and how to behave themselves, and it kept them from a great many of the sins to which the Gentile nations round about them were given. Yet we have this expression in Scripture, "The curse of the law," and read, "For as many as are of the works of the law are under the curse: for it is written, Cursed is every one that continueth not in all things which are written in the book of the law to do them."

When God gave that law, He pronounced a blessing on all who kept it, and declared that they would receive life thereby. "The man which doeth those things shall live by them" (Rom. 10: 5), but on the other hand, He said, as quoted here, "Cursed is every one that continueth not in all things which are written in the book of the law to do them." Every one who recognizes in that law the divine will as to the life of man here on earth and yet fails to measure up to it comes under its curse. And who is there today who has ever kept this law? I know people say, "If we do the best we can, will that not be enough?" Scripture negatives any such thought. In James we read, "Whosoever shall keep the whole law, and yet offend in one point, he is guilty of all" (James 2: 10). We know how true that is in regard to human law. Suppose that I as a citizen of the United States violated none of the laws of my country except one, by violating that one law I have become a law-breaker, and am therefore subjected to the penalty of the broken law. When we speak of people being under "the curse of the law" we mean that they are subject to the penalty of the broken law, and the penalty is death, spiritual and eternal. "The soul that sinneth, it shall die" (Ezek. 18: 20). Therefore the law is well called "the ministration of death" and "the ministration of condemnation" (2 Cor. 3: 7, 9), for all who are under the law but have failed to keep it are under condemnation, they are condemned to death, and therefore under the curse. But our Lord Jesus Christ has died to deliver us from the curse of the law.

Can we not deliver ourselves? Though we have broken it in the past can we not make up our minds that from this moment on we will "turn over a new leaf," and be very careful to observe every precept of the moral law of God? In the first place, we could not do that. It is impossible for men with fallen natures to fully keep the holy law of God. Take that particular commandment, "Thou shalt not covet;" you cannot keep yourself from coveting though you know it is

wrong to do so. You look at something your
neighbor has and involuntarily your heart says,
"I wish that were mine." On second thought, you
say, "That is very unworthy; I should really rejoice for my neighbor;" but still, have you not
coveted? The apostle Paul says that as far as
the other commandments were concerned his life
was outwardly blameless. He was alive without
the law until the commandment came, "Thou
shalt not covet." "But sin, taking occasion by
the commandment, wrought in me all manner of
concupiscence" (Rom. 7: 7, 8). And so he was
slain by the law that he could not keep. But suppose you were able to keep it from this very day
until the last day of your life, would not that
undo and make up for all the wrong-doing of the
past? Not at all. The past failure still stands
on God's record. "God requireth that which is
past" (Eccl. 3: 15).

"But that no man is justified by the law in the
sight of God, it is evident: for, The just shall live
by faith." Notice, no man is justified by the law
of God, no man ever has been justified by the law
of God, no man ever will be justified by the law
of God. In Romans 3 we read, "Now we know
that what things soever the law saith, it saith to
them who are under the law: that every mouth
may be stopped, and all the world may become
guilty before God. Therefore by the deeds of

the law there shall no flesh be justified in His sight: for by the law is the knowledge of sin" (Rom. 3:19, 20). In other words, God did not give the law to save man, He gave the law to test him, to make manifest man's true condition. And that explains a passage that puzzles some, "The law was added because of transgressions" (Gal. 3:19). It was really given in order to give to sin the specific character of transgression.

I was strolling across the park the other day when I suddenly looked down and saw almost at my feet a sign, "Keep off the grass." I was on the grass, but the moment I saw the sign I hurried to get on to a path. If I had continued to walk on the grass after seeing the sign I would be a transgressor. I was not a transgressor before this, for I did not know I was doing wrong. I saw other people walking on the grass, and did not realize that there were certain sections where this was not allowed. I did not know that it was forbidden in that particular place. Until the law sin was in the world, and men were doing wrong in taking their own way, but "where no law is, there is no transgression" (Rom. 4:15). God set up His law to say, as it were, "Keep off the grass." Now if they walk on the grass they are transgressors. If men disobey God they transgress. The sinfulness of man's heart is shown up by the fact that men do deliberately and wilfully disobey. It is impossible to be justified by the law, for to be justified is to be cleared from every charge of guilt. The law brings the charge home, the law convicts me of my guilt, and the law condemns me because of that guilt.

It was written in the prophets, "The just shall live by his faith" (Hab. 2: 4), so it was made known even in Old Testament times that men were to be justified, not by human effort, but by faith. Three times those words are quoted for us in the New Testament. In the epistle to the Romans the apostle says, "I am not ashamed of the gospel of Christ: for it is the power of God unto salvation to every one that believeth; to the Jew first, and also to the Greek. For therein is the righteousness of God revealed from faith to faith: as it is written, The just shall live by faith" (Rom. 1: 16, 17). In the epistle to the Hebrews we have exactly the same words quoted, "The just shall live by faith" (Heb. 10: 38). And here we have them in the epistle to the Galatians. It has been very well said that these three epistles expound that text of six words, "The just shall live by faith."

How do men become just before God? As we have already remarked, Romans answers that question and expounds the first two words, "The just." It tells us who the just are, those who believe in the Lord Jesus Christ. But if justified by faith, how is one maintained before God in that position? Is it not now by works of their own? Galatians answers that and puts the emphasis on the next two words, "The just *shall live* by faith." And what is that power that sustains and strengthens and enables just men to walk with God through this world, living an unworldly life, even as "Enoch walked with God: and he was not; for God took him" (Gen. 5:24)? Again the answer comes to us as in Hebrews the last two words are expounded, "The just shall live *by faith.*" It takes three epistles in the New Testament to expound one Old Testament text of only six words, "The just shall live by faith." It gives us an idea of how rich and full the Word of God is.

But if "the just shall live by faith" then men never can be justified by efforts of their own, for verse 12 tells us, "And the law is not of faith: but, The man that doeth them shall live in them." The law did not say, "The man who *believes* shall live," but, "The man who *does* shall live." The latter might seem to us to be the right thing; if a man does right he ought to live. The trouble is, man does not do right. We read, "All have sinned, and come short of the glory of God" (Rom. 3:23). If one commandment out of ten has been violated that man has forfeited all claim to life. Suppose a man falling over a precipice reached out his hand as he went over, and caught hold of a chain fastened to some stump in the cliff, and there hung on to the chain. The chain has ten links. How many would have to break to drop the man into the abyss below? Only one. The law is like that chain; when you sinned the first time you broke the link and down you went, and you are in the place of condemnation if not saved. You never can fit yourself for the presence of God by any works of righteousness that you can do. The law says, "The man which doeth these things shall live in them," but men have failed to do, and therefore are condemned to die.

Now see the glorious message of reconciliation! "Christ hath redeemed us from the curse of the law!" How did He do it? "Being made a curse for us: for it is written, Cursed is every one that hangeth on a tree." Here was One who had never violated God's law, here was the holy, eternal Son of God, the delight of the Father's heart from all eternity, who came into the world, who became Man, for the express purpose of redeeming those who were under the curse of the law. He Himself said, "The Son of Man came not to be ministered unto, but to minister, and to give His life a ransom for many" (Matt. 20: 28). But if He Himself has violated that law, He is subject to its penalty and never can redeem us; but how careful the Word of God has been to show that He never came under that penalty. He was holy in nature from the moment He came into the world. The angel said to Mary, His mother, "That Holy Thing which shall be born of thee shall be called the Son of God" (Luke 1:35). His life was absolutely pure as He went through this scene. He magnified the law and made it honorable by a life of devotion to the will of God. "He was in all points tempted like as we are, yet without sin" (Heb. 4:15). Sinless, though tempted; and at last God "made Him to be sin for us, who knew no sin; that we might be made the righteousness of God in Him" (2 Cor. 5:21). He against whom God had nothing, voluntarily took our place, went to the cross, and there paid the penalty that we should have paid. If I had to pay, eternity would be too short for it, but He, the Eternal One, hung on the cross, settled to the utmost farthing every claim that the offended law had against me, and now I receive Him, trust Him as my Saviour, and what is the result? I am delivered from the curse of the law.

> "Free from the law, O happy condition!
> Jesus hath bled, and there is remission,
> Cursed by the law and bruised by the fall,
> Christ hath redeemed us once for all.
>
> "Now we are free—there's no condemnation,
> Jesus provides a perfect salvation;
> 'Come unto Me,' oh, hear His sweet call!
> Come, and He saves us once for all."

Has your soul entered into this?

I shall never forget, after struggling for so long to work out a righteousness of my own, the joy that came to me when I was led to look by faith at yonder cross, an empty cross now.

"I saw One hanging on the tree,
 In visions of my soul,
Who turned His loving eyes on me
 As near His cross I stole."

I knew He was there on my behalf. He, the sinless One, was suffering there for me, the sinner, and I looked up to Him. In faith I could say, "Lord Jesus, I am Thy sin; I am Thine unrighteousness. Thou hast none of Thine own, but art bearing mine." And I looked again, and that cross was empty and my Lord's body had been laid in the tomb. "He was delivered for our offences," and buried out of sight as I deserved to be buried out of sight. But I looked again and that tomb too was empty, and He came forth in triumph, "He was raised again for our justification" (Rom. 4: 25). I looked not to the cross now but to the throne of God, and by faith I saw Him seated there, a Man exalted at God's right hand, the same Man who stood dumb in Pilate's judgment-hall, and did not say a word to clear Himself because I could not be cleared unless He died for me.

Who would want to work out a righteousness of his own when he can have one so much better through faith in the Lord Jesus Christ? "Christ hath redeemed us from the curse of the law, being made a curse for us: for it is written, Cursed is every one that hangeth on a tree."

And now because of that, the blessing of Abraham may come to the Gentiles in Christ Jesus; we may receive the promise of the Spirit through faith. "That the blessing of Abraham might come on the Gentiles through Jesus Christ; that we might receive the promise of the Spirit through faith." What is "the blessing of Abraham?" Long ago God had said, "In thee and in thy seed shall all nations of the earth be blessed." But centuries rolled by and the nations of the Gentiles were left outside; they were outside the pale, strangers to the covenant of promise, they knew nothing of the blessing of Abraham, nor what God had promised through his seed. But now Christ has died, not for Jews only but for the Gentiles also, and because of His work the message goes out to the whole world that God can save every one who believes on the Lord Jesus, and all believers become in faith the children of Abraham and are sealed by the Holy Spirit of God. The blessing of Abraham is justification by faith for every believer, even as "Abraham believed God, and it was counted unto

him for righteousness" (Rom. 4: 3). The apostle
draws attention to the fact that when God said
to Abraham, "In thy Seed shall all nations of the
earth be blessed," He was not referring merely
to the nation that should spring from him but to
one individual Person, for it had been settled in
the purpose of God from eternity that the Christ
was to be born of Abraham's lineage.

"Brethren, I speak after the manner of men;
Though it be but a man's covenant, yet if it be
confirmed, no man disannulleth, or addeth thereto." When men make covenants we expect them
to live up to them. God made a covenant of unconditional grace to Abraham long years before.
Later the law came in, but did that invalidate the
covenant of pure grace made to Abraham? "To
Abraham and his Seed were the promises made.
He saith not, And to seeds, as of many; but as
of one, And to thy Seed, which is Christ."
Through the Lord Jesus, then, the blessing of the
covenant goes out to every poor sinner who will
believe in Him. "And this I say, that the covenant, that was confirmed before of God in
Christ, the law, which was four hundred and
thirty years after, cannot disannul, that it should
make the promise of none effect." God was not
playing fast and loose with Abraham when He
gave him this unconditional covenant of grace.
He did not say, "If you do thus and so, and if you

do not do certain things, all the world will be blessed through your seed." But He said, unconditionally, "In thee and in thy seed shall all nations of the earth be blessed." It is not a question at all of human effort; it is not a question of something we earn.

When the apostle discusses this same subject in Romans 4, he says, in the opening verses, "What shall we say then that Abraham our father, as pertaining to the flesh, hath found? For if Abraham were justified by works, he hath whereof to glory; but not before God. For what saith the Scripture? Abraham believed God, and it was counted unto him for righteousness. Now to him that worketh is the reward not reckoned of grace, but of debt" (vers. 1-4). What does that mean? It means that if you had to do something to earn your salvation you would not be saved by grace. Suppose you work six days for an employer, and at the end of that time he comes in a supercilious kind of attitude, hands you an envelope, and says, "You have been working well the last six days, here is a little gift, I want to give you this as a token of my grace." You look at it and find it contains your wages, and you say, "Sir, I do not understand; this is not a gift. I earned this." But the man says, "I want you to feel that it is an expression of my appreciation." "No," you would say, "you owe me this;

you are in my debt, for I earned this money." If
I could do anything to save my soul I would put
God in debt to save me, but all God does for me
He does in pure grace. And so we read, "To him
that worketh not, but believeth on Him that justifieth the ungodly, his faith is counted for righteousness" (Rom. 4:5). And though the law
came four hundred and thirty years after this
promise of grace for all nations through Abraham's seed, it did not alter God's purpose; it was
given only in order to increase man's sense of his
need, to make him realize his sinfulness and help-
lessness, and lead him to cast himself on the infinite grace of God.

"For if the inheritance be of the law, it is no
more of promise: but God gave it to Abraham by
promise." If it comes through self-effort it is
not a question of promise at all. But God gave
it to Abraham by promise, and, "The promise,"
Peter says, "is unto you, and to your children,
and to all that are afar off, even as many as the
Lord our God shall call" (Acts 2:39). Perhaps,
reader, you have been struggling for years to fit
yourself for God's presence, you have been trying hard to work out a righteousness of your
own, "trying to be a Christian." Let me beg of
you, stop trying, give it up! You cannot become
a Christian by trying any more than you could
become the Prince of Wales by trying. You are

what you are by birth. You are what you are as a sinner by natural birth, and you become a child of God through second birth, through believing on the Lord Jesus Christ. The blessing of Abraham is yours when you receive it by faith.

CHAPTER EIGHT

THE LAW AS CHILD-LEADER UNTIL CHRIST

(Gal. 3: 19-29)

"Wherefore then serveth the law? It was added because of transgressions, till the seed should come to whom the promise was made; and it was ordained by angels in the hand of a mediator. Now a mediator is not a mediator of one, but God is one. Is the law then against the promises of God? God forbid: for if there had been a law given which could have given life, verily righteousness should have been by the law. But the Scripture hath concluded all under sin, that the promise by faith of Jesus Christ might be given to them that believe. But before faith came, we were kept under the law, shut up unto the faith which should afterwards be revealed. Wherefore the law was our schoolmaster to bring us unto Christ, that we might be justified by faith. But after that faith is come, we are no longer under a schoolmaster. For ye are all the children of God by faith in Christ Jesus. For as many of you as have been baptized into Christ have put on Christ. There is neither Jew nor Greek, there is neither bond nor free, there is neither male or female: for ye are all one in Christ Jesus. And if ye be Christ's, then are ye Abraham's seed, and heirs according to the promise."

WE have been considering in our studies of the earlier part of this chapter the relationship that the law had, the law as given at Sinai, to the unconditional promise of grace which God gave to Abraham 430 years before, and we have seen that the law coming in afterwards could not add to nor take away from

117

the covenant already made.   That naturally leads
to the question of verse 19, "Wherefore then
serveth the law?"   If the law did not add anything to what God had given by promise to
Abraham, and surely it could not take anything
from it, what was its purpose?   Why did God
give it at all?   The apostle answers, "It was
added because of transgressions, till the seed
should come to whom the promise was made; and
it was ordained by angels in the hand of a mediator."   I think perhaps we may understand it
better if we read it, "It was added with a view
to transgressions," in order that it might make
men see the specific character of transgression,
and thus deepen in each soul a sense of his sinfulness and his need.

We are all so ready to excuse ourselves, to say
if we had known better we would not have done
the wrong thing.   How often you hear people
say, "I do the best I know, and endeavor to do
the best I can."   But where has a man or woman
ever been found who could honestly utter those
sentences?   Have you always done the best you
knew?   Have you always done the best you
could?   If you are absolutely honest before God,
you know that you have not.   Again and again
we have all sinned against light and knowledge,
we have known far better than we have done.
Thus we have failed to glorify God, and by going

contrary to His revealed will we have proven ourselves not only sinners but transgressors.

Both in the original language of the New Testament and that of the Old Testament, there is a word for "sin" which literally means to "miss the mark." I remember having this brought before me when working among the Laguna Indians of New Mexico. One day my interpreter, a bright Indian, said, "I am going to spend the day hunting; would you like to go with me?"

I am no hunter, but I went with him for the exercise. He had a fine new rifle which he was very eager to try out. He gave evidence of his prowess with that weapon. Standing on one side of a canyon he would say, "Do you see that creature moving yonder?"

At first I could not possibly see it, but as he pointed it out I would see something that was just a moving speck away over on the opposite wall.

He would say, "Wait a minute," and level his rifle, and the next moment I would see the creature that looked like a small speck leap into the air and then drop down dead. He was a wonderful shot with a rifle, but when we got home he said to me, "I want to show you what I can do with our old weapon, for I have kept up with the bow and arrow. That seems so typical of our people that I have wanted to keep it up."

So we went into the field, and the Indian hunter set up a very small twig of a willow-tree, and enacted a scene something like that described in Scott's "Ivanhoe." He fitted the arrow to the string and said, "Now I am going to split that twig in two." Letting fly the arrow he shot right by the twig but did not touch it. "Oh," he said, "I have sinned."

For the moment I did not ask him why he used that expression.

Then he said, "I didn't take the wind into account, as I should have done." He fitted another arrow to the string, and let it fly, and split that twig right in two. I could hardly believe that any one could do such a thing.

He said, "There! I did not sin that time."

I said to him, "Why did you use that term 'sin'? You were not doing anything wrong when you did not hit that wand. Why did you say, 'I sinned,' and when you did hit it, 'I didn't sin that time'?"

"Oh," he said, "I was thinking in Gowaik (that is the language of the Laguna Indians) and speaking in English. In our language 'to sin' means 'to miss the mark'."

"That is a very singular thing," I said, "for in the Greek and Hebrew 'to sin' is 'to miss the mark'."

That is what is involved in the expression,

"All have sinned, and come short of the glory of God" (Rom. 3:23). But in the law we have something more than that. God has set up a standard of righteousness. The law with its ten definite ordinances, "Thou shalts and thou shalt nots," makes known to man exactly what God demands of him. Now if man sins knowing the revealed will of God, if he fails to obey that law, it is evident that he is not only a sinner but a transgressor. He has definitely violated a specific command of God; he has crossed over the line, as it were, and, "Sin by the commandment becomes exceeding sinful" (Rom. 7:13). That was one reason for which God gave the law—that men might have a deeper sense of the seriousness of self-will which is the very essence of sin, of rebellion against God. When God gave the law He gave it in the hands of a mediator, and Moses sprinkled the book of the covenant and also the people with the blood of the covenant, testifying to the fact that if man fails to keep his side of the covenant he must die, but also signifying that God would provide a Saviour, a Redeemer.

"Now a mediator is not a mediator of one, but God is one." Two contracting parties suggests the thought of the need of a mediator, but when God gave His promise to Abraham there was only one. God gave the Word, and there was nothing to do on Abraham's part but to receive it. He

did not covenant with God that he would do thus
and so in order that God's promise might be fulfilled, but God spoke directly to him and committed Himself when He said, "In thee shall all
nations be blessed" (Gal. 3:8). The question
arises, Is the law against the promises of God by
bringing in certain terms which were not in the
original promise? Does the law set the promises
to one side? God forbid. But a certain principle
was laid down in the law which declared that
"the man that doeth them shall live in them"
(ver. 12), and if any man had been found to do
these things perfectly he could have obtained life
on the ground of the law. But the law said to
man, "The soul that sinneth, it shall die" (Ezek.
18:14), and no man was ever found who could
keep it. "If there had been a law given which
could have given life, verily righteousness should
have been by the law."

A gentleman said to me in California one night,
"I do not like this idea of being saved by Another.
All my life I have never wanted to feel indebted
to other people for anything. I do not want anybody's charity, and when it comes to spiritual
things I do not want to be saved through the
merits of anybody else. According to what you
said tonight, if I keep the law perfectly I will
live and will owe nothing to any one. Is that
right?"

I said, "Well, yes; it is."

He said, "I am going to start **in on that.**"

I said, "How old are you?"

"Around forty."

"Suppose you came to years of accountability somewhere around twelve; you are nearly thirty years too late to begin, and Scripture says, 'Cursed is every one that continueth not in all things which are written in the book of the law to do them' (ver. 10). Therefore, because the law cannot give life, you will never be able to earn anything on that ground." He went away very disgruntled.

"But the Scripture hath concluded all under sin." If God has concluded all under sin, must all men be lost? No; all have been concluded under sin "that the promise by faith of Jesus Christ might be given to them that believe." God would have all men recognize their sinfulness in order that all might realize their need and come to Him proving His grace. He puts all men on one common level. Romans says, "There is no difference: for all have sinned" (Rom. 3:22, 23). Men imagine that there are a great many differences. One man says, "Do you mean to tell me that there is no difference between a moral man and a poor reprobate in the gutter?" Of course there is a great deal of difference, not only as far as the standard of society is concerned, but

also as to their own happiness and the estimate
of their neighbors; but when it comes to a question of righteousness, "There is no difference:
for all have sinned." All may not have sinned
in the same way, they may not have committed
exactly the same transgressions, but "all have
sinned," all have violated God's law.

A gentleman once said to a cousin of his, "I do
not like that idea about there being no difference,
it is repugnant to me. Do you mean to tell me
that having tried all my life to live a decent and
respectable life, God does not see any difference
between me and people living lives of sin and iniquity?"

She said to him, "Suppose that you and I were
walking down the street together, and we passed
some place of interest, perhaps a museum, that
we were eager to see. We went to the window
and inquired about the admission fee, and were
told it was $1.00. I looked into my purse and
said, 'Oh, I have left my money at home: I
have only 25c.' You looked at your money and
found you had only 70c. Which one of us would
go in first?"

"Well," he said, "under such circumstances
neither of us would get in."

"There would be no difference, and yet you
would have a great deal more money than I; but

as far as having what was necessary to pay our way in, there is no difference."

God demands absolute righteousness of sinners before they enter heaven. "There shall in no wise enter into it any thing that defileth" (Rev. 21: 27). You may have your 95c. worth of righteousness while I do not have a nickel's worth of it, but neither of us can get in unless we have our hundred cents, and there is no difference. "There is none righteous, no, not one" (Rom. 3: 10). Remember that God has said that, not some zealous, earnest preacher or evangelist, but God Himself by the Holy Spirit. And the law was given to demonstrate that fact. But if men take the place of unrighteousness before God, if they take the place of being lost sinners, and own their sin and guilt, what then? "The Scripture hath concluded all under sin, that the promise by faith of Jesus Christ might be given to them that believe." In other words, when men come to the place where they realize the fact that they cannot earn eternal life by any effort of their own, and are ready to receive it as a free gift, that moment it is their's. "He that believeth on the Son hath everlasting life" (John 3: 36). "Verily, verily, I say unto you, He that heareth My word, and believeth Him that sent Me, hath everlasting life, and shall not come into condemnation; but is passed out of death into life" (John 5:24).

But now the apostle shows another use for the law. Paul says, in ver. 23, "But before faith came," that is, "before *the* faith," because it was made known clearly and definitely that God was justifying men by faith alone in His blessed Son, "we were kept under the law"—he speaks now as a Jew—"we were kept under the law, shut up unto the faith which should afterwards be revealed." The Gentiles at that time did not have the law, but the Jews did. God gave the Jew that law, and he was looked upon as a minor child under rules and regulations. "Wherefore the law was our schoolmaster to bring us unto Christ, that we might be justified by faith." That word rendered "schoolmaster" is exactly the word that we have Anglicized by the term "pedagogue," a school-teacher. But the original word was not exactly a school-teacher, it really means a child-leader, a child-director, and was the name applied in ancient Greek households to a slave who had the care of the minor children. He was to watch over the morals of the child, protect him from association with others who were not fit for his companionship, and take him day by day from the house to the schoolroom. He there turned him over to the schoolmaster, but at the end of the day he would get him and bring him back home again. The apostle says here, and very beautifully, I think, "The law was our child-leader, our child-director, until Christ." That is, God did not leave His people without a code of morals until Jesus came to set before us the most wonderful moral code the world has ever known, and the law served in a very real way to protect and keep them from much of the immorality, iniquity, vileness, and corruption found in the heathen life round about them. As long as the people lived in obedience, in any measure, to that law, they were saved from a great deal of wickedness and evil.

"The law was our child-leader," perhaps not exactly to *bring* us to Christ, but, "The law was our child-leader *until* Christ." "The law was given by Moses, but grace and truth came by Jesus Christ" (John 1:17). Now Christ has come we have come to the door of the schoolroom of grace, and we have learned the blessed truth of justification by faith alone in Him whom God has set forth to be the propitiation for our sins. We are no longer under a child-director.

We are here told that we are not only freed from the law as a means of attempting to secure justification, but are also freed from that law as a means of sanctification, for we have so much higher a standard in Christ risen from the dead, and are to be occupied with Him. As we are taken up with Him the grace of God teaches us that, "Denying ungodliness and worldly lusts, we should live soberly, righteously, and godly, in this present world" (Titus 1: 12). For instance, suppose I as a Christian by some strange mishap had never even heard of the Ten Commandments, suppose it were possible that I had never known of them; but on the other hand I had been taught the wonderful story of the gospel, and had been entrusted with some of the books of the New Testament showing how a Christian ought to live. If I walk in obedience to this revelation, I live on a higher, on a holier, plane than he who only had the Ten Commandments. Anyone having the wonderful teaching that came from the lips of the Lord Jesus Christ, and the marvelous unfolding of the epistles showing what a Christian ought to be, has this new standard of holiness, which is not the law given at Sinai, but the risen Christ at God's right hand, and as I am walking in obedience to Him my life will be a righteous life, and so, "After that faith is come we are no longer under the pedagogue."

Then he adds, "Ye are all the children (sons) of God by faith in Christ Jesus;" from Him we receive life. To whom does God communicate eternal life? To all who put their trust in His blessed Son. "He that hath the Son hath life; and he that hath not the Son of God hath not life" (1 John 5: 12). And so we can see why our Lord Jesus stresses, "Except a man be born again, he

cannot see the kingdom of God" (John 3:3).
There must be the impartation of the divine life.
This makes us members of God's family—a new
and wonderful relationship.

"For as many of you as have been baptized into
Christ have put on Christ." He probably has two
thoughts in mind here. Outwardly we put on
Christ in our baptism. That ordinance indicates
that we professedly have received the Lord Jesus
Christ, but I think also he has in view the baptism of the Holy Spirit, and by that we are
actually made members of Christ and, in the fullest, deepest sense, we put on Christ. And now as
members of that new creation, "there is neither
Jew nor Greek," national distinctions no longer
come in.   In this connection there is "neither
Jew nor Greek, there is neither bond nor free,
there is neither male nor female: for ye are all
one in Christ Jesus." He does not ignore natural
distinctions. Of course we still retain our natural
place in society, we remain servants or masters,
we remain male or female, but as to our place in
the new creation, God takes none of these distinctions into account. All who believe in the Lord
Jesus Christ are made one in Him, "members of
His body, of His flesh, and of His bones" (Eph.
5: 30). How we need to remember this!

"Ye are all one in Christ Jesus. And if ye be
Christ's, then are ye Abraham's seed, and heirs

according to the promise." To be "in Christ" and to be "Christ's," comes to exactly the same thing, "all one in Christ Jesus." "And if ye be Christ's (if you belong to Him), then are ye Abraham's seed, and heirs according to the promise." Because you too have believed God as Abraham did (Abraham "believed God, and it was counted unto him for righteousness"—Rom. 4: 3), it is counted to you for righteousness. And so every believer forms part of Abraham's spiritual seed. There is both the spiritual and the natural seed of Abraham. "They which be of faith are blessed with believing Abraham" (Gal. 3: 9). I hope we are clear as to this distinction between law and grace.

Some years ago I took with me to Oakland, California, a Navaho Indian. One Sunday evening he went to our young people's meeting. They were talking about this epistle to the Galatians, about law and grace, but they were not very clear about it, and finally one turned to the Indian and said, "I wonder whether our Indian friend has anything to say about this."

He rose to his feet and said, "Well, my friends, I have been listening very carefully, because I am here to learn all I can in order to take it back to my people. I do not understand what you are talking about, and I do not think you do yourselves. But concerning this law and grace, let me see if I can make it clear. I think it is like this. When Mr. Ironside brought me from my home we took the longest railroad journey I ever took. We got out at Barstow, and there I saw the most beautiful railroad station with a hotel above it, I have ever seen. I walked all around and saw at one end a sign, 'Do not spit here.' I looked at that sign and then looked down at the ground and saw many had spitted there, and before I think what I am doing I have spitted myself. Isn't that strange when the sign say, 'Do not spit here'? I come to Oakland and go to the home of the lady who invited me to dinner today and I am in the nicest home I have ever been in in my life. Such beautiful furniture and carpets I hate to step on them. I sank into a comfortable chair, and the lady said, 'Now, John, you sit there while I go out and see whether the maid has dinner ready.' I look around at the beautiful pictures, at the grand piano, and I walk all around those rooms. I am looking for a sign; the sign I am looking for is, 'Do not spit here,' but I look around those two beautiful drawing-rooms, and cannot find a sign like this. I think, What a pity when this is such a beautiful home to have people spitting all over it—too bad they don't put up a sign! So I look all over that carpet but cannot find that anybody have spitted there. What a queer thing! Where the sign says, 'Do not spit,' a lot of people spitted; here where there is no sign, nobody spitted. Now I understand! That sign is law, but inside the home it is grace. They love their beautiful home and want to keep it clean. I think that explains this law and grace business," and he sat down.

CHAPTER NINE

THE ADOPTION OF SONS

(Gal. 4: 1-7)

"Now I say, That the heir, as long as he is a child, differeth nothing from a servant, though he be lord of all; but is under tutors and governors until the time appointed of the father. Even so we, when we were children, were in bondage under the elements of the world: but when the fulness of the time was come, God sent forth His Son, made of a woman, made under the law, to redeem them that were under the law, that we might receive the adoption of sons. And because ye are sons, God hath sent forth the Spirit of His Son into your hearts, crying Abba, Father. Wherefore thou art no more a servant, but a son; and if a son, then an heir of God through Christ."

IN this section of the epistle the apostle makes a very interesting distinction, which, if thoroughly understood, will help greatly in enabling us to see the relative place of Old Testament believers and that of those in the present glorious dispensation of the grace of God. We need to remember that in all dispensations it was necessary that men be born again in order to become the children of God, and new birth has always been, on the part of adults at least, by faith in the divine revelation. We are told in James 1: 18, "Of His own will begat He us with the Word of truth, that we should be a kind of firstfruits of His creatures." What is true of us in this age has been true of believers in all ages. Each one was begotten by the Word of truth. Of

133

course, in the case of infants not yet come to years of accountability, God acts in sovereignty, regenerating them by His divine power apart from personal faith in the Word when they are too young to know it. Jesus has said, "It is not the will of your Father in heaven that one of these little ones should perish," but it is just as necessary that children be born again as in the case of adults, for, "That which is born of the flesh is flesh, and that which is born of the Spirit is spirit." There must be new birth on the part of every person who would enter the kingdom of God. But there are great dispensational distinctions marked out in Holy Scripture. In Old Testament times believers were all God's children, but they were not definitely recognized as His sons. In this age it is different. All of God's children are also His sons. Do you ask what is the difference? Well, the distinction is one that we today perhaps would not think of making, but when Paul wrote the epistle to the Galatians all his readers would understand it very clearly. In that day, minor children were not recognized as their father's heirs until, when they came of age, he took them down to the forum, answering to our court-house, and there officially adopted them as his sons. From that time on they were no longer considered as minor children, but recognized as heirs. Old Testament saints, the apostle

shows us, were in the position of children. New
Testament saints, since the coming of the Holy
Spirit at Pentecost, are acknowledged by God as
His sons by adoption. The Holy Spirit Himself
is the Spirit of adoption. When He is received
in faith, at the very moment of our conversion
we are marked out as God's sons and heirs. This
is confirmed in Rom. 8: 14-17: "For as many as
are led by the Spirit of God, they are the sons of
God. For ye have not received the spirit of bondage again to fear; but ye have received the Spirit
of adoption, whereby we cry Abba, Father. The
Spirit itself beareth witness with our spirit, that
we are the children of God: and if children, then
heirs; heirs of God, and joint-heirs with Christ;
if so be that we suffer with Him, that we may be
also glorified together."

The divinely-directed reasoning of the apostle
in these first seven verses in Galatians 4 is very
striking and beautiful in its orderly presentation
of the theme. He tells us, "Now I say, That the
heir, as long as he is a child, differeth nothing
from a servant," that is, a bondman, "though he
be lord of all." Take a young child in the home
before he has attained his majority. He may be
heir actually to vast wealth, but he is not permitted to have his own way, nor enter into the
possession of his patrimony. He is to be kept in
the place of subjection for discipline and train-

ing. His place in the home is practically no different than that of a servant. In fact, he himself has to be subject to the servant, as ver. 2
tells us; he is under guardians and stewards, or
tutors, until the time appointed of the father.
This is all perfectly plain and does not take an
erudite mind to understand it. Then note the
application. The apostle shows that the people
of Israel, God's earthly people, were in this state
of nonage. The apostle Paul identifies himself
with these as a Jew and says, "Even so we, when
we were children, were in bondage under the
elements (or principles) of the world." That is,
they were under the law, and the law speaks to
man in the flesh. It was given by God in order
to impress upon him his duties and responsibilities. It had no power in itself to produce the
new life, though it could guide the children of
God and show them the path they should take
through the world. It was really, however, an
almost intolerable bondage to those who did not
enter into the spiritual side of it. But now since
the new age has come in, the age of grace, a wonderful change has been brought about. We read:
"But when the fulness of the time was come, God
sent forth His Son, born of a woman, born under
the law, to redeem them that were under the law,
that we might receive the adoption of sons." "The
fulness of the time" was, of course, the comple-

tion of the prophetic periods as given in the Old
Testament. One would think particularly of the
great prophecy of the seventy weeks of Daniel.
When at last the time had arrived that Messiah
was destined to appear, God fulfilled His Word
by sending His Son into this scene to be born of a
woman, and that woman an Israelite under law.

Now observe one thing here. We meet certain
professed Christians today who deny what is
is called the Eternal Sonship of Christ. They tell
us He was not Son from eternity. They admit
He was the Word, as set forth in John 1: 1, but
they say He became the Son when He was born
on earth. Verse 4 definitely denies any such
teaching. "God sent forth His Son to be born of
a woman." He was the Son before He ever
stooped from the heights of glory to the virgin's
womb. It was the Son who came in grace to become Man in order that we might be saved. This
same truth is set forth in 1 John 4: 9, 10: "In
this was manifested the love of God toward us,
because God sent His only begotten Son into the
world that we might live through Him. Herein
is love, not that we loved God, but that He loved
us, and sent His Son to be the propitiation for
our sins." Nothing could be clearer than the
two definite statements in these verses. God sent
His Son, sent Him into the world, sent Him from
heaven, even as John 3: 16 declares: "God so

loved the world that He gave His only begotten Son." We dishonor the Lord Jesus Christ if we deny His Eternal Sonship. If He be not the Eternal Son, then God is not the Eternal Father. Someone has well asked, "Had the Father no bosom till Jesus was born in Bethlehem?" He came from the bosom of the Father, to be born into this world, in order that He might be our Kinsman-Redeemer.

He was born under the law. He took His place before God here on earth as an Israelite, subject to the law of God. He kept that law perfectly; sinless Himself, He never could come under its curse because of His own failure. Therefore, He was able to go to the cross and give Himself up to death to bear the curse of the broken law, that He might redeem them that were under the law, "that we," says the apostle, "might receive the adoption of sons." He met all that was against His people and brought them out into a place of full liberty where God could publicly own them as His sons, no longer children in the servant's place but heirs of God, joint-heirs with Jesus Christ. The testimony to this was the giving of the Holy Spirit. So in ver. 6 we read, "And because ye are sons, God hath sent forth the Spirit of His Son into your hearts, crying Abba, Father." This is true of all believers, for we need to remember that since the bringing in of the

new dispensation in all its fulness, every believer
is indwelt by the Holy Spirit, and thus sealed and
anointed. "If any man have not the Spirit of
Christ," we are told, "he is none of His." So
there is no such person in the world today as a
true Christian who is not indwelt by the Spirit
of God. We have the Spirit of the Son, and because He dwells in our hearts we now look up
with adoring love into the face of God and cry
"Abba, Father." "Abba" is the Hebrew word for
"Father." Our English word is the translation
of the Greek *'pateer,'* and so we have Jew and
Gentile united through grace, addressing God as
members of one family, as His children by birth
and His sons by adoption, and crying "Abba,
Father."

The apostle's conclusion follows very naturally:
"Wherefore, thou art no more a servant but a
son; and if a son, then an heir of God through
Christ." The old condition, which prevailed
throughout the centuries before Jesus came into
the world and died for all our sins upon the cross,
rose again for our justification, ascended to
heaven, and in unity with the Father sent the
Holy Spirit, that has come to an end. Believers
are no longer in the servant's place, but by the
reception of the Spirit are God's recognized sons,
and so heirs of all His possessions through Christ
Jesus our Lord.

In this connection it is interesting to notice that after the resurrection of the Lord Jesus from the dead, He said to Mary, "Go to My brethren, and say unto them, I ascend unto My Father, and your Father; and to My God and your God" (John 20:17). In this He fulfilled the prophecy written so long before, "I will declare Thy name unto My brethren" (Ps. 22:22). Though the Holy Spirit had not yet come, the Lord anticipates the full glory of the new dispensation by recognizing all the redeemed as His brethren, and thus He speaks of "My Father and your Father, My God and your God." Notice, He does not say, *our* Father and *our* God. There was good reason for this. God was His Father in a unique sense; He was His Father from eternity. This is not true of us. He is our Father when we receive Christ in faith as our Saviour. And so in regard to the other expression, "My God." It is written, "In the beginning was the Word, and the Word was with God, and the Word was God." Therefore God was His God in a different sense to that in which He is our God. He is our God because He is our Creator. We are merely creatures, while He Himself created all things. And so while there cannot be exactly the same relationship, yet the same Person who is His Father and His God is now our Father and our God, because we are sons of God through faith in Christ Jesus.

Oh, may our hearts enter more into the precious-ness of this, and as we realize something of the dignity of this wonderful place that God has given us, may we seek grace to so live in this scene as to bring glory to His name.

Remember, there is a certain sense in which He has entrusted the honor of His name to us. He said to Israel of old, "Thou shalt not take the name of the Lord thy God in vain." This did not refer to what we call swearing or profanity, but they were called by the name of the Lord and were responsible to magnify His name. Instead of that, the apostle Paul says of them, "Through you the name of God is blasphemed among the Gentiles." That is, the Gentiles saw so much that was wicked and corrupt in the behavior of God's earthly people that they said, "If these people are like their God, then He must be a very unholy Being indeed." Oh, my brethren, are we so be-having ourselves that men, "seeing our good works, glorify our Father which is in heaven?" Do they say, as they behold the grace of God in our lives, "How marvellous must be the love and the holiness of the God to whom these people be-long, and whose sons they profess to be!" It is as we walk in obedience to His Word that we magnify the grace which has saved us and put us into this blessed place of sons and heirs.

CHAPTER TEN

THE ELEMENTS OF THE WORLD

(Gal. 4: 8-20)

"Howbeit then, when ye knew not God, ye did service
unto them which by nature are no gods. But now, after
that ye have known God, or rather are known of God,
how turn ye again to the weak and beggarly elements,
whereunto ye desire again to be in bondage? Ye observe
days, and months, and times, and years. I am afraid of
you, lest I have bestowed upon you labor in vain. Brethren, I beseech you, be as I am; for I am as ye are: ye
have not injured me at all. Ye know how through infirmity of the flesh I preached the gospel unto you at the
first. And my temptation which was in my flesh ye despised not, nor rejected; but received me as an angel of
God, even as Christ Jesus. Where is then the blessedness ye spake of? For I bear you record, that, if it had
been possible, ye would have plucked out your own eyes,
and have given them to me. Am I therefore become your
enemy, because I tell you the truth? They zealously
affect you, but not well; yea, they would exclude you,
that ye might affect them. But it is good to be zealously
affected always in a good thing, and not only when I am
present with you. My little children, of whom I travail
in birth again until Christ be formed in you, I desire to
be present with you now, and to change my voice; for I
stand in doubt of you."

"HOWBEIT then, when ye knew not God, ye
did service unto them which by nature
are no gods." We have seen in this
epistle that the Galatians, who had been brought
out of heathen darkness into the light and liberty
of the gospel through the ministry of the apostle

Paul, had fallen under the charm—shall I say?—
of certain judaizing teachers who were carrying
them into subjection to the law of Moses, telling
them that unless they were circumcised and kept
the law of Moses they could not be saved, that
while they began in faith, they had to complete
their salvation through works of their own, ac-
quiring merit by obedience to the commands of
the law. The apostle has been showing them
that the law could only condemn, could only kill,
could not justify, could not give life, neither
could it sanctify, and that our sanctification is as
truly by faith as is our justification.

Now he reasons with them, trying to show the
folly of their course in giving up Christianity
with all its liberty and light for the twilight and
bondage of Judaism. "Why," he says, "you were
heathen when I came to you. You were enslaved
to heathen customs, you served those that you
esteemed to be gods who really are not gods, you
were worshippers of idols, and you know that
in those days you were misled by pagan priest-
craft. There were certain things you could not
eat, places you could not go, things you could not
touch. There were different kinds of offerings
that you had to bring, there were charms against
evil spirits, and amulets, and talismans. You
were slaves to worldly customs in those days of
your heathenism. The thing that amazes me is

that you should be willing to go into another bondage after having known something of the liberty of grace."

"But now, after that ye have known God, or rather are known of God, how turn ye again to the weak and beggarly elements, whereunto ye desire to be in bondage?" Notice that expression, "After that ye have known God, or rather are known of God." There are the two sides to it. We often say to people, "Do you know Jesus?" But it means more to realize that Jesus knows you, to be able to say, "Thank God, He knows me, and He knew about me in my sin, and He loved me and gave Himself for me." We sometimes say, "Have you found Jesus?" Of course the Word of God says, "Seek, and ye shall find," and the Lord bids us to "call upon Him while He is near," but it is a more wonderful truth that He seeks us. We have heard of the little boy who was approached by a Christian worker who said to him, "My boy, have you found Jesus?" And the little fellow looked up with a perturbed expression and said, "Why, please, sir, I didn't know He was lost; but I was, and He found me." That is it.

"I was lost, but Jesus found me,
    Found the sheep that went astray;
Threw His loving arms around me,
    Drew me back into His way."

God knew me long before I knew Him. He knows me now, since I have trusted Christ, as His child, and Paul says, "Isn't it a shame that after you have known God, or rather have been known of God, after you have come into this blessed relationship with Him as your Father, if you really know what it is to be born again, isn't it strange that you would turn now to as legal a system as that from which you were delivered when first brought to a saving knowledge of the Lord Jesus Christ?" "How turn ye again to the weak and beggarly elements, whereunto ye desire again to be in bondage?" Someone might say, "But what do you mean? They were turning to law, to observing Jewish feasts and Jewish sabbaths, Jewish ceremonies. But they never knew those things in their heathen days. Why does he say, 'How turn ye *again'?"* The principle was exactly the same. Why do the heathen go through their forms and ceremonies? Because they hope to gain merit and save their souls. Why did the Jews go through all their rites and ceremonies? That they might please God in that way, and so gain merit and eventually save their souls. The principle is just the same, whether you try to save yourself by offering your own child or the dearest thing you have on a heathen altar, whether you keep the seventh-day Sabbath, as some people do today, and thereby hope to save themselves, or whether you observe the heathen feast-days and hope to please the heathen gods thereby. The Jewish festivals have been fulfilled in Christ, and we are not going back to them, hoping to please God by their observance. They had their place once, and men of faith could observe them in obedience to the Word of God, but that place is not theirs now, because "Christ is the end of the law for righteousness to every one that believeth" (Rom. 10:4). All these ceremonies were merely shadows of things to come. Now that the reality is come, why go back to the shadow? We are not going to be occupied with the type since we have the Antitype; we are not going to be occupied with pictures when we have the Reality. The worldly principle, of course, is to try to merit salvation by works of your own.

There are only two religions in the world, the true and the false. All forms of false religion are alike, they all say, "Something in my hand I bring," the only difference being in what that something is. But the true religion, the revelation from heaven, leads a man to sing, "Nothing in my hand I bring." Christianity says, "Not by works of righteousness which we have done, but according to His mercy He saved us, by the washing of regeneration, and renewing of the Holy Ghost" (Titus 3:5). We see Christians today who turn to symbols and pictures as a means of helping them spiritually, but they are just going back to the elements of the world. If you were to ask a heathen, "Is this idol your god?" some would say, "Yes," but an intelligent heathen would reply, "No; it is not exactly that I consider that idol as my god, but it represents my god; it helps me to enter into communion with my god." You see just the same thing in Christendom where some churches are filled with images. They are not images of Mars, Jupiter, Venus, or Isis, or Osiris, but images just the same—images of Saint Joseph, Saint Barnabas, Saint Paul, the twelve apostles, the blessed Virgin Mary, and even of Christ. Candles are burning in front of them and people bow before them. We ask, "Why do you not worship God? Why worship these images?" And they answer, "We do not worship them; we reverence them, and they are simply aids to worship. These images help to stir up our spirits and help us to worship."

I heard a Protestant minister speaking to a group of ministers and he said, "I find that it is very helpful to have before me a very beautiful picture of the thorn-crowned Christ." He mentioned a painting by a certain artist, and said, "I have that framed; and when I want to come to the Lord I like to drop everything else and sit and contemplate that picture for a while, and I begin to realize more and more what He has done for me. That draws out my heart in worship and adoration." "How turn ye again to the weak and beggarly elements, whereunto ye desire again to be in bondage?" There is no painter on earth who can paint my Christ. You need to go to the Bible to get that picture. If you want to be stirred up and put in a worshipful spirit, sit down over your Bible and read the fifty-third chapter of Isaiah, or the account in the Gospels of what Christ accomplished, and as you are occupied with the truth of God your heart will be drawn out in worship. You do not need pictures to help you to worship. These are just the "weak and beggarly elements" of the world. In the dispensation of the grace of our Lord Jesus Christ we are to worship in "spirit and in truth."

So the apostle says, "I am sorry to see you go back to these things"—"Ye observe days, and months, and times, and years." That is, they were going back to the Jewish Sabbaths and other holy days and festivals, the Jewish Sabbatical year and the year of Jubilee. But, you see, these things are not binding on us today. Why? Because the Sabbath day of the Jews has found its fulfilment in Him who said, "Come unto Me, all ye that labor and are heavy laden, and I will give you rest" (Matt. 11:28). "There remaineth therefore a rest (a true Sabbath-keeping) for the people of God." We have found our Sabbath in

Christ, and so we observe the first day of the week, the day of His resurrection, not in order to gain merit but because we are glad to have the privilege of coming together as a company of worshipping believers and to take advantage of the opportunity to preach the gospel of the grace of God. That seventh-day Sabbath was the memorial of Israel's deliverance from Egypt. That does not apply to us, but we have found its fulfilment in Christ. Some may ask, "Are you quite certain that the Sabbath of the law is included among the shadows?" Yes, turn to Colossians 2: 16, 17: "Let no man therefore judge you in meat, or in drink, or in respect of an holy day, or of the new moon, or of the sabbath days: which are a shadow of things to come; but the body is of Christ." Do you not see?—it was the Sabbath of old, one day's rest in seven. Now I have Jesus, and I have seven days' rest in seven. I have rest in Him continually, and am delivered from the Sabbath of the law.

Then there were sacred months. There was the month in which they had the passover and the feast of the firstfruits. Then the seventh month, in which was the great day of atonement and the feast of tabernacles. But all of which those months and feasts speak has been fulfilled in Christ. He is the true passover: "Christ our Passover is sacrificed for us: therefore let us keep the feast, not with old leaven, neither with the leaven of malice and wickedness; but with the unleavened bread of sincerity and truth" (1 Cor. 5: 7, 8). The feast of the firstfruits had its fulfilment in the resurrection of Christ, and it was He who said, "Except a corn of wheat fall into the ground and die, it abideth alone: but if it die, it bringeth forth much fruit" (John 12:24). Christ fell into the ground in death, and now has become the firstfruits of them that slept, and we worship with adoring gratitude for all that this means to us. The great day of atonement has had its fulfilment in the cross. The Lord Jesus Christ was the sacrificed Victim whose precious blood makes atonement for the soul. We read, "The life of the flesh is in the blood: and I have given it to you upon the altar to make an atonement for your souls: for it is the blood that maketh an atonement for the soul" (Lev. 17: 11). That is all fulfilled in Jesus. And He is the true fulfilment of the feast of tabernacles, the feast which carries us on to His coming back again when He will bring in everlasting righteousness. They were all given to point forward to the coming of the blessed Son of God, and His wondrous work.

"Ye observe days, and months, and times, and years." Many in Israel had fallen into the evil habit of consulting astrologers and others, and so were known as observers of times, but that was

distinctly contrary to God's mind, and He links it
up with demons. Christians have nothing to do
with anything like that. Then they observed
sacred years. There was the Sabbatical year,
every seventh year had to be set apart as a Sabbath to the Lord. You cannot pick out certain
parts of the law and keep them only; if you are
bound to keep the seventh-day Sabbath, you are
bound to keep the seventh-year Sabbath also.
But Paul says that as Christians we are delivered
from all this. It was only bondage and we are
free from it.

"I am afraid of you, lest I have bestowed upon
you labor in vain." He really stood in doubt as
to whether they were truly converted. He re-
membered how they had confessed their sins, and
the joy they had, and now he says, "Was that not
genuine?" One may often feel like that about
people. Some make a good start and apparently
seem to be real Christians, but the next thing you
know they are taken up with some most unscriptural thing, and you wonder whether it was all a
mistake. If people are saved, they are sealed by
the Holy Spirit. He is the Spirit of Truth and
He comes to guide them into all truth. Thank
God, sometimes they are recovered, and then you
know they were real; but if never recovered, we
read, "They went out from us, but they were not
of us; for if they had been of us, they would no

doubt have continued with us: but they went out, that they might be made manifest that they were not all of us" (1 John 2:19).

Now he turns directly to these converts of his, and in the most tender way he says, "Brethren, I beseech you, be as I am; for I am as ye are: ye have not injured me at all." What does he mean? He is practically saying, "There was a time in my life when I observed all these things that you are going into now; when all my hope of heaven was based upon working out a righteousness of my own; and I was very punctilious about all these things that you now are taking up. I observed the Passover, I kept the feast of firstfruits, the ordinances of the great day of the atonement, and kept the feast of tabernacles. I did all these things that you are undertaking to do. I was careful about meats and drink, I looked upon certain foods as unclean and would have nothing to do with them, but I came to you as one of you. You did not know anything about the law, and I came to you as a man utterly delivered from the law of Moses, completely freed from it. I wish you would come over to where I am. Take your place now with me; I am not under law but under grace, and I want you to be under grace rather than under law." Before God, they were actually so, of course, if truly saved, but he would have them so in spirit.

He tells us elsewhere how he stood, "I am become all things to all men, if by any means I may save some. To the Jews I became as a Jew, that I might gain the Jews; to them that are under the law, as under the law, that I might gain them that are under the law; to them that are without law, as without law (being not without law to God, but under the law to Christ), that I might gain them that are without law" (1 Cor. 9:20, 21).

Let me illustrate Paul's position. Let this desk indicate it. He stands in the center between the two extremes. Over to the right are those under the law, the Jews; to the left are those without the law, the Gentiles who do not know anything about the law of Moses. Now he says, "I do not belong in either company since I am saved by grace, but stand here between the two, and being regenerated I am subject to Christ. In order that I may reach the Jew I go over there where he is, and am willing to sit down with him and partake of the kind of food he eats, and to go with him to his synagogue, in order that I may have an opportunity to preach to him. And I will use the law of Moses to show him his sin, and the prophets to show him the Saviour. Then I go to the Gentiles, but I do not preach the law of Moses to them." He could say, "When I came among you I took my place as a man not under law but

in the liberty of grace, and preached Christ to
you as the Saviour of all who believe. I wish you
would appreciate that enough to stand with me.
You leave me and go to the place God took me out
of before He saved me. Do you not see the mistake you are making? You are giving up grace
for law."

"Ye know how through infirmity of the flesh I
preached the gospel unto you at the first. And my
temptation which was in my flesh ye despised not
nor rejected; but received me as an angel of God,
even as Christ Jesus." He sought to touch their
hearts by reminding them of those early days
when he came to Antioch in Pisidia, and to Iconium, Lystra and Derbe, and preached the Word
among them. All of these were Galatian cities.
Did he come with pomp and ceremony, marvelous
costumes, and candles and images? No; nothing
like that. He came not as a great and mighty
ecclesiastic, as one professing to have authority
over them, but as a lowly man preaching Christ
and Him crucified. "Ye know how through infirmity of the flesh I preached the gospel unto you
at the first."

Paul was used of God to heal many sick people, but he never healed himself, and did not ask
anybody to heal him except God. He prayed for
deliverance three times, but God said, "I am not
going to deliver you but—My grace is sufficient

for thee," and Paul answered, "Most gladly therefore will I rather glory in my infirmities, that the power of Christ may rest upon me" (2 Cor. 12: 9). He was a sick man for years as he preached the gospel. He would come in among people, weak and tired and worn, and if there was not money enough to support him he would go to work and make tents to earn money for bread, and then at night would go and look for people to whom to preach Christ. He commended the gospel to these Galatians by his self-denying service and his readiness to suffer. As they (in those days, poor heathen) looked upon him they wondered that he should so love them, and they marvelled at his message, and believed it, and were saved. Now he says, "You have lost all that; you do not care anything about me any more; you have gone off after these false teachers, and you have lost your joy." "Where is then the blessedness ye spake of? For I bear you record, that, if it had been possible, ye would have plucked out your own eyes, and have given them to me." I take it that the suffering he endured had to do with his eyes. He probably had some affliction of the eyes that made it difficult for him to read and to see an audience, and it made his appearance mean when he stood upon the platform. Possibly they said, "Poor Paul! If we could give him our eyes we would gladly do so!" That is the way they once felt. "Am I therefore become your enemy, because I tell you the truth?" It was these evil teachers that had upset them.

"They zealously affect you, but not well; yea, they would exclude you, that ye might affect them." In other words, they have come to make a prey of you with their false teaching, trying to affect you adversely in order that you might rally around them, for they want to get up a little party of their own. They are not seeking your good, but trying to extend their own influence. "It is good to be zealously affected always in a good thing, and not only when I am present with you." That is, It is good for a man to be zealous in what is right, it is good to go after people with the truth and bring them into the light, and they who had started in the truth should have continued in it.

And now in his deep affliction he exclaims, "My little children, of whom I travail in birth again until Christ be formed in you." In other words, I remember when you were saved, I went through the very pangs of birth in my soul, and now I am going through it all again because I am in such anxiety about you. "I desire to be present with you now, and to change my voice; for I stand in doubt of you." In other words, "I am writing some strong things to you, but I would like to talk tenderly, lovingly, to you if I were only there.

I am not sure about you." False religion never can give certainty, but the blessed, glorious gospel of the grace of God does. It fully assures us of complete and final salvation if we believe God. Who then would turn away deliberately from the liberty that we have in Christ to the bondage of some false system?

CHAPTER ELEVEN

A DIVINE ALLEGORY

(Gal. 4: 21-31)

"Tell me, ye that desire to be under the law, do ye not hear the law? For it is written, that Abraham had two sons, the one by a bondmaid, the other by a freewoman. But he who was of the bondwoman was born after the flesh; but he of the freewoman was by promise. Which things are an allegory: for these are the two covenants; the one from the mount Sinai, which gendereth to bondage, which is Agar. For this Agar is mount Sinai in Arabia, and answereth to Jerusalem which now is, and is in bondage with her children. But Jerusalem which is above is free, which is the mother of us all. For it is written, Rejoice, thou barren that bearest not; break forth and cry, thou that travailest not: for the desolate hath many more children than she which hath an husband. Now we, brethren, as Isaac was, are the children of promise. But as then he that was born after the flesh persecuted him that was born after the Spirit, even so it is now. Nevertheless what saith the Scripture? Cast out the bondwoman and her son: for the son of the bondwoman shall not be heir with the son of the freewoman. So then, brethren, we are not children of the bondwoman, but of the free."

"TELL me, ye that desire to be under the law, do ye not hear the law?" We have already noticed that while the Galatians were a Gentile people who had been saved by grace, they had fallen under the influence of certain Judaizing teachers who were trying to put them under the law. They said, "Except ye be circumcised after the manner of Moses, ye cannot be saved" (Acts 15: 1), and so in this letter the apostle Paul has taken up the great question of Law and Grace and has been expounding it, clarifying it, making clear that salvation is not by works of the law but entirely by the hearing of faith.

Undoubtedly these Jewish teachers who had gotten into the Christian company were referring the believers back to the Old Testament, and they could give them scripture after scripture in which it seemed evident that the law was the supreme test, and that God had said, "The man which doeth those things shall live by them" (Rom. 10: 5), and, "Cursed is every one that continueth not in all things which are written in the book of the law to do them" (Gal. 3: 10). And so they sought to impress upon these believers the importance of endeavoring to propitiate God, of gaining divine favor by human effort.

Now he says, "You desire to be under the law; do you? Do you want to put yourself under the law of Moses? Why do you not hear the law? Why do you not carefully read the books of the law and see just what God has said?" He uses the term "law" here in two different ways. In the first instance as referring to Moses' law, the law given at Sinai with the accompanying rules and regulations, statutes and judgments, that were linked with it, but in the second, as refer-

ring to the books of the Law. "Tell me, ye that
desire to be under the law (the legal covenant),
do ye not hear the law (the books of the law in
which God tells us of the covenants) ?"

Then he turns them back to Genesis and says,
"For it is written, that Abraham had two sons,
the one by a bondmaid, the other by a freewoman." We know that story. Abraham's wife
was Sarah, and God had promised that Abraham
and Sarah should be the parents of a son who
was to be the precursor of the coming Seed in
whom all nations of the earth should be blessed,
but the years passed by and it seemed as though
there was to be no fulfilment of that promise.
Finally, losing hope, Sarah herself suggested that
they should descend to the lower custom of the
people of the nations around them, and that
Abraham should take another woman, not exactly
to occupy the full status of a wife, but one to be
brought into the home as a concubine. Abraham
foolishly acceded to that and took Hagar. As a
result of that union a son was born who was
called Ishmael, and Abraham fondly hoped that
he would prove to be the promised one through
whom the Messiah should come into the world.
But God said, "No; this is not the one. I told
you you should have a child of Sarah, and this
one is not the promised seed." Abraham pleaded,
"O that Ishmael might live before Thee!" (Gen.

17: 18). But God said, as it were, "He can have a certain inheritance, but he cannot be the child of promise. In due time Sarah herself shall have a child, and in that child My covenant will stand fast."

The apostle now shows us that these events had a symbolic meaning. He does not mean to imply that they did not actually take place as written. They did. Scripture says in 1 Corinthians 10: 11, speaking of Old Testament records, "Now all these things happened unto them for types: and they are written for our admonition, upon whom the ends of the world are come." Notice, "All these things happened." Some people say they did not happen, that they were just myths, or folk-lore, or something like that, but the Holy Ghost says, "All these things happened." And so what you read in the Word concerning different Old Testament characters, the nations, cities, and so on, all these are to be received as historic facts. During the last hundred years when the voice of archeology has been crying out so clearly and loudly, not one thing has been discovered to refute anything written in Scripture, while thousands of discoveries have helped to bear witness to and authenticate the Bible record. It does not need to be authenticated, of course, as far as faith is concerned, for we believe what God has said. However, these important

discoveries have helped in a large measure to shut
the mouths of skeptics who would not believe the
statements of Scripture to be true. Abraham
lived, Sarah lived, Hagar was a real personage,
the two sons were real personages. From Ishmael
came the Arabs, from Isaac, the Hebrews. From
the beginning the two boys did not get on together, and these nations were not friendly. That
explains the trouble in Palestine today. They
could not get on in the beginning, and cannot today. But the apostle undertakes to show that
these mothers and their sons had symbolic sig-
nificance.

"But he who was of the bondwoman was born
after the flesh (and so he speaks of all who are
only born after the flesh); but he of the freewoman was by promise" (Isaac was the child of
grace). It would have been absolutely impossible
from a natural standpoint for Abraham and
Sarah to become parents at the time Isaac was
born. It was a divine manifestation, a miracle.
Isaac was a child of promise, and hence the child
of grace. The apostle tells us that these things
are an allegory. All through the Word God has
used allegories in order that we might receive
great moral, spiritual, and typical lessons from
these incidents, and here the Spirit of God Himself unfolds one of them for us.

"Which things are an allegory: for these are

the two covenants; the one from the mount Sinai, which gendereth to bondage, which is Agar. For this Agar is mount Sinai in Arabia, and answereth to Jerusalem which now is, and is in bondage with her children. But Jerusalem which is above is free, which is the mother of us all." These two women represent the two covenants, Sarah, the Abrahamic covenant, and Hagar, the Mosaic covenant. What was the difference between these two? The Abrahamic covenant was the covenant of sovereign grace. When God said to Abraham, "In thee and in thy Seed shall all nations of the earth be blessed," He did not put in any conditions whatsoever. It was a divine promise. God said, "I am going to do it; I do not ask anything of you, Abraham, I simply tell you what I will do." That is grace. Grace does not make terms with people; grace does not ask that we do anything in order to procure merit. Many people talk about salvation by grace who do not seem to have the least conception of what grace is. They think that God gives them the grace to do the things that make them deserving of salvation. That is not it at all. We read, "Being justified freely by His grace" (Rom. 3:24), and that word "freely" literally means "gratuitously." The same word is translated "without a cause" in another portion of Scripture. It is said of the Lord Jesus Christ that the Scripture was fulfilled which was written concerning Him, "They hated Me without a cause" (John 15:25). Jesus never did anything to deserve the bad treatment that men gave Him, and you and I cannot do one thing to deserve the good treatment that God gives us. Jesus was treated badly by men freely; we who are saved are treated well by God freely. I hope that you understand this wonderful fact, and that your soul is thrilling with the joy of it! What a marvelous thing to be saved by grace! One reason that God saves people by grace is that, "It is more blessed to give than to receive," and He must have the more blessed part.

Years ago a wealthy lady in New York built a beautiful church. On the day of dedication her agent came up from the audience to the platform and handed the deed of the property to the Episcopal Bishop of New York. The bishop gave the agent $1.00 for the deed, and by virtue of the $1.00, which was acknowledged, the property was turned over to the Episcopal Church. You say, "What a wonderful gift!" Yes; in a certain sense it was, for the passing over of $1.00 was simply a legal observance. But after all, in the full Bible sense it was not a gift, for it cost $1.00; and so the deed was made out not as a deed of gift but as a deed of sale. It was sold to the Episcopal Church for $1.00. If you had to do one thing in order to be saved, if you had even to raise your hand, to stand to your feet, had but to say one word, it would not be a gift. You could say, "I did thus and so, and in that way earned my salvation," but this priceless blessing is absolutely free. "If by grace, then is it no more of works: otherwise grace is no more grace. But if it be of works, then is it no more grace: otherwise work is no more work" (Rom. 11: 6). That is what the Spirit of God tells us in the Word.

And so we see the covenant of grace illustrated in Sarah. God had said to Sarah, "You shall have a child, and that child will be the means of blessing to the whole world." It seemed impossible that that could ever be, but in God's good time His Word was fulfilled, at last through Isaac came our Lord Jesus Christ who brought blessing to all mankind. Hagar, on the other hand, was a bondwoman, and she speaks of the covenant of law, of the Mosaic covenant, made at mount Sinai, for there God said, "The man that doeth those things shall live in them," but no man was ever found who could keep that perfectly, and therefore on the ground of law no one ever obtained life. Sarah, who typifies grace, became the mother of the child of promise; Hagar typifies law, and became the mother of the child of the flesh. The law speaks only to the flesh, while the believer is the child of promise and has been born of divine power. "Except a man be born again, he cannot see the kingdom of God" (John 3:3). Why is it that people generally are so ready to take up with legality and so afraid of grace? It is because legality appeals to the natural mind.

I remember going through Max Muller's set of translations of Oriental Sacred Literature, in thirty-eight large volumes. I read them through in order to get an understanding of the different religious systems in oriental lands, and found that though they differed in ten thousand things, they all agreed on one thing, and that is that salvation was to be won by self-effort, the only difference being as to what the effort was. All taught salvation by works, and every religion except that which is revealed from heaven sets people doing something or paying something in order to win divine favor. This appeals to the natural man. He feels intuitively that God helps those that help themselves, and that if he does his best, surely then God will be interested enough to do something for him. But our best amounts to absolutely nothing. "All our righteousnesses are as filthy rags" (Isa. 64:6), and the sooner we learn that we have no goodness of our own, that we have nothing to present to God with which to earn our salvation, the better for us. When we learn that, we are ready to be saved by grace alone. We come to God as poor, needy, helpless

sinners, and through the work that the Lord
Jesus Christ has done for our salvation we who
believe in Him become the children of promise.

Hagar typified Jerusalem which is here on
earth because Jerusalem at that time was the center of the legal religion. But Sarah typifies Jerusalem above "which is the mother of us all," or
literally, "our mother." The law is the earthly
system, it speaks to an earthly people, to men
after the flesh, whereas grace is a heavenly system which avails to children of promise. Jerusalem above is "our mother." Why? Because
Christ is above. Christ has gone up yonder, and
having by Himself made purification for sins He
has taken His seat on the right hand of the
Majesty in the heavens and there He sits exalted,
a Prince and Saviour, and from that throne grace
is flowing down to sinful men.

> "Grace is flowing like a river,
>   Millions there have been supplied;
> Still it flows as fresh as ever,
>   From the Saviour's wounded side;
>   None need perish,
>   All may live since Christ has died."

Have you trusted this Saviour? Have you received that grace? Can you say, "Yes, I am a
citizen of heaven; Jerusalem above is my
mother"? Even Abraham looked for that heavenly city. God promised him an inheritance on
earth, and some day his children will have that

They are trying to get it now after the flesh, and are having a very hard time. Some day in accordance with the promise, they shall have it, and then it will be all blessing for them. That will be after their eyes are opened to see the Lord Jesus Christ as their Messiah. A great many people are troubled about Palestine. I am deeply interested in what is going on over there, and recognize in it a partial fulfilment of the Word, but the reason why the Jews were driven out of Palestine 1900 years ago was because they "knew not the time of their visitation," and when their own Saviour came they rejected Him. They said, "We have no king but Cæsar." And when Pilate asked, "What shall I do with Jesus which is called Christ?" they cried, "Away with Him, away with Him! Crucify Him!" (John 19: 15), "His blood be on us, and on our children" (Matt. 27: 25). How terribly that malediction has been answered through the centuries. That does not excuse the wickedness of the persecution of the Jews, but it is an evidence of divine judgment. They would not have the Saviour, and they have been under Cæsar's iron heel ever since. But now they are going back to Palestine. Have they changed in their attitude, in their thoughts? Have they turned to God and confessed the sin of crucifying the Lord of glory? No. Then how can they expect blessing as they go back to the land? No wonder there is trouble, trouble which will continue and increase until the dark and dreadful days of the Great Tribulation. They are but the children of Hagar, but some day when the Church has been caught up to be with the Lord, and God turns back to Israel, a remnant from them will be saved. "They shall look upon Me whom they have pierced, and they shall mourn for Him, as one mourneth for his only son" (Zech. 12:10), and when they own as Saviour and Lord, Him whom once they rejected, He will cleanse them from their sins; He will take them back to the land; He will bring them into blessing; He will destroy all their foes; and they themselves will become a means of blessing to the whole earth. That is the divine program as laid down in the Word of God.

I should like to urge any Jewish friends to search their own Scriptures. Will you not turn to your own Bible and read chapter 53 of the book of Isaiah, Psalm 22, Psalm 69, the last three chapters of the book of Zechariah, and then if you have a New Testament, read the epistle to the Hebrews and the Gospel of Matthew, and see if the Spirit of God will not show you what is the whole trouble with Israel to-day? All their troubles have come upon them because they sought the blessing not after the Spirit but after the flesh, and so refused the promised Seed when

He came. And you Gentiles, if you are seeking
salvation by church-membership, by observing
ordinances, by charity, by your own good works,
prayers, and penances, can you not see that you
too are seeking the blessing after the flesh when
God would give it to you on the ground of pure
grace? Oh, that you might become children of
Sarah, of the covenant of grace, who can say,
"Thank God, Jerusalem above is our mother."
"Our citizenship," says the apostle, "is in heaven;
from whence also we look for the Saviour, the
Lord Jesus Christ" (Phil. 3:20). And Abraham,
we are told, "looked for a city which hath founda-
tions, whose Builder and Maker is God" (Heb.
11:10). Abraham is in heaven, and all his spiritual children who have died in the past are with
him there. The Lord Jesus tells of the poor beg-
gar, the child of Abraham, who died and was carried by the angels to Abraham's bosom. All the
redeemed who have passed off the scene are in
this same glorious paradise where Abraham is,
and by-and-by, when Jesus comes, we all shall join
that glad throng.

And then, not only now but through the millennial age, how many will be the children of God!
So the apostle quotes from Isaiah 54:1: "Rejoice,
thou barren that bearest not; break forth and
cry, thou that travailest not: for the desolate hath
many more children than she which hath an hus-

band." What a strange scripture! First notice
its character. The chapter that precedes it is
Isaiah 53. There we have the fullest, the most
complete prophecy of the coming into the world
of the Lord Jesus, His suffering and death and
resurrection, that is to be found anywhere in the
Bible. Isaiah seems to see Him suffering, bleeding, and dying on the cross, and he says: "He
was wounded for our transgressions, He was
bruised for our iniquities: the chastisement of
our peace was upon Him; and with His stripes we
are healed. All we like sheep have gone astray;
we have turned every one to his own way; and
the Lord hath laid on Him the iniquity of us all"
(Isa. 53: 5,6), and the prophet closes that chapter
with the wonderful words, "He bare the sin of
many, and made intercession for the transgressors" (ver. 12). And then the very next word,
when you come to chapter 54, is *"Sing!"* There
is enough there to make you sing: "He bare the
sin of many, and made intercession for the transgressors. Sing!" Of what shall we sing? Of the
matchless grace that God has manifested in
Christ. Paul translated that word, "Sing," "Rejoice." Why? Because Jesus has died, the sin
question is settled, and now God can let free grace
flow to poor sinners. Grace in the past had been
like a woman who was forsaken and alone, and
longed to be the mother of children, but wept and

mourned alone. And on the other hand here is legality typified by another woman, and she has thousands of children, people who profess to be saved by human effort, saved by their own merits. Yes; legality is a wonderful mother, she has a vast family, and poor grace does not seem to have any children at all. But now the gospel goes forth, and what happens? Grace, the one forsaken, neglected, becomes the mother of more children than legality. "For it is written, Rejoice, thou barren that bearest not; break forth and cry, thou that travailest not: for the desolate hath many more children than she which hath an husband." And so grace now has untold millions of children, and there will be millions more in the glorious age to come.

> "Millions have reached that blissful shore,
> Their trials and their labors o'er,
> And still there's room for millions more.
> Will you go?"

"Now we, brethren, as Isaac was, are the children of promise." Are you sure that is true of you? Have you believed God's promise? He has promised a full, free, and eternal salvation to every one who trusts His Son. We who have believed are children of promise. But the children of legality cannot understand this. No one hates grace as much as the man who is trying to save himself by his own efforts.

"But as then he that was born after the flesh persecuted him that was born after the Spirit, even so it is now." During the dark ages, for over 1,000 years, the doctrines of grace were practically lost to the Church, and many were trying to save themselves by penances, by long weary journeys, by thousands and thousands of prayers repeated over and over, by giving of their wealth to endow churches and build monasteries. The children of legality were a great host, and God opened the eyes of Martin Luther, John Knox, John Calvin, William Farel, and a host of others, and they found out that while men had been trying to save themselves by human effort it was the will of God to save poor sinners by grace. Luther took hold of the text, "The just shall live by faith," and the truth began to ring out all over Germany and Europe and then spread to Britain, and soon bitter persecution broke out and people cried, "Put them to death, these people who believe in salvation by grace, who do not believe that they can be saved by penances and human merit; burn them, starve them, shoot them, behead them, do everything possible to rid the world of them!" They do not get rid of them in those ways today, but the world still hates and detests the people who are saved by grace. If you come into a community where people are go· ing on in a smug self-righteousness, imagining they are going to heaven by church-attendance, because they were baptized as babies, were confirmed at twelve years of age, have given of their money, and have attended to their religious duties, and you ask, "Are you saved?" their answer will be, "Nobody can ever know until they get to the judgment-seat, but I am trying to be." "Well," you say, "you can be sure;" and you tell them of salvation by grace, and they exclaim, "What is this? What detestable fanaticism!" and at once they will begin to persecute you. The children of the flesh cannot stand the children of the Spirit.

"Nevertheless what saith the Scripture? Cast out the bondwoman and her son: for the son of the bondwoman shall not be heir with the son of the freewoman." God says, "My children are the children of promise; My children are those who are saved by grace." Do you know the blessedness of the reality of it in your own soul?

"So then, brethren," the apostle concludes, "we are not children of the bondwoman, but of the free." In other words, we have nothing to do with the legal covenant but we are the children of the covenant of grace.

> "Grace is the sweetest sound
>   That ever reached our ears,
> When conscience charged and justice frowned,
>   'Twas grace removed our fears."

Chapter Twelve

FALLING FROM GRACE

(Gal. 5: 1-6)

"Stand fast therefore in the liberty wherewith Christ
hath made us free, and be not entangled again with the
yoke of bondage. Behold, I Paul say unto you, that if
ye be circumcised, Christ shall profit you nothing. For
I testify again to every man that is circumcised, that he
is a debtor to do the whole law. Christ is become of no
effect unto you, whosoever of you are justified by the
law; ye are fallen from grace. For we through the
Spirit wait for the hope of righteousness by faith. For
in Jesus Christ neither circumcision availeth any thing,
nor uncircumcision; but faith which worketh by love."

IN chapters 5 and 6 we have the third division,
the practical part, of this letter. He shows
us what the result should be in our daily
lives if we have laid hold of the blessed truth that
salvation is altogether by grace through faith in
Christ Jesus, and so begins like this, "Stand fast
therefore." Wherefore? Because of the finished
work of Christ through which all who believe
have been not only delivered from the judgment
due to their sins, not only delivered from the
penalty of the broken law, but delivered from the
law itself and en-lawed to Christ. The believer
now walks in a place that was never known before. He is down here in this world, it is true,
but he is neither without law, nor yet under law,
but is subject to the Lord Jesus Christ, and so is

brought into a glorious liberty—liberty, of course, not to do the will of the natural man, not to obey the dictates of the flesh, but liberty to glorify God, to adorn the doctrines of Christ by a holy, triumphant life as he passes through this scene. This is the liberty into which Christ has brought us, and now to go back to some legalistic system such as that of Judaism or those prevailing in Christendom today, is to become "entangled again with the yoke of bondage."

Through the centuries that the Jews were under the law, not one of them found salvation through practising the ceremonial law or obeying the law given at Mt. Sinai, because every man failed, and it put them all under condemnation. But Christ has brought us into liberty. How foolish then to go back under law which only engenders bondage. Paul could say, I was in that bondage once, but I was delivered from it. You heathen people never knew that bondage, but you do know something of the liberty of Christ. Are you going now into the bondage out of which God delivers every Jew He saves? It is folly to take a step like that. But if you mean to do it, you had better go the whole length, for you cannot take certain commands and say, "I will obey those things," for God says, "Cursed is every one that continueth not in all things which are written in the book of the law to do them" (Gal. 3: 10).

"Behold, I Paul say unto you, that if ye be circumcised, Christ shall profit you nothing." That is, if they depended upon the rite of circumcision for the salvation of their souls they were ignoring Christ. He is not saying that if somebody had been misled for the moment and had accepted the teaching of these Judaizers, he lost Christ; but if their dependence was upon these things, they have set Christ at naught. "For I testify again to every man that is circumcised, that he is a debtor to do the whole law." If you take the first step, go the whole length, for the law is one. You cannot take from it what you please and reject the rest. "Christ is become of no effect unto you, whosoever of you are justified by the law; ye are fallen from grace." Of course the real meaning is, that if one is seeking justification by law, he is seeking to be right with God on the basis of his own human efforts. You say, "Well, God commanded His people to do them." Yes, in the Old Testament; but we read that "the law was our schoolmaster (our child-leader) until Christ," but now that Christ has come we are no longer under the child-leader. If you go back to law, you set Christ to one side; you cannot link the two principles of law and grace.

In Romans we are told that if salvation is "by

grace, then is it no more of works: otherwise grace is no more grace. But if it be of works, then is it no more grace: otherwise work is no more work" (Rom. 11:6). It must be one or the other. Either you earn your salvation by efforts of your own, or you accept it as the free gift of God. If you have trusted Christ as your Saviour you have received it as a gift. If you did anything to deserve it, if you worked for it, if you purchased it, it would not be a gift. So we read, "To him that worketh is the reward not reckoned of grace, but of debt. But to him that worketh not, but believeth on Him that justifieth the ungodly, his faith is counted for righteousness" (Rom. 4:4, 5). Therefore, if you turn back to law after you have known Christ, you are deliberately setting your Saviour to one side. "Ye are fallen from grace."

That is an expression that a great many people are interested in. A man came to a friend of mine, a Methodist minister, and said, "I understand that you Methodists believe in falling from grace; is that so?"

He said, "I understand that you Presbyterians believe in horse-stealing."

"No, we do not."

"Well, don't you believe that it is possible for a man to steal horses?"

"Yes, but we wouldn't do it."

"Well, we believe it is possible for men to fall from grace, but we do not believe in doing it."

But what do we mean by falling from grace? Here we have the expression in Scripture, "Ye are fallen from grace." Really, a better translation is, "Ye are fallen away from grace"—you have turned away from grace. Does this mean that if a man is once a Christian but falls into some kind of sin, he loses his salvation and is no longer a Christian? If it meant that, every believer ceases to be a Christian every day, because there is not a person anywhere that does not fall into some kind of sin every day—sins of thought, of word, or of deed. But falling from grace is not sinking into sin, into immorality or other evil-doing, but it is turning from the full, clear, high Christian standard of salvation by grace alone to the low level of attempting to keep one's salvation by human effort. Therefore, a man who says, "I am saved by grace, but now my continuance depends on my own effort," has fallen from grace. That is what it is to "fall from grace."

I do not care what it is you imagine you have to do in order to keep saved; whatever it is, you put yourself on legal ground if after believing on the Lord Jesus Christ you think that your salvation is made more secure by baptism, by taking the Lord's Supper, by giving money, by joining the church. If you do these things in order to

help save your soul, you have fallen from grace—
you fail to realize that salvation is by grace alone,
God's free unmerited favor. Someone asks,
"Don't you believe in doing those things?" Indeed, I do; not in order to save my soul, but out
of love for Christ.

> "I would not work my soul to save,
> That work my Lord has done;
> But I would work like any slave
> From love to God's dear Son."

Christian obedience is not on the principle of law
but of love to Christ.

It is the grace of God working in the soul that
makes the believer delight in holiness, in righteousness, in obedience to the will of God, for real
joy is found in the service of the Lord Jesus
Christ. I remember a man who had lived a life
of gross sin. After his conversion one of his old
friends said to him, "Bill, I pity you—a man that
has been such a high-flier as you. And now you
have settled down, you go to church, or stay at
home and read the Bible and pray; you never
have good times any more."

"But, Bob," said the man, "you don't understand. I get drunk every time I want to. I go
to the theater every time I want to. I go to the
dance when I want to. I play cards and gamble
whenever I want to."

"I say, Bill," said his friend, "I didn't understand it that way. I thought you had to give up these things to be a Christian."

"No, Bob," said Bill, "the Lord took the 'want to' out when He saved my soul, and He made me a new creature in Christ Jesus."

We do not make terms with the Lord and say, "If You will save me, I won't do this, and I will do that," but we come throwing up our hands and saying, "Lord, I cannot do a thing to save myself; Thou must do it in Thine own free grace or I am eternally lost." Now if as Christians we stoop down from that high level and still try to make ourselves acceptable to God by some human effort, we have fallen from grace. Yes, we do believe it is possible to fall from grace, and we also believe that about three-fourths of Christendom have fallen from grace. I do not mean that they won't get to heaven, but I do mean that many real Christians have come down to a very low level. They are so occupied with their own efforts instead of with the glorious finished work of our Lord Jesus Christ.

"For we through the Spirit." Everything for the believer is through the Spirit. The Holy Spirit has come to dwell in us, and God works His works in us by the Spirit. And so instead of human efforts, instead of trying to do something in order to earn divine favor, we yield ourselves to the Holy Spirit of God that He may work in and through us to the glory of our Lord Jesus Christ. "For we through the Spirit wait for the hope of righteousness by faith." What is the hope of righteousness? It is the coming again of our Lord Jesus Christ and our gathering together unto Him. We are now made the righteousness of God in Christ, and yet every day we mourn over our failures; we do not rise to the heights we desire. Every night we have to kneel before God and confess our sins. But we are looking on in glad hope to the time when Jesus will come back again and transform these bodies of our humiliation, and then we shall be fully like Him.

> "Soon I'll pass this desert dreary,
>   Soon will bid farewell to pain,
> Nevermore be sad or weary,
>   Never, never sin again."

"When He shall appear, we shall be like Him; for we shall see Him as He is" (1 John 3: 2).

"For in Jesus Christ neither circumcision availeth any thing, nor uncircumcision; but faith which worketh by love." Whether a man is a Jew or a Gentile it does not make any difference, whether he has been a rigid law-keeper or an idolator, there is no difference, "For all have sinned, and come short of the glory of God" (Rom. 3: 23). When people put their trust in the Lord Jesus Christ the Holy Spirit comes to dwell in them, and they are said to be "in Christ," and,

"There is therefore now no condemnation to them which are in Christ Jesus" (Rom. 8:1), for we are forever linked up with His Son, the Lord Jesus Christ. Our human works and religious ceremonies count for nothing as far as justifying the soul. What does count? "Faith which worketh by love." And as we walk in fellowship with the Lord Jesus Christ, as our hearts are taken up with Him, as faith makes Christ real ("Faith is the substance of things hoped for, the evidence of things not seen," Heb. 11:1), we shall find that it is the substantiating of the things for which we hope, the assured conviction of the reality of things that our eyes have never seen. Faith tells us Jesus lives, faith tells us that the sin question is settled, that we are in Christ. As we go on in faith looking to Him, drawing from Him new supplies of grace day by day, faith worketh by love, and love is the fulfilling of the law, and therefore we do not need to be under the law in order to live aright. It is the only natural thing now for Christians to seek to live for the glory of our Lord Jesus Christ.

A physician came into a room where I was visiting a family where a dear child was very ill. She was the apple of the mother's eye. The doctor said, "Now, Mrs. So-and-So, there is one thing I would suggest. Because of the condition the little one is in, I would not let anyone else take

care of her but yourself. It is going to mean a
great deal to the child to have you care for her.
She is in a very nervous condition." Do you think
that mother found that a hard law to obey? Her
mother-heart led her to respond at once, "Yes,
Docor, I will see that no one else looks after the
baby. I will do all I can for her." Was that
legality? No, it was "faith working by love." So
with the Christian. All our obedience springs
from heart-devotion to the Lord Jesus Christ. We
delight to do good, we delight to help others, we
delight to preach His Word, to minister to those
in need and distress, we delight in what Jesus Himself calls "good works," because we love Christ and
we want to do those things of which He approves.
Anything else than this is to "fall from grace."

CHAPTER THIRTEEN

FAITH WORKING BY LOVE

(Gal. 5: 7-15)

"Ye did run well; who did hinder you that ye should
not obey the truth? This persuasion cometh not of Him
that calleth you. A little leaven leaveneth the whole
lump. I have confidence in you through the Lord, that
ye will be none otherwise minded: but he that troubleth
you shall bear his judgment, whosoever he be. And I,
brethren, if I yet preach circumcision, why do I yet
suffer persecution? Then is the offence of the cross ceased.
I would they were even cut off which trouble you. For,
brethren, ye have been called unto liberty; only use not
liberty for an occasion to the flesh, but by love serve one
another. For all the law is fulfilled in one word, even in
this: Thou shalt love thy neighbor as thyself. But if ye
bite and devour one another, take heed that ye be not
consumed one of another."

PAUL now goes on to show that Christian liberty is not license to live after the flesh, but
it is liberty to glorify God. Notice how he
pours out his heart to them as he thinks of their
defection. He says, "Ye did run well." That is,
he looks back over their earlier years and reminds
himself of their first devotion and joy, how consistent they were, how they sought to glorify the
Lord. But their testimony has been marred, their
earlier love has been lost, they no longer are such
devoted, active servants of the Lord Jesus Christ

185

as once they were. They have been turned aside by false teaching.

"Ye did run well; who did hinder you that ye should not obey the truth?" What was it that turned them aside? It was their acceptance of the idea that although they were justified by faith they could be sanctified only by the law, and that is a very common error today. A great many people think that while the law cannot justify, yet after all, when one is justified, it is obedience to the law that sanctifies. But the law is as powerless to sanctify as it was to justify. It is of no use to try to put the old nature under law. You have two natures, the old, the carnal, and the new, the spiritual. That old nature is just as black as it can be, and the new is as white as it can be. The old is just as evil as it can be, and the new is as good as it can be. It is of no use to say to the old nature, "You must obey the law," because the carnal mind is not subject to the law of God. On the other hand, you do not need to say that to the new nature, because it delights in the law of God. So our sanctification is not of the law. These Galatians had lost sight of this.

And so in verse 8 the apostle says, "This persuasion cometh not of Him that calleth you." The word translated "persuasion" might be better rendered "persuasibleness." This persuasibleness, this readiness on your part to be persuaded by

these false teachers, "cometh not of Him that
calleth you." People are as easily changed in their
religious views as they are in their political
views. They are one thing one day, and another
thing the next. They start out all right, and then
the first false teacher that comes along gets their
attention, and if he quotes a few scripture verses
they say, "It sounds all right; he has the Bible
for it," and so they go from one thing to another
and never get settled anywhere. The apostle says
that this readiness to be persuaded by human
teachers is not of God. If you were walking with
God you would be listening to His voice and hearing His Word, and would be kept from over-
persuasibleness.

"A little leaven leaveneth the whole lump," we
are told in verse 9. This same sentence is found
in 1 Corinthians 5: 6, where Paul warns the
saints against the toleration of immorality in
their midst. An evil man was among them. He
was living in sin and they seemed powerless to
deal with it, like some churches today who have
never had a case of discipline for years, tolerating all kinds of wickedness. They do not dare to
come out and deal with it. These Corinthians
were glorying in the fact that they were broad-
minded enough to overlook this man's adultery
and incest, and Paul says to them, "If you are
going to do this, you must face the fact that 'a

little leaven leaveneth the whole lump.' Others
looking on will say, 'If the Church of God does
not take a stand against these things, why should
we be so careful?' "

Here in Galatians, the apostle is not speaking
of wickedness in the life but of false doctrine, and
says that if they do not deal with it in the light
of God's Word they will find that it too is like
leaven, and "A little leaven leaveneth the whole
lump," and the time will come when they will
have lost altogether the sense of the grace of
God. It is interesting to notice that in the Word
of God leaven is always a picture of evil. A great
many people do not see that. They talk about
"the leaven of the gospel." In Matthew where
the Lord Jesus says, "The kingdom of heaven is
like unto leaven, which a woman took, and hid in
three measures of meal, till the whole was
leavened" (Matt. 13: 33), their idea is that the
three measures of meal represents the world, and
the woman is the Church putting the leaven, the
gospel, into the world, and by-and-by the whole
world will be converted. We have been at it now
for nearly 2,000 years, and instead of the world
getting converted, the professing Church is getting unconverted.

Think of issuing a decree to blot out the name
of Jehovah from all texts written on the walls of
any church in Germany—Germany, the land of

the Reformation; Germany, where Luther led the people away from the darkness of corruption—and think of that country attempting to blot out the name of Jehovah today! We are not converting the world very fast. Think of Russia where the Gospel was introduced over 1500 years ago, and today every effort is being made to destroy the testimony that remains in that land. It will take millennium after millennium if ever the world is to be saved by our testimony. But that is not our program. We read, "When the Son of Man cometh, shall He find faith on the earth?" (Luke 18: 8). "As it was in the days of Noe, so shall it be also in the days of the Son of Man" (Luke 17: 26). Corruption and vileness filled the world in the days of Noah, and so today corruption and vileness fill the world. "They did eat, they drank, they married wives, they were given in marriage, until the day that Noe entered into the ark, and the flood came, and destroyed them all" (Luke 17: 27). We see the same things happening now, and some day the Lord's people are going, not into the ark, but they are going to be caught up to meet the Lord in the air, and then the awful flood of judgment will be poured out on this poor world. The parable does not mean that the gospel will go on until the whole world is converted; it means the very opposite. The three measures of meal represented the meal-offering, and the meal-offering was the food of the people of God and typified Christ, our blessed, holy Saviour. There was to be no leaven in the meal-offering, for that was a type of evil. The leaven is the evil teaching corrupting the truth. Jesus indicated three kinds of leaven. He said, "Beware of the leaven of Herod, beware of the leaven of the Pharisees, beware of the leaven of the Sadducees." The leaven of Herod was political corruption and wickedness, that of the Pharisees was self-righteousness and hypocrisy, and that of the Sadducees was materialism. Of any of these it may be said, "A little leaven leaveneth the whole lump." The thing that stops its working is to expose it to the action of fire, and when we judge these things in the light of the gospel of Christ they can work no longer.

But though Paul warns these Galatians he does not give them up. He feels sure that they will come out all right, for he knows how real they were in the beginning. "I have confidence in you through the Lord, that ye will be none otherwise minded: but he that troubleth you shall bear his judgment, whosoever he be." What a solemn word that is! God has said, "Be not deceived; God is not mocked: for whatsoever a man soweth, that shall he also reap" (Gal. 6: 7). And we are told, "There is no respect of persons with God" (Rom. 2: 11). How that ought to keep our hearts

as we see men in high places today guilty of
heinous crimes against civilization. We shudder
as we see how hopeless it is for the nations to
contend with these men and their evil principles.
How the tyrants of earth still defy God! But,
depend upon it, He is going to take things in His
own hands one of these days, and judgment is
coming as surely as there is a God in heaven. For
God has said, regarding Abraham's seed, "Cursed
be every one that curseth thee, and blessed be he
that blesseth thee" (Gen. 27: 29), and the man
who is dealing cruelly with Abraham's seed is
already under the curse of God. That judgment
some day will fall. We can be sure of that. There
is no way out, because God has decreed it. Men
may trifle with God for the moment, they may
question because He seems to wait a long time,
but the Greeks used to say, "The mills of the gods
grind slowly, but they grind exceeding small." In
every aspect of life the truth remains that God is
a God of judgment, and, "By Him actions are
weighed" (1 Sam. 2: 3).

Paul then says, "And I, brethren, if I yet preach
circumcision"—suppose I preached all these
legalistic things, would I be persecuted as I am
now? Surely not. But if I did that, I would not
be true to my great commission. "Why do I yet
suffer persecution? Then is the offence (the
scandal) of the cross ceased." What does he

mean by "the scandal of the cross"? It was a scandalous end to a human life to have to die on a cross. The cross was like the gallows today. Cicero said, "The cross, it is so shameful it never ought to be mentioned in polite society." Just as a person having a relative who had committed murder and was hung for it, would not want to speak about it, so people felt about the cross in those days. Yet the Son of God died on a cross. Oh, the shame of it! The Holy One, the Eternal Creator, the One who brought all things into existence, went to that cross and died for our sins. Paul practically says, You are setting that cross at naught if you introduce any other apparent means of salvation in place of the death Jesus died to put away sins. And then he cries, "I would they were even cut off which trouble you." Or literally, "I would they would cut themselves off that trouble you," these men who would pervert the gospel of Christ.

In verse 13 he comes back to the theme of liberty, "For, brethren, ye have been called unto liberty"—you have been set free, you are no longer slaves, you are free men—"only use not liberty for an occasion to the flesh." Do not say, "Well, now, I am saved by grace and therefore I am free to do as I like." No; but, I am saved by grace and so I am free to glorify the God of all grace! I have liberty to live for God, I have liberty to magnify the Christ who died for me, and I have liberty to walk in love toward all my brethren. It is a glorious liberty this, the liberty of holiness, of righteousness. "But by love serve one another." Having been called into this liberty be willing to be a servant. Our blessed Lord set us the example; He took that place on earth: "If I, then, your Lord and Master, have washed your feet; ye also ought to wash one another's feet" (John 13: 14). Through love we delight to serve. Look at that mother caring for her little babe. She has to do many things her heart does not naturally delight in. Is her service a slavery as she waits upon her babe? Oh, no; she delights to do that which love dictates, and so in our relation to one another, how glad we ought to be to have the opportunity of serving fellow-saints. "By love serve one another."

"For all the law is fulfilled in one word." It is as though he says, You talk about the law, you insist that believers should come under the law; why don't you stop to consider what the law really teaches? "All the law is fulfilled in one word, even in this: Thou shalt love." The man who loves will not break any of the commandments. If I love God as I should, I will not sin against Him. Look at Joseph, exposed to severe temptation, greater perhaps than many another has gone through, and yet his answer to the

temptress was, "How shall I do this great wickedness and sin against God?" He loved God and
that kept him in the hour of temptation. And
when it comes to dealing with our fellows, if we
love our neighbor as ourselves we won't violate
the commandments. We won't lie one to another,
we won't bear false witness, no one will commit
adultery, there will be no violation of God's law,
we will not murder. No wrong will be done to
another if we are walking in love. "All the law
is fulfilled in one word, even in this: Thou shalt
love thy neighbor as thyself." The Holy Spirit
who dwells in every believer is the Spirit of love,
and the new nature is a nature which God Himself has implanted, God is love and therefore it
is natural for the new nature to love. When you
find a believer acting in an unloving way, doing
an unkind thing, you may be sure that it is the
old nature, not the new, that is dominating him
at that moment. Oh, to walk in love that Christ
may be glorified in all our ways! It was said of
early Christians, even by the heathen about them,
"Behold how they love one another!" Can that
always be said of us? Or must it be said, "Behold how they quarrel; behold how they criticize;
behold how they backbite one another; behold
how they scandalize one another." What a shame
if such things could be said of us! "All the law

is fulfilled in one word, even in this: Thou shalt love."

Now on the other hand, if one fails in this, "If ye bite and devour one another, take heed that ye be not consumed one of another." If you would tear one another's reputations to pieces, find fault with one another, quarrel with one another, be careful, for the natural result will be that you will be "consumed one of another." Do you know why many a testimony that was once bright for God today is in ruins? It is because of a spirit of quarrelsomeness, fault-finding, and murmuring, comes in among the people of God, and God cannot bless that. If you and I are guilty of that, we ought to get into God's presence and examine our ways before Him; yea, plead with Him to search our hearts, and confess and judge every such thing as sin in His sight in order that we may be helpers and not hinderers in His service.

"If ye bite and devour one another, take heed that ye be not consumed one of another." "Well," someone says, "I always hate myself if I say anything unkind, and I make up my mind never to do it again." The trouble is that you have not yielded that tongue of yours to the Lord Jesus Christ. You remember the word, "Present your bodies a living sacrifice, holy, acceptable unto

God, which is your reasonable service" (Rom. 12: 1). A number of people have presented almost every part of their bodies except their tongues. They have kept the tongues for themselves, and they allow them to wag on and on until gradually they bring in a lot of sorrow and grief among the people of God. Won't you say, "Lord, this tongue of mine was given me to glorify Thee; I have used it so often to find fault with others, to injure the reputation of a brother or a sister, to speak unkindly or discourteously about other people. Lord Jesus, I give it to Thee, this tongue that Thou hast bought with Thy blood. Help me to use it from this time on solely to glorify Thee. And in using it to glorify Thee, I shall be using it to bless and help others, instead of to distress and hinder them."

You may never yet have come to Jesus, and possibly you are saying, "Is there a power such as you speak of that can lift a person above a life of sin, enabling him to so live?" Yes, there is; come to the Lord Jesus Christ, put your trust in Him, receive Him as your Saviour, enthrone Him as Lord of your life, and you will find that everything will be different, everything will be new. You will have a joy, a gladness, that you have never been able to find in all the devious ways of this poor world. He says, "Behold, I stand at the door, and knock: if any man hear

My voice, and open the door, I will come in to him, and will sup with him, and he with Me" (Rev. 3: 20). Fling wide the door of your heart today, and say:

> "Come in, my Lord, come in,
>   And make my heart Thy home.
> Come in, and cleanse my soul from sin,
>   And dwell with me alone."

He will be so glad to come in and take control, and everything will be made new in the light of His presence.

CHAPTER FOURTEEN

LIBERTY NOT LICENSE

(Gal. 5: 16-26)

"This I say then, Walk in the Spirit, and ye shall not fulfil the lust of the flesh. For the flesh lusteth against the Spirit, and the Spirit against the flesh: and these are contrary the one to the other: so that ye cannot (or, may not) do the things that ye would. But if ye be led of the Spirit, ye are not under the law. Now the works of the flesh are manifest, which are these; Adultery, fornication, uncleanness, lasciviousness, idolatry, witchcraft, hatred, variance, emulations, wrath, strife, seditions, heresies, envyings, murders, drunkenness, revellings, and such like: of the which I tell you before, as I have also told you in time past, that they which do such things shall not inherit the kingdom of God. But the fruit of the Spirit is love, joy, peace, longsuffering, gentleness, goodness, faith, meekness, temperance: against such there is no law. And they that are Christ's have crucified the flesh with the affections and lusts. If we live in the Spirit, let us also walk in the Spirit. Let us not be desirous of vain glory, provoking one another, envying one another."

THE present section of this epistle brings before us the truth, in a very marked way, of the two natures in the believer. It is important to remember that when God saves us He does not destroy the carnal nature which we received at our natural birth. The new birth does not imply the elimination of that old carnal nature, neither does it imply a change in it, but rather the impartation of an absolutely new nature born of the Holy Spirit of God, and these

198

two natures abide side by side in the believer in
the Lord Jesus Christ. This explains the conflict
that many of us have known since we have been
converted. In fact, I need not have said, "many
of us," for all converted people know at one time
or another something of that conflict between the
flesh and the Spirit. Jesus said, "That which is
born of the flesh is flesh"—that is, the old nature
—"that which is born of the Spirit is spirit"—
that is the new nature, and these two natures
abide side by side until we receive the redemption
of the body which will be at the coming again of
our Lord Jesus Christ, when He will transform
this body of our humiliation and make it like
unto the body of His glory. Then we will be delivered forever from all inward tendency to sin.
Until then we have to learn, and sometimes by
very painful experiences, that the carnal nature,
that old nature, "is not subject to the law of God,
neither indeed can be" (Rom. 8: 7).

That old nature is so corrupt, so vile, that it
can never be sanctified, and the new nature is so
pure, so holy, that it does not need to be sanctified. So there is no mention in Scripture of the
sanctification of the old nature. What is it then
that needs to be sanctified? It is the man himself, and he is sanctified as he learns to walk in
accordance with the dictates of the new nature.
He is directed by the Holy Spirit of God, for the

believer is not only born of the Spirit but indwelt by the Spirit.

We are not to confound new birth by the Spirit with the reception of the Spirit. New birth is the operation of the Spirit of God. He it is who produces the new birth through the Word. We receive the Word in faith, we believe the Word, and the Spirit of God through the Word brings about new birth. The apostle James says, "Of His own will begat He us with the word of truth" (James 1: 18). The apostle Peter says, "Being born again, not of corruptible seed, but of incorruptible, by the Word of God, which liveth and abideth for ever. . . . And this is the Word which by the gospel is preached unto you" (1 Pet. 1:23, 25). And when I believe that Word I am born again; that is an inward change. It is the impartation of a new life; it is eternal life. But there is something more than that. It was always true in all dispensations, from Adam down to the day of Pentecost, that wherever people believed God's Word they were born again, but the Holy Spirit Himself as a divine Person had not then come to dwell within them. Now since Pentecost, upon believing, we are sealed with the Holy Spirit of God. He creates the new nature, and then comes to indwell the one who is thus born again, and as the believer learns to recognize the fact that the Spirit of God dwells within him, and as he turns everything over to His control, he finds deliverance from the power of inbred sin.

Notice how the apostle puts it here: "This I say then, Walk in the Spirit and ye shall not fulfil the lust (or, the desire) of the flesh." It is so easy to fulfil the desire of the flesh. We must not link with that word "lust" the idea that it always means things base and unclean. The word itself simply means "desire," and whatever the desire of the flesh is it is always hateful to God. Here may be one who desires all kinds of carnal indulgences, and we have no difficulty in realizing the vileness of that, but here is another who desires worldly fame, the praise and adulation of his fellows, and that is also the lust of the flesh, or mind, and is as obnoxious to God as the other. Any kind of a carnal or fleshly desire is a lust, and if we would be delivered from walking according to these selfish lusts we must walk in the Spirit.

It is one thing to have the Spirit indwelling us, and quite another to walk in the Spirit. To walk in the Spirit implies that the Holy Spirit is controlling us, and we can walk in the Spirit only as our lives are truly surrendered to Christ. Somebody says, "Well, then, I understand you mean to tell us that all believers possess the Holy Spirit, but that many of us have never received the second blessing, and are not filled with the

Spirit." I do not find the term, "second blessing," in Scripture, though I admit that in the lives of many Christians there is an experience that answers to what people call "the second blessing." Many Christians have lived for years on a rather low, somewhat carnal, worldly plane. They love the Lord, they love His Word, they love to attend the ordinances of His house, they enjoy Christian fellowship, and seek to walk as upright men and women through this world, but they have never truly yielded themselves and all their ransomed powers wholly to the Lord. There is something they are keeping back, some controversy with God, and as long as this continues there will always be conflict and defeat, but when one comes to the place where he heeds the Word, "I beseech you therefore, brethren, by the mercies of God, that you present (that you surrender, hand over) your bodies a living sacrifice, holy, acceptable unto God, which is your reasonable service" (Rom. 12: 1)—when one makes that surrender there is indeed in the life what answers to a kind of second blessing; that is, the Spirit of God is now free to take possession of that believer, and operate through him and use him for the glory of God in a way He could not do as long as that man or woman was not wholly surrendered to the Lord.

We speak a great deal about "full surrender,"

and yet, I am afraid, some of us use the term in a very careless way. It is of no use to speak of being fully surrendered to God if I am still seeking my own interest. If I am self-centered, if I am hurt because people do not praise me, or if I am lifted up because they do, then the Spirit of God does not have His way with me. If Christ Himself is not the one object before my soul, if I cannot say, "For me to live is Christ," if my great concern is not that Christ should be magnified in me whether by life or by death, then I am not yet wholly surrendered to Him. If I cannot say from the heart, "Not my will, but Thine," there is no use in talking about being surrendered to Christ. The surrendered believer is no longer seeking his own but the things which belong to Christ Jesus. That is the man who "walks in the Spirit." "Walk in the Spirit, and ye shall not fulfil the lust of the flesh."

The conflict is shown in verse 17: "For the flesh lusteth (or desireth) against the Spirit, and the Spirit against (or contrary to) the flesh: and these are contrary the one to the other." It is not exactly, "So that ye *cannot* do the things that ye would," for God has made provision that we might do the things that we would, but it should be rendered, "So that ye *may not* do the things that ye would." Here is conflict in the believer's breast. The flesh desires one thing, the Spirit

another, and as long as there is not a full surrender to the will of God these two are in constant warfare, and therefore the believer may
not do the things that he would. I rise in the
morning and say, "Today I will not allow that
tongue of mine to say one unkind thing, one un-
Christlike word." But some unexpected circumstances arise, and almost before I know it I have
said something for which I could bite my tongue.
The thing I never meant to do I did. And, on
the other hand, things I meant to do I did not
do. What does that tell me? There is conflict.
The Spirit of God has not His complete right of
way in my heart and life, and because of this
conflict I may not do the things that I would.
I am hindered, and my life is not a life of full
surrender as God intended it to be. How many
of us know this experimentally. Oh, the defeated
lives, the disappointed lives, even of people who
are real Christians, who know the blessedness of
being saved by the precious blood of the Lord
Jesus Christ and who long to glorify God, and
yet are constantly defeated. Why? Because the
Spirit of God does not have His supreme place
in their lives.

"But if ye be led of the Spirit, ye are not under
the law." We are not to think that the way of
deliverance is by law-keeping. I may say, "From
now on I mean to be very careful, I will obey

God's law in everything. That surely will result in my practical sanctification." But no; I am disappointed again. I will find that the will to do good is present with me, but how to perform it is another thing, and so I have to learn that my sanctification is no more through the law than my justification. What then? He tells us, "If ye be led of the Spirit, ye are not under the law." If you yield to the Spirit of God, if He has the control of your life, if you are led by Him, then the righteousness of the law is fulfilled in us who walk not after the flesh but after the Spirit. And in order that we may not misunderstand, he brings before us the lusts of the flesh, that we may be able to drag these things out into the light, that we may see them in all their ugliness, so that if any of them have any place in our hearts and lives we may judge them in the presence of God. We often run across people today who say that they do not believe in the depravity of human life, but these are the things that come from the natural man; and even the believer, if he is not careful, if he is not walking with God as led by the Spirit, may fall into some of them.

"Now the works of the flesh are manifest (they are evident), which are these: Adultery, fornication, uncleanness, lasciviousness." Maybe some of you think or say, "I wish he would not use those words; I do not like them; they are nasty words." My dear friends, let me remind you, there is nothing the matter with the words; it is the sins that are expressed in these words that are so nasty. Many people who do not like the words are living in the sins, and God drags things out into the light and calls sin by name. There are people living in the sin of adultery who do not like to hear their wickedness called by name. Take the words of the Lord Jesus, "Whosoever shall put away his wife, saving for the cause of fornication, causeth her to commit adultery: and whosoever shall marry her that is divorced committeth adultery" (Matt. 5: 32). There are those who are committing adultery according to that passage, and others who are contemplating it. If you have allowed yourself any unholy love, permitting yourself any unholy familiarity with one with whom you have no right to seek to enter the married relationship, you yourself are guilty in God's sight of the sin that is mentioned here. "Fornication, uncleanness, lasciviousness," that is, vile, filthy thoughts indulged in. You cannot hinder evil thoughts coming into your mind, but you can help indulging in them. Lasciviousness is indulging in thoughts that are unclean and vile and unholy. People sometimes come to me in great distress and say, "Evil thoughts come to me, even when I am praying, and I wonder sometimes whether I am really converted or not." That is the flesh manifesting itself. These things may come to you, but do you indulge in them? A Welshman said, "I cannot help it if a bird alights on top of my head, but I can help it if he builds his nest in my hair," and so you may not be able to help it if evil thoughts come surging into your mind, but you can help indulging in those thoughts.

"Idolatry," putting anything in the place of the true and living God. "Witchcraft." "Oh," you say, "that is out-moded. They used to burn witches." But what is witchcraft? It is a word that implies "having to do with the dead," and I think that Chicago has a good many witches in it. Often while passing along the street I see such signs as "Spiritualist medium," or something like that, people pretending to have traffic with the dead. That is witchcraft, and it is an abomination in the sight of God. "Hatred." This is a sin which we all have to guard against. Scripture says, "Whosoever hateth his brother is a murderer" (1 John 3: 15). Hatred comes from the old nature. "Variance"—quarrelsomeness. There are many of us who would shrink from those first sins, but we are not very easy to get along with, we are dreadfully touchy, and this is as truly an evidence of the old nature, as those other "works of the flesh." "Emulations," a constant desire to excel other people, to get the admiration of others. Here is a preacher who has some little gift, and he is upset because some other preacher has greater recognition. Here is one who sings a little, and someone else who also sings excites more admiration, and there is trouble about it. Here is a Sunday School teacher, and some other teacher seems to be preferred before her, and she is in a frenzy and almost ready to quit her work. Trace these things back to their source and you will find they all come from the flesh, and therefore they should be judged in the sight of God. And then, "wrath." That is anger. There is an anger that is holy, but that wrath to which you and I usually give way is very unholy. The only holy anger is anger with sin. "Be ye angry, and sin not" (Eph. 4: 26). The old Puritan said, "I am determined so to be angry as not to sin, therefore to be angry at nothing but sin." And then "strife," resulting in "seditions." The two words are intimately linked together. All these things are sinful. "Heresies," a school of opinion set up opposed to the truth of God. "Envyings." Scripture says, "Be content with such things as ye have" (Heb. 13:5). Someone has a better house than I have, someone else has a better car than mine, and I envy him. The Arab said, "Once I felt bad and I complained because I had no shoes, until I met a man who had no feet." There is not one of us but has far more than he deserves. Why should we envy anyone else? Suppose some people have magnificent mansions and I have only a hut.

> "A tent or a cottage, why should I care?
> They're building a palace for me over there!"

"Be content," says the Spirit of God, "with such things as ye have." When you reach that place life will be very much happier for you.

"Murders." Think of putting murder with such sins as emulations and envyings! Many a murder has resulted from these very sins, and, you know, murder does not consist in sticking a knife into a man or blowing his brains out with a revolver. You can murder a man by your unkindness. I have known many a person who died of a broken heart because of the unkindness of those from whom they had a right to expect something different. God give us to manifest so much of the love of Christ that we will be a blessing to people instead of a curse to them. Then "drunkenness." Surely I do not need to speak of this to Christians. This too is a work of the flesh. Then "revellings." The world calls it "having a good time" in a carnal way. "And such like: of the which I tell you before, as I have also told you in time past, that they which do such things shall not inherit the kingdom of God." Here he uses the present continuous tense: "That they that are in the habit of doing such things, they whose lives are characterized by such things." If people are characterized by these things they prove that they are not Christians at all. Real Christians may fall into them, but they are miserable and wretched until they confess them, but unsaved men revel in them and go on without judging them. These things come from the flesh.

Now we have the opposite—the fruit of the Spirit. "But the fruit of the Spirit is love, joy, peace, longsuffering, gentleness, goodness, faith, meekness, temperance: against such there is no law." You notice the word here is "fruit," for we do not read in the Bible of the "fruits" of the Spirit, but of the "fruit." This ninefold fruit springs from the new nature as one is actuated by the Holy Spirit of God. "Love," the very essence of the divine nature. "Joy,"—Scripture says, "The joy of the Lord is your strength" (Neh. 8:10). "Peace," that is more than happiness, that is a deep-toned gladness that is unruffled and untroubled by all the trials of earth. "Longsuffering," this leads you to endure uncomplainingly. "Gentleness," some of us are so gruff and so rough, but the Christian should cultivate the meekness, the gentleness of Christ. "Faith," in the sense of confidence in God. "Meekness." We are not meek by nature; the natural man is always pushing himself forward. The spiritual

man says, "Never mind me; recognize others; I
am willing. to remain in the background." Wherever you find this pushing spirit you may know
that one is still walking in the flesh. When you
find the desire to give godly recognition to others
you will find one walking in the Spirit. And then,
"temperance" is just self-control, the whole body
held under in subjection to the Spirit of God.
"Against such there is no law." You do not need
law to control a man thus walking in the Spirit.

"And they that are Christ's have crucified the
flesh with the affections and lusts." It does not
say, "They that are Christ's *should* crucify the
flesh." They have done so when they put their
trust in the Lord Jesus. They trusted in the One
crucified in their behalf, and therefore can say,
"I have been crucified with Christ: nevertheless
I live" (Gal. 2: 20). It is a settled thing. If you
have crucified the flesh, if you have recognized
the fact that Christ's crucifixion is yours, then do
not live in that to which you have died. "If we
live in the Spirit, let us also walk in the Spirit."
If we have this new life, if linked up now with
our risen Christ, then let Him control our ways,
let us be yielded to Him, let us walk in the Spirit,
let us not be desirous of fame or glory, let us not
seek anything that would lead to empty boasting,
provoking one another, saying and doing things

that may pain others needlessly, or envying one another.

Some of you may say, "That is a tremendously high standard, and I am afraid I can never attain to it." No; and I can never attain to it in my own strength, but if you and I are yielded to the Holy Spirit of God and allow Him to make these things real in our lives, then we will indeed attain to the ideal set before us here, but it will not be ourselves, it will be Christ living in us manifesting His life, His holy life, in and through the members of our body. God give us to know the reality of it!

CHAPTER FIFTEEN

GRACE IN ACTION

(Gal. 6: 1-10)

"Brethren, if a man be overtaken in a fault, ye which are spiritual, restore such an one in the spirit of meekness; considering thyself, lest thou also be tempted. Bear ye one another's burdens, and so fulfil the law of Christ. For if a man think himself to be something, when he is nothing, he deceiveth himself. But let every man prove his own work, and then shall he have rejoicing in himself alone, and not in another. For every man shall bear his own burden. Let him that is taught in the Word communicate unto him that teacheth in all good things. Be not deceived; God is not mocked: for whatsoever a man soweth, that shall he also reap. For he that soweth to his flesh shall of the flesh reap corruption; but he that soweth to the Spirit shall of the Spirit reap life everlasting. And let us not be weary in well doing: for in due season we shall reap, if we faint not. As we have therefore opportunity, let us do good unto all men, especially unto them who are of the household of faith."

WE are now to consider a number of special admonitions having to do with the manifestation of grace, in our attitude toward our brethren generally and toward the world outside, for where grace is active in the soul there will always be kindly consideration of others. Where a spirit of censoriousness prevails, or where malice and bitterness fill the heart, one may be certain that, for the time being at least, the one who manifests such a disposition has lost the sense of his debtorship to the grace of God.

In the first instance, we have the case of a brother who has failed, though not wilfully. The Spirit of God says, "Brethren, if a man be overtaken in a fault." He did not set out with intention to sin. He was not endeavoring to stifle his conscience, but sudden temptation proved too much for him, as for instance, in the case of the apostle Peter, who really loved the Lord, but when challenged as to being one of His disciples was so filled with fear that he denied the One he had declared he would never forsake. It is important to distinguish between wilful, deliberate sin, when one has put away a good conscience and definitely embarked upon a course of evil, and sudden and unexpected failure because of overwhelming temptation taking one off his guard. How many fall under such circumstances! Perhaps it is the power of appetite or of fleshly passion. It may be a question of a quick temper or unjudged pride and vanity. One goes on unconscious of danger, finds himself in circumstances for which he was not prepared, and before he realizes what is transpiring, he has sinned against the One who loves him most. It is easy for others who do not understand the hidden springs of action to blame such a one very severely, particularly if his fault is of such a character as to reflect discredit upon the testimony of the Lord. The easiest way in such a case is to insist on immediate excision, excommunicating the wrong-doer from all Church privileges. But here a better way is unfolded to us. Paul writes, "Ye which are spiritual, restore such an one in the spirit of meekness; considering thyself, lest thou also be tempted." It is no evidence of spirituality to give way to harsh judgment, but rather to manifest compassion for the one who has failed and to seek to bring him back to fellowship with God. It is only in the spirit of meekness that this can be done. A hard, critical spirit will drive the failing one deeper into sin and make it more difficult to recover him at last. But a loving, tender word, accompanied by gracious effort to recover, will often result in saving him from further declension.

If we remember what we ourselves are and how easily we too may fall, we will not be over-stern in dealing with others. It is not that we are called upon to excuse sin. That must be dealt with faithfully, for we are told in the law, "Thou shalt in any wise rebuke thy neighbor, and not suffer sin upon him." But we are to point out the way of deliverance; considering our own need of divine help continually in order that we may be kept from sin, we will know better how

to deal with those who in the hour of temptation
have missed their path.

Then we have a precious word as to that
mutual concern for others which should ever
characterize believers: "Bear ye one another's
burdens, and so fulfil the law of Christ." The
law of Christ is the law of love, and love seeks
to help others in their distress and share the load
with them. If anyone thinks himself superior to
such service and stands upon his dignity, he is
but manifesting his own littleness, for "if a man
think himself to be something, when he is
nothing, he deceiveth himself."

Each one should recognize his own individual
responsibility to God, and therefore he is to be
careful that his own work is in accordance with
God's revealed mind, as indicated in His Word.
As he thus walks obediently he will know that
joy which comes from fellowship with God and
will not depend on others for his happiness. It
is a recognized principle of Scripture that each
man must bear his own responsibility, and this is
the meaning of verse 5, where the word "burden"
suggests something quite different to its use in
verse 2.

Verse 6 lays down a principle of wide applica-
ion: "Let him that is taught in the Word communicate unto him that teacheth in all good
things." If God has used another to instruct and

help me in the way of life, I, on my part, should be glad to do what I can to be of help and assistance to him. It is not simply that preachers entirely given to the work of the Lord should be sustained by the gracious gifts of those to whom they minister, though that is involved in it, but it is a constant giving and receiving in all walks of life. He who seeks only to be benefited by others and is not concerned about sharing with them, will have a Dead Sea kind of a life. It is said that nothing can live in that body of water because it has no outlet, and though millions of tons of fresh water pour into it every week, evaporation and mineral deposits make it so bitter and acrid that it cannot sustain life. He who is more concerned about giving to others than about receiving for himself will be constantly fresh and happy in his own experience and will enjoy all the more the good things ministered to him.

It is a remarkable fact that it is in this connection, what we might call the principle of "giving and receiving," that the Holy Spirit directs our attention most solemnly to the kindred law of "sowing and reaping." It never pays to be forgetful of the future. He who acts for the present moment only is like one who is indifferent to the coming harvest, and so either thinks to save by sparse sowing, or else recklessly strews obnoxious seeds in his field, sowing wild oats, as people say, and yet hopes to reap a far different kind of harvest. We reap as we sow. This is insisted on again and again in Scripture. Here we are told, "Be not deceived, God is not mocked; for whatsoever a man soweth that shall he also reap." Elsewhere our Lord has laid down the same principle. He asks, "Do men gather grapes of thorns, or figs of thistles?" And He declares that "every good tree bringeth forth good fruit; but a corrupt tree bringeth forth evil fruit" (Matt. 7: 16, 17). Israel sowed the wind, the prophet exclaimed, and he predicted they would reap the whirlwind (Hos. 8: 7). Men who sow wickedness reap the same, asserted Eliphaz (Job 4: 8). This is so self-evident that it needs no emphasis. Yet how easily we forget it, and how readily we hope that in some strange, unnatural transformation our sinful folly will be so overruled as to produce the peaceable fruits of righteousness. But whether it be in the case of the unsaved worldling, or the failing Christian, the inexorable law will be fulfilled—we reap what we sow. How important then that we walk carefully before God, not permitting ourselves any license which is unbecoming in one who professes to acknowledge the Lordship of Christ. "For he that soweth to his flesh shall of the flesh reap corruption; but he that soweth to the Spirit shall of the Spirit reap life everlasting" (ver. 8). It is not that we *earn* everlasting life by our behavior; we receive it as a gift when we believe on the Lord Jesus Christ (John 3:36). But we now have eternal life in dying bodies, and in a scene of contrariety, where everything about us is opposed to that new and divinely-implanted nature which we were given in regeneration. Soon, at our Lord's return, we shall enter into life in all its fulness, and then, at the judgment-seat of Christ, we shall reap according to our sowing. They who live for God now will receive rich reward in that day. And they who yield now to the impulses of the flesh and are occupied with things that do not glorify God will suffer loss.

How timely then the admonition: "Let us not be weary in well doing," coupled with the sure promise, "For in due season we shall reap if we faint not" (ver. 9). We are so apt, having begun in the Spirit, to seek to finish in the flesh, as in the case of these Galatians. But only that which is of the Spirit will be rewarded in the day of manifestation. That which is of the flesh—even though seemingly religious—will only produce corruption and bring disappointment at last.

In closing this section the apostle reverts to the general principle of verse 6, now extending it to include all men everywhere. The spiritual man is one who sees things from God's standpoint, therefore he cannot be insular, self-centered, or indifferent to the needy souls all about him. "As we have therefore opportunity, let us do good unto all men, especially unto them who are of the household of faith" (ver. 10). Thus we will imitate Him whose life was laid out in doing good, both to the unthankful and the godless, and to the little flock who waited for the consolation of Israel. As we seek, by the power of the indwelling Spirit, to maintain the same attitude toward our fellow-men, whether sinners or saints, we fulfil the righteousness of that law which says, "Thou shalt love thy neighbor as thyself." We do not need to put ourselves under the law to do this. We only need to recognize our relationship to the glorified Christ, who is the Head of that new creation to which, by grace, we belong.

Are we ever on the watch for such opportunities to manifest the goodness of God to those with whom we come in contact, and thus magnify the Lord, whose we are and whom we serve? Having been so wondrously dealt with ourselves, how can we do other than seek to exemplify in our dealings with others the mercy and loving-kindness which has been shown toward us?

This is indeed to live on a higher plane than law. It is the liberty of grace, which the Holy Spirit gives to all who recognize the Lordship of Christ.

CHAPTER SIXTEEN

GLORYING IN THE CROSS

(Gal. 6: 11-18)

"Ye see how large a letter I have written unto you with mine own hand. As many as desire to make a fair show in the flesh, they constrain you to be circumcised; only lest they should suffer persecution for the cross of Christ. For neither they themselves who are circumcised keep the law; but desire to have you circumcised, that they may glory in your flesh. But God forbid that I should glory, save in the cross of our Lord Jesus Christ, by whom the world is crucified unto me, and I unto the world. For in Christ Jesus neither circumcision availeth any thing, nor uncircumcision, but a new creature. And as many as walk according to this rule, peace be on them, and mercy, and upon the Israel of God. From henceforth let no man trouble me: for I bear in my body the marks of the Lord Jesus. Brethren, the grace of our Lord Jesus Christ be with your spirit. Amen."

THERE is something about verse 11 that I think lets us right into the heart of the apostle Paul. He was some distance away from Galatia when word came to him that Judaizing teachers had come in among the different assemblies, and were teaching the believers that unless they were circumcised and kept the law they could not be saved. He saw that this meant to step down from the truth of grace altogether. The believer does not obey in order to be saved, but because he is saved. He delights to glorify

221

the One who has redeemed him, and his obedience springs from a heart filled with gratitude to that One who gave His life for him. He does not try to make himself fit or to keep himself fit for heaven. The apostle was so much disturbed by what he heard that he sat right down and penned this letter. It glows with the white heat of his burning zeal for the gospel of God. As we have already remarked, it was not a usual thing for men to write their own letters in those days. Letter-writing was a distinct occupation, as it is still in the different cities of the East; and if a man had a good deal to do he would engage one of these professional letter-writers just as here and now a man who has much correspondence engages a stenographer. He would not attempt to handle it all himself. And so ordinarily the apostle dictated his letters to various persons. They wrote them out, and he signed them and sent them on. But in this case apparently he had no amanuensis close at hand, and he was so stirred in his spirit, that he felt he could not lose a moment in getting a letter off, and so sat right down and wrote it himself. He refers to this in verse 11, "Ye see how large a letter I have written unto you with mine own hand." It is not really a large letter. Compared with the Epistle to the Romans this is a very short one. It is not more than one-third the length of First

Corinthians, and only about one-half the length of the Second Epistle to the Corinthians. Compared with other writings in the New Testament it is brief indeed; but we get help here if we consult a more critical translation. It should read, "You see with what large characters I have written unto you with mine own hand." And that indicates not only that he was not used to letter-writing, but we gather besides that he had some kind of affliction with his eyes, and was not able to see well. You remember the time he was on trial in Jerusalem, and the high priest commanded him to be smitten on the mouth, and indignantly he shouted out, "God shall smite thee, thou whited wall" (Acts 23:3), and somebody said, "Do you speak evil of God's high priest?" At once he apologized and said, "I did not know that he was the high priest." He ought to have known, for there Ananias stood, doubtless in his priestly robes, but if Paul were at the other end of the room with poor eyesight he might not have recognized the man. And then there are other scriptures that give similar suggestions. He had already said in this letter, "I bear you record, that, if it had been possible, ye would have plucked out your own eyes, and have given them to me" (Gal. 4:15). They would not have wanted to do that unless his sight were poor. So I take it that possibly this was the affliction which he had to endure for many years, and therefore when he sat down to write he was like a half-blind person writing in big sprawling letters. And realizing that he was not sending a neat manuscript such as an amanuensis would have prepared, he apologized for it by saying, "You see with what large characters I have written unto you with mine own hand." I think that manuscript with its large letters ought to have touched the hearts of those Galatians, and should have made them realize how truly he loved them, how concerned he was about them, that he could not wait to write them in the ordinary way, but must send off this epistle as quickly as it could be produced.

Then he concludes with these words, "As many as desire to make a fair show in the flesh, they constrain you to be circumcised." If it could have been possible to keep the Christians within the fold of Judaism and make of them one more Jewish sect, they would have been saved from a great deal of persecution they had to suffer. And so the apostle says, these emissaries from Jerusalem going about among you have not your good at heart, but they want to make a fair show in the flesh; they want to show a great many adherents to what they teach, but do not take the place of separation to the name of the Lord Jesus Christ. I could go with them and make a fair show in the flesh too, and would not have to suffer persecution for the cross of Christ. That cross was not only the place where the Lord Jesus suffered for our sins but is the symbol of separation. It told out the world's hatred of the Son of God, and Paul had identified himself with the One whom the world spurned, and therefore he gloried in that cross.

When people take legal ground and tell you that salvation is by human effort, they themselves never live up to their own profession. You may have heard some say, "I do not think people have to be saved by the blood of the Lord Jesus Christ; I think if everybody does the best he can, that is all that can be expected." Did you ever see a man who did the best he could do? Have you always done the best you knew? You know you have failed over and over again, even in those things that you knew to be right, things you did not do that you should have done, and things you did that you knew you should not have done. Therefore, to talk about being saved by doing the best you can is absurd. No man has ever done his best, except, of course, our holy, spotless Saviour, the Lord Jesus Christ.

Somebody says, "It is gospel enough for me to follow the Sermon on the Mount." That is saying a good deal. Did you ever see a man who did that, or have you done it? Test yourself by it.

Read Matthew 5, 6, and 7, and just test yourself honestly; check yourself, and see how far you fall short of the precious precepts of this wonderful address given by the Lord Jesus Christ. There is no question but that you and I ought to live up to it. It indicates the type of life that should characterize every believer. But if you have not lived up to the Sermon on the Mount, either as a matter of attaining or maintaining salvation, at once you put yourself out of court. You have not lived it out, and I am afraid you never will, and therefore you can be very thankful indeed that God is saving poor sinners by grace. Someone else says, "I believe if we keep the law God gave at Sinai (it is holy, just, and good, the apostle himself tells us), it is all that God or man could require of us." So far as actual living is concerned, I suppose it is; but again I put the question, Have you kept it? Do you know of any one who has ever kept it? Let us keep in mind the words, "Whosoever shall keep the whole law, and yet offend in one point, he is guilty of all" (James 2:10). So on this ground there is no hope for any of us. "If we fail," some say, "God has provided the sacraments." But those who talk in that way are never certain that they are keeping the sacraments correctly. How do you know that you are keeping them perfectly? You may fail in purity of purpose as you take the

Lord's Supper, or in baptism. Even they who count on being saved through self-effort do not keep the law perfectly. We all fail, and therefore we need to recognize the fact that salvation is only through the free, matchless grace of God.

They would like to have you follow on in their ways in order that they might glory in your flesh, says the apostle. Men like to get a following, they like to have people join with them in any particular stand they take. It ministers to the pride of the natural heart to be able to head up a large group.

In opposition to all this human effort Paul sets the cross of our blessed Saviour: "But God forbid that I should glory, save in the cross of our Lord Jesus Christ, by whom the world is crucified unto me, and I unto the world." When he said these words he was not thinking just of the wooden instrument on which Jesus died, and he certainly was not thinking of a cross on a steeple of a church, or on an altar of a church, nor yet of a cross dangling from a chain at the waist or throat, or worn as an ornament. When he wrote of "the cross of our Lord Jesus Christ," he was thinking of all that is involved in the crucifixion of the blessed Saviour on that tree. The cross of Christ is the measure of man's hatred to God. Think of it! God sent His Son into the world! Millions of people talk about it at the

Christmas season, and the merchants today are encouraging people to observe His birth so· that they may sell more goods. You will find that even a Jewish merchant will wish you a merry Christmas if you purchase something from him. But remember this, the world has already told us what it thinks of Christ. It may celebrate His birth by gifts one to another, they may put on glorious concerts and have great festivals in the name of the Christ born in Bethlehem, but this world has shown what it thinks of Jesus by hurrying Him to a Roman cross. When Pilate asked, "What shall I do then with Jesus which is called Christ?" they cried out with one accord, "Let Him be crucified" (Matt. 27:22), and that is the Christ they profess to worship today, the Christ they have crucified. They will even celebrate Christmas in the taverns of our cities, celebrate the birth of Christ by drinking and carousing on Christmas-eve and Christmas-day, and they will call that keeping the birth of Jesus. But the Christ of Bethlehem is the Christ of the cross, and the world has given its sentence concerning Him. They said, "We will not have this Man to reign over us." "Well," the apostle says, "I glory in siding with the Man whom the world rejected." When he says, "God forbid that I should glory, save in the cross of our Lord Jesus Christ," it is just another way of saying, "My boast, my joy, my delight is in the One whom the world has crucified."*

Then the cross of Christ was the place where God has told out His love in utmost fulness. "Herein is love, not that we loved God, but that He loved us, and sent His Son to be the propitiation for our sins" (1 John 4: 10). When man did his worst, God did His best. When man said, "Away with Him! Crucify Him!" God accepted Him as the substitute for sinners, and the judgment that our sins deserved fell on Him. God made His soul an offering for our sin. And so when Paul says, "I glory in the cross of our Lord Jesus," he means, I glory in the love that gave Jesus to die for me, a sinner.

But he has shown that Christ's death is my death and I am to take my place with Him, recognizing His death as mine. In chap. 2:20 we read, "I am crucified with Christ: nevertheless I live; yet not I, but Christ liveth in me: and the life which I now live in the flesh I live by the faith of the Son of God, who loved me, and gave Himself for me." When Paul says, "I glory in the cross of Christ," he means this then:—I accept the cross of Christ as my cross; I accept His death as my death; I take my place with Him as one who has died to the world, to sin, and to self,

---

*This address was given at the Christmas season.

and henceforth I am not under law but under
grace. Law crucified my Saviour. He met its
claims upon that cross, and now, having satisfied
all its demands, I am delivered from its authority and am free to walk before God in grace, seeking to glorify Him in a life of happy obedience
because I love the One who died there to put away
my sin. All this, and much more, is involved in
the expression, "God forbid that I should glory,
save in the cross of our Lord Jesus Christ, by
whom," he says, "the world is crucified unto me,
and I unto the world."

Christian, have you taken that stand? Do you
realize that Christ's cross means absolute separation from the world that rejected Him? That
is what we confess in our baptism; that is what
Christian baptism means. I have heard of many
a believer who pondered a long time before taking the step of being buried in baptism because
afraid he would not be able to live out what was
set forth in this beautiful ordinance, and, of
course, apart from Christ we could not. But
what is involved? A recognition that I have died
with Him, that I have been buried with Him, and
that this is an end of me as a man after the flesh.
Therefore, I have been raised with Christ to walk
in newness of life.

I remember some brethren who were talking
about a Christian's relationship to oath-bound

secret societies. (This Book tells me concerning the Lord Jesus that He said, "In secret have I said nothing" (John 18: 20), therefore I know that He never was inside of an oath-bound secret order, and He has called upon me to be a follower of Him.) One of these brethren said to the other, "You belong to such-and-such an order."

"Oh, no," he said; "I do not."

"Why, you do; I was there the night you were initiated, and once a member of that you are a member until death."

"Exactly; I quite admit what you say, but I buried the lodge member in Lake Ontario."

He meant that in his baptism the old order came to an end.

I have heard of a dear young woman once a thorough worldling, but at last she was brought to a saving knowledge of the Lord Jesus. Her friends came on her birthday one evening to give her a surprise party, and wanted to take her with them to a place of ungodly worldly amusement. She said, "It is good of you to think of me, but I could not go with you; I never go to those places."

"Nonsense," they said; "you have often gone with us."

"But," she said, "I have buried the girl that used to go to those places."

"Not I, but Christ liveth in me."

Christian baptism should speak of separation from the world that crucified the Lord Jesus Christ. Look at Israel. They had been slaves to Pharaoh, and there is old Pharaoh on the other side of the sea, shouting, "You come back here and serve me; put your necks under the yoke of bondage again." And I think I hear them say, "Good-bye, Pharaoh; the Red Sea rolls between us; we have been crucified to Egypt and Egypt to us." That is it, "I have been crucified with Christ: nevertheless I live; yet not I, but Christ liveth in me." And so the world is crucified to me and I to the world. Let me say a word of warning here. Many a Christian has judged the vile, filthy, corrupt, polluted things of the world who has never judged the brilliant, cultured, esthetic world. But the brilliant, cultured world is just as vile in the sight of God as the corrupt, disgusting, filthy world that many walked with, in days before they were converted. You can get out of fellowship with God by association with the cultured world, as truly as by going down into the world's base and ungodly places of vulgar amusement.

Oh, Christian, keep close to the footsteps of the flock of Christ, and do not let them meet you in any other field. Here is real circumcision. Circumcision was an ordinance that signified the death of the flesh. "For in Christ Jesus neither circumcision availeth anything, nor uncircumcision, but a new creature," or, literally, "a new creation." And that is the whole thing. You and I through the cross have passed out of the old creation, if saved, and are now in the new creation of which Christ is the glorified Head. See to it that in your associations, in your pleasure, in your amusement, in your religious life, you keep in that sphere where Christ is owned as Head and Lord.

And then he adds, "And as many as walk according to this rule"—what rule? He has not laid down any rule. Yes, he has said we are a new creation. That is the way to test everything that may be put before me. Is it of the new creation or is it of the old? If it is of the old, it has nothing for me. I belong to the new and am to walk according to this rule. "As many as walk according to this rule, peace be on them, and mercy," for they will always need mercy. They will never attain perfection in this life, but God never forgets His own. Sometimes we may drift so far that we forget Him, we may even feel as though our hearts are utterly dead toward Him, as though He has forsaken us, but remember what He says, "I will never leave thee, nor forsake thee" (Heb. 13:5). There is a double negative in the original, it is, "I will never, never leave thee, nor forsake thee." It is unthinkable that the blessed Lord should ever give up one who has put his trust in Jesus, and so He always deals with us in mercy, restoring our souls when we fail.

Then the apostle uses a very peculiar expression, "And upon the Israel of God." Whom does he mean by "the Israel of God"? I do not think he is referring to the Church as such, for he has just referred to that when speaking of the new creation. I think he recognizes as the true Israel those of God's earthly people who really accept the testimony of God and who own their sin and trust the Saviour whom God has provided. "They are not all Israel, which are of Israel" (Rom. 9: 6). That a man happens to be born of the seed of Abraham does not make him a son of Abraham. Because a man happens to be born of Israel this does not make him an Israelite. He must have the faith of Abraham to be blessed with faithful Abraham, and he must receive the Saviour who came through Israel if he is going to be a true Israelite.

Now that these Judaizers have made so much of a distinguishing mark upon the body through an ordinance and have said that a man that did not bear that mark was unclean and unfit for Christian fellowship, Paul says, I have a better mark than anything you may talk about. "From henceforth let no man trouble me: for I bear in my body the marks of the Lord Jesus." What did he mean by that? His very body had been wounded many times for Jesus' sake, when those cruel stones fell on him at Lystra, when beaten with stripes his body was branded; but he glories in these things and says, "I bear in my body the marks of the Lord Jesus." Someone has said, "When we get home to heaven God is not going to look us over for medals but for scars." I wonder whether we have received any scars for Jesus' sake. Many of them are not physical scars, they are scars of the heart, but it is a great thing to have the brand-marks of the Lord Jesus.

And now Paul closes this epistle without any salutations. Most of his letters contain a great many salutations to various people, but here he does not send any special message to any of them because, you see, they were playing fast and loose with the things of God, and there would be no use, after giving them this stern message, to placate them by sending cordial salutations to the brethren in Christ as though nothing had happened to hinder fellowship. So he merely says, "The grace of our Lord Jesus Christ be with your spirit. Amen." God grant that every one of us may enjoy that grace!

EPHESIANS
(In The Heavenlies)

THE SPHERE
OF CHRISTIAN PRIVILEGE

✓ ✓ ✓

"Paul, an apostle of Jesus Christ by the will of God, to the saints which are at Ephesus, and to the faithful in Christ Jesus: Grace be to you, and peace, from God our Father, and from the Lord Jesus Christ. Blessed be the God and Father of our Lord Jesus Christ, who hath blessed us with all spiritual blessings in heavenly places in Christ" (Eph. 1:1-3).

✓ ✓ ✓

THERE is nothing redundant in God's Word. Men write books and very frequently pad them in order to give quantity as well as quality, but there is nothing like that in the Bible. God's words are tried—"as silver tried in a furnace of earth, purified seven times"—and therefore we may well give our most careful attention to every item and every expression used.

With what great outstanding theme does this epistle deal? It opens up the truth of the privileges and responsibilities of the Church as the Body and Bride of Christ. It brings before us our position as believers; as quickened, raised, and seated in Christ in heavenly places.

There are very remarkable correspondences between certain Old Testament books and New Testament epistles. The Epistle to the Romans, for instance, answers to Exodus; the Letter to the Hebrews is the counterpart of Leviticus; and this Epistle to the Ephesians is the New Testament book of Joshua. In Joshua we have the people of Israel entering upon the possession of their inheritance. In Ephesians believers are called upon to enter by faith now into the possession of that inheritance which we shall enjoy in all its fulness by-and-by. We are far richer than we realize. All things are ours, and yet how little we appropriate! It is said in the prophecy of Obadiah that when the Lord returns and His kingdom is established, the people of Israel shall "possess their possessions." This is a challenge to us. Do you possess your possessions? Or are your heavenly estates like castles in Spain about which you dream, but never really make your own? I trust the Spirit of God may lead us into the present enjoyment of our portion in Christ.

For our purpose the epistle may be divided very simply, without breaking it up into many portions which would be difficult to carry in our memories. We shall divide it into two parts, the first three chapters giving us the doctrinal unfolding, and the last three, the practical outcome;

the first division gives us our inheritance, and the last, the behavior that should characterize those who are so richly blessed. That is the divine order; instruction in the truth first, practice in accordance with the truth afterwards. Now let us look particularly at these opening verses.

We are struck at once by the name of the writer, Paul. Thirteen New Testament epistles begin with the word "Paul." Another one is undoubtedly from Paul, but begins with the magnificent word "God." I refer to the Epistle to the Hebrews. Do we stop to inquire as often as we should how this man ever came to be called Paul? That was not his name originally. His name in the first place was Saul. He was a Benjamite, and bore the name of the first king, who came from the tribe of Benjamin. For many years this man was a haughty, self-righteous Pharisee, proud of his genealogy, of his religion, of his personal devotedness, until one day he had a meeting with our Lord Jesus Christ. Have you had such a meeting? From that moment on everything was changed for him. He could say:

> "I was journeying in the noon-tide,
>   When His light shone o'er my road;
> And I saw Him in the glory,
>   Saw Him, Jesus, Son of God.
>
> Marvel not that Christ in glory
>   All my inmost soul hath won;
> I have seen a light from heaven,
>   Far beyond the brightest sun."

It was that vision of Christ that changed Saul the Pharisee, into Paul, the humble, lowly servant of Christ. He did not use the new name immediately, you remember. It seems to have been taken after he won his first outstanding Gentile convert in the Isle of Cyprus—after the conversion of Sergius Paulus; and it appears to have been given him in recognition of his apostolic ministry. It means "the little one," a wonderful name for one who once thought himself so great; but that is what Christ does for one. "What things were gain to me, those I counted loss for Christ. Yea, doubtless, and I count all things but loss for the excellency of the knowledge of Christ Jesus my Lord: for whom I have suffered the loss of all things, and do count them but dung, that I may win Christ" (Phil. 3: 7, 8). All that Saul gloried in, Paul flung away for Jesus' sake; and he was content to be little, "less than the least of all saints," that in him Christ Jesus might show forth all long-suffering.

I remember going to a colored camp-meeting, and the dear black folk were singing a little ditty that went like this:

> "The quickest way up is down,
>   The quickest way up is down;
> You may climb up high, and try and try,
>   But the quickest way up is down."

How long it takes some of us to learn that! We are always trying to become somebody, and forgetting that, "Whosoever will save his life shall lose it: and whosoever will lose his life," says Jesus, "for My sake shall find it" (Matt. 16:25). Blessed it is when the princely Saul becomes the little Paul as he bows at the Saviour's feet.

Paul calls himself an apostle. Just what is an apostle? The word might be translated "a messenger," "a sent one," "one sent on a mission," and so there is a certain sense in which every missionary is an apostle. But there is a higher sense in which the word "apostle" refers to those who were specially commissioned by our Lord Jesus Christ to go forth in the world and carry the truth through which the Church was instituted. Paul was not among those who knew the Lord on earth, but he was ordained an apostle to the nations by His personal appointment when the risen Christ appeared to him that day on the Damascus turnpike. He said to him, "I have appeared unto thee for this purpose, to make thee a minister and a witness both of these things which thou hast seen, and of those things in the which I will appear unto thee" (Acts 26:16). And so Paul could go forth, the apostle of the Lord Jesus Christ, saying:

> "Christ the Son of God hath sent me
>   Through the midnight lands;
> Mine the mighty ordination
>   Of the piercéd hands."

He was an apostle of Jesus Christ by the will of God.

I do not like to touch upon critical questions in connection with these studies, and yet I must do so here. Some people do not notice divine names carefully, and that is the reason why those who copied the manuscripts were not always particular whether they wrote "Jesus Christ," or "Christ Jesus," but here it should be "Christ Jesus." Peter, James, John, and Jude spoke of our blessed Lord as "Jesus Christ." Why? Because "Jesus" is His human name and in resurrection He was made Lord and Christ. They knew Him on earth as "Jesus," the self-humbled One. But Paul never knew Him in that way; he never knew Him as "Jesus" on earth; he had his first sight of Him in the glory, and his soul was so thrilled with what he beheld that he never thought of Him as other than the glorified One. So he invariably writes in the original text, "Christ Jesus," and his message is in a peculiar sense called "The gospel of the glory." The other disciples walked with Him on earth, and delighted to dwell on what He was when here, and so they speak of Him as "Jesus Christ." Any critical version will make this distinction clear.

Paul is a messenger, a sent one of Christ Jesus "by the will of God." It was no mere idle thought of his that sent him forth on this mission. It was not that he concluded it would be the best way to spend his life. He who saved him commissioned him, and sent him forth to be a teacher of the Gentiles in faith and verity; and so he insists on the divine character of his commission, "An apostle of Christ Jesus by the will of God."

A simple cobbler was being introduced to a rather dignified clergyman, and when the cobbler said, "I didn't get your name," the clergyman replied, "The Reverend Doctor Blank, by the will of God." The cobbler said, "And I am John Doe, cobbler by the will of God; I am glad to meet you, sir." It is a great thing, whatever your station in life may be, to recognize it as "by the will of God." Am I a preacher of the gospel? It should be only because I have heard a divine call urging me forth and thrusting me out. Am I a merchant? Has it been given to me to make money for the glory of God? Then let me remember that I am a merchant by the will of God, and I should be sure that I am where God's will has placed me, and should seek to be faithful to Him.

The apostle addresses himself, though not to two classes of people as one might suppose, "To the saints which are at Ephesus, and to the faithful in Christ Jesus." That might suggest that the term "saints" took in all believers and that "the faithful" included a spiritual aristocracy, but it might better be rendered, "To the saints which are at Ephesus, even the believers in Christ Jesus." In other words, it is faith in Christ Jesus which constitutes a person a saint. Are you a saint? You say, "I wouldn't like to go so far. I am not sinless yet." A saint is not a sinless person; a saint is a separated person, separated to God in Christ Jesus. People have an idea that if you live a very saintly life, eventually you may become a saint. God says, "Do you believe in My Son? Have you trusted Him? Very well, then, I constitute you a saint; be sure that you live in a saintly way." We do not become saints by saintliness, but we should be characterized by saintliness because we are saints.

In verse 2 we have the apostolic salutation, "Grace be to you, and peace, from God our Father, and from the Lord Jesus Christ." He is not referring at all to the grace that saves. These people were already saved. He tells them, "By grace are ye saved through faith; and that not of yourselves: it is the gift of God: not of works, lest any man should boast" (Eph. 2:8, 9). It is a great thing to have that settled. So many of us never seem to get anything settled. We come to Christ, but lack positive conviction and definite assurance. That comes out in a great many of the hymns we sing. How hard it is to get hymns that are absolutely scriptural. In a meeting some time ago I was giving a message on "The Indwelling Holy Spirit." At the close of the service, the dear pastor stood up and said, "In the light of this splendid address, let us sing, 'Holy Spirit, faithful Guide, ever near the Christian's side,'" and I felt my heart sink as I thought, "After I have spent forty minutes trying to show them that the Holy Spirit is not merely at our side, but dwells in us, they haven't got it yet." Then they came to that last gloomy verse, and I said, "Please don't sing such words as these:

> "'When our days of toil shall cease,
> Waiting still for sweet release;
> Nothing left but heaven and prayer,
> Wond'ring if our names are there;
> Wading deep the dismal flood,
> Pleading nought but Jesus' blood.'"

What a mixture! I refuse to sing it. I *know* my name is there!

I do not understand how it is that Christians are so slow in laying hold of divine truth. Here in our verse the apostle means grace to keep, to preserve us, not grace to save. For the believer that is already settled for eternity, but we need daily grace for daily trials.

How does one obtain this grace? "We have not an high priest which cannot be touched with the feeling of our infirmities; but was in all points tempted like as we are, yet without sin. Let us therefore come boldly unto the throne of grace, that we may obtain mercy, and find grace to help in time of need" (Heb. 4:15, 16). We were saved by grace, we began with grace, but we need grace every step of the way that we might triumph over the world and over the natural propensities of our poor hearts; for as Christians we have the nature of the old man in us still, and it will readily manifest itself if not subdued and kept in place by grace divine.

"Grace be to you, and peace." This is not peace *with* God which was made for us by the blood of Calvary's cross. Every believer in the Lord Jesus should know what it is to have peace with God, "Being justified by faith, we have peace with God through our Lord Jesus Christ" (Rom. 5:1). But this is the peace *of* God, garrisoning our hearts as we move along toward our heavenly home, the same peace that filled the heart of Jesus when here on earth. May I use an illustration of Dr. W. I. Carroll's right here? Jesus said to His disciples in the ship, "Let us go over to the other side." Where were they going? To the other side. When they got into the boat, He went to sleep in perfect peace, and in the middle of the night the elements raged, the devil stirred up a terrific tempest, but it could not drown Him. It was impossible that the boat in which He sailed should founder; but the disciples were terrified and they aroused that Holy Sleeper and said, "Master, carest Thou not that we perish?" Jesus, wakened from His sleep, looked at them, and said, "O ye of little faith." Little faith! With the thunder roaring, the lightning flashing, the wind blowing a gale, and the sea raging, why, you surely could not blame men for being afraid! But you see, Jesus did not say to them, "Let us go out into the middle of the lake and get drowned." He said, "Let us go over to the other side," and they should have rested on His word. They would have had the same peace that He had if they had believed His word.

Do the trials of the way sometimes test your soul? Do you wonder what will become of you? This is what will become of you: If worst comes to worst and you starve to death, you are going Home to heaven! Thousands of people are dying and going to a lost eternity, but no matter what comes to you, if you are saved, you are going Home! As we realize that we are in His hand, the peace of God, like a military garrison, keeps our hearts and saves us from all doubt and fear.

"Grace be to you, and peace, from God our Father." Do you love to dwell on those words, "From God our Father"? The blessed Lord came to reveal the Father, and the Holy Spirit gives us to know the Father, and one of the first evidences that a man is born of God is that he lifts his heart to heaven and says, "Father." This is a different thing from the God of the

Lodge Hall, from the God of the Modernist, from the doctrine of the universal Fatherhood of God and brotherhood of man. That is not what the apostle is talking about. He has been addressing saints, believers in Christ Jesus, and when he speaks to them, he says, "God our Father." It is only by regeneration, only by the second birth, that we enter into this blessed relationship. Scripture declares that those who have never been regenerated are of the flesh, they are not the children of God, and our Lord Jesus said to certain ones, "Ye are of your father the devil, and the lusts of your father ye will do" (John 8: 44). That does not sound very much like the universal Fatherhood of God and the brotherhood of man! People tell me that is what Jesus came to teach. I defy anyone to find any such thing anywhere in all the teaching of our Lord Jesus Christ. He said to Nicodemus, "Except a man be born again, he cannot see the kingdom of God" (John 3: 3). In that very verse He denies the universal Fatherhood of God and brotherhood of man. I know all men are brothers in Adam and we are one in sin, but it is only by a new birth that I become a brother of the saints and a child of God.

"Grace be to you, and peace, from God our Father, and from the Lord Jesus Christ." How the Holy Ghost delights to give Him His full title, "the Lord Jesus Christ." He is Lord of all, and therefore all men are called upon to subject themselves to Him. Notice verse 3, for in this we properly begin the study of the epistle: "Blessed be the God and Father of our Lord Jesus Christ." He has said before that God is our Father, and now points out that in a peculiar sense God sustains that relationship to the Lord Jesus Christ. He is the God of our Lord Jesus Christ because Jesus became Man, and as Man He looks up to the Father as His God. He is the Father of our Lord Jesus Christ because Christ is God the Son from all eternity. What a wealth of instruction is bound up in that expression, "The God and Father of our Lord Jesus Christ." It was not until the resurrection that He revealed this blessed relationship. He said to Mary, "Go to My brethren, and say unto them, I ascend unto My Father, and your Father, and to My God, and your God" (John 20: 17). He does not say, "I ascend to *our* God and *our* Father." His relationship is different to ours. He was not simply a man brought into union with God, but He was the Son of God, come down to earth in grace, who became Man for our redemption.

Farther on in this epistle there are two prayers, one in the last part of this chapter, and the other in chapter three, and they accord in a very striking way with these titles. In chapter 1: 17 Paul prays that "the God of our Lord Jesus

Christ" may do certain things; and then when we turn over to chapter 3:14 we read, "For this cause I bow my knees unto the Father of our Lord Jesus Christ." Why the difference? Because in the first prayer he is speaking of the divine counsels and power, and so he addresses himself to God. In the second prayer he takes into consideration our relationship to God and addresses himself to "the Father of our Lord Jesus Christ." Scripture is wonderfully accurate.

"Blessed be the God and Father of our Lord Jesus Christ, who hath blessed us with all spiritual blessings in heavenly places in Christ." Notice, "He *hath* blessed us." The apostle is not speaking of something that may be ours when we get to heaven, but right here and now I have been blessed with every spiritual blessing in Christ Jesus. People often ask me if I have obtained the second blessing yet, and I generally say, "Second blessing? Why, I am somewhere up in the hundreds of thousands as far as that goes, if you refer to experience; but actually I obtained every blessing that God has for a redeemed sinner when I put my trust in the Lord Jesus Christ." He does not just give us a little now and a little later, but gives us everything in Christ. It is all yours. Enter into it and enjoy it. It is one thing to have the blessings and another thing to make them yours. I read recently about a man in Montana for whom search had

long been made. Some years ago a British noble-
man died, leaving an estate which, as he had no
children, would go to the nearest heir. This man
away out west was the nearest heir, living in poverty, and just eking out a struggling existence
when they found him and gave him the news that
the estate was his. It was his all the time, but he
did not know it. What did he do when he found
it out? Did he say, "Well, it is a good thing to
know that I have something to fall back on and
some day I will go and look into it?" No, he
went down town, and on the strength of it bought
himself a new suit and a ticket, and started to
Great Britain. I read an interview which the
reporters had with him. They said, "Where are
you going?" He answered, "To take possession
of my estate." You and I are richer far than he
was, but do we really take possession by faith
of the things that are ours in Christ?

You may say, "But name some of these things
that are ours." He has blessed us with the blessing of forgiveness of our sins, with justification
from all things, with sanctification in Christ, with
a robe of perfect righteousness, with a heavenly
citizenship, by giving us a place in the Body of
Christ, by making us heirs of His riches in Christ
Jesus! And yet how some of us struggle along,
eking out a poor, wretched, miserable existence!
We act as spiritual paupers when we ought to be
living like millionaires.

"Who hath blessed us with all spiritual blessings in heavenly places in Christ." God has
made Christ Jesus to be unto us wisdom, righteousness, sanctification, and redemption, and yet
for six years after I was converted I was still
seeking righteousness and sanctification. But
one day I woke up to the fact that it was all
mine in Christ Jesus, and that I had simply to
appropriate and enjoy it.

Now notice he says, "In heavenly places." My
blessings are all yonder, and He calls me in the
Spirit to rise to my heavenly citizenship and live
in this world as a heavenly man should live, drawing from the glory all the resources I need that
I may be more than conqueror day by day, as
I pass through this scene.

Notice how carefully you have to read Scripture. "Who hath blessed us with all spiritual
blessings in heavenly places in Christ." What a
mistake it would be to translate that, "with
Christ." Do you see the difference? How often
we hear people misquote it, and say, "He hath
raised us up together, and made us sit together
in heavenly places *with* Christ Jesus." Nothing
of the kind. We are not seated together *with*
Christ; we are seated *in* Him. He is there as
our representative, and that is an altogether different thing from being seated *with* Him. We
have "everything *in* Jesus and Jesus everything!"
Mark, this does not mean that we are only

blessed and seated together in Christ when we have a real, good, happy, spiritual meeting. Sometimes when we have a good meeting and the people think they have been helped, some well-meaning brother closes in prayer and says, "O Lord, we thank Thee that we have been sitting together in heavenly places in Christ Jesus this morning." I say to myself, "The dear brother hasn't got it yet. He thinks because there is a glow in his heart, because he feels happy, that means he is sitting in heavenly places in Christ." But I am sitting in heavenly places in Christ just as truly when I am oppressed with the trials of the way, as I am when I am flourishing and have everything that heart could desire. It is a question of fact: Christ is there in the heavenlies, and God sees me in Him. I am blessed in Him and all the treasures of heaven are at my disposal, and I am to draw upon them as I have need in order that I may be happy, in order that I may rejoice as I go forth in His service down here.

OUR ELECTION
AND PREDESTINATION

✔ ✔ ✔

"According as He hath chosen us in Him before the foundation of the world, that we should be holy and without blame before Him." (Put the stop right there.) "In love having predestinated us unto the adoption of children by Jesus Christ to Himself, according to the good pleasure of His will" (Eph. 1: 4, 5).

✔ ✔ ✔

IN verse 3 the apostle gives thanks to "The God and Father of our Lord Jesus Christ"—the Source of all our blessings—"who hath blessed us with all spiritual blessings in heavenly places in Christ." And now he carries our minds back to the past eternity that we may be brought to realize that salvation is altogether of God, not at all of ourselves. An old hymn puts it this way:

> "'Tis not that I did choose Thee,
> For, Lord, that could not be,
> This heart would still refuse Thee,
> But Thou hast chosen me."

And again in another that we know well, we are taught to sing:

"Jesus sought me when a stranger
   Wand'ring from the fold of God;
He to rescue me from danger
   Interposed His precious blood."

It was God Himself who purposed our salvation in the past eternity. It is Jesus Christ who wrought out our salvation upon the cross when the fulness of time had come. It is God the Holy Spirit who convicts us and brings us to repentance and to a saving knowledge of the grace of God as revealed in Christ. We cannot take any credit to ourselves for our salvation. A little boy was asked, "Have you found Jesus?" He looked up and said, "Please, sir, I didn't know He was lost; but I was, and He found me." We did not have to do the seeking after Him, He sought us because of the love that was in His heart from eternity.

"According as He hath chosen us in Him before the foundation of the world." This, of course, is the truth of election. Again and again believers are spoken of as elect people, as children chosen of God. Mr. Spurgeon said, "God certainly must have chosen me before I came into this world or He never would have done so afterwards." He set His love upon us in the past eternity. This troubles people sometimes; and yet how could it be otherwise? God who is infinite in wisdom, with whom the past and the future are all one eternal *now*, purposed in His heart before the

world came into existence, that He was going to
have a people who would be to the praise and
glory of His grace for all eternity, and He looked
down through the ages and saw us as those for
whom He would give His Son in order to add to
the glory of the Lord Jesus Christ. It is wonderful to see how intimately the joy of Christ and
our salvation are linked together. John Bunyan
said, "Oh, this Lamb of God! He had a whole
heaven to Himself, myriads of angels to do His
bidding, but these could not satisfy Him. He
must have sinners to share it with Him."

You notice in verse 3 he uses the double title,
"The God and Father of our Lord Jesus Christ."
It is God who purposes it this way, it is God who
plans, it was God who chose us in Christ before
the foundation of the world; and, notice, it is
not that He chose the Church as such, but He
chose every individual who was to be a member
of that Church, to be one with Christ for eternity.
You say, "I do not understand that." I don't
either. Whenever I come to consider a subject
like this, God's electing grace and predestinating
love, I remind myself that the Word says, "My
thoughts are not your thoughts, neither are your
ways My ways, saith the Lord. For as the
heavens are higher than the earth, so are My
ways higher than your ways, and My thoughts
than your thoughts" (Isa. 55:8, 9). But it may
help us a little if we consider this apart from the
question of the fall of man.

Before the world was made, before sin came in, God chose us in Christ to be with His Son for all eternity. The fact that sin came in did not alter God's purpose. He is still going to carry it out in spite of all that Satan has done to wreck His fair creation. The purpose of God is according to His grace, grace to those who could not earn it, who did not deserve anything but eternal judgment. Somebody has well said, "The truth of election is a family secret." It is not something that we go out and proclaim to the world. We read, "Cast not your pearls before swine," and swine, you know, are unclean. We are not to go to unsaved men in the uncleanness of their sin and talk about election. They would not understand it at all; but it is a family secret that God loves to whisper in the ears of His beloved children.

It has been pictured in this way. Here is a vast host of people hurrying down the broad road with their minds fixed upon their sins, and one stands calling attention to yonder door, the entrance into the narrow way that leads to life eternal. On it is plainly depicted the text, "Whosoever will, let him come." Every man is invited, no one need hesitate. Some may say, "Well, I may not be of the elect, and so it would be useless for me to endeavor to come, for the door will not open for me." But God's invitation is absolutely sincere: it is addressed to every man, "Whosoever

will, let him take of the water of life freely"
(Rev. 22: 17). If men refuse to come, if they
pursue their own godless way down to the pit,
whom can they blame but themselves for their
eternal judgment? The messenger addressed
himself to all, the call came to all, the door could
be entered by all, but many refused to come and
perished in their sins. Such men can never blame
God for their eternal destruction. The door was
open, the invitation was given, they refused, and
He says to them sorrowfully, "Ye will not come
unto Me, that ye might have life." But see, as
the invitation goes forth, every minute or two
some one stops and says, "What is that?" "The
way to life," is the reply. "Ah, that I might find
the way to life! I have found no satisfaction in
this poor world." We read, "She that liveth in
pleasure is dead while she liveth." "I should
like to know how to be free from my sin, how to
be made fit for the presence of God." And such
an one draws near and listens, and the Spirit of
God impresses the message upon his heart and
conscience and he says, "I am going inside: I will
accept the invitation; I will enter that door," and
he presses his way in and it shuts behind him.
As he turns about he finds written on the inside
of the door the words, "Chosen in Christ before
the foundation of the world." "What!" he says,
"had God His heart fixed on me before ever the
world came into being?" Yes, but he could not

find it out until he got inside. You see, you can pass the door if you will, you can trample the love of God beneath your feet, you can spurn His grace if you are determined to do it, but you will go down to the pit and you will be responsible for your own doom.

There is no such thing taught in the Word of God as predestination to eternal condemnation. If men are lost, they are lost because they do not come to Christ. When men do come to Christ, they learn the wonderful secret that God has foreknown it all from eternity, and that He had settled it before the world came into existence that they were to share the glory of His Son throughout endless ages. D. L. Moody used to say in his quaint way, when people talked about the subject of election, "The whosoever wills are the elect, and the whosoever won'ts are the non-elect." And so you can settle it for yourself whether you will be among the elect of God or not.

When asked to explain the doctrine of election a colored brother once said, "Well, it's this way, the Lord done voted for my salvation; the devil done voted for my damnation; and I done voted with the Lord, and so we got into the majority." The devil seeks my eternal loss and God seeks my eternal blessing, and my heart says, "I will." I then know that I am among those chosen in Christ before the foundation of the world. Let

me link this up with another scripture, 2 Thess.
2: 13, "But we are bound to give thanks always
to God for you, brethren, beloved of the Lord,
because God hath from the beginning chosen you
to salvation through sanctification of the Spirit
and belief of the truth." There you have the purpose of God in the past eternity. God had from
the beginning chosen you unto salvation, and He
is carrying out His purpose through the work of
the Holy Spirit and belief of the truth on the part
of the one who hears the message.

Then again listen to the Apostle Peter, "Elect
according to the foreknowledge of God the
Father, through sanctification of the Spirit, unto
obedience and sprinkling of the blood of Jesus
Christ: Grace unto you, and peace, be multiplied"
(1 Pet. 1: 2). There you have exactly the same
order. God the Father foreknew us from eternity,
but it was up to us whether or not we would
yield to Christ. When we did yield in the obedience of faith, we took our places beneath the
sprinkled blood of Jesus and our salvation was
eternally assured. People try sometimes to put
the whole responsibility upon God and say, "If
God has not chosen me, I cannot be saved." If
you will trust in Christ, you may know that God
has chosen you.

You remember that striking illustration which
the Spirit of God Himself gives us in the last of
the book of Acts. When Paul and his company

were on their way to Rome, a terrific storm arose, and they were casting out some of the cargo in order to lighten the ship, but finally they gave up in despair. And then an angel appeared and spoke with Paul, and Paul called for the captain of the ship and said, "Be of good cheer: for there shall be no loss of any man's life among you, but of the ship. For there stood by me this night the angel of God, whose I am, and whom I serve, saying, Fear not, Paul; thou must be brought before Caesar: and, lo, God hath given thee all them that sail with thee" (Acts 27: 22-24). There was God's foreknowledge. Every one in that ship would be brought through safely, they would all land in Italy, not one of them would be lost. But a little while afterwards Paul noticed something going on among the sailors. They were fitting out a boat and were preparing to launch it into the sea, putting some provisions into it and getting ready to cut away and leave the ship. And Paul said to the captain, "Except these abide in the ship, ye cannot be saved" (Acts 27: 31). Had he not already told them that none should perish? That was God's side. Then he said, "Except these abide in the ship, ye cannot be saved"—that was their side. They were responsible to see that no one left the ship, and so it is in regard to the doctrine of election and man's responsibility. Every one who is saved will be in heaven because he was chosen in Christ before the foundation of the world, and yet every man who is ever saved will be there because as a poor guilty sinner he put his personal trust in the Lord Jesus Christ. You may say, "I can't harmonize this." You do not need to do so; just believe it and go on your way rejoicing.

Look a little farther, "According as He hath chosen us in Him before the foundation of the world, that we should be holy and without blame before Him." God, who foresaw all who would put their trust in Christ, provided a means whereby all our sin and iniquity could be settled for, in order that we might be presented holy and without blame before Him. This, of course, involves the work of the cross. Redemption was not an after thought with God, it was all provided for when He decided to bring into existence creatures who could give Him voluntary love and service.

The question may be asked, "Why did not God who knows all things create a race of people who could not have sinned, who could not have spurned Him nor hated Him, but who would always have done that which was right in His sight, who would always have loved and obeyed Him? Is not God in some sense responsible for sin because He created a creature weak enough to sin? Could He not have created one so strong that he could not have sinned?" Certainly He could. He could have made creatures that could not have failed Him. He has given us samples of this in the lower world. He has made creatures who never deviate one hair's breadth from the purpose of their being. Dr. Leander Keyser, who is not only a great theologian, but a great naturalist, says, "I have studied birds for over forty years and have had thousands of them under my observation, and I say to the honor of the bird kingdom that I have never known an unchaste bird." Do you see what that means? God makes those little feathered creatures to act according to His own thought for them. Think of the Mourning Dove who, if it loses its mate, remains widowed all of its life. God has constituted it that way, and could have so constituted mankind that they could not have deviated from the path of rectitude. But the determination to create a man or woman who could give Him loyal obedience, loving service, and voluntary devotion, necessitated the creation of men and women who could turn away from God if they wanted to, refuse to obey Him if they so desired. Otherwise there would have been no freedom in their love, devotion, reverence, and affection, and God was willing to take all the risk that He did take in order to have beings in this universe who would give Him glad and free-hearted love and devotion. So when sin came in, the Saviour was given, and the Seed of the woman has bruised the serpent's head and now, through the work of Christ,

God can present us in His glorious presence holy
and without blame in Him. It is not what we are
naturally in ourselves, but what we are in Christ
Jesus.

Now notice in verse 5 we have another word
that troubles people. We read, "In love having
predestinated us." You will notice that I began
reading verse 5 with the last part of verse 4. I
put the period after the word "Him"—"That we
should be holy and without blame before Him."
Our Authorized Version puts it this way, "That
we should be holy and without blame before Him
in love," but there is something deeper than that.
I read it, "That we should be holy and without
blame before Him," and then start the next
clause, "In love having predestinated us unto the
adoption of children by Jesus Christ to Himself,
according to the good pleasure of His will." One
is not so afraid of the word *predestinated* when
the sentence begins that way. There is no arbi-
trariness there, but it is all "in love." Predestination is a manifestation of the love of the Father.
As it is God who chose us in grace, it is the
Father who has predestinated us to the adoption
of children. Nowhere in the Bible are people
ever predestinated to go to hell, and nowhere are
people simply predestinated to go to heaven. Look
it up and see. We a e chosen in Christ to share
His glory for eternity, but predestination is always to some special place of blessing.

Turn to Romans 8:29: "For whom He did foreknow, He also did predestinate to be conformed to the image of His Son, that He might be the firstborn among many brethren." Predestinated to what? Predestinated "to be conformed to the image of His Son." You see, predestination is not God from eternity saying, "This man goes to heaven and this man to hell." No, but predestination teaches me that when I have believed in Christ, when I have trusted Him as my Saviour, I may know on the authority of God that it is settled forever that some day I am to become exactly like my Saviour. It settles the question of the security of my salvation. Whatever my present unsatisfactory experiences may be, some day I shall be altogether like the One who has redeemed me.

"Having predestinated us unto the adoption of children by Jesus Christ to Himself." That word "adoption" perplexes some. They say, "Does it mean that we are only adopted children and not really born children? A born child is one thing; a child who may not be at all related to the family, but is brought in and adopted, is another. Does it mean adopted in that sense?" This word literally means, the full placing as sons. We might read it, "Having predestinated us unto the son-placing through Jesus Christ unto Himself." It will help us to understand it if we bear in mind that in the days when our Bible was written, ε man might have a number of wives and some who were really his slaves. He would have to select those children among whom he wished to divide his estate for he might not wish it divided among this motley company. He would take those whom he selected down to the forum, and there confess them openly before the proper authority as his sons and then go through a ceremony of adoption. From that day on they were recognized as his heirs. We have been born into the family of God by regeneration and thus made children of God. We have received the Holy Spirit, who is the Spirit of adoption, and God has marked us out as those who will share everything with the Son for all eternity. We are adopted sons and born again children.

"In love having predestinated us unto the adoption of children by Jesus Christ to Himself, according to the good pleasure of His will." Our Lord is the One through whom all this blessing comes. You know there is a beautiful passage in the Old Testament which speaks of the coming Saviour as a "nail in a sure place" (Isa. 22:23). The simile is taken from the tent-life of the Arabs. Pegs were fitted into the upright poles of their dwellings, upon which they hung their garments and blankets, and upon similar pegs the women hung the utensils they used. Scripture pictures all kinds of vessels hung on one of these nails fastened in a sure place, and it says, "And they shall hang upon him all the glory of his father's house" (Isa. 22:24). So the Lord Jesus Christ having accomplished redemption has become that "nail in a sure place," and every one of us are hung upon Him. If the nail goes down, we all go down; if Christ fails, then we all go down together, but since Christ will never fail, then He will sustain every one of us right on to the very end. That is the truth that is revealed here.

How this truth of election and predestination and of sonship emphasizes the preciousness of our Lord Jesus Christ! Say it over and over to your soul until your whole being is thrilled, "Lord Jesus, I owe it all to Thee." Then you will begin to understand why one enraptured with His love could sing:

> "Jesus, the very thought of Thee
>   With sweetness fills my breast;
> But sweeter far Thy face to see,
>   And in Thy presence rest."

Every blessing for time and eternity we owe to Him. Is it according to our poor thoughts? Oh, no. According to our apprehensions, according to the strength of our faith, according to our devotedness? Not that. What then? "According to the good pleasure of His will." You know some people are afraid of the will of God, really afraid of it. And yet it is the will of God that you and

I who put our trust in the Lord Jesus should share the Saviour's glory for all eternity; and in revealing His will to us step by step along the way He would have us become more and more conformed to Him down here. Oh, to be able to say from the heart, "I welcome Thy sweet will, O God." The greatest mistake any Christian can make is to substitute his own will for the will of God.

Remember, it is the will of God that every saved one should eventually be with Christ and like Christ forevermore.

> "I know not where His hand shall lead,
>   Through desert wastes, o'er flowery mead;
>   'Mid tangled thicket set with thorn,
>   'Mid gloom of night or glow of morn;
>   But still I know my Father's hand
>   Will bring me to His goodly land."

If you are still unsaved, the most fearful mistake *you* can ever make is to suppose that if you should yield yourself to the will of God it would take away from your peace and happiness and joy. The only real peace, the only real happiness, the only real joy for created beings is found in falling in with the will of God. That will planned our redemption, that will purposed our salvation, and that will secures our place in the glory for all eternity.

ACCEPTED IN THE BELOVED

✓ ✓ ✓

"To the praise of the glory of His grace, wherein He hath made us accepted in the Beloved" (Eph. 1:6).

✓ ✓ ✓

YOU will at once recognize the fact that this verse does not in itself constitute a complete sentence. It is part of a rather lengthy sentence which began with the third verse. We have been climbing one of God's wonderful mountain peaks from that verse, and now we have reached the top. Standing here we are privileged to look below us and see the depths from which we have come, and then look beyond and see the glory that is before us.

There is no room for human boasting. Our salvation is according to the good pleasure of God's will, to the praise of the glory of His own grace, that no man may have opportunity to give himself any credit whatsoever. It is to the praise of the glory of God's grace that He hath made us accepted in the Beloved. I hope we are all clear about grace. We are constantly preaching about it, singing about it, and reading about it, and yet how few there are who really enter into the precious fact that our salvation is altogether of grace. No matter how many times one may preach on salvation by grace, every time he rises to face an audience there are scores and possibly hundreds who are still strangers to the grace of God. Let us never forget that grace is God's free unmerited favor lavished upon those who deserve nothing but His judgment. You cannot earn grace, you cannot earn His loving-kindness.

You may remember the case of the woman who attempted the assassination of Queen Elizabeth. She was dressed as a man page, and had secreted herself in the queen's boudoir awaiting the convenient moment to stab her to death, not realizing that the queen's attendants would be very careful to search the rooms before her majesty was permitted to retire. Hidden there among the gowns they found this woman and brought her into the presence of the queen. They took from her the poniard which she had hoped to plant in the heart of her sovereign. She realized that her case, humanly speaking, was hopeless, and so she threw herself down on her knees and pleaded and begged the queen as a woman, to have compassion upon her, a woman, her intended assassin, and to show her grace. Queen Elizabeth looked at her quietly, and coolly said, "If I show you grace, what promise will you make for the future?" The woman looked up and said, "Grace that hath conditions, grace that is fettered by precautions, is no grace at all." Queen Elizabeth caught it in a moment and said, "You are right; I pardon you of my grace," and they led her away a free woman. History tells us that from that moment Queen Elizabeth had no more faithful devoted servant than that woman who had intended to take her life.

Remember grace that hath conditions, grace that is fettered by precautions, that insists upon pledges and promises for the future, is no grace at all. Grace is favor freely shown to those who deserve only judgment, and so we read that our salvation is to the praise of the glory of His grace, and when at last we get home to heaven, He shall have all the praise and all the glory. We will gratefully acknowledge in His blessed presence that left to ourselves we would have gone on to everlasting judgment, that it was He who showed us our deep, deep need. Looking down upon us He pitied us as we were hurrying on to endless woe and He gave His Son to die. This is the grace of our Lord Jesus that led Him to go to Calvary's cross and settle the claim that we never could have settled. And so by grace, and by grace alone, have we been saved.

Observe what grace has done for us: "Wherein He hath made us accepted in the Beloved." There are several other suggested translations of this passage. It might be rendered, "To the praise of the glory of His grace, which He hath freely bestowed upon us in the Beloved," or "To the praise of the glory of His grace wherein He has taken us into favor in the Beloved." But all these different renderings suggest just exactly the same thing, that the saved sinner does not stand before God in any righteousness of his own, that he does not plead any merit of his own before the divine throne, but that through grace he has been received to the very heart of God. Not merely forgiven, not merely justified, not merely washed from his sins or cleansed from his defilement, but received in loving-kindness to the very heart of God according to the Father's estimate of His own beloved Son. In the seventeenth chapter of John our blessed Lord speaks to the Father of His own, of you and of me, if we have believed in Him, for He was praying for those "who shall believe on Me through their word." Thus He included all believers to the very end of time, and speaking of such He says to the Father, "That the world may know that Thou hast loved them, as Thou hast loved Me." I could not believe that if it were not in my Bible; I could not believe that God, the Holy One, loves me a poor sinner in myself, a poor sinner who never retires at night without having to lift my heart to Him in penitence and confess my failures, as He loves the Lord Jesus Christ, His holy, spotless Son.

We do not have far to go for the proof of His

love. It is seen in that God commended His own love toward us in that He sent His Son to be the propitiation for our sins. If He gave His Son for me, then He must love me as greatly as He loves His Son, or He never would have permitted Him to die for me. And then again, you remember that kindred passage in the fourth chapter of First John, "That we may have boldness in the day of judgment; because as He is, so are we in this world," that is, as He is in relation to judgment. He has already passed through the judgment and will never have to go into it again. He will never again know the forsaking of God, the enshrouding of His soul with the blackness of darkness, the taste of the bitter cup, the agony, shame, and curse of the cross. All that is in the past. He went through it all for us and now so truly are we linked up with Him that, "As He is, so are we in this world."

A very interesting volume has been recently published, giving the story of the life and work of Dr. Usher, who for a great many years carried on medical missionary work in Turkey. In this wonderful story he relates one incident that illustrates in a very striking way what we have before us. He tells how a very notable member of the Turkish movement had become governor of a certain province, in which the mission hospital and schools were located. This man was very learned and of great determination, but a very rigid

Mussulman. He had made up his mind to act in accordance with one of the old laws of Turkey stating that foreigners coming into the country should be allowed to live there for one year, but if at the end of that time they had not become Mohammedans, they would have to leave Turkey. That law had been a dead letter for a great many years, but he made up his mind that he would banish all the missionaries, Catholic and Protestant, from his province.

However, he decided that he would be fair, and he would give them all an opportunity to become Mohammedans, and so during the month of Ramadan, their annual fast, he invited all these missionaries to a great feast in his home. You see, they could feast at night but not in the daytime. As all these missionaries received the message, they knew it to be a summons, for according to Turkish law it would never do to make excuses, for the invitation to dine with the governor was tantamount to a command. Dr. Usher sat on the left hand of the governor, and the Chaldean Catholic bishop sat on his right hand, with the other missionaries on either side, and a number of the attendants of the governor in waiting.

By-and-by, turning to the Catholic bishop, the governor said, "My lord bishop, will you tell me how you think a man can enter paradise?" The bishop answered, "I will say that I believe

through the merits of Jesus Christ, God can forgive my sins and take me to paradise." "Not at
all," said the governor; "I cannot believe that God
is less righteous than I am, and I do not believe
it would be righteous for God because of His
friendship for another, to forgive a sinner and
take him to paradise. If some one here had become indebted to the government and I had to put
him in prison, and some one said, 'That man is a
friend of mine, for my sake I beg you let him go
free,' no matter how much I would desire to
please my friend, I would be an unrighteous governor to let him go free simply because of my
friendship for some one who was interested in
him. I do not believe that God is less righteous
than I." The Chaldean bishop had not another
word to say and sat there looking puzzled. Dr.
Usher felt that something tremendous was at
stake, and he knew that he would be questioned
next, so he lifted his heart to God, remembering
the word, "When they deliver you up, take no
thought how or what ye shall speak: for it shall
be given you in that same hour what ye shall
speak" (Matt. 10: 19). He prayed, "Lord, by Thy
Spirit give me now the message." The governor
turned and said, "What would you say? How
may a man be assured of an entrance into paradise?" Dr. Usher replied, "Your Excellency, will
you permit me to use your own illustration, only
to change it slightly? Let us think of you not

merely as the governor of this province, but as the king. You have one son, the prince, whom you love tenderly. Suppose that I am the man who is in debt to the government, owing a sum so vast that I could not pay one part out of a thousand. In accordance with the law, I am laid hold of and cast into prison. Unworthy as I am, your son is a friend of mine: he has a deep interest in me and a real love for me. He seeks you out and says, 'My father, my friend is in prison for a debt which he owes the government, and which he cannot pay. Will you permit me to pay it all for him in order that he may go free?' And you say to him, 'My son, since you are so interested and willing to pay the debt yourself, I am willing that it should be so, and more than that, I will participate with you in it.' And so he goes to the proper authority and pays my debt in full, leaving nothing to be demanded. He takes the receipt, and comes down to me in my prison cell. I could treat him in three ways. When he comes to me and says, 'Brother, your debt is paid and you may go free,' I could turn in haughtiness and say, 'No; I refuse to be under obligation to anybody,' forgetting that my debt is already an obligation and that I am now only entering into one of loving-kindness, whereas I was before obligated by law. Or suppose I say, 'I will never leave this prison unless I can pay the debt myself.' I would have to remain in the

prison, for I could not settle the debt. Then, I
might look at the receipt and say, 'Yes; but I
can't believe it; there is some mistake about it.
I can't believe that you would take such an interest in me. I dare not leave; let me remain here.
I would be afraid to go out lest the first police
officer would arrest me again.' But he might say,
'Man, it is foolish for you to talk like that.' And
if he should insist on drawing me out of the
prison, I should go slinking down the street and
trembling as I thought of my debt, and my home
would become a prison for I would be afraid to
look out of the window or go to the door. I
would have no assurance if I did not believe the
message that your son brought. But in the third
place I could rise up and fall at the feet of the
prince, your son, and say, 'I can never repay you
for what you have done for me, but I shall seek
to show by my life how grateful I am.' And so
I would go free. Let us suppose that on some
later day I see the prince riding down one of the
streets of the city, and I notice that some one
has let a great pile of cord-wood lie in the street
which hinders him from going by. Would I try
to get some one to get this out of the way? No;
but how glad I would be to run out and clear a
passage for the prince. If he should say, 'Thank
you; let me pay you for your labor,' I would say,
'Oh, no; you paid my debt; it is a joy for me to
do something to show my gratitude.' "

The Turkish governor was listening carefully and watching intently, and suddenly a light shone, and he said, "Oh, then, Mr. Usher, is this the reason why you have a hospital here in Turkey? Is this why you establish these schools and why you missionaries are giving your lives for our people? It is not trusting to earn your way into paradise?" "No," said Dr. Usher; "our way into paradise is settled because Jesus has paid the debt, and now we serve because we love Him." The Turkish governor was thoughtful again and then looked up and said, "You used the illustration of my son paying the debt, and you suggested by that that you meant that God has a Son; but God is one God; He does not beget, and He is not begotten. I cannot accept the idea that God should come down to this world and beget a Son." Dr. Usher said, "But, Your Excellency, when God speaks to us He has to use our language. His thoughts are above our thoughts and His words above our words. We speak to one another in different tongues. If I were to say to you in English, 'In a little while I am going home,' it would mean something altogether different from the message which would be conveyed in Turkish, for in Turkish there is no word for home. I would have to say, 'In a little while I am going to the house;' but I do not mean that I am going to the building, I mean that I am going to the love of my wife and children whether there is a

building or not. That constitutes home for me.
And, you see, our poor human language has no
word to express the infinite mystery of the relation between the Father and the Son, for it is not
such a relationship as you and I know; it is one
that existed from all eternity."

The governor felt he could not banish them,
and allowed the work to go on and was himself
dismissed from his position because of his grace
and kindness in protecting the missionaries. They
have always hoped that deep in his heart he
turned to Christ.

Our blessed Lord saw us in our deep need. He
paid for us, and having settled the debt He has
now brought us into the royal family, washed us
from every stain of sin, robed us in garments of
glory and beauty and given us a seat at the table
of the King. He has taken us into favor in the
Beloved so that the Father's thoughts of Christ
are His thoughts of love for us who trust Christ.
Out of this, you see, springs the obedience of
faith; out of this springs the earnest desire to so
labor, so work, so live for God that in that coming
day when we meet our Saviour in the glory, we
shall be acceptable to Him and shall hear Him
say to us, "Well done, thou good and faithful
servant; enter thou into the joy of thy Lord"
(Matt. 25:21).

He does not mean that we enter paradise because of our service, but that entering heaven in

all the infinite value of the Person and work of Christ we share His joy through the ages to come because of devotion to the One who loves us and gave Himself for us.

REDEMPTION BY HIS BLOOD

✓ ✓ ✓

"In whom we have redemption through His blood, the forgiveness of sins, according to the riches of His grace" (Eph. 1: 7).

✓ ✓ ✓

WE have noticed that we were thought of and our happiness planned for by God long before the world began, that when the fulness of time had come, He sent the Lord Jesus Christ into the world to carry out the divine purpose, and that since His death and resurrection, since His ascension to God's right hand in heaven, He has made us accepted in the Beloved. In verse 7 we have the basis of it, "In whom we have redemption." I wish that we might have that firmly fixed in our minds. We do not have to pray, "Take all my guilt away;" we do not have to plead with God to save or to justify us, because these things are blessedly settled and settled for eternity, if we have trusted the Lord Jesus Christ. And so we do not hope some day to receive the redemption of our soul. We have redemption, we have "redemption through His blood, the forgiveness of sins, according to the riches of His grace."

Many of you know that there are three very distinct words used in the New Testament for *redemption.* One of these words means simply to go into the market and buy, "to purchase;" and when you buy a thing, of course it is yours. We have been bought with a price, even the precious blood of the Lord Jesus Christ. We have been redeemed to God by Him and belong to Him. He purchased us, He paid the price for us, made us His own. We sold ourselves for nothing, but we have been redeemed without money, even the precious blood of Christ.

There is another word, a little fuller word, for *redemption,* and this means "to buy out of the market," so that that which has been purchased shall never be put on sale again. For instance, when one went into the slave-market of old and saw a certain slave for sale, and said, "I will purchase this person," when the money was paid the slave was handed over to the purchaser. Then he put into the hand of the slave a legal paper, a writ, which granted him complete freedom—that is the meaning of the second word, "to buy out of the market," never to be placed in jeopardy again. It is the word that is used where Peter tells us we have been redeemed not with "corruptible things, as silver and gold . . . but with the precious blood of Christ, as of a lamb without blemish and without spot: who verily was fore-ordained before the foundation of the world, but was manifest in these last times for you, who by Him do believe in God, that raised Him up from the dead, and gave Him glory; that your faith and hope might be in God" (1 Pet. 1: 18-21). We have been "bought out of the market," we are not going to be put on sale any more. We are free.

The third word is the one found in our text. It is a Greek compound, the first part, *apo,* means "away from," going away from something or some condition, and the second part, *lutrosis,* means "to be free," "to be loosed," and so it means literally, "to be loosed away" from something. We have been loosed away from the curse of the law that once hung over us. We have been loosed away from the judgment of God toward which we were one time speeding, loosed away from the guilt of our sins. That is why I won't sing, "Take all my guilt away." My guilt was taken away, for we have been loosed away from the entire question of guilt. God will never permit that question to be raised again. It was raised with His own blessed Son at Calvary's cross when all the judgment that my guilt deserved fell on Him, and now I can say:

> "Death and judgment are behind me,
>   Grace and glory are before;
> All the billows rolled o'er Jesus,
>   There exhausted all their power."

Why, it ought to thrill our souls and fill us with
a flood of joy continually. No wonder we sometimes sing:

> "Redeemed, redeemed, from sin and all its woe.
> Redeemed, redeemed, eternal life to know,
> Redeemed, redeemed, by Jesus' blood!
> Redeemed, redeemed! Oh, praise the Lord!"

If we should hold our peace when we realize
what grace hath wrought on our behalf, the very
stones would cry out.

Then notice the price of our redemption—"In
whom we have redemption through His blood."
No less a price would do; no less a price would
have availed to set us free, to deliver us from the
curse and the judgment once hanging over us.
In Old Testament times the sinner came to the
altar bringing a lamb or a goat from the flock,
or a bullock from the herd, or, if very poor, two
turtle-doves, two young pigeons. These were
slain, the blood poured out, and they were offered
upon the altar and consumed by the fire of divine
judgment, a typical sacrifice for sin. But,

> "Not all the blood of beasts
>   On Jewish altars slain,
>   Could give the guilty conscience peace
>   Or wash away its stain."

Why? Because there was not sufficient value in
those creatures that were offered up through all
past dispensations. They did not have intrinsic

worth. When that blood was shed and was sprinkled upon the altar and upon the poor sinner, it was powerless to avail, it was powerless to settle the sin question; but, thank God, in our Lord Jesus Christ we see a sacrifice of infinite worth.

People try to reason sometimes as to the extent of His atonement. Some theologians have talked about a limited atonement, for they believe that our blessed Lord made an atonement for a certain elect company only, and that outside of that company there is no possibility of salvation for anyone. Let me say this soberly, seriously, and knowing in my very soul that I have the backing of the Word of God—If every sinner who has ever lived in the world and every sinner who will ever live were to come to God in faith owning his sin and guilt and putting his trust in the Lord Jesus Christ, so infinite is the value of the work of the cross, of the life that was there given, of the precious blood that was there shed, that every sinner could be redeemed from judgment, be freed from every charge, and still there would be untold value in the atonement of Christ which would avail for the sinners in a million universes like this one. There is no measuring the atoning value of the blood of Jesus. I remember hearing a Roman Catholic priest say that one drop of the precious blood of Jesus could wash away all the sins that have ever been committed in this world.

He was right, because, you see, on the one hand, you have finite sinners, and on the other hand, you have the infinite atonement of the Son of God. "We have redemption through His blood." Do you fear then to rest upon this wonderful gospel truth? Do you fear then to trust your soul to the blessed Saviour who there died for your sins on the cross?

Dr. Joseph Parker of London, the noted English preacher, who for many years proclaimed the Word of God in the great City Temple, tells in his autobiography that there was a time when he gave too much attention to the modern theories of his day. Men were reasoning and speculating and undervaluing the Word of God and he found himself, as he read their books and mingled in their meetings, losing his grip intellectually upon the great fundamental doctrine of salvation alone through the atoning blood of the Lord Jesus Christ. But he tells us that there came into his life the most awful sorrow that he ever had to bear. His devoted wife, whom he loved so tenderly, was stricken, and in a few short hours was snatched away from him, He was unable to share his grief with others, and walking through those empty rooms of his home with a breaking heart, his misery felt for some footing in modern theory and there was none, "And then," he said, addressing a company of his Congregational brethren, "my brethren, in those hours of darkness, in those hours of my soul's anguish, when filled with doubt and trembling in fear, I bethought myself of the old gospel of redemption alone through the blood of Christ, the gospel that I had preached in those earlier days, and I put my foot down on that, and, my brethren, I found firm standing. I stand there today, and I shall die resting upon that blessed glorious truth of salvation alone through the precious blood of Christ."

> "On Christ the solid Rock I stand,
> All other ground is sinking sand."

Redemption by blood—in what way does the blood of Christ save us? The blood is the life. The Word of God tells us, "The life of the flesh is in the blood: and I have given it to you upon the altar to make an atonement for your souls" (Lev. 17: 11). Of what blood is He speaking? What blood is given upon the altar to make an atonement? It is the precious blood of Christ, of which all these sacrifices of old were simply typical. Upon the cross God gave Jesus, and there He gave up His life when He poured out His blood. It is through the giving of His life, and not through our imitating the life of Jesus, that we are saved. It is through the outpouring of the life of Jesus in the shedding of His blood that we find redemption. "The Son of God, who loved me, and gave Himself for me" (Gal. 2: 20). And so we have redemption through His blood, and this necessarily involves the forgiveness of sins.

This subject of forgiveness of sins perplexes people sometimes. Forgiveness is presented in Scripture in three very distinct aspects. First, there is eternal forgiveness, and that is what the apostle is speaking of here. Every believer is eternally forgiven the moment he comes to God through Jesus. He stands before God justified, every trespass forgiven and as clear before the throne of God as if he had never committed a sin. He never again has to come to God suing for forgiveness, for He has forgiven all his trespasses. But you may say, "Well, do you mean by that, all my trespasses up to the hour of my conversion?" I mean something far more than that, something far better than that. I mean that the believer's sins, all of them, past, present, and whatever sins may be committed in the future, were all taken into account and were all atoned for when Jesus died, and the moment a man trusts in Him, all the value of that atoning work is put down to his account and every sin is forgiven. That is the first great aspect of forgiveness.

In the second place, there is the restorative forgiveness of the Father. The eternal forgiveness is God's forgiveness—God, the Judge of all. The moment my responsibility for my actions as a sinner ended, that moment my responsibility as a child having to do with my Father began, and if

I fail (and I do, and you do), I come to Him not to beg forgiveness, for that is settled in the cross, but I come knowing that, "If we confess our sins He is faithful and just to forgive us our sins, and to cleanse us from all unrighteousness." When as a believer I fail, I come to God as my Father and tell out the story of my failure and my sin; and I know on the authority of the Word of God, that as I confess my sin, it is put away and my communion with the Father is restored. Sin on the part of the believer does not affect his life, for his life is hid with Christ in God, but it does affect his communion with the Father, and that is not restored again until the failing believer comes confessing his sins. Then he receives restorative forgiveness.

The third aspect has been called "governmental forgiveness." It has to do with the temporal consequences of sin. I think of a Christian man whom I have known for a great many years, who in his unsaved days was an inebriate, giving himself to drunkenness for years. Though that man lived a wonderful Christian life for over thirty years, he suffered all his life in his body because of his early sins. Sometimes he was tempted to wonder whether God had really forgiven him when the punishment of sin seemed to be going on in his body. Again and again you will find this. God permits temporal punishment to follow sin, but when the believer learns to take everything as from the hand of God and bows to the will of God, He sometimes even grants him governmental forgiveness and restores the body, restores the years that the locusts have eaten, and brings back temporal blessings that one might have supposed were forever forfeited.

Upon what is all this based? It is "according to the riches of His grace." It does not say "*out* of the riches of His grace," but "*according* to the riches of His grace." Can you estimate the riches of God's grace? How rich is He in grace? Is He a millionaire? More than that. Is He is a multi-millionaire? More than that. Is He a billionaire, a trillionaire? More than that. Shall I go on? It is useless, for God's grace is infinite, and you and I have been blessedly saved, forgiven, redeemed, "according to the riches of His grace." I repeat, it is not merely *out* of the riches of His grace. Here is a millionaire to whom you go on behalf of some worthy cause. He listens to you and says, "Well, I think I will do a little for you," and he takes out his pocketbook and selects a ten-dollar bill. Perhaps you had hoped to receive a thousand from him. He has given you *out* of his riches, but not *according* to his riches. If he gave you a book of signed blank checks all numbered, and said, "Take this, fill in what you need," that would be *according* to his riches.

We who are saved may well rejoice, for we have been forgiven, we have been redeemed, not *out* of the riches of God's grace but *"according* to the riches of His grace." Do you get it? If you do, you will never feel poor again. And you owe it all to the work of the cross, to the blessed One who there died, and through eternity we are going to join with all the redeemed up yonder and ascribe all power and praise and honor and glory to the Lamb that was slain, "who redeemed us to God by Thy blood out of every kindred, and tongue, and people, and nation" (Rev. 5:9).

May I quote the beautiful words of one of our Christian poets, as emphasizing this precious truth?—

> *"O spotless Lamb, my Sacrifice,*
> *Thou art my soul's salvation;*
> *In God's eternal counsel, Thou,*
> *Before the earth's creation,*
> *Wert slain; our God had planned it all*
> *Ere Satan caused Thy creatures' fall*
> *That shrouded them in darkness.*
> *Naught we could do the gulf to span*
> *'Twixt God and sinful fallen man,*
> *Created in God's likeness.*
>
> *"God saw us in our deep, deep need,*
> *He undertook to save us;*
> *'Twas not a trifling thing to Him,*
> *His very best He gave us.*
> *Then mercy's fountain to reveal,*
> *Our weary, sinsick souls to heal,*
> *His Father-heart not sparing,*
> *From Godhead's fullest glory, He*
> *Sent His own Son to earth—I see*
> *Him now my burden bearing.*

"Oh, love of God, how great and strong
  Beyond all human telling!
Oh, wondrous gift! The Father's Son,
  All doubt and gloom dispelling,
The Lord of glory comes to earth,
A Virgin chosen gave Him birth,
  His bed a lowly manger;
Angels adoring hover near,
Shepherds the great glad tidings hear,
  But to Thine own a stranger.

"In adoration, praise, and love,
  My heart is bowed before Thee;
I trust Thy grace, believe Thy Word.
  It full assurance gives me
That all my sins are washed away
By Thine own blood! Oh, let me stay
  Close by Thy side forever.
I am Thine own, and Thou art mine!
Who from Thy heart and love sublime,
  And joy and peace, can sever?"

—H. A. M.

THE DISPENSATION OF THE FULNESS OF TIMES

✦ ✦ ✦

"Wherein He hath abounded toward us in all wisdom and prudence; having made known unto us the mystery of His will, according to His good pleasure which He hath purposed in Himself: that in the dispensation of the fulness of times He might gather together in one all things in Christ, both which are in heaven, and which are on earth; even in Him: in whom also we have obtained an inheritance, being predestinated according to the purpose of Him who worketh all things after the counsel of His own will: that we should be to the praise of His glory, who first trusted in Christ. In whom ye also trusted, after that ye heard the word of truth, the gospel of your salvation: in whom also after that ye believed, ye were sealed with that Holy Spirit of promise" (Eph. 1: 8-13).

✦ ✦ ✦

GOD has many counsels but only one purpose, and that purpose is fully brought before us in these verses. In carrying out this purpose He has His counsels in regard to the people of Israel and to the nations of the Gentiles. "In thee shall all the families of the earth be blessed," He said to Abraham. And He has His formerly hidden counsel, now made

known, in regard to the Church which is "the
fulness—the completion—of Him that filleth all
in all." He has His counsels in regard to the
glorious coming kingdom, when our Lord Jesus
shall reign from the river to the ends of the earth.
But all these are but different parts of His one
glorious purpose.

"He hath abounded toward us in all wisdom
and prudence." We may think of this first of all
as the display of His divine wisdom and intelligence; but there is more than that, there is the
subjective side. "He hath abounded *toward us*
in all wisdom and prudence—intelligence." That
is, God, through His Word, through the revelation
of His purpose given to His believing people, to
those who search His Word, believe His Word,
and enter into His truth, gives wisdom and intelligence in divine things which no one else ever
had in all the ages of the past. While there were
unnumbered saints of God in former dispensations, none had the intelligence in divine things
which you and I ought to have.

Even "the angels of His might" never had the
intelligence of His wonderful plan that the weakest Christian may now have if he will. We are
told that angels are learning the wisdom of God
in us. He never gave to them a complete revelation of what was coming; but they are learning
the wisdom, the counsels, the purpose of God, as
they behold His grace displayed in us. The

Church then is an object-lesson to angels. It was given to us to enter into these things, and not merely for intellectual gratification but in order that the truth might build us up in Christ, might form us morally and make us what God would have us be. "And every man that hath this hope set on Him purifieth himself even as He is pure" (1 John 3:3). We are not to view divine mysteries simply as lines of truth upon which to exercise our human intelligence; but we are to be sanctified through the truth. The revelation that God has given should so grip our souls and exercise our consciences that it will lead us to behave as a people who are truly strangers and pilgrims down here, looking for that glorious era which Christ will bring in when He returns.

"He ha⁺h abounded toward us in all wisdom and intelligence," as this word, "prudence," really means. "Having made known unto us the mystery of His will." We need to remind ourselves that this word, "mystery," so frequently used in the New Testament, does not necessarily mean something mysterious, something difficult of apprehension, but rather a secret which no one could understand until it was revealed. The mysteries of the kingdom of heaven, the mystery of lawlessness, of Babylon, the great mystery of Christ and the Church, the mystery of the rapture, the mystery of Israel's present rejection, as illustrated in the olive tree of Rom. 11, once hidden secrets which no man could understand, are now opened up to the people of God, and so it is the responsibility of a minister of Christ to expound these mysteries to the saints. We read that such are "stewards of the mysteries of God" (1 Cor. 4: 1). From the treasure that God has given them they draw things new and old, and open them up to God's people so that they may enter into the good of them.

What is the mystery of His will? "Having made known unto us the mystery of His will, according to His good pleasure which He hath purposed in Himself: that in the dispensation of the fulness of times He might gather together in one all things in Christ, both which are in heaven, and which are on earth; even in Him." Here, succinctly, clearly, in one brief verse, we have the summing up of the mystery of God. Everything is working on to this one *near-at-hand* "divine event toward which the whole creation moves," when God will head up everything in Christ.

What is meant by a "dispensation?" The word, "dispensation," is used a number of times in the English New Testament, and other words are also used to translate the same Greek word, sometimes "stewardship," "order," "administration," and here "dispensation." We find that the original word has been brought right over into English; it is our word "economy." "That in the economy of the fulness of times He might head up everything in Christ." What is an economy? An economy is an ordered condition of things. Domestic economy is the ordering of a house. But the economy of one house is not necessarily the economy of every other house. If Christians would only bear that in mind, it would save a great deal of confusion. Then there is political economy. The ordering of the affairs of one nation is not the economy of another. The economy of Soviet Russia is not, and I hope will never be, that of the United States of America; the economy of Fascist Italy is not the economy of Democratic England. These nations have their own ways of ordering their affairs, and if one came from Soviet Russia to the United States and attempted to order his conduct according to the economy of Russia, it would not be tolerated here. It might be lawful and right there, but not here. And so there are these various economies running through the Word of God. A dispensation, an economy, then, is that particular order or condition of things prevailing in one special age which does not necessarily prevail in another.

There is a difference between a dispensation and an age. An age is a period of time in which a particular economy prevails. There was the economy before the flood when God was dealing with men according to conscience. We do not know just how God's children met and carried on a public testimony in those days. All that we have concerning that particular time is given us in two or three brief chapters. But after the flood, there was a new economy; civil magistracy was instituted by God for the restraint of human conduct. Then we see God calling Abraham out, and making him to be the beginning of a new race of people to whom He entrusted a new economy, the promise of the coming Seed through whom all nations of the earth should be blessed. And then at Mount Sinai the law was given to the people of Israel. That economy was in force until our blessed Lord cried, "It is finished," on Calvary's cross. Now in the present age of the grace of God, we have this wonderful dispensation of the Holy Spirit, in which the gospel of God is being sent out into all the world. There is no one favored nation, but God's grace goes out to all nations. We are not under law as a principle either of salvation or of life, but we are under grace, saved by Christ, kept by Christ, called upon to walk in Christ to the praise of the glory of His grace. By-and-by there will be another glorious economy, "The dispensation of the fulness of times." That will be in the last glorious age, which has been called ever since the dawn of the Christian era, "The Millennium," "The Reign of Righteousness," when,

> "Jesus shall reign where'er the sun,
> Does his successive journeys run;
> His kingdom spread from shore to shore,
> Till moons shall wax and wane no more."

It is not a dispensation of blessing merely for this world, but heaven and earth will be brought into wonderful unity, and heavenly saints and earthly saints will find their headship in Christ.

"That in the dispensation of the fulness of times He might gather together in one all things in Christ, both which are in heaven, and which are on earth; even in Him." How important then that we know something about what God is doing, that we understand intelligently our dispensational place in the ways of God. Into what confusion of mind many Christians have fallen because, though they are living in this age and are under our special dispensation, they are trying to behave according to another dispensation, confusing law with grace.

How many Christians need to understand these distinctions! They are in confusion of mind all their lives because they do not see the difference between God's order for the house of Israel of old, and for the house of God, the Church, which is the "pillar and ground of the truth," in this present age, to be succeeded by the glorious dispensation of the fulness of times yet to come in what we generally call the Millennium. St. Augustine said, "Distinguish the ages, and the Scriptures are plain."

So God has revealed to us His purpose of grace. He has opened up the good pleasure of His will that we might understand what His plan is for

Israel, the Church, and the world. What a wonderful time it will be when everything unChristian will be put down, when the authority of the Lord Jesus Christ will be owned not only by all in heaven but by all on earth. This is the time referred to in Colossians 1:20: "Having made peace through the blood of His cross, by Him to reconcile all things unto Himself; by Him, I say, whether they be things in earth, or things in heaven." Notice there are only two spheres when Scripture speaks of the future reconciliation. It never includes the sad, unhappy abode of the lost; it simply says that all things in heaven and all things in earth are some day to be reconciled to God through Jesus Christ. But Scripture also speaks of the subjugation of all things, of how God is going to subdue all things to Christ, "That at the name of Jesus every knee should bow, of things in heaven, and things in earth, and things under the earth." All created intelligences will own the authority of our Lord Jesus Christ, but all in heaven and all on earth are to be reconciled to Him in the dispensation of the fulness of times, when He will "gather together in one all things in Christ, both which are in heaven, and which are on earth; even in Him."

And when the apostle, speaking as a Jew by nature, as one who belongs to the people to whom the message first came, says, "In whom also we have obtained an inheritance, being predestinated

—being marked out beforehand—according to the purpose of Him who worketh all things after the counsel of His own will: that we should be to the praise of His glory, who first trusted in Christ," literally, "who pre-trusted in Christ." God has made wonderful promises to Israel, to be fulfilled when "they shall see the King in His beauty," and shall cry, "This is our God; we have waited for Him." Israel in that day will be born again and will turn to the Lord. But Paul himself, an Israelite, says, "We (he and his companions) have already trusted in Christ — we have pre-trusted in Him before this day of His glorious revelation."

"In whom ye (Gentiles) also trusted, after that ye heard the word of truth, the gospel of your salvation: in whom also after that ye believed, ye were sealed with that Holy Spirit of promise." You see, first those of the kindred according to the flesh, and then those of the nations who were alienated and enemies from God by wicked works.

Notice that the greatest objective then for all Christians is that which so many of God's beloved people sometimes neglect, it is the truth of the coming again of our Lord Jesus Christ. The Church's complete blessing awaits His coming, every individual's blessing awaits His coming, the redemption of our bodies awaits His coming, the conversion of Israel awaits His coming, and the full redemption of all the Gentile peoples awaits

the coming of our blessed Saviour. How we
should long for this great event, watch for it as
one watches for the morning. Frances Havergal
has expressed the Christian's attitude in a beautiful way:

"Thou art coming, O our Saviour!
   Coming, God's anointed King!
Every tongue Thy Name confessing,
   Well may we rejoice and sing.
Thou art coming! Rays of glory
   Through the veil Thy death has rent,
Gladden now our pilgrim pathway,
   Glory from Thy presence sent.

"Thou art coming! Thou art coming!
   We shall meet Thee on Thy way;
Thou art coming! We shall see Thee,
   And be like Thee on that day.
Thou art coming! Thou art coming!
   Jesus, our beloved Lord;
Oh, the joy to see Thee reigning,
   Worshipped, glorified, adored!

"Thou art coming! Not a shadow,
   Not a mist, and not a tear,
Not a sin, and not a sorrow,
   On that sunrise grand and clear.
Thou art coming! Blessed Saviour,
   Nothing else seems worth a thought:
Oh, how marvelous the glory,
   And the bliss Thy pain hath bought.

"Thou art coming! We are waiting
   With a 'hope' that cannot fail,
Asking not the day or hour,
   Anchored safe within the veil.

> Thou art coming! At Thy table
>   We are witnesses of this,
> As we meet Thee in communion,
>   Earnest of our coming bliss."

May it be ours to enter more and more fully, by reverent, prayerful study of and meditation upon the Word of God, into the apprehension of the glorious purpose of His grace that we may walk *now* in the light of that coming dispensation when Christ shall see of the travail of His soul and shall be satisfied!

SEALED WITH THE HOLY SPIRIT

✦ ✦ ✦

"In whom ye also trusted, after that ye heard the word of truth, the gospel of your salvation: in whom also after that ye believed, ye were sealed with that Holy Spirit of promise, which is the earnest of our inheritance until the redemption of the purchased possession, unto the praise of His glory" (Eph. 1: 13, 14, R. V.).

✦ ✦ ✦

YOU will notice that these verses carry us back in thought to what has immediately preceded in verse 12. There the Apostle Paul says, "That we should be to the praise of His glory, who first trusted in Christ," and he speaks as a representative believer from Israel. The gospel of God was to the Jew first. Those who received the message on the day of Pentecost were all of Israel, although they came from the many different parts of the world into which they had been scattered because of their sins. Wherever the message went it was to the Jew first in those early days, and the Apostle Paul, himself a Jew, could speak of the glorious privileges which belonged to them who had become the people of God in Christ.

In verse 13 he turns to the Gentile converts; therefore the words are especially appropriate as applied to ourselves, "In whom ye also trusted." Notice the different pronoun. It is "ye," Gentiles. "In whom ye also trusted, after that ye heard the word of truth." He does not necessarily imply any lengthy period after they had heard the word of truth. It might be rendered, "In whom ye also trusted, upon hearing the word of truth." The gospel message believed results in immediate salvation. It is not necessary that people go through a long season of soul-exercise and travail of spirit after hearing the gospel before they are converted to God. A man may hear the message for the first time, and hearing, believe and live. Yet one can quite understand the pitiful question of the Chinese woman who had lived in the darkness of paganism all her life. Some itinerant missionaries came to her village, and for the first time, she feared the only time, she heard the message of grace. She came trembling and said, "It is a wonderful story. I have never heard it before, and you are leaving us tomorrow. I may never hear it again, but I believe it. Do you think once is enough to make my soul secure?" Yes, once is enough!

> "Once for all, O sinner, receive it,
> Once for all, O brother, believe it:
> Cling to the cross, the burden will fall,
> Christ hath redeemed us once for all."

Most of us have heard it over and over again. I wonder how many can take these words to ourselves, "In whom ye also trusted, after that ye heard the word of truth, the gospel of your salvation." The gospel is indeed the "good spell." That is the exact meaning of the Anglo-Saxon word, "gospel." Some of the words that we think of as slang are really ground deep in our language. We speak of a soap-box orator as a "spellbinder," and think of that as slang, but the fact is, the word "spell" was used in that way centuries ago. The gospel is the good spell, the good message, God's good news for poor lost sinners; it is God's good news about His blessed Son. It cannot be too often emphasized that the gospel is not good advice to be obeyed; it is good news to be believed. It is something that God has told us about the Lord Jesus Christ, and when we believe the message, we are saved. Now, following our salvation, we are sealed with the Holy Spirit—"In whom also after that ye believed, ye were sealed with that Holy Spirit of promise." A good many have been misled by the rendering here given. "In whom also after that ye believed—" they have thought that this necessarily implied an interval between believing and being sealed with the Spirit; but I would call your attention to the fact that we have exactly the same words as in the previous part of the verse: "In whom ye also trusted, after that ye heard the word of truth."

Not necessarily a week or a month, or yet ten minutes after, but *upon hearing*. And so we read in the latter part of the verse that *upon believing* we were sealed with the Holy Spirit.

There is, of course, a difference between the Holy Spirit's regenerating work and the sealing. The difference is as great as that between building a house and moving into it. You may move into it the moment it is ready. When the Spirit of God creates a man anew in Christ Jesus, that moment a house is built, a temple is prepared, and then the blessed Holy Spirit of God moves in and takes possession of him. "Ye were sealed with that Holy Spirit of promise." That is, the Spirit who had been promised in past ages and by our blessed Lord when here on earth, has now come to indwell every believer. Three times in the New Testament we read of the believer being sealed with the Spirit. We find it here, and in 2 Cor. 1: 22, "Who hath also sealed us, and given the earnest of the Spirit in our hearts," and then in our same epistle (chap. 4: 30), "Grieve not the Holy Spirit of God, whereby ye are sealed unto the day of redemption." These are the only three direct references to the sealing of the Holy Spirit in connection with the believer, but in John 6: 27 we read of the blessed Lord Himself that He was sealed. "Labor not for the meat which perisheth, but for that meat which endureth unto everlasting life, which the Son of Man shall give unto you:

for Him hath God the Father sealed." You remember when He came forth from His baptism in the Jordan, the Spirit of God descended like a dove and abode upon Him, and a voice from heaven said, "This is My beloved Son, in whom I am well pleased" (Matt. 3: 17). That is the sealing of the blessed Saviour. It is always interesting to note that it is in the sixth chapter of John's Gospel, where He dwells upon the fact that He is the Living Bread which came down from heaven, which if a man eat he shall live forever, that our Lord speaks of Himself as sealed.

A seal was a stamp, a mark of ownership, a mark of approval. You go to the grocery store and get a loaf of bread, and it has a little stamp on it, or perhaps it has the name of the bakery or the trade mark impressed upon the bread. This was done by pressing the dough into the pan which had the name in the metal. That name upon the loaf of bread is the maker's guarantee. It is as though he says, "I stand back of this bread." It is just so with our blessed Lord. He is the Bread of God, the Living Bread, the Bread of Life, and God the Father sealed Him when He gave Him the Holy Spirit without measure. And now when we believe in Him, trust Him as our Saviour, the same blessed Holy Spirit comes to live in us. God the Father seals us by the Spirit, and says, as it were, "This man, this woman, belongs to Me; henceforth I stand back of him, I own him as Mine."

It is a remarkable thing that the only two epistles in which we read of sealing by the Spirit are Corinthians and Ephesians. Corinth and Ephesus were great centers of the lumber industry in ancient times. A raft of logs would be brought from the Black Sea and notice sent to the different lumber firms that the raft was in the harbor. These firms would send their men out and they would look over the logs and make their selection. One would say, "I will take those logs," another, "I will take these," and they would pay down a little earnest money and then cut a certain wedge upon each log that the firm had agreed to take. This was called the seal. The logs might not be drawn out of the water for many weeks, but each was sealed by the mark of the firm that had undertaken to purchase them. I was standing on a high bridge at St. Cloud, Minn., watching a lumber jam, and as I saw the men working I said to my friend, "Do all these logs belong to one firm?" "Oh, no," he said; "there are representatives of many different firms working here in the Minnesota woods." "Well," I asked, "how on earth can they distinguish between the logs?" He showed me from the bridge how they were marked, so that when they reached their destination down the river, the various firms would be able to select their own logs. Though you and I are still tossing about on the waters of this poor scene we have been sealed by the Holy Spirit of promise, and when the appointed day comes and the blessed Lord takes His own to be with Himself, that will be the day of the redemption of His purchased possession, and He will take out of this world all who have been sealed with His Spirit. We will go to be with Him in yonder bright glory.

We may well remember the word, "Grieve not the Holy Spirit of God, whereby ye are sealed." He who has come to dwell within us will abide with us forever. When the Spirit of God once takes up His abode in a believer, He never leaves him in life or in death, until presented faultless in the presence of the glory of our Lord Jesus Christ. The bodies of our beloved dead in Christ are in the keeping of the Holy Spirit, and living saints are indwelt by the Spirit and will be until called hence to be forever with the Lord.

This enables us to understand the transition of thought as we pass to verse 14. In verse 13 the Holy Spirit is a seal, and in verse 14 He is the earnest, "Which is the earnest of our inheritance until the redemption of the purchased possession, unto the praise of His glory." I mentioned the lumber-dealer paying down a small sum as an earnest, the rest to be paid in full when the logs were drawn out of the water. Our blessed God has given us the Holy Spirit as the earnest, the pledge, that eventually we are to be taken out of this scene and fully conformed to the image of

His Son. Now we are privileged to appropriate in a small measure what we shall have in all its fulness when we get home to heaven. Everything of Christ which we enjoy at all, we enter into by the Holy Spirit.

"If here on earth the thoughts of Jesus' love
Lift our poor hearts this weary world above,
If even here the taste of heavenly springs
So cheers the spirit, that the pilgrim sings,

"What will the sunshine of His glory prove?
What the unmingled fulness of His love?
What hallelujahs will His presence raise?
What but one loud eternal burst of praise?"

What will it mean when we see Him face to face, when the last vestige of sin and infirmity will disappear, and we shall be like Him for whom we wait? We shall be to "the praise of His glory." Think of it! Every saint of God, every redeemed one, every sinner saved by grace divine, will add to the glory, to the satisfaction of the heart of God throughout eternity. It was in order that we might thus be won for Christ, that we might be set apart for Himself, that our blessed Lord came in grace from the throne in heaven down to the cross of Calvary. It was that He might redeem us to God with His own blood and make us suited habitations for the Holy Spirit's indwelling, that He saved us and made us His own.

PAUL'S FIRST PRAYER FOR THE SAINTS

✓ ✓ ✓

"Wherefore I also, after I heard of your faith in the Lord Jesus, and love unto all the saints, cease not to give thanks for you, making mention of you in my prayers; that the God of our Lord Jesus Christ, the Father of glory, may give unto you the spirit of wisdom and revelation in the knowledge of Him; the eyes of your understanding being enlightened; that ye may know what is the hope of His calling, and what the riches of the glory of His inheritance in the saints, and what is the exceeding greatness of His power to us-ward who believe, according to the working of His mighty power, which He wrought in Christ, when He raised Him from the dead, and set Him at His own right hand in the heavenly places, far above all principality, and power, and might, and dominion, and every name that is named, not only in this world, but also in that which is to come: and hath put all things under His feet, and gave Him to be the Head over all things to the Church, which is His body, the fulness of Him that filleth all in all" (Eph. 1: 15-23).

✓ ✓ ✓

WE have in this letter two prayers offered by the Apostle Paul, not only for the Ephesians but for all the people of God. The first is our present passage and the second is found in chapter three. Notice that he says, "I also, after I heard of your faith in the

Lord Jesus, and love unto all the saints, cease not to give thanks for you, making mention of you in my prayers." He offers his petition for those who are already saved. When people are born of God, one of the first evidences that they possess a new nature is that they feel a sense of dependence upon the Lord and begin to pray, first for themselves, and then their hearts go out in intercession for others. When the Lord sent Ananias to Saul of Tarsus, he objected, saying, "Lord, I have heard by many of this man, how much evil he hath done to Thy saints at Jerusalem, and here he hath authority from the chief priests to bind all that call on Thy name." But the Lord replied, "Behold, he prayeth." This was an evidence of a real work begun in the soul of the erstwhile persecutor of the Church of God, and so Ananias went to him in confidence and laid his hands upon him, saying, "Brother Saul, the Lord, even Jesus, that appeared unto thee in the way as thou camest, hath sent me, that thou mightest receive thy sight, and be filled with the Holy Ghost," and he commanded him to be baptized. It is as natural for the renewed man to pray as it is for the natural man to breathe.

Note how the apostle tells the saints of his confidence in them. He had heard with joy of the way they had been growing in grace, of their faith in the Lord Jesus and love unto all the saints. Where faith is genuine, it will always be manifested by love; not merely to our own peculiar group, but love unto all the saints. This term "saints" is an all-inclusive one, taking in every individual who has been born into the family of God. Some have an idea that all the saints are in heaven, but we do not need to pray for those who are in the presence of the Lord over yonder. Believers on earth are called saints, and for them we need to make intercession.

Paul prays for three distinct things, but first he asks, "That the God of our Lord Jesus Christ, the Father of glory, may give unto you the spirit of wisdom and revelation in the knowledge of Him." Earlier in the chapter, we have already seen how in verse 3 he exclaims, "Blessed be the God and Father of our Lord Jesus Christ." Because the Eternal Son became Man for our redemption, it is right to speak of the God of our Lord Jesus Christ. Because His relationship is ever that of Son, it is equally right to speak of God as His Father. This first prayer is addressed to "the God of our Lord Jesus Christ." When we come to consider the second prayer we shall find that it is addressed to the Father. When we think of God as such, we think of Him as Creator, the Source of all counsel and wisdom ("God is light"), and we notice that in this particular prayer the apostle is especially occupied with the counsels or purpose of God. The other is addressed to the Father because it has to do with the family relationship. "God is love" as well as light.

It is very remarkable how exactly divine titles are used in Holy Scripture. He prays, "That the God of our Lord Jesus Christ, the Father of glory" (or excellence)—all glory proceeds from Him, and glory is but the manifestation of divine excellence—"may give unto you the spirit of wisdom and revelation in the knowledge of Him." He does not mean that you must receive the Holy Spirit in some new and second way. If a Christian, you have the Holy Spirit dwelling in you, but He who indwells you delights in His special work of opening up the things of Christ and revealing them to His saints. How does He do that? By giving insight into the truth already revealed in the Word of God. All Scripture is divinely inspired. Holy men of God spake as they were moved by the Holy Spirit, but the merely natural man reads the Word and sees nothing in it, because he is not acquainted with its Author. The believer who is indwelt by the Holy Spirit reads, and in reading hears the voice of God. So there is all the difference in the world between reading this Book in a cold intellectual way and reading it in the presence of God, depending upon His blessed Holy Spirit to open up its truth to heart and mind. It is then that He acts as the Spirit of wisdom and revelation, giving the believer to enjoy precious things never seen before.

Have you not often heard some servant of God expounding the Word in such a way that it came home to your heart in wondrous power and blessing? Perhaps you said, "It is strange; I have read that passage over and over again, and yet I never saw it like that before. I do not understand how it is that when I read the Bible myself I fail to appreciate these things." Often the real trouble is we do not spend enough time in the presence of God, looking to Him to open up His truth to us.

I remember years ago, while my dear mother was still living, I went home to visit the family, and found there a man of God from the north of Ireland. I was a young Christian at the time, engaged in gospel work. He was a much older man, an invalid, dying of what we then called "quick consumption." He had come out to Southern California, hoping climatic conditions would be of some help to him. But it was evident that he was too far gone to be recovered to health again. He lived, by his own desire, in a small tent out under the olive trees a short distance away from our home. I went out to see him there. I can remember how my heart was touched as I looked down upon his thin worn face upon which I could see the peace of Heaven clearly manifested. His name was Andrew Fraser. He could barely speak above a whisper, for his lungs were almost gone, but I can recall yet how, after a few words of introduction, he said to me, "Young man, you are trying to preach Christ; are you not?" I replied, "Yes, I am." "Well," he whispered, "sit down a little, and let us talk together about the Word of God." He opened his well-worn Bible, and until his strength was gone, simply, sweetly, and earnestly he opened up truth after truth as he turned from one passage to another, in a way that my own spirit had never entered into them. Before I realized it, tears were running down my face, and I asked, "Where did you get these things? Could you tell me where I could find a book that would open them up to me? Did you learn these things in some seminary or college?" I shall never forget his answer. "My dear young man, I learned these things on my knees on the mud floor of a little sod cottage in the north of Ireland. There with my open Bible before me, I used to kneel for hours at a time, and ask the Spirit of God to reveal Christ to my soul and to open the Word to my heart, and He taught me more on my knees on that mud floor than I ever could have learned in all the seminaries or colleges in the world." It was not many weeks after this that he was absent from the body and present with the Lord, but the memory of that visit has always remained with me and is a most precious recollection. Is it not true that most of us do not stay long enough in the presence of God? We do not get quiet enough to let Him talk to us and reveal His mind to us.

"Meditation," someone has said, "is becoming a lost art in our day." To meditate is really to chew the cud. Just as the cattle take their food in the rough and then ruminate and get the sweetness and the good out of it, so the believer needs to read the Word and then spend time quietly in the presence of God, going over it again and again, ruminating, chewing the cud, until it becomes truly precious to his heart. Of old the Israelites were forbidden to eat the flesh of any animal that did not chew the cud and part the hoof. The parted hoof is a foot that rises above the filth of this world. It has been well said that it is a great thing when the mouth and the foot agree, when we feed on the Word and walk in the power of the truth. It is when one thus gets into the presence of God that the Holy Spirit delights to take of divine things and show them unto us. It is thus we grow in the knowledge of Christ. That is one reason why the Spirit came. Every believer to a certain extent has the knowledge of Christ, but the original word implies more than that. It is not merely knowledge as such; it is really super-knowledge, or full knowledge. "That the God of our Lord Jesus Christ, the Father of glory, may give you the Spirit of wisdom and revelation in the full knowledge of Him." Perhaps you know Him as your Saviour, as the One who has redeemed you from everlasting destruction,

as the glorious Head of the Church, with whom
you are linked by the Holy Spirit. He would
have you go on to know Him better, for there are
riches in Christ that you may be sure you have
never yet entered into. We cannot afford to be
negligent, or to let other things crowd out the
blessing we might have by giving more time to
the teaching of the Holy Spirit.

> "Oh, the pure delight of a single hour
> That before Thy throne I spend,
> As I kneel in prayer, and with Thee, my Lord,
> I commune as friend with friend."

We sing these words sometimes and sing them
rather glibly, but how much do we know of the
reality of spending an hour in His presence,
learning more of Him as the Spirit of God unfolds precious things that otherwise our hearts
would never enter into?

We have already remarked that there are three
distinct petitions in this prayer. He asks,

1. "That the eyes of your heart being enlightened, ye may know what is the hope of His
   calling."
2. "And what the riches of the glory of His
   inheritance in the saints."
3. "And what is the exceeding greatness of
   His power to us-ward who believe, according to the working of His mighty power."

Notice, it is "That the eyes of your heart being
enlightened." Our Authorized Version reads,

"The eyes of your understanding," but it is not merely the intellect he has in view, it is the heart. Christians understand with the heart. It is "with the heart man believeth unto righteousness." It is with the heart that we enter into divine realities. One may be very brilliant intellectually, but that does not guarantee for a moment that he will have an understanding of spiritual things. It is only as the heart is exercised before God, as the eyes of the heart are opened, that spiritual things will be discerned. That is one reason why people must be born again, otherwise they cannot understand the things of God.

Perhaps an illustration will help to make clear what I mean. Some people are born into the world with a remarkable musical sense, and some have none at all. Now a man who has no sense of tone cannot become a musician, no matter how others may seek to instruct him. Such an one might go to listen to the most wonderful oratorio, but it would all be meaningless to him if he had no appreciation of music. He would really have to be born again, as it were, in order to appraise it aright, and so in regard to spiritual things, one must have a new nature if he would enter into them appreciatively.

But if the eyes of the heart are opened, then one may understand something of "the hope of His calling." Do you understand "what is the hope of His calling?" It is that to which we have already had our attention drawn in the earlier part of the chapter: "He hath blessed us with all spiritual blessings in heavenly places in Christ; according as He hath chosen us in Him before the foundation of the world," that we should be holy and without blame before Him. This is the hope of His calling; that some day we shall see Him as He is and be like Him. Our God has chosen us for this, and He is never going to give up until we attain to the full stature of men and women in Christ Jesus.

Then, in the second place, that we may apprehend the riches of the glory of His inheritance in the saints. Earlier in the chapter we read of the riches of His grace; here we have the riches of His glory. We are enjoying the riches of His grace now and we shall enter into and enjoy the riches of His glory by-and-by. Notice this expression, "The riches of the glory of His inheritance in the saints." What does that mean? It does not mean that the saints are His inheritance, as some would have us believe, but it does mean that when He takes possession of His inheritance, He is going to take possession of it through His saints. It is not our inheritance in Him, observe, but His inheritance in us. Of old the land of Canaan was His inheritance, but He took possession of it through His people Israel. By-and-by He will take possession of a redeemed universe through His saints and we shall reign with Him.

Who can apprehend our part in that glory? What will it be when we are with Him and like Him when He returns to reign, and we shall sit with Him upon His throne and God will take possession of His inheritance in His saints!

Then observe the third petition: "What is the exceeding greatness of His power to us-ward who believe, according to the working of His mighty power." You see, Christians are not storage batteries. How often we hear people praying, "O God, give me more power," and you would think that we were a little bit like these ever-ready flashlights that you can open up and put a battery in, then press a button and get a light. You would imagine that as Christians, the Lord puts a power battery into us, presses a button, and then we shine for Him. Nothing of the kind! We have power only as we are living in fellowship with Him who is the Source of all power, and as we are walking in fellowship with Him, the same power works in and through us that wrought in Christ when God raised Him from the dead. That was the fullest manifestation of divine power the world has ever known.

Our attention is not called to the power that created the heaven and the earth, to the power that brought the people of Israel out of Egypt, parted the Red Sea, and led them in triumph to the Land of Canaan, nor to the working of mighty miracles through the Lord and His apostles, but to the greatest manifestation of the power of God of which we know anything, the resurrection of the Lord Jesus Christ. This is the same power that works in believers who walk in fellowship with Him: "According to the mighty power which He wrought in Christ when He raised Him from the dead and set Him at His own right hand in the heavenly places, far above all principality, and power, and might, and lordship, and every name that is named, not only in this world, but also in that which is to come." By these expressions, "principality," "power," "might," "dominion," we are to understand the countless hosts of angelic beings, glorious sinless spirits serving our blessed Lord, and also serried ranks of evil angels opposed to God and His Christ.

Our Lord went down into the depths, into the grave, descended into the lower parts of the earth, and Satan and his hosts rejoiced when they saw Him under the power of death. But God has raised Him from the dead and taken Him up to His right hand in the highest glory, where as Man He sits today enthroned. The wonderful thing that the apostle dwells on here is that the power that did all that for the Lord Jesus is the power that works in us as believers if we do not hinder it by our frivolity and worldliness. Do not, I beg of you, ever complain again that you have no power to meet temptation, that you have no power to rise above some sinful habit. If you find yourself in that condition it is because you are out of fellowship with God. Get right with Him. Judge the sin that has hindered communion and then, as when you make the electrical connection the power flows through the wire to operate the mighty machinery, so you will be in living touch with God, and divine power will work in and through you to enable you to triumph over sin and live to His glory.

We are told that Christ has gone up "above all principality, and power, and might, and dominion, and every name that is named, not only in this world, but also in that which is to come." And then we are told that He has put all things under His feet. We do not yet see everything subject to Him, but we do see Him seated in the heavenlies above all things, as evidence that all shall eventually acknowledge His rightful sway. Then we have an added word which was never revealed in Old Testament times but is now made known in this dispensation of grace: "And gave Him to be Head over all things to the Church which is His Body, the fulness of Him that filleth all in all." A head without a body is incomplete. The marvelous thing is that the Church is the completeness of Christ; during all this present age He is manifesting Himself through the Church to the world. Some day the members of the Body will be with the Head in the glory, and the one new man will be manifested in all his perfection. Is it not a wonderful thing then to realize this: that our blessed Lord would in this sense be incomplete without us? Think of it! We were poor lost sinners of the Gentiles, deserving nothing but the judgment of God, but now through His grace we have been saved, and not only that but made members of His Body, the Body of Christ, the completeness of Him that filleth all in all. What a hallowed responsibility this puts upon us to represent Him aright in this world; to manifest His grace, His holiness, His love, His hatred of sin, His compassion for the lost, His desperate earnestness in seeking to reach lost men and make known to them the riches of His grace. We are left here to carry on His work in the scene where He was crucified. May God give us to rise to a proper sense of our hallowed responsibility and thus to make Him known as we should.

THE CHRISTIAN'S PAST, PRESENT AND FUTURE

✓ ✓ ✓

"And you hath He quickened, who were dead in trespasses and sins; wherein in time past ye walked according
to the course of this world, according to the prince of the
power of the air, the spirit that now worketh in the children
of disobedience: among whom also we all had our conversation in times past in the lusts of our flesh, fulfilling the desires of the flesh and of the mind; and were by nature the
children of wrath, even as others. But God, who is rich in
mercy, for His great love wherewith He loved us, even
when we were dead in sins, hath quickened us together with
Christ (by grace ye are saved); and hath raised us up
together, and made us sit together in heavenly places in
Christ Jesus: that in the ages to come He might show the
exceeding riches of His grace in His kindness toward us
through Christ Jesus" (Eph. 2: 1-7).

WHILE holding meetings in Southern California I took the inter-urban car one
Saturday to go from Los Angeles to a
well-known beach resort. We had hardly left the
city when a rather peculiar-looking lady (I suppose she was a lady; at any rate, she was of the
feminine persuasion), attired in a strange garb
that made her look as though she was dressed up
in red bandanna handkerchiefs pieced together,

and who wore a shawl on her head with a lot of spangles over her forehead, came and sat down beside me, and said, "How do you do, gentleman? You like to have your fortune told?" I said, "Are you able to tell my fortune?" She held out a winsome little palm and said, "Cross my palm with a silver quarter, and I will give you your past, present, and future." "You are very sure you can do that if I give you a quarter?" I said. "You see, I am Scotch, and should hate to part with a quarter and not get proper exchange for it." She looked bewildered for a moment, but then said very insistently, "Yes, gentleman, I can give you your past, present, and future. I never fail; I have wonderful second sight. Cross my palm with a quarter. Please, gentleman. I will tell you all." I said, "It is really not necessary, because I have had my fortune told already, and I have a little Book in my pocket that gives me my past, present and future." "You have it in a book?" she said. "Yes, and it is absolutely infallible. Let me read it to you," I said, and I pulled out my New Testament. She looked startled when she saw it, but I turned to this second chapter of the Epistle to the Ephesians and said, "Here is my past, 'And you hath He quickened, who were dead in trespasses and sins: wherein in time past ye walked according to the course of this world, according to the prince of the power of the air, the spirit that now worketh in the children of disobedience: among whom also we all had our conversation in times past in the lusts of our flesh, fulfilling the desires of the flesh and of the mind, and were by nature the children of wrath, even as others.' " "Oh, yes," she said; "it is plenty, I do not care to hear more." "But," i said, as I held her gently by the arm, "I want to give you my present also, 'But God, who is rich in mercy, for His great love wherewith He loved us, even when we were dead in sins, hath quickened us together with Christ, (by grace ye are saved;) and hath raised us up together and made us sit together in heavenly places in Christ Jesus.' " "That is plenty, gentleman," she said; "I do not wish to hear any more." "Oh, but," I replied, "there is more yet, and you must get it; and you are not going to pay me a quarter for it either. I am giving it to you for nothing. It is my past, my present, and my future. Here is the future, 'That in the ages to come He might show the exceeding riches of His grace in His kindness toward us through Christ Jesus.' " She was on her feet, and I could not hold on any tighter lest I should be charged with assault and battery, and she fled down the aisle, saying, "I took the wrong man! I took the wrong man!"

You know how interested people are in trying to delve into the mysterious and unknown. If it were not for this bump of curiosity that so many have, these fortune-tellers and spirit-mediums, who can tell you how to make immense sums of money but are themselves as poor as church mice, would all have to die of starvation. People want to know the things that God has not revealed. But it is amazing to see how indifferent they are to the very important revelation that He has given us in His Word. He has made known the past, the present and the future of the universe, of the nation of Israel, of the great Gentile nations, of the Church of God, and then — what comes home to every Christian—of every individual believer in the Lord Jesus Christ.

"And you hath He quickened." You will notice that the words, "hath He quickened," are in italics. That means that there is nothing in the original to answer to them, and yet we actually seem to need them to fully bring out the thought of the Greek, for in the original the verb comes in the fifth verse, and in order to make it read smoothly in English it is necessary to put in these words. To be quickened is to be made to live. Because we were dead we needed to receive divine life. "You hath He quickened, who were dead in trespasses and sins: wherein in time past ye walked according to the course of this world." What a past! We were utterly beyond any ability to save ourselves, for a dead man can do nothing to improve his condition, and every unsaved person is dead, dead toward God, dead spiritually. If you are out of Christ, you have never had one

pulse-beat toward God, you are dead in trespasses
and sins. Sin has not only made man guilty so
that he needs forgiveness, but sin has sunk the
human race into a state of spiritual death so that
men need divine life. That is why we must be
born again. Being born again is receiving new
life from God through faith in the Lord Jesus
Christ.

Of course, there are degrees of sinfulness, there
are degrees along moral lines. We would not for
a moment say everybody is just as corrupt, just as
vile, just as wicked, just as despicable, as everybody else. That would not be true; and yet if people are dead, they are dead. The beautiful little
maid, the daughter of Jairus, had been dead only
a few minutes when the blessed Lord reached her
father's house, but she was dead, she was lifeless.
Fair to look upon, lovely and sweet, no doubt, in
the eyes of her beloved parents, like a beautiful
marble statue, but although there was not the
corruption that there might have been, she was
dead nevertheless. Turn over to Luke's Gospel
and you find that as the blessed Lord came to the
village of Nain they were carrying a young man
out to bury him. He was dead. Dead perhaps a
day or two. In the land of Palestine they generally bury the dead either on the day that life
ceases or the day immediately following. So this
young man was dead longer than the little maid,
but life was just as truly extinct in her case as

in his. Then you have the blessed Lord at the
grave of Lazarus. The sisters told Him not to
roll the stone away, for their brother had been
dead four days and would already be offensive.
Corruption had set in, but the Lord Jesus brought
new life to that man. In every instance it took
exactly the same mighty, quickening power to restore the dead. Only the Son of God could speak
life to the daughter of Jairus, to the young man
of Nain, and to Lazarus. So we were dead, every
one of us, we who are now saved. Some were
deeply corrupted because of sin, others perhaps
did not know so much of its vileness and corruption, but all alike were dead before God and needed new and divine life.

"Dead in trespasses and sins." Notice the difference between the two expressions. Sinning is
missing the mark. Trespass is the violation of a
definite law. We see the sign, "No trespassing,"
and know that that means that we cannot pass a
certain boundary without being guilty of trans-
gressing. You and I are guilty on both counts.
We are sinners, for we have taken our own way;
and we are trespassers, because we have actually
transgressed what we knew to be the revealed will
of God; and so we are dead to God in our natural
condition. Yet we are able to walk—"Wherein
in time past ye walked according to the course of
this world."

We were dead toward God and could not take

one step with Him. Dr. Gaebelein relates that he was holding meetings in a Y. M. C. A. auditorium, and one day the secretary showed him a card which he was in the habit of passing out. It read, "I promise faithfully henceforth to lead a religious and Christian life," and then there was a place to sign one's name. The secretary said, "How do you like that? Isn't that a pretty good way of putting it?" Dr. Gaebelein said, "How on earth can a dead man live any kind of a life? What is the use of putting a card like that into the hands of a dead sinner, and having him sign it and say, 'I promise faithfully henceforth to lead a religious and Christian life?' You cannot live a life for God until you receive a life from God." You can live according to the world, live a moral life and what some people call a religious life, but that is only "according to the course of this world." For, after all, the world admires morality and religion. If you are a young man looking for a wife, you do not look in the vilest part of the city for some poor wretched characterless girl, you try to find one who has a bit of religion and morality; and a young woman looking for a husband does the same. People have an idea that morality and religion are necessarily Christian. Of course a Christian ought to be characterized by both, but from a much higher motive than the world. The course of this world is often a religious and a moral course, but in independence of Christ.

A little group of Greek philosophers were talking together five hundred years before Christ, and the question was asked, "What is the briefest possible definition of a man?" Plato said, "Man is a two-legged animal." One of them went out, and brought in a rooster. He held him up and said, "Behold Plato's man!" Then one exclaimed, "I have it; man is a religious animal." That is it. There is not another creature in the world but man that ever lifts his eyes toward God and heaven, that ever feels a sense of responsibility to a higher power, and therefore man is incurably religious. Even the atheist is incurably religious. He worships himself, he is his own god. So, we say, the course of this world may be a religious and a moral course. On the other hand, it may be a vile, abominably wicked, sinful course, but it is all the same, it is "the course of this world," and that is the course in which we walked before we were born again.

"According to the prince of the power of the air." He is, of course, the devil. When living in our sins, the devil was our master and we were led by his will.

"The spirit that now worketh in the children of disobedience (those who refuse obedience to God) ; among whom also we all had our conversation (our manner of living, our desire) in times past in the lusts of our flesh, fulfilling the desires of the flesh and of the mind." We sometimes think of the word "lust" as though it referred only to one degrading kind of sin, but it is unlawful desire of any kind. There are just as truly lusts of the mind as lusts of the flesh. Pride, vanity, self-will, covetousness, independence of God—these are all lusts of the mind, and they are just as vile in the sight of God as the lusts of the flesh. In the first three chapters of the Epistle to the Romans we have God's picture of the lusts of the flesh, and in the first three chapters of First Corinthians we have God's picture of the lusts of the mind. One kind is just as sinful as the other.

"And were by nature the children of wrath, even as others." That is, we were born in sin, we were born of a race that is unclean, unholy, and obnoxious to the eyes of God, but God had purposes of grace and of loving-kindness, which He has carried out through Christ Jesus, for the salvation of that sinful race.

Do you recognize the picture of your past? Maybe this is your present instead of your past. If it is, God grant that it may become your past, and that you will be through with this kind of thing forevermore. Life is found alone in Christ.

Now look at the present, as given us in verses 4-6. "But God," how much that expression, *"But God,"* means. We have God coming in now. We were dead, helpless, unable to do one thing to retrieve our dreadful circumstances, but God came in. Of old God came in when this world was "without form and void; and darkness was upon the face of the deep . . . and God said, Let there be light: and there was light;" so when we were dead in trespasses and sins, God came in and spoke the word of living power. "But God, who is rich in mercy." In what is He not rich? We saw in the first chapter that He is rich in grace and rich in glory, and here we read that He is rich in mercy. There are infinite resources of mercy for the vilest sinner. There is no one for whom there is no mercy. "God, who is rich in mercy, for His great love wherewith He loved us" —it all came out of the heart of God. There was not a thing about us to commend us to God but, "God so loved the world that He gave His only begotten Son, that whosoever believeth in Him should not perish, but have everlasting life." "In this was manifested the love of God toward us," in that "He sent His only begotten Son into the world, that we might live through Him." "Herein is love, not that we loved God, but that He loved us, and sent His Son to be the propitiation for our sins." Because we were dead, He sent Jesus to give us life; because we were guilty, He sent Jesus to be the propitiation by bearing our sins in His own body on the tree.

"God, who is rich in mercy, for His great love wherewith He loved us, even when we were dead in sins, hath quickened us together with Christ."

The whole human race is dead in trespasses and sins. The Jewish part of the race had the revelation from God, and yet they sought to be justified on the ground of works. But these were dead works, and the Jews were just as truly dead in trespasses and sins as the Gentiles, the great godless world outside. But now God comes in and works in power, and by the living Word He speaks to the dead Jews and to the dead Gentiles, and the Word brings life, and they believe it and are quickened together. They who had been separated before, between whom was a middle wall of partition, are become one in Christ Jesus. That is the meaning of this word, "together." God breaks down the barriers separating Jews and Gentiles and makes them one in Christ through believing, giving us life together *with* Christ. Not merely *in* Christ, but *"with* Christ." Why does He put it that way? There was a time when because of my sins Jesus Christ lay dead in the grave, but, having completed the work that saves, God quickened Him from the dead and brought Him back in triumph from the tomb. Christ's resurrection is the pledge of ours. We believe in Him and are brought forth from the place of the dead and quickened with Him. He is the Saviour, we are the saved, and together we form one blessed company of which He is now the glorified Head.

"By grace ye are saved," and grace precludes all thought of merit. We were not saved because we prayed so earnestly, repented so bitterly, turned over a new leaf, made restitution for past sins, tried to do good, kept the law and obeyed the sermon on the mount, or anything else that we could do, but we were saved by grace, and grace is God's unmerited favor to those who merited the opposite.

In a certain Bible Conference a great number of preachers attended the meetings every day, and some of them were a bit upset because the Conference speaker was telling the people that if they were saved once, they are saved for all eternity. So in trying to press the truth one day, I said, "We are not *being* saved if we hang on to the end, but we have already *been saved*. It is a settled thing." I wish we could understand that.

I am afraid that there are a great many people who imagine that when they come to Christ, it is just the beginning and that they are really on probation; if they keep on and are good enough, they will be saved at last. I cannot understand people who close their prayer with, "Now, O Lord, save us at last." I refuse to say "Amen" to that, for I have already been saved. It is a settled thing, and no one is saved for a time and then becomes unsaved, because in order to become unsaved you would have to become unborn, and how can that be? A saved person has been quickened from the dead, born into the family of God, given a new life, and that life is eternal. If that life could ever be forfeited, it would only be **proba-tionary** life, dependent upon one's ability to keep it. I have eternal life, and it is not dependent upon my obedience but on the living Christ to see me through to the very end. Do not ever say you are saved if you do not mean that you are saved for eternity. If people ask you if you are saved and you believe you will be saved at last, you will have to say, "Well, not yet; but I hope to be if God and I can only hold out together!" But if you have already trusted the Lord Jesus and believe the Word, say, "Yes, thank God, I am saved for eternity through the precious, atoning blood of the Lord Jesus Christ."

It is one thing to be saved and have eternal life, to be taken out of that state of death, but it is another thing to be presented before God in all the perfection of His blessed Son. It is this of which we read in verse 6, "And hath raised us up together, and made us sit together in heavenly places in Christ Jesus." You notice it is not *with* Christ Jesus. We are quickened with Him —He was quickened from the dead and so we are quickened with Him—but here it says, "He hath raised us up together, and made us sit together in heavenly places in Christ Jesus." Some of these days we shall be caught up and shall be *with* Christ; but that will be when we all get home to glory. While still here, God sees us *in* Christ. We are represented by Him and in Him. As the high priest of old had the names of the Israelites upon his breast and upon his shoulders when he went into that holy place, and they were all seen in their high priest, so we are seen in Christ, and every moment of our lives He is giving us a perfect representation before the throne of God. I am just as truly raised up together and sitting in heavenly places in Christ Jesus when I am lying flat on my back in the hospital as I am when in the meeting. God sees me up there in Christ. Do not drag it down to mere experience. It is a blessed fact that is true of every Christian. It is a great thing to have our experience answer to our standing, and that comes through walking in fellowship with Him.

But what about our future? "That in the ages to come He might show the exceeding riches of His grace in His kindness toward us through Christ Jesus." "The ages to come"—that takes us a long way on, a long way beyond the Millennium. The Millennium is "the age to come," and here we have "the ages to come." That is the Greek expression for eternity. It consists of untold millions of ages running on forevermore. Through all the ages to come God is going to exhibit the exceeding riches of His grace. Some of these days I am going to have a part in a great exhibition, when from the ends of the earth there will be gathered together all the redeemed of the Lord. Then God will demonstrate to all created intelligences how it has been the delight of His heart to show great grace to great sinners. That is our future—a future that does not depend on our faithfulness but on His, who saved us by grace in order that we might show His glories forevermore.

GOD'S WORKMANSHIP

✓ ✓ ✓

"For by grace are ye saved through faith; and that not of yourselves: it is the gift of God: not of works lest any man should boast. For we are His workmanship, created in Christ Jesus unto good works, which God hath before ordained that we should walk in them" (Eph. 2: 8-10).

OUR God is very jealous that there should be no slight put upon the Person and work of His blessed Son. God loves poor sinners so much that He sent His Son into the world to be the propitiation for our sins, but He loves His Son so much that He will not permit anyone in heaven who ignores the work that the Lord Jesus Christ accomplished. It is only through His finished work that any of us have title to a place over yonder, and so our salvation is entirely by grace.

As I was meditating on this verse, I thought, "Dear me; what shall I say about it that has not been said a hundred times already?" But it cannot be otherwise, for in trying to present the salvation of God one must dwell on such a passage as this over and over again, for that is the very heart of the matter.

Salvation is entirely by grace, and grace utterly precludes the thought of human merit. Were there any question of merit on our part, it would not be grace. "To him that worketh is the reward not reckoned of grace, but of debt" (Rom. 4: 4). If you work, you put the one by whom you are employed into your debt, and he does not get out of your debt until he has paid for your labor. Therefore, if by works of ours, if by any effort of ours, we could earn God's salvation, we would put God in our debt, and He could not get out of it until He had taken us home to heaven as a reward, as payment for what we had done. But no works of ours, no efforts of ours, no labor that we could perform, could ever put away the guilt of one sin; and so we are shut up to grace, to unmerited favor. It is not only unmerited favor, but it is favor against merit, for we have merited the very opposite.

"By grace are ye saved." Notice the apostle does not say, "By grace are ye being saved," or, "By grace will ye be saved eventually," but he is declaring something which is already true of every believer in the Lord Jesus Christ. It is not, "By grace shall ye be saved if ye abide in the present place," but "By grace *are* ye saved," because the work of redemption is already consummated. Therefore, our salvation is looked at by God as something that is finished and complete. If there were any possibility that somehow along the way to heaven I might lose the salvation of God, it could not be said that I am already saved, but rather that I am being saved. But, thank God, not only is the work that saves finished, but the salvation is looked upon as an accomplished fact. It might be translated. "By grace have ye been saved."

"Through faith," this is the agent. Faith is simply the hand that lays hold of the gift that God presents to me. Believing the gospel, I am saved. Some people, I think, are in danger of making a saviour of their faith, for they say, "Well, if I could only believe firmly enough, if I could believe in the right way, I think I would be saved." It is not a question of how you believe; it is a question of whom you believe. Paul says, "I know whom I have believed, and am persuaded that He is able to keep that which I have committed unto Him against that day" (2 Tim. 1 : 12). Do not make a saviour of your faith. The Saviour is Christ, and faith lays hold of Him. Then lest there should be any idea in the mind of the redeemed one that in some sense at any rate he deserves credit for coming to Christ and believing this message, the apostle immediately adds, "And that not of yourselves: it is the gift of God."

Take the message as a whole again, "By grace are ye saved through faith; and that not of yourselves: it is the gift of God." Theologians have questioned as to whether "not of yourselves" means the salvation or the faith. We may apply it to the whole subject in question, "By grace are ye saved, and that not of yourselves." The grace, the salvation, are not of yourselves. "By grace are ye saved through faith, and that not of yourselves." The faith is not of yourselves; it is all the gift of God. But somebody says, "If faith is the gift of God and God is not pleased to give me that gift, how can I believe?" Scripture says, "Faith cometh by hearing, and hearing by the Word of God." God gives the gift of faith to all who give heed to the message of the gospel. After the Spirit of God brings that message home to the heart, it is thoroughly possible for men to resist the Holy Ghost. It is possible on the other hand to give heed to the ministry of the Spirit, and thus be led on to personal faith in the Lord Jesus Christ. Faith is a gift, and apart from it you can never be saved, but in order that we may have faith, "God so loved the world, that He gave His only begotten Son, that whosoever believeth in Him should not perish, but have everlasting life." Refuse the Word, and there will never be faith; give heed to the Word, and faith cometh by hearing. And so of it all it may be said, "Not of works, lest any man should boast."

Old John Nelson, one of Wesley's preachers, was a poor, godless, blaspheming blacksmith until God saved him, and after that he became one of the early Methodist preachers, and proclaimed in power the gospel of the grace of God and won many to a saving knowledge of the Lord Jesus Christ. One day he was talking to a very self-righteous man who said, "I don't need your Saviour; my life is all I need. I can present my own life to God, and I am satisfied He won't be hard on me. If anybody gets into heaven I shall, because of the good I have done, because of the way I have lived." "Look here," said John Nelson; "if you got into heaven, you would bring discord there. All in heaven will be saved sinners, and we are going to sing, 'Glory to the Lamb that was slain and hath washed us from our sins in His own blood.' You couldn't sing that, and so you would bring discord. You would be singing, 'Glory to me because by my own good life and consistent living, my charity and good behavior, I fitted myself for heaven.' If the angels caught you doing that, they would take you by the nape of your neck and throw you over the wall." That is a rather crude way of putting it, but he knew the truth of salvation by grace. David says, "My soul shall make her boast in the Lord." I have no goodness of my own, no faithfulness, no merit, but I shall boast in Him.

In the tenth verse we read, "For we are His workmanship, created in Christ Jesus unto good works, which God hath before ordained that we should walk in them." The word translated "workmanship" is used only twice in the New

Testament, here in Ephesians and in the first chapter of Romans where Paul is speaking of the testimony of creation. He says in verse 20, "For the invisible things of Him from the creation of the world are clearly seen, being understood by the things that are made, even His eternal power and Godhead; so that they are without excuse." In the original, one Greek word is translated here, "the things that are made." That word is *poiema*. From it we get our English word "poem." Creation is God's poem, witnessing to His eternal power and glory. The very stars in the heaven are,

> "Forever singing as they shine,
> The hand that made us is divine."

That word is used again only in this second chapter of the Epistle to the Ephesians, and here it is translated "workmanship," which means something that someone has made. So we read that, "We are His workmanship (we are His poem), created in Christ Jesus unto good works."

What a wonderful piece of literature a poem is! How different from any prose! It takes a man or woman of a peculiar cast of mind to produce a worthwhile poem. There is something artistic about it, and all the hard work in the world could not enable you to produce one unless you have the poetic instinct. It is a very artistic thing to play an organ, and I might sit down and work away on it from now until I became decrepit and aged, but I would never get music out of it because I have no music in me. You have to be a musician in order to bring the music out of an organ, and you have to be a poet in order to write poems. If God were other than He is, He never could have brought this universe into existence nor saved one poor sinner. Creation is God's first poem, but redemption is His second poem, and you and I who are saved constitute the syllables in God's great poem of redemption. Every one is set in the right place by God Himself, "We are His workmanship," and therefore He is given all the credit, for He has done it all through His Son.

We are created in Christ Jesus, quickened unto newness of life with Him and represented before God in Him—"Created in Christ Jesus unto good works." Notice the order. He has already told us that we are not saved by good works, but now says that we must not ignore good works, for one of the purposes for which He has saved us is in order that we might do good works. In the general epistles there are two great sayings: "This is a faithful saying, and worthy of all acceptation, that Christ Jesus came into the world to save sinners" (1 Tim. 1: 15). But in Titus 3: 8 we read, "This is a faithful saying, and these things I will that thou affirm constantly, that they which have believed in God might be careful to maintain good works. These things are good and profitable unto men." You see the place good works have, they **are** not to be ignored, but they are not meritorious. We are not saved by them, but we are created in Christ Jesus *unto* good works. In other words, springing from the fact that we have been saved, because we are God's workmanship, God's great redemptive poem, our lives should now be musical, should be rhythmical and lyrical, and every one of us should fit into the place where He has set us in this great epic of redemption.

"We are His workmanship, created in Christ Jesus unto good works, which God hath before ordained that we should walk in them." Do you believe in foreordination? If you are a Christian, you are foreordained to behave yourself, to do good works, to live a life well pleasing unto God. That is what He has marked out for you. The Christian's pathway is a life lived in subjection to Him.

MADE NIGH BY THE BLOOD
OF CHRIST

✓ ✓ ✓

"Wherefore remember, that ye being in time past Gentiles in the flesh, who are called Uncircumcision by that which is called the Circumcision in the flesh made by hands; that at that time ye were without Christ, being aliens from the commonwealth of Israel, and strangers from the covenants of promise, having no hope, and without God in the world: but now in Christ Jesus ye who sometimes were far off are made nigh by the blood of Christ. For He is our peace, who hath made both one, and hath broken down the middle wall of partition between us; having abolished in His flesh the enmity, even the law of commandments contained in ordinances; for to make in Himself of twain one new man, so making peace; and that He might reconcile both unto God in one body by the cross, having slain the enmity thereby: and came and preached peace to you which were afar off, and to them that were nigh. For through Him we both have access by one Spirit unto the Father" (Eph. 2: 11-18).

✓ ✓ ✓

WE have already taken up the question of the past, present and future of the individual believer. In this passage, the apostle addresses converted Gentiles collectively and speaks of converted Jews collectively. He says in verse 11, "Wherefore remember, that ye being in time past Gentiles in the flesh, who are called

Uncircumcision by that which is called the Circumcision in the flesh made by hands: that at that time ye were without Christ, being aliens from the commonwealth of Israel, and strangers from the covenants of promise, having no hope, and without God in the world."

Of old God had called one man, Abraham, out from the world and made him the depositary of certain promises. Afterwards He gave to his seed the covenant of works, the Mosaic covenant at Mt. Sinai, and by that God separated the people of Israel from all the other people of the world. Those outside of Israel were called Gentiles. It is a remarkable thing that in the Old Testament God is never said to have made a covenant with the Gentiles as such. After the days of Noah, His covenants were all made with Israel, and His promises were all made to Israel. He made many wonderful promises *about* the Gentiles, but He made none to them, and therefore, when Christ came into the world and the gospel first began to be preached, it could be said that those who were Gentiles in the flesh, like ourselves, "were without Christ, being aliens from the commonwealth of Israel, and strangers from the covenants of promise, having no hope, and without God in the world."

Israel had a very definite hope. God had promised certain things to them. But the Gentiles had no such hope, they were outside of all this,

and therefore without God in the world. It was
not merely that they worshiped idols, that they
bowed down to gods of wood and stone, but the
point was they did not know the true God at all.
They were godless, "atheists," in the world. But
now, through the coming of our Lord Jesus
Christ and through His death on Calvary's cross,
wondrous blessing flows forth to the nations of
the Gentiles, blessings of which they had never
dared to dream in the past.

"Now in Christ Jesus ye who sometimes were
far off are made nigh by the blood of Christ."
You see the Jew occupied a place of nearness to
God through covenant relationship, while the
Gentile was far off, being a stranger to it all. But
the Jew through his failure to keep his part of the
covenant of works, had himself become personally
alienated from God, so that, after all, in His sight,
as we read in the Epistle to the Romans, "There
is no difference, for all have sinned, and come
short of the glory of God." Therefore, the same
grace that flowed out to Israel is the grace that
overflows to the Gentiles. The Jews never obtained salvation on the ground of merit, or because they were God's peculiar people marked off
from the nations of the world by the covenant of
circumcision, nor because of the sacrifices which
they offered throughout the legal dispensation.
Those of them who were saved owed everything
to the matchless grace of God which gave the

Lord Jesus Christ, their promised Messiah, to die for their sins upon that cross of shame. And that same mighty Sacrifice which was offered upon the tree avails for all men everywhere who put their trust in Him. And so, although no covenant has been made with the Gentiles, although the new covenant of which we read in Jeremiah and in Hebrews is never said to have been made with the Church, but is to be made with Israel and Judah in the last days, yet every believing Gentile comes under all the spiritual blessings of the new covenant the moment he trusts in Christ, because it is all pure grace.

The shedding of the blood of our Lord Jesus Christ was the greatest crime ever perpetrated on the face of this earth. It involved the awful sin of deicide. When a man murders another, he is held responsible for taking the life of his fellow-man, but when a man stretches forth his hand against God incarnate, what can be said about his guilt! Yet that is the awful crime in which Jews and Gentiles participated. When the Lord Jesus Christ was nailed to Calvary's tree and His blood poured forth, it was the manifestation of the world's greatest sin, but it also became the greatest possible manifestation of the infinite love and grace of God. That which declares the enormity of man's sin and the corruption of his heart is that which manifests the love of God to the greatest extent. All this was foreseen.

Peter could say, "Him, being delivered by the determinate counsel and foreknowledge of God, ye have taken, and by wicked hands have crucified and slain" (Acts 2: 23). Yet this same Jesus is now made Lord and Christ, and through Him all who believe, as the Apostle Paul says, "are justified from all things." We sometimes sing:

> "The very spear that pierced His side
> Drew forth the blood to save."

That Roman spear-point driven into the very heart of the Son of God tells out the wickedness of the heart of man, but that cleansing blood rushing forth to wash away our sins tells how God has loved us, how wonderfully the grace of God has abounded over all our sins. We who sometimes were far off, we poor, wretched Gentiles, alienated from God by wicked works, and enemies in our minds, have now by putting our trust in Him been brought into a place of nearness that the law could never give even to Jews, and the Jew who believes in Him has been brought into this same blessed place. Together we have been "made nigh by the blood of Christ."

The blood of beasts that was shed of old could never settle the sin question because there was not sufficient intrinsic value in the victim, but in the case of our Lord Jesus Christ we see the Holy, the Just, the Sovereign of the skies, stooping to man's estate. He had to be who He is in order to do what He did, and because He is the infinite God become Man His blood has atoning value that no other blood could have. Thus we are made "nigh by the blood of Christ." We may well sing:

"So near, so very near, to God,
    Nearer I could not be;
  For in the person of His Son,
    I am as near as He.

"So dear, so very dear, to God,
    Dearer I could not be;
  The love wherewith He loves the Son,
    Such is His love to me."

Dear Christian, does your heart enter into it? Do you realize that the very moment you came, a feeble trembling sinner, and reached out the hand of faith, laid hold of the testimony of God concerning His blessed Son, that moment by the precious blood of Christ you were brought into such an intimate relationship to God that you could not be drawn any closer? Of course, when it comes to communion that is another thing, for in that sense there are times when we are nearer to Him than at others. But we have been "made nigh by the blood of Christ." Not made nigh by the sincerity of our repentance, by the strength of our faith, by the depth of our devotion, by the gladness of our spiritual experience, but made nigh by the blood. We owe everything for eter-

nity to the precious atoning blood of our blessed
Lord, and He who shed that blood, He who died
for our sins upon the cross, is Himself our peace.

We read, "Being justified by faith, we have
peace with God." That is not merely an experience of calmness in the soul, but it is the blessed
realization that the sin question has been fully
settled, that that which separated between our
souls and God has been done away, done away in
the cross, and so Christ Himself is our peace. You
see I am not called upon to be occupied with my
feelings, but with Christ. I may be very happy
today, and then circumstances may arise tomorrow which cause the clouds to overshadow my
soul and hide the sunshine of God's face, and I
may be in darkness, doubt, difficulty, and perplexity, but my peace remains unchanged.

> "Peace with God is Christ in glory,
>   God is just and God is love;
> Jesus died to tell the story,
>   Foes to bring to God above."

And so when I get disgusted with myself and
my own poor experience, I can look away from
self and look up by faith to Him, the blessed
Christ of God seated there on the right hand of
the Majesty in heaven, and say, "Yonder is my
peace, my heart rests in Him. God rests in Him,
and I rest in Him." Has your soul entered into
it? I hope we make these things practical, so

that they do not become mere doctrinal statements to us but realities that sink into the depths of our beings.

"For He is our peace, who hath made both one." What does He mean by, "Hath made both one?" Does He mean that He hath made Christ and us one? That is blessedly true, but that is not what is spoken of here. He was speaking a little farther back of two opposite companies, the circumcision and the uncircumcision, the Jew and the Gentile, the covenant people and those who are strangers to the covenants of promise. But when Christ died, He died for both, and we who believe from both of these companies are now reconciled to God, and therefore we read, "He hath made both one." And so my Jewish brother and I, his Gentile brother, are one in Christ.

"And hath broken down the middle wall of partition between us." I think the apostle is referring, as an illustration, at any rate, to the wall in the temple of old, separating the court of the Gentiles from the court of the Israelites. On this wall there was an inscription which was dug up just a few years ago, and it read, "Let no Gentile, let no man of the nations, go beyond this wall on pain of death." But the apostle says, "He hath broken down the middle wall of partition between us."

"Having abolished in His flesh the enmity, even

the law of commandments contained in ordinances; for to make in Himself of twain one new man, so making peace." What does he mean by that new man? It is the Body consisting of redeemed Jews and Gentiles here on earth and our glorious Head, our Lord Jesus Christ, in heaven. Redeemed sinners united by the Holy Spirit to Christ in heaven from now on form one new man, and so in a double sense peace has been made between the individual soul and God, and between Jew and Gentile, once separated by this middle wall of partition. In order that peace might be made between the individual soul and God, the law of commandments contained in ordinances had to be abolished.

That law pronounced a curse and condemnation on all who violated it. It was the Jews' pride and boasting that they were custodians of the law of God, and so they were, and yet they did not realize that it but put them all under the curse. They thought they were a blessed people and a privileged people to have the law of God, but alas, alas, they had broken the law, and God said, "Cursed is every one that continueth not in all things that are written in the book of the law to do them" (Gal. 3: 10). But the blessed Lord Jesus went to the cross and was made a curse for us—"As it is written, Cursed is every one that hangeth on a tree" (Gal. 3: 13). And so by enduring the cross, by bearing the judgment, He

has "abolished in His flesh the law of commandments contained in ordinances." And now both
Jews and Gentiles come to God on the same basis,
as sinners, but as sinners for whom Christ died.
Out of these two companies, when redeemed, you
have the new man of which Christ is the Head.

Then in verse 16 he uses the other term, "In
one Body," and says, "That He might reconcile
both unto God in one body by the cross, having
slain the enmity thereby." He has slain the enmity by taking our place upon the cross and bearing the judgment for us. We read that He has
made in Himself of Jew and Gentile one new
man. That takes in, as we have said, the Body
on earth and the Head in Heaven. Now we read,
"That He might reconcile both unto God in one
Body." Why not say, "That He might reconcile
both unto God in one new man"? It is because
Christ does not have to be reconciled to God, but
the Body must be reconciled to Him, for we who
form the Body were all poor sinners, we were
once on our way to everlasting ruin, but we have
been reconciled unto God in one Body. How are
we reconciled to God? You remember, our blessed
Lord came into the world to manifest the love of
God to sinners, and we read, "God was in Christ
reconciling the world unto Himself." But what
was the result? Did men receive Him gladly? Did
they own Him as Saviour and Lord? Instead of
that they nailed Him to the cross of shame. But

love that was stronger than death, love that the
many waters of judgment could not quench, led
Him to go down into the darkness of the tomb
for us, and now through faith in the risen Christ
who died for our sins, the enmity has been ban-
ished and we have been reconciled to God. And
so in resurrection power, having settled the sin
question, having completed the work that makes
atonement, the blessed Lord returned to this very
world that rejected Him. He appeared here for
forty days in His resurrection body, and gave the
message of the gospel to His disciples to carry
into the world. He "came and preached peace."
He sent forth the good news of peace to you which
were afar off, poor sinners of the Gentiles dying
in ignorance and darkness, and to you which were
nigh, Jews to whom His Word had come, who
had the oracles of God, who had light that the
Gentiles knew nothing of, but who joined with the
Gentiles in crucifying the Lord of glory. In the
love of His heart the message goes to you as well
as to the world outside. He "came and preached
peace to you which were afar off, and to them
that were nigh."

In the next verse we have a wonderful statement: "For through Him—" Through whom?
The resurrected Christ who ever lives at God's
right hand to make intercession for us. "For
through Him we both" (that is, we Jews and we
Gentiles who were once far off) now "have ac-

cess by one Spirit unto the Father." Of old there was no immediate access to God. That unrent vail told of a God hidden in the dark. God was not able to come out to man because of the fact that the sin question was not settled, and man could not go in to God for there was no way for his sins to be cleansed. But now the death of Christ has rent the separating vail.

> "The vail is rent! Our souls draw near
>   Unto a throne of grace;
> The merits of the Lord appear,
>   They fill the holy place.

> "His precious blood has spoken there,
>   Before and on the throne:
> And His own wounds in heaven declare,
>   The atoning work is done.

> " 'Tis finished! Here our souls have rest,
>   His work can never fail:
> By Him, our Sacrifice and Priest,
>   We pass within the vail.

> "Within the holiest of all,
>   Cleansed by His precious blood,
> Before the throne we prostrate fall,
>   And worship Thee, O God!"

Through Him we both have access, immediate access, by one Spirit, the Holy Spirit, who was given by God at Pentecost, baptizing believing Jews and Gentiles into one Body, and has made us both members of this one new man. We both have access by one Spirit unto the Father. What a wonderful thing it is to be a Christian! What a wonderful thing it is not only to have your sins forgiven but to have been brought into the family of God, and to have been made a fellow-member with other believers of the Body of Christ. Not only that, but to be accepted of God and to be as near to the heart of God as His own beloved Son. Not only that, but to have immediate access at any moment into His own blessed presence within the holiest in the power of the Holy Spirit. And all this rests on the infinite value of the blood of the Lord Jesus Christ. "Made nigh by the blood of Christ."

BUILT TOGETHER FOR A HABITATION OF GOD

✦ ✦ ✦

"Now therefore ye are no more strangers and foreigners,
but fellow-citizens with the saints, and of the household of
God; and are built upon the foundation of the apostles
and prophets, Jesus Christ Himself being the chief corner
stone; in whom all the building fitly framed together groweth unto an holy temple in the Lord: in whom ye also are
builded together for an habitation of God through the Spirit"
(Eph. 2: 19-22).

✦ ✦ ✦

IN this second chapter we have had brought
before us in a very vivid way our relationship to the Father as those who have been
quickened together with Christ. We have been
regenerated, we have been made members of the
family of God, the same divine life having been
communicated to every one of us, and thus we are
brought into this living relationship with the
Father. And then we have seen our new relationship to Christ. We are now made members of
His Body. The Body of Christ is looked at in
Scripture in two very distinct aspects. First, as
comprising all believers from Pentecost to the
coming again of our Lord Jesus Christ to call us
all to meet Him in the air. In other words, all

saints of this dispensation constitute the Body of
Christ. But then it is looked at in another way.
In Corinthians it is the aggregate of believers
upon the earth at a given time. All Christians
today constitute the Body of Christ as now manifest in the world, and all Christians throughout
the entire dispensation constitute the Body of
Christ as it will be for all eternity. We saw that
in the Body of Christ all distinctions between
Jews and Gentiles who believe in the Lord Jesus
Christ are done away, the middle wall of partition is broken down, and we are one in Him.

Now we go on to consider our relationship to
the Holy Spirit, and find that we have been constituted a habitation in which God by the Holy
Spirit dwells during the time of our sojourn on
the earth, and in which He will dwell throughout
all the ages to come. Two different figures are
used, one the Tabernacle, as set forth in the book
of Exodus, and the other the glorious Temple, as
depicted for us in the books of Kings and Chron-
icles. The Tabernacle represents the temporary
condition, the Temple the eternal condition which
will abide forever, and so we read in verse 19,
"Now therefore ye are no more strangers and
foreigners, but fellow-citizens with the saints, and
of the household of God."

We have noticed in our earlier study that
throughout this letter the apostle says "ye" when
he is addressing Gentiles and "we" when he

speaks of Jews. He was a Jewish believer, and speaks of "we who first hoped in Christ," and then speaks of "ye who also trusted, after that ye heard the word of truth, the gospel of your salvation." So now he says, "Ye are no more strangers and foreigners, but fellow-citizens with the saints, and of the household of God." We have seen that the Gentiles were "strangers from the covenants of promise." They were outside, they did not belong to that special elect nation of Israel, but alas, many in Israel failed to enter into their holy privilege, and so we are told elsewhere that they are not all Israel who are of Israel, but God called out a remnant from Israel, and that remnant by accepting the Lord Jesus Christ as their Saviour were baptized into Jesus Christ and were made living stones in the house of God. And now Gentiles who believe, though having no part nor lot in this matter, are brought in, too, and are no longer "strangers and foreigners, but fellow-citizens with the saints."

What do we mean by "saints"? Simply that we are now linked with Israel after the flesh? Not at all. They forfeited all rights from an earthly standpoint. It is those in Israel who believe in the Lord Jesus Christ who are here called saints, and so when he says we are "fellow-citizens with the saints," he means that the Gentiles who believe in the Lord Jesus Christ are as truly united to Christ now by the Spirit as our Jewish breth-

ren who believe in the same blessed Saviour. A
"saint" is a holy one, but holiness is not a question primarily of experience. A "holy one" is one
set apart to God. People often think of saints as
those who have already attained to perfect holiness, but that is not the divine thought at all.
Every one who puts his trust in the blessed Lord
has been set apart to God in Christ, and thus is
constituted a saint. But now having been made a
saint, one is called upon to live in a saintly way.
We do not become saints by holy living, but because God has constituted us saints we are called
to holy living.

So we read that we have been made "fellow-
citizens with the saints." What citizenship is
that? It is a heavenly citizenship. We read in
Philippians, "Our citizenship is in heaven." Philippi was what the Romans called a colony, but
they used that term in a different sense from
what we use it today. A Roman colony was a
city that had been characterized by some special
devotedness to the Roman imperial government,
and in order to reward the citizens of that place
for their loyalty and faithfulness the title "Colonia" was conferred upon that city. That meant
that from that time on every free-born person
living in that place was constituted a Roman citizen, and had just exactly the same rights and
privileges as though he were free born in Rome.

It was some years before Paul wrote that letter

to the Philippians that the Romans were in conflict with the people to the north and to the east of Macedonia, and when the Roman legions reached Philippi they found the citizens of that place had already raised a great army to assist, and had provided vast resources to meet the army. So delighted was the Roman general with their generosity and loyalty that he sent back to Rome a splendid report. The Senate then met and conferred upon them the title "Colonia," which means that every Philippian could then say, "I am a Roman citizen." However, Philippi was in Macedonia, and of course the people had certain duties to that government, but Philippi was governed directly from Rome, and had a representative of the Roman government there. See how the apostle applies it here. We are in this world sinners saved by grace and linked to our blessed Lord Jesus Christ, though He is rejected by this world. And now God so appreciates devotion to His blessed Son in this the day of His rejection, that He says, "I am going to confer upon every one who trusts Him, upon every one who owns His Lordship during this time when the world is spurning Him, the title of 'Colonia.' They are heavenly citizens; they belong to heaven." Though in the world, we are "fellow-citizens with the saints." We have our duties, our responsibilities to the world in which we live, but our prime duty, our prime responsibility, is to heaven with which we have to do because we are citizens of that blessed country and belong to the household of God.

Now he uses the figure of a building, and says, "And are built upon the foundation of the apostles and prophets, Jesus Christ Himself being the chief corner stone." You remember this same figure is used in other places in the New Testament. In the third chapter of First Corinthians we read of the building that God is erecting in the wonderful gospel days. You have it again in the sixth chapter of Second Corinthians where we read of the temple of God, and also in the second chapter of the first epistle of Peter, where believers are likened to living stones built upon *the* Living Stone, our Lord Jesus Christ.

In the Old Testament when Solomon's temple was erected on Mount Moriah, in order that there might be a level platform upon which the great superstructure should stand, vast stones were brought and mortared into the solid rock, and then stones were fitted into that temple. At the end of seven years it was the most wonderful sanctuary that the world had ever known up to that time. But there was a peculiarity about the construction. It went up without the sound of a hammer, because the stones were quarried out below; they were also cut, shaped and polished down there, and then placed upon that platform and cemented together without the use of a work-

man's hammer. So today no one can hear a
sound as a living stone is fitted into the temple
of God, but God by the Holy Ghost is quarrying
out these living stones from the depths of sin, and
He is lifting them up by His mighty power and
building them upon Christ, the great foundation.

> "View the vast building, see it rise!
> The work how great, the plan how wise!
> Nor can that faith be overthrown
> That rests upon the Living Stone."

Some day this temple will be completed, but
it is now in course of construction. Every believer is a living stone. In Africa, India, China,
and the islands of the sea, God is finding these
living stones and they are being built into this
glorious structure. It will remain for eternity the
glorious sanctuary in which God will display the
riches of His grace to all created intelligences.
What a wonderful thing to be a living stone in
that temple! You see no man can make himself
a living stone, only the Spirit of God can do that,
and therefore it is only those who have believed
in the Lord Jesus Christ who are placed in this
wonderful building.

"And are built upon the foundation of the
apostles and prophets, Jesus Christ Himself being
the chief corner stone." Does he mean that the
apostles and prophets are the foundation? Not
at all. He means that they are built upon the

foundation that they laid. What foundation did they lay? Paul says, "Other foundation can no man lay than that is laid, which is Jesus Christ" (1 Cor. 3: 11). So the apostles and the prophets proclaimed the truth concerning the Lord Jesus Christ, and upon that foundation this glorious temple is being builded. You say, "But what prophets are these? We have no difficulty about the apostles for we know they are the apostles of the new dispensation. Do the prophets include the Old Testament prophets?" We answer, They preached Christ. Who preached a more glorious gospel than Isaiah? Listen to His wonderful words, "He was wounded for our transgressions, He was bruised for our iniquities: the chastisement of our peace was upon Him; and with His stripes we are healed." Listen to Jeremiah, "This is His name whereby He shall be called, The Lord our Righteousness" (Jer. 23: 6). Listen to Zechariah, "Awake, O sword, against My Shepherd, and against the Man that is My Fellow, saith the Lord of hosts: smite the Shepherd, and the sheep shall be scattered: and I will turn Mine hand upon the little ones" (Zech. 13: 7). And so we might go on. In this sense the prophets of the Old Testament joined with the apostles of the New Testament in setting forth the truth of a crucified and risen Saviour, but if he had in mind these Old Testament prophets, we might expect him to say "prophets and apostles," for these Old Testament prophets came long before the apostles did. But, you see, he reverses it and says, "And are built upon the foundation of the apostles and prophets." Would it not be rather this that just as there were apostles of the New Testament dispensation so there were also the prophets? We read, for instance, of certain prophets and teachers at Antioch. Some of the writers of the New Testament, as Mark and Luke, were not apostles but were prophets, and so I take it that we are to limit this to the New Testament workmen, those who were raised up of God at the beginning to lay the foundation, to preach Christ, to proclaim the gospel. It is upon this glorious proclamation that the temple of God has been building through the centuries.

"Built upon the foundation of the apostles and prophets, Jesus Christ Himself being the chief corner stone." "There is none other name under heaven given among men, whereby we must be saved" (Acts 4: 12). Christ is the One Mediator between God and man. Only those who put their trust in Him are built into this holy temple. Only those who have been saved through His death, His shed blood, and His glorious resurrection are members of His Body. Only those who have rested their souls for eternity upon the work that He accomplished upon Calvary have been quickened together with Him and are thus brought into the family of God. These are our brethren. Others are our fellow-men, in whom we are deeply interested, over whom we yearn with the compassion of Christ. But we dare not take that sacred term of "brethren" and apply it those who reject our Lord Jesus Christ, who trample His blood under their feet, for it is upon His work alone we rest. We remember He said to Peter, "Whom say ye that I am?" and Peter answered, "Thou art the Christ, the Son of the living God." And Jesus said, "Blessed art thou, Simon Bar-jona: for flesh and blood hath not revealed it unto thee but My Father which is in heaven. And I say unto thee, that thou art Peter, and upon this rock I will build My Church." What rock? That Christ is the Son of the living God. "On this rock I will build My Church." This is the one foundation. It was laid in death when Jesus died upon the tree and now in resurrection the Spirit is building this glorious temple upon Christ.

But now, as we said, the temple is not yet finished. As long as there are still poor sinners to be brought in, the temple is not complete. If you should ask for my opinion as to how near we are to the finished temple, I would say that I think there are a very few more stones to be put in, just one here and there in the roof, and then it will be complete. It might be that the last living stone to be placed in the building will be placed there today, and then the work will be done.

"In whom all the building, fitly framed to-

gether," that is, every one is fitted by the Holy
Spirit into his or her exact place as a living stone.
"In whom all the building fitly framed together
groweth—that is progress, not completion, it is
not that it has grown up but—"groweth unto an
holy temple in the Lord." And when it is all completed, what a dwelling-place for God and the
Lamb it will be. What a wonderful sanctuary
through all the ages to come. When you think of
being a living stone in that glorious building,
does it not bring to your soul a sense of the importance of holy living, of devotedness to Christ,
of so behaving yourself that He will delight in
dwelling in you? Whereas in 1 Corinthians 3
and 2 Corinthians 6 the temple of God is the entire Church, in 1 Corinthians 6 the temple of the
Holy Spirit is the individual. In 1 Corinthians
3:16 we read, "Know ye not that ye are the temple of God, and that the Spirit of God dwelleth
in you?" And then speaking of the enemies outside, he says, "If any man defile the temple of
God, him shall God destroy; for the temple of
God is holy, which temple ye are." In 2 Corinthians 6:16 we read, "What agreement hath the
temple of God with idols? for ye are the temple
of the living God; as God hath said, I will dwell
in them, and walk in them; and I will be their
God, and they shall be My people." And it is because the Church collectively comprises the temple of God that the command comes, "Wherefore

come out from among them, and be ye separate, saith the Lord, and touch not the unclean thing; and I will receive you." But now look back at 1 Corinthians 6: 19. You will find that he changes the figure to the individual. "What? Know ye not that your body is the temple of the Holy Ghost which is in you, which ye have of God, and ye are not your own?" Here we find the word is, "your body," not "your bodies." The individual is the temple of the Holy Ghost which is in him. Addressing the whole company he says that collectively they form the temple of God but each individual believer's body is the temple of the Holy Ghost. What godliness should characterize us, what piety, what separation from the world, what faithfulness to Christ should mark us!

Coming back to verses 20, 21 of Ephesians 2, the temple is spoken of, but in verse 22 we have, I believe, the thought of the tabernacle. He has been speaking of the whole company of believers, and now comes back to address any group of believers at a given time, like this church at Ephesus. "In whom ye also are builded together for an habitation of God through the Spirit." That is a finished product right here on the earth, like the tabernacle which could be placed at a given place today, taken down tomorrow, and moved elsewhere. It was made of a number of boards which had been fitted together, covered with gold, and united by bands. Then on each board there were two tenons which went down into sockets of silver. Beautiful curtains covered the united framework. Once those boards had been trees out in the desert, as you and I were poor sinners having no hope in the world, cut down by the work of the Spirit of God, planed and fitted together by the Spirit and now made the abiding place of God. They were covered with gold—made the righteousness of God in Christ. The curtains speak of all His perfections sheltering His own. This is the picture that is used here. You as a company of Christians are builded together for an habitation of God through the Spirit.

Do we realize this as much as we should? Any assembly or church of the living God (and I use this in the strictest New Testament sense, a company of called-out believers) is the habitation of God through the Spirit. That is why the Church should be kept holy, that is why unsaved people should have no part in its fellowship, because they are not members of the true Church. That is why Christians who are members of that Church should be careful to eschew all worldliness and everything that would dishonor the Lord Jesus Christ. May God give us to so live that we shall glorify His name in this scene.

THE REVELATION OF THE MYSTERY

✶ ✶ ✶

"For this cause I Paul, the prisoner of Jesus Christ for you Gentiles, if ye have heard of the dispensation of the grace of God which is given me to you-ward: how that by revelation He made known unto me the mystery; (as I wrote afore in few words, whereby, when ye read, ye may understand my knowledge in the mystery of Christ) which in other ages was not made known unto the sons of men, as it is now revealed unto His holy apostles and prophets by the Spirit; that the Gentiles should be fellow-heirs, and of the same Body, and partakers of His promise in Christ by the gospel: whereof I was made a minister, according to the gift of the grace of God given unto me by the effectual working of His power. Unto me, who am less than the least of all saints, is this grace given, that I should preach among the Gentiles the unsearchable riches of Christ; and to make all men see what is the fellowship of the mystery, which from the beginning of the world hath been hid in God, who created all things by Jesus Christ: to the intent that now unto the principalities and powers in heavenly places might be known by the Church the manifold wisdom of God, according to the eternal purpose which He purposed in Christ Jesus our Lord: in whom we have boldness and access with confidence by the faith of Him. Wherefore I desire that ye faint not at my tribulations for you, which is your glory" (Eph. 3: 1-13).

✶ ✶ ✶

THE apostle comes now to the unfolding of that great secret which had been in the heart of God from eternity, but in this glorious dispensation of grace has at last been fully revealed. It is my thought we should see that in a very special sense Paul was the chosen one to make known this mystery in all its fulness. On the other hand we need to guard against the idea that no others participated in this knowledge, for in verse 5 of the portion we have just read we note that he declares, "It is now revealed unto His holy apostles and prophets by the Spirit." Others, therefore, shared with him in this blessed knowledge, but preeminently he was the apostle of the mystery.

No one else speaks of the Body of Christ, among all the New Testament writers. To Paul this revelation came first that he might communicate it to others. But the truth that Jew and Gentile were to be blessed alike on the ground of pure grace was made known to the twelve. Our Lord sets forth this truth in John 10: 4, 16. "His own sheep" from the Jewish fold, and "other sheep" of the Gentiles were to form "one flock" under the fostering care of "one Shepherd." Peter's vision of the sheet let down from heaven set forth the same glorious mystery. But the revelation of the one Body was the special truth committed to Paul and made known in germ at the very time of his conversion, as the words, "Why persecutest thou Me?" imply. To touch a saint on earth was to touch the Head in heaven. Thus was he taught the unity of the Body and its union with the glorified Head.

We might say it was because of this very truth that he was in prison at the time he wrote the Ephesian letter. This I think is involved in the expression "I, Paul, the prisoner of Jesus Christ for you Gentiles." You will remember that in his defence on the temple stairs at Jerusalem, it was when he announced that he had been commanded by the Lord to go unto the Gentiles that the ire of his Jewish hearers was stirred to the depths, and they cried, "Away with such a fellow from the earth; it is not fit for him to live." We, therefore, who are Gentiles by nature, have special reason to be grateful to Paul for his faithfulness in proclaiming the purpose of God concerning our part in the divine program. Because of this he suffered obliquy and shame, and spent many weary months in prison rather than surrender in the least degree the truth of God committed to him.

Here, as in Colossians, he indicates that his was a double ministry. First, he speaks (ver. 2) of the dispensation of the grace of God which was given him. A dispensation, as we have seen, is a stewardship. Paul, like every true New Testament preacher, was a steward of the grace of God. Notice how the Apostle Peter also speaks in his first epistle, 4: 10, "As every man has received the gift, even so minister the same one to another as good stewards of the manifold grace of God." Grace, we have already observed, is God's un-

merited favor to those who have deserved the
very opposite. It is this that is proclaimed in the
gospel. And this, of course, is the first part of
the mystery. The apostle goes on to show that
he was not only a minister of the gospel, but in
a special sense a minister of this now revealed
secret.

He says that by revelation the mystery was
made known to him, and he calls it the "mystery
of Christ." It is God's wonderful secret concerning the glory of His blessed Son. How good it is
to know that Christ's glory and our salvation are
eternally linked and can never be separated.
Speaking of the mystery he says, "As I wrote
afore in few words." This, I take it, refers to
what he had already said in chapter 1: 9-13. He
will now elaborate that more fully. He had also
written before to others concerning this mystery,
as, for instance, to the Romans in chapter 16:
25, 26; to the Corinthians, see the first epistle,
chapter 2: 7; and in others of his letters we have
similar references. I mention this because of the
unwarranted position taken by some that the
mystery was never revealed until Paul's impris-
onment. On the contrary, he had been proclaiming
it from the very beginning, both by voice and
pen.

Now what is this mystery which in other ages
was hidden from the sons of men? We are told
in verse 6: "That the Gentiles should be fellow-

heirs and of the same Body, and partakers of His promise in Christ by the gospel." In what does this differ from the Old Testament declaration that God would bless the Gentiles through Israel? The great difference, I take it, is this: According to the Old Testament prophets the day is coming when Israel will be restored to covenant relationship with God and will be brought into a place of special blessing here on the earth, and the Gentile nations living at that time will be blessed with and in subjection to them. But the great truth for our age is, that God is now calling out a people for the heavens to be the Body and Bride of His Son throughout the ages to come, and through whom He will administer the affairs of a redeemed universe. This Body is composed of those who were once by nature Jews and others who were Gentiles, but who have both been brought into the new creation by a second birth and united to the Lord Himself by the Spirit, thus becoming one Body with Him and each other. It was this great truth that Paul was specially called to minister "according to the gift of the grace of God," which had been bestowed upon him. The Holy Spirit effectually worked in and through him to bring lost sinners of the Gentiles into this wonderful place of privilege and inalienable blessing.

Note how meekly the apostle speaks of himself, even in connection with this great ministry committed to him, which was enough to have turned any ordinary man's head. He says, "Unto me, who am less than the least of all saints, is this grace given." He was not exalted by the abundance of the revelation made known to him, but accepted it as a divine trust which he was to minister for the glory of God and the blessing of others. Alas, what a different spirit often actuates some today, who, getting a little smattering of truth, are carried away by their fancied superior intelligence, and manifest the most shocking pride and conceit because of the imagined inferiority of other believers who have not yet attained to their knowledge of the truth! Surely every new divine revelation to our souls should only humble us the more as we realize that we have nothing that we have not received. Apart from divine grace, we would still be in nature's darkness and ignorance. Paul took the very lowest place as he went about preaching among the Gentiles the unsearchable riches of Christ. To those who were in the greatest spiritual poverty he proclaimed the possibilities of wealth beyond the power of human tongue to express, and he would have all men enter into the blessedness of this, and enjoy in reality the fellowship of the mystery, or, as we might render it, the communion of this secret. Men form their secret societies and delight to meet in hidden places to enjoy together mysteries that others cannot share. The Christian is through grace already a member of the society of the redeemed, a fellowship divinely formed by the indwelling of the Holy Spirit, and as such can enjoy with fellow-believers the marvelous secret which God has now made known. From the beginning of the world it has been hidden in Himself, He who created all things by Jesus Christ. Observe, it was not simply hidden in the Bible, as though the Old Testament contained this message and we only needed to ferret it out. But it was hidden in God, and could not have been apprehended by man at all excepting by divine revelation. Upon the rejection of the Lord Jesus Christ by Israel, and the descent of the Holy Spirit to bear witness to the perfection of His finished work, it pleased God to make known this mystery. Even angels, whether good or bad, had no knowledge of it until it was given to God's saints on earth. This, I understand, is what is involved in the remarkable statement of verse 10, "To the intent that now unto the principalities and powers in heavenly places might be known by (or really, through) the Church, the manifold wisdom of God." That is, the unseen hosts of glorious beings in the heavens, as well as the vast armies of fallen spirits dominated by Satan, are learning, as they observe what God is doing here on earth in His Church, the many-sided wisdom of God, "according to the purpose of the ages, which He purposed in Christ Jesus our Lord." One of our poets has written:

"Through the ages
One unceasing purpose runs."

The humble student of the Word of God can see unfolded in the New Testament the great purpose that God had in mind, when He created the universe and man and counseled with Himself to take out of that world from the children of Adam a vast company who would be united to His blessed Son throughout eternity. All will work out for the glory of Christ Jesus, our Lord.

In Him we now have immediate access with fullest confidence into the presence of God. We are so intimately linked up with Him, so truly one with Him, that we can approach the throne of grace without dread or fear, knowing that all we ask in His name, that is, by His authority, the Father delights to do.

No wonder the apostle could glory in suffering because of this great truth, and he would not have the saints become discouraged because of his trials, but he rather would have them remember that whatever tribulation he was passing through was on their behalf and for their glory.

To the extent that we enter into and appropriate these precious things for ourselves, will be our practical sanctification—our separation from the world and worldly-religious systems that ignore entirely the truth of the mystery of the one Body. He who thus apprehends his unity with

Christ, and hence with all who are in Christ, cannot be sectarian in heart or practice, but must of very necessity embrace all believers in his fellowship and interest.

To profess to hold the truth of the one Body is one thing. To be held by it is quite another. It is an amazing thing to realize that so intimate is the link that binds all believers to each other and to our glorified Head in heaven that everything I say or do as a Christian has an effect for good or ill on all my fellow-members, just as every part of the human body affects every other part. How careful this should make us in our walk and our attitude toward one another.

LECTURE XIII.

PAUL'S SECOND PRAYER FOR THE SAINTS

�　✔　✔

"For this cause I bow my knees unto the Father of our Lord Jesus Christ, of whom the whole family in heaven and earth is named, that He would grant you, according to the riches of His glory, to be strengthened with might by His Spirit in the inner man; that Christ may dwell in your hearts by faith; that ye, being rooted and grounded in love, may be able to comprehend with all saints what is the breadth, and length, and depth, and height; and to know the love of Christ, which passeth knowledge, that ye might be filled with all the fulness of God. Now unto Him that is able to do exceeding abundantly above all that we ask or think, according to the power that worketh in us, unto Him be glory in the Church by Christ Jesus throughout all ages, world without end. Amen" (Eph. 3: 14-21).

✔　✔　✔

WE have two prayers in this precious epistle. In the first chapter we have the prayer for knowledge, and in the third, the prayer for love. After reading the first prayer we naturally find ourselves looking out over the great sphere of God's eternal purpose, trying to take in the scope of His wonderful pre-arranged divine plan. But, as we read the second prayer and meditate upon it, we find ourselves looking up in adoring gratitude, with our hearts going out in love to the One who first loved us.

As we try to expound this prayer I want you to think of seven words that I believe will help us to get its scope. We read in verse 14, "For this cause I bow my knees unto the Father of our Lord Jesus Christ." The expression, "I bow my knees," is a very beautiful one and suggests intensity of feeling. Have you ever noticed that if you are just quietly engaged in prayer or meditation, you may sit, perhaps, as I often do, in a comfortable big chair with your open Bible before you, and as one thought or another comes, you close your eyes and lift your heart to God in prayer? Or, when you come together with God's people, you love to stand in holy silence before God joining with some one who is leading in prayer. But when you are intensely in earnest, when something has fairly gripped you that stirs you to deepest supplication, you find yourself almost irresistibly forced to your knees.

"For this cause—" For what cause? Because of his deep interest in the people of God, because of his desire that they should enter fully into their privileges in Christ, and understand the great mystery of which he had spoken. "For this cause I bow my knees unto the Father of our Lord Jesus Christ." We noticed that the first prayer is addressed to the God of our Lord Jesus Christ, for God as such is the Source of all counsels, but this second prayer, which has to do more with family relationship, is addressed to the Father of our Lord Jesus Christ. Divine titles are used most discriminately in the Word of God; never in the careless way that we so often use them. We might not think it made any difference whether one said, "I address myself to the God of our Lord Jesus," or, "I bow my knees to the Father of our Lord Jesus," but it made a great deal of difference to the apostle. It indicated the different thoughts that were in his mind.

When I think of God, I think of the Maker of all things, the Planner of all things who fitted the ages together. But I think of the Father as the One from whose bosom the eternal Son came into this world, becoming Man for our salvation. Ere He left this scene He said to Mary, "I ascend unto My Father, and your Father; and to My God, and your God" (John 20: 17). There, you see, you have the two thoughts: God the Source of all counsels; the Father, the Source of all affections —family affection, the very center of family relationship.

"I bow my knees unto the Father of our Lord Jesus Christ, of whom the whole family in heaven and earth is named." "The whole family" is undoubtedly a correct rendering here, and yet "every family" would be just as correct, and you probably will want to ask yourself the question:

"What conveys to my mind the most precious thought?" "The whole family"—that means that all saints in earth and heaven constitute one great family of born again ones, and are thus linked up with the Father. But I am thinking, too, of the great hosts of angels never redeemed by the blood of Christ because they have never fallen, and even those who fell found no Saviour. The angels, too, own the Fatherhood of God, but they are servants, waiting on the family. And then there is the family of the Old Testament saints. There was the antediluvian family, the patriarchal family, the Israelites, those who were truly of Israel. All these were families through the past dispensations. And then there is the Church of this age of grace, and by-and-by there will be the glorious kingdom family. There are dispensational distinctions, but all receive life from the same blessed Person, and all together adore and worship Him. Notice that the whole family is located in heaven and on earth. Those who are dead to us are living to God above.

Now you have the prayer proper. First there is our *endowment*. "That He would grant you, according to the riches of His glory." You may come to God in prayer for anything, and realize that since you have such a marvelous endowment as that, you do not need to fear to present your petitions to God. You cannot ask too much. You remember the man who came to a king asking

for something, and the king gave to him out of
his abundant treasure until the suppliant said,
"Your Majesty, that is too much! That is too
much!" The king smiled and said, "It may seem
too much for you to take, but it is not too much
for me to give." And so our blessed God gives
out of His abundance. "Able to do exceeding
abundantly above all that we ask or think." He
does not say, as we sometimes think, "Able to do
exceeding abundantly above all that we *can* ask
or think," for we could be like little children asking for the moon, but he says that He does for
us, "exceeding abundantly above all that we ask
or think." When we come to Him in the name of
Jesus, bringing our petitions, there is more in
that great endowment fund than we can ever
exhaust.

"According to the riches of His glory." "According to," not "out of the riches of His glory."
We have noticed the difference between these two
expressions when commenting on a similar
passage found in chapter one, so we need not repeat the illustration we used then. But it means
much to the soul when one truly sees this distinction.

Then observe the next phrase. We have in it,
our *enduement*. "To be strengthened with might
by His Spirit in the inner man." Do you sometimes feel your limitations, your weakness, your
lack of intensity of purpose, your powerlessness

when it comes to living for God and witnessing for Him? Do you feel as though you might as well give up for the little you accomplish? Do you say, "If I only had more strength, how different it might be"? Listen! The excellency of the power is of God, not of us, and the Holy Spirit who dwells within us is ready to work in and through us to the glory of our Lord Jesus Christ. So the prayer is that we may be "strengthened with might by His Spirit in the inner man." You know we are not walking storage-batteries. Some people have an idea that this is practically what the Christian should be. You hear people pray, "O God, give me more power, fill me with power." The idea they have is that the old battery is pretty well run down. "Put another one in, Lord," is what they seem to say. No, you are not a storage-battery; you are in connection with the great eternal dynamo, and the Holy Spirit works in and through you to the glory of the Lord Jesus Christ as you are yielded to Him. He Himself is the source of all power, and that power is to be used by the people of God.

The next word is *enthronement*. "That Christ may dwell in your hearts by faith." Is this not the same thing as when in another epistle He speaks of Christ reigning? Is it not Christ sitting upon the throne of our hearts dominating, controlling us for the glory of God, His blessed pierced hands guiding and directing everything?

It is not Christ received as an occasional visitor, not Christ recognized merely as a guest, but Christ abiding within as our living, loving, blessed Lord: Christ dwelling in the heart by faith. You remember the little couplet,

> "If Christ is not Lord of all,
> He is not Lord at all."

He does not want the second place. He must have the first if your life is going to be that which it should.

The next thing is our *establishment*. "That ye, being rooted and grounded in love." He uses a figure here that you will find in other of his epistles, "rooted and grounded." The two terms are very different. When I was a boy, the school-teacher used to tell me that I must not mix my metaphors. For instance, I should not start with the figure of a ship and change to that of a rail-road in the same sentence. But the Holy Ghost is wonderfully independent in His use of metaphors. "That ye, being rooted and grounded in love." Rooted like a tree, and grounded like a building which is raised upon a great foundation. Rooted and grounded in what? In love. What is love? That is the great rock foundation upon which we build, for God is love, and he who is rooted in love is rooted in God, and therefore, the right-eous shall flourish like the palm tree. The believer is like the trees, for they draw their nourishment

from the living God Himself. What a Christian
character will be built when one is founded upon
this Rock, building upon God Himself, rooted and
grounded in love!

And now we have our *enlightenment.* "That
ye may be able to comprehend with all saints."
You will never be able to take it all in, but you
comprehend a little, and another a little, and I a
little, and with all the saints together we begin
to get some idea of God's wonderful purpose of
grace. Therefore, we need one another, we need
fellowship, we need to be helpers of each other's
faith. The feeblest, the weakest member of the
Body of Christ is necessary, for God may give to
some feeble crippled brother what some strong
active Christian may never get at all. "That ye
may be able to comprehend with all saints what
is the breadth, and length, and depth, and height."
Of what? Some say of love. What has He been
speaking about in this chapter? God's wonderful
purpose of the ages, God's great plan. It is that
by the Spirit you may be able to comprehend with
all saints what is the breadth, and length, and
depth, and height of that vast system of grace
which God is working out through the ages of
time and which will be consummated in the ages
to come.

In school I was told that no solid could have
more than three dimensions, length, breadth, and
thickness; but we have here length, breadth,

depth, and height—four dimensions. Could you draw a picture of this? Could you draw an illustration of length, breadth, depth, and height? How would you do it? Some of the old Greek philosophers used to reason about a possible fourth dimension, and with them it was a kind of weird spiritual dimension. After all, that is not so bad. You remember that Spanish prisoner whose bones were discovered when Napoleon's soldiers opened the prison of the Inquisition. There in an underground dungeon they found the skeleton of the prisoner, flesh and clothing all long since gone, but the remnants of an ankle bone with a chain attached to it were still there. There upon the wall they saw cut into the rock with a sharp piece of metal a cross, and above it in Spanish, the word for height, and below it the word for depth, and on one arm the word for for length, and on the other the word for breadth. As that poor prisoner of so long ago was starving to death, his soul was contemplating the wonder of God's purpose of grace, and to Him the figure of the cross summed it all up — the length, the breadth, the depth, the height!

Next he prays that we may "know the love of Christ which passeth knowledge." Surely this is our *enlargement*. We glory as we enter into the knowledge of the love of Christ; but what a strange expression is this! He prays that we may know the unknowable. "The love of Christ that passeth knowledge." See that darling little babe in the mother's arms, looking up and cooing and responding to the mother's smile. You or I might say, "Let me take the little one," and hold out our hands, and it would look at us and cling the more tightly to the mother, and if we should insist on taking it, it might utter a piercing cry which would say, "I do not know you; I do not know whether you love babies or not, but I know my mother's love and can trust her." And yet, what does the baby know of the love of a mother? What does it understand about the reasons behind a mother's love? But it enjoys it nevertheless. And so the youngest saint in Christ knows the love of the Saviour, and the oldest saint, the most mature saint, is still seeking to know in greater fulness that love that passeth knowledge.

> "Oh, the love of Christ is boundless,
>   Broad and long and deep and high!
> Every doubt and fear is groundless,
>   Now the Word of faith is nigh.
> Jesus Christ for our salvation,
>   Came and shed His precious blood;
> Clear we stand from condemnation,
>   In the risen Son of God."

Then notice the last point in this prayer, "That ye might be filled with all the fulness of God." Or properly, "That ye might be filled unto all the fulness of God." This is our *enrichment*. When our translators said, "Filled with all the fulness of God," they meant well, but you could not hold all the fulness of God. Solomon said, "Even the heaven of heavens cannot contain Thee." Yet we read that He dwells in the heart of him that is humble and contrite. Walking by the seaside one time, some one touched the real meaning of this word. He picked up one of the beautiful sea-shells and put it down in the sand where the water had ebbed for a moment or two, and then as they watched, the sea came rolling in and the shell was filled, and he said, "See! Filled unto all the fulness of the ocean." So you and I as we live in fellowship with God may be filled unto His fulness. We are in Him and He is in us, and thus the prayer is answered.

And now notice the closing wonderful benediction. "Now unto Him that is able to do above all we ask"; is that what is written? No; that is not enough. Is it, "Able to do abundantly above all that we ask"? That is not enough. Is it, "Able to do exceeding abundantly above all that we ask?" Still that does not reach the limit. "Unto Him that is able to do exceeding abundantly above all that we ask or think." You need not fear to come to God about anything. Are you troubled about present circumstances? Have you availed yourself of the abundant resources of God? If things are right in your heart and you come to God and make connections there, you can be sure of a wonderful answer. "Unto Him that is able to do exceeding abundantly above all that we ask or think, according to the power that worketh in us"—this divine energy which works through poor feeble creatures such as we are— "Unto Him be glory in the Church by Christ Jesus throughout all ages, world without end. Amen." He is the One in whom God will find His pleasure throughout all eternity.

THE WALK WORTHY OF
OUR CALLING

✝ ✝ ✝

"I therefore, the prisoner of the Lord, beseech you that ye walk worthy of the vocation wherewith ye are called. With all lowliness and meekness, with longsuffering, forbearing one another in love; endeavoring to keep the unity of the Spirit in the bond of peace. There is one Body, and one Spirit, even as ye are called in one hope of your calling: one Lord, one faith, one baptism, one God and Father of all, who is above all, and through all, and in you all" (Eph. 4: 1-6).

✝ ✝ ✝

IN chapters one to three we have been studying the doctrinal section of this letter to the Ephesians. We now take up the practical part, that which has to do with our lives as those who through grace have been made members of Christ. Notice how tenderly the apostle leads us to this. He says, "I therefore, the prisoner of the Lord, beseech you that ye walk worthy of the vocation wherewith ye are called."

Wherever grace rules in the soul, "I command" is changed to "I beseech." You do not find the apostle lording it over the faith of the people of God, but graciously, tenderly pleading with them, rather than sternly ordering their behavior. He speaks of himself in a way that certainly must have gone home to the heart of every one who read this letter in its original setting, for these Ephesians had been brought to know the Saviour's love through him, and the link between a preacher and those who have been brought to Christ as a result of his ministry is a very real one. Hearts are very closely bound together when they stand in that relationship. What must they have felt to realize that the man of God to whom they owed so much was lying in a Roman prison, and he was there not because of any ill-doing on his part, but because of his faithful proclamation of the gospel which had meant so much to them. He was a prisoner of the Lord, and from his prison-cell he writes this letter, beseeching them to walk worthy of the vocation wherewith they are called.

Our vocation is, of course, our calling. Paul refers to that which he has been previously opening up in these other chapters. He has been putting before us the blessedness of the new life, that all who believe on the Lord Jesus Christ are members of that one Body of which He is the exalted Head in heaven, and that all such have been builded together for a habitation of God by the Spirit. In view of the fact that we have been redeemed to God by the precious blood of Christ; in view of the fact that I am a member now of His body, of His flesh, and of His bones; in view of the fact that I am a living stone built into that temple of God by the Holy Spirit, that temple in which He dwells, my behavior is to be ordered of God, I am to walk worthy of the vocation wherewith I am called. Elsewhere we are told to walk worthy of God and of the Lord.

"With all lowliness and meekness, with longsuffering, forbearing one another in love." I spent quite a little time over this verse. It went home to my own heart, for every expression in it was a challenge to me, and I kept asking myself the question, "To what extent have I risen to the standard that is here set forth? I must present this to others as the divine standard for a Christian's behavior. To what extent am I measuring up to it?" And the more I carefully examined every expression both in the English and in the original Greek, the more humiliated and ashamed before God I was as I realized how far short I have often come—I am afraid, I always come—from living out what we have here. Every word is important.

"With all lowliness." That word is found only once elsewhere in the New Testament and that is in the Epistle to the Philippians, chapter 2:3. "Let nothing be done through strife or vainglory; but in lowliness of mind let each esteem other better than themselves." The original word means "modesty," that is, an utter lack of self-assertiveness, that which is so characteristic of us as fallen creatures—we who have nothing to be proud of and yet are sometimes proud of our very crudity and ignorance. A young minister arose in a Methodist Conference and said, "I am against education. I don't believe in education. I read no books except the Bible; I don't profess to know nothing about literature or anything of that kind; I am just an ignorant man. But the Lord has taken me up, and is using me, and I am not at all interested in schools or colleges or education. I am proud to be just what I am." An old preacher arose and said, "Do I understand that our dear young brother is proud of his ignorance? If so, all I have to say is that he has a great deal to be proud of." Most of us are that way; we are proud of the very thing of which we ought to be ashamed. We begin to boast of our attainments and ability, even as children. One of the first things parents must learn in training their children is to curb that natural tendency to boastfulness. But as Christians, how completely we should be delivered from this. We have nothing that we have not received. Every blessing we have we owe to divine grace. With what modesty, then, should we behave ourselves!

The word "meekness" is found eight times in the New Testament. I should like, if there were time, to turn to every one of the passages, but I would remind you of this, that it is used of our blessed Lord Himself. The apostle says, "We be-

seech you by the meekness and gentleness of
Christ," and Christ says, "Take My yoke upon
you, and learn of Me; for I am meek and lowly in
heart: and ye shall find rest unto your souls"
(Matt. 11:29). The root of the original word
really means "humility," a spirit that never takes
offence. Somebody says something unkind about
me. I flare up in a moment. Why? Because I
am not meek. They said of Jesus, "He has a
devil," and He meekly endured it. They said, "Say
we not right that Thou art a Samaritan?" But
He answered them not. "When He was reviled,
He reviled not again; when He suffered, He
threatened not." That is meekness.

And then the next word, "longsuffering." This
is a favorite word of the apostle, and we also find
it used twice by the Apostle Peter. It is found
twelve times in the New Testament. It means
literally, "to endure with unruffled temper." Do
you know very much about longsuffering? "Well,"
you say, "I would not mind if what she said about
me had been true, but when I know it isn't true,
I can't stand it." Therefore, the need of longsuffering. It is the flesh which talks like that.
That does not come from the new nature but from
the old. Many years ago I had a friend, a little,
odd German brother, whose name was George.
Sometimes he would fly off and lose his temper,
but it always brought him back to earth if one
looked at him quietly and said, "Is that old George

or new George talking?" In a moment the tears would come; and even now, though he has been gone thirty years, I can hear him say, "That's old George; new George would neffer behafe that way. I must take that old George and inflict punishment upon him. He has no right to behafe like that." Yes, the old nature is quick to take offence, quick to flare up if not properly appreciated, but the new nature just bows in meekness and lets the waves and billows pass over and is undisturbed thereby.

The last word here is "forbearing." "Forbearing one another in love." This word occurs only once otherwise in the New Testament and that is in Colossians 3:13. There we have a very similar expression to that which is before us here: "Forbearing one another, and forgiving one another, if any man have a quarrel against any: even as Christ forgave you, so also do ye." Literally, forbearance means "to put up with." Now taking all that into account I thought I would try to translate that verse myself. I am going to give you the Authorized Version first, and then my own translation. "With all lowliness and meekness, with longsuffering, forbearing one another in love." My translation is, "With all modesty and humbleness of spirit, with unruffled temper, lovingly putting up with all that is disagreeable in other people." That is a literal rendering of the original. That is the Spirit of Christ. As we meditate upon it and think of all that is involved in it, how can we do other than hang our heads in shame and confess that in many things we all offend, but seek grace that we may be so yielded to the control of the Holy Spirit of God that these things may indeed become real in our lives?

The apostle goes on, "Endeavoring to keep the unity of the Spirit in the bond of peace." Others have translated it, "Giving diligence to keep the unity of the Spirit in the bond of peace." Observe, he does not say, "Giving diligence to keep the unity of the Body." We do not have anything to do with that. We do not have to preserve the unity of the Body. God is looking after that. He has bound every believer up in a bundle in Christ, has given His blessed Holy Spirit to dwell within, and He links them one to another, and to the blessed Head in heaven. The Body of Christ is always complete as God looks at it. People talk about "these heartless divisions that rend the Body of Christ," but they do not rend the Body of Christ. You see, the Body of Christ is not composed of all the different sects and denominations. If you were to gather all the different Catholic sects together, the Roman Catholic, the Greek Catholic, the Chaldean Catholic, the Anglican Catholic, the Coptic Catholic, etc., and then gather all the Protestant sects together and unite them all in one big church, that would not be the Body of Christ. That would contain a great many

people who are in the Body of Christ but it would
also include a great many who are not. On the
other hand, after you had gathered all these denominations and sects together, there would be a
great many outside that would be members of the
Body of Christ, for "The Church, which is His
Body," and the Church, which some call the visible
Body of Christ, are not the same thing. The Body
of Christ consists only of those who are regenerated and born again by the Holy Spirit and linked
to Christ in glory by the Spirit's baptism, and all
the divisions in Christendom cannot rend that
Body. But what have they done? They certainly
have denied the unity of the Spirit. The apostle
would have us recognize this unity which God
Himself has constituted, and so he says, "Endeavoring to keep the unity of the Spirit in the bond
of peace."

The Spirit unites us to that Body which He has
formed, and now He says, "I want you to recognize it." When you meet with fellow-believers, do
you endeavor to keep the unity of the Spirit, do
you realize that you belong to them and they belong to you? "But," you say, "they do not see
things the way I do." If they belong to Christ,
they belong to you and you to them. We are to
do this in the uniting bond of peace. Some years
ago I was taken ill in the midst of a series of
meetings at Minneapolis. After my fourth address
I went out one Sunday noon to take dinner, and

right after the meal I tumbled over, and when I regained consciousness I had a fever of one hundred and two degrees and was ill with typhoid. I was down for six weeks. As soon as I had strength enough to start home my friends helped me to the station. I could not walk alone, but they assisted me, and the porter was very courteous. He made up a berth and put both mattresses on, and let me recline there all day long. The first morning as I lay there with a lot of pillows behind me, I took out my Bible and was getting my morning portion. Of course you never start the day without at least a little portion from the Word of God; do you? You do? Well that is why you have so many bad days. I was reading from the Word of God when a rather stout-looking German lady came walking by, and she stopped and said, "Vat's dat? A Bible?" I said, "Yes." "Vell, you haf your morning worship all by yourself? Vait," she said, "I go get my Bible and we haf it together." She came back and settled herself on my couch and said, "Var are you reading?" A little later a tall gentleman came by, and stopped and said, "Reading the Bible! Vell, I tank I go get mine, too." He was a Norwegian, and he came back with his Bible, and in a few minutes I was amazed at the people who crowded around. They did the same thing every day, and we had a delightful time all the way to California. I would get my Bible, and then they would begin to come, and sometimes there would be as many as twenty-eight Bibles. The conductor would go all through the cars and say, "The camp-meeting is beginning in car number so-and-so. Any wanting to take advantage are invited." They sometimes got so full they would start a hymn, sometimes we would have a little prayer, and sometimes it would be only the Bible reading, and they would ask questions. That went on until we reached Sacramento, where some of the cars were to be cut off and go down the valley. So the people from the other cars came in to say good-bye, and this dear German sister came and said, "Oh, it has been just like a camp-meeting all the way. It has fed my soul. I am going to Turlock, but I want to ask you, What denomination are you?"

"Well," I said, "I belong to the same denomination that David did."

"What was that? I didn't know that David belonged to any."

"David said, 'I am a companion of all them that fear Thee and keep Thy precepts.'"

"Yah, yah," she said; "that is a good church to belong to."

Why, dear friends, I suppose if we had interrogated those people, we would have found that we belonged to a dozen different sects, but the blessed thing was, we found we were all one in Christ. Oh, that we might "endeavor to keep the unity of the Spirit in the bond of peace," not in contentiousness, not in quarreling, but all alike seeking to glorify the Lord Jesus Christ, our Saviour.

In the last three verses the apostle brings before us a sevenfold unity. Notice; "There is one Body, and one Spirit, even as ye are called in one hope of your calling; one Lord, one faith, one baptism, one God and Father of all, who is above all, and through all, and in you all." Seven different unities all linked up in one. One great confession, and yet it is easy to see that there are three distinct spheres indicated, becoming larger and larger. Verse four speaks of that unity which is absolutely vital, "There is one Body." That is the Body of Christ, and, as we have seen, that Body is composed only of people who have been washed from their sins in the blood of our Lord Jesus Christ, regenerated by the Word and by the Spirit, and thus made members of Christ. Then in the second place, "There is one Spirit," and this is the one Holy Spirit by whose operation we have been baptized into the Body of Christ. We read in 1 Corinthians 12:13, "For by one Spirit are we all baptized into one Body, whether we be bond or free; and have been all made to drink into one Spirit." "One Body, and one Spirit," and then, "one hope"—"Even as ye are called in one hope of your calling." All believers have the same blessed hope, the hope of some day, some day soon, beholding the face of our Lord Jesus

Christ and being transformed into His image. All real believers are included here—one Body, one Spirit, one hope of your calling.

But now the second sphere is a little bit wider. It does not necessarily include only those who are born again. It may include those who have made a profession which is not real. "One Lord, one faith, one baptism." You see, there are those who say, "Lord, Lord," who have never been born again. Jesus says that in the day of judgment many shall come to Him and say, "Lord, Lord, have we not prophesied in Thy name? and in Thy name have cast out devils? and in Thy name have done many wonderful works? And then will I profess unto them, I never knew you: depart from Me, ye that work iniquity." Take, for instance, the part of the world which we speak of as Christendom. What do people write at the head of their letters? They write 1936.* And what does that mean? It means, in the year of our Lord 1936. I suppose every racketeer and gangster in Chicago dates his letters that way. "Why call ye Me, Lord, Lord, and do not the things which I say?" (Luke 6:46). There are lots of hypocrites in Christendom who call Him Lord, and yet show by their lives that they have never been born again.

---

*This lecture was delivered in 1936.

Then there is the one faith. This is not the
faith by which we are saved, but the faith of the
Christian Church, the faith which was once for
all delivered to the saints. It is the one standard
of truth that God has given to be proclaimed in
the world, it is that which the apostle calls *the
faith*. Faith in Christ is confidence in Jesus, but
the faith is the body of the Christian doctrine.

Then there is baptism, the outward expression
of allegiance to Christ. Some say, "Do you think
that baptism here is water baptism, or the baptism of the Spirit?" I say without a moment's
hesitation, "Water baptism," for we have seven
unities. We have already had the baptism of the
Spirit, "one Body, one Spirit," and we do not have
the Spirit repeated here. If it were the baptism
of the Spirit, you would have only a sixfold unity,
but baptism is the outward expression of allegiance to Christ. A man may profess to belong to
Christ and be baptized, but that does not prove
he is really born again. The mark of Christ has
been put upon some men and yet they have never
truly received Him into their hearts. What a solemn thing this is! I wonder if any of you are in
the wider circle, you have never been born again,
you are not in the first circle but are among those
who have made profession, whether real or not,
and, therefore, are in the second circle. Can it
be that you have made a profession of Christ, that
the mark of Christ has been put upon you, that

you have been baptized in the name of the Father
and of the Son and of the Holy Ghost, and yet
have never trusted Christ? What an awful thing
for a lost one in the pit of woe to have to say, "I
bore Christ's mark on earth; I was baptized in
recognition of His death and suffering, and yet
here I am lost for all eternity because I did not
trust that Saviour who suffered for me."

Notice the third circle. This is very much wider
than the others, for it takes in God's relationship
to the entire creation. "One God," and as such
He is in relationship to all His creatures, "and
Father of all, who is above all, and through all,
and in you all." This is not the modern doctrine
of the universal Fatherhood of God and the universal brotherhood of man, but it means that God
is the Creator of all men. "One God and Father
of all, who is above all, and through all, and in
you all." He is a distinct Personality. This is not
pantheism, not God as a principle, but God, a
divine Personality, and yet immanent in grace,
not far from any one of us.

He is the living God, the divine Personality, the
transcendent God, God over all, pre-eminent, directing all things, pervading everything. He is
"in you all." That is the distinction between
God's attitude toward the world as a whole and
toward those who have been born again—"in you
all." If you have accepted Christ, if you have
trusted Him, God dwells in you. What a wonder-

ful truth, what a marvelous thing this is! He says, "I will dwell in them, I will walk in them." As we walk the streets we can realize that God is walking with us, and so we may well come back to the exhortation with which we began, "Walk worthy of the vocation wherewith ye are called."

GIFTS FROM THE ASCENDED CHRIST

✓ ✓ ✓

"But unto every one of us is given grace according to the measure of the gift of Christ. Wherefore He saith, When He ascended up on high, He led captivity captive, and gave gifts unto men. (Now that He ascended, what is it but that He also descended first into the lower parts of the earth? He that descended is the same also that ascended up far above all heavens, that He might fill all things.) And He gave some, apostles; and some, prophets; and some, evangelists; and some, pastors and teachers; for the perfecting of the saints, for the work of the ministry, for the edifying of the Body of Christ: till we all come in the unity of the faith, and of the knowledge of the Son of God, unto a perfect man, unto the measure of the stature of the fulness of Christ" (Eph. 4: 7-13).

✓ ✓ ✓

OUR attention in these verses is especially drawn to the gifts that the ascended Christ has bestowed upon His Church for its edification, its upbuilding. First observe that there are gifts for all—"Unto every one of us is given grace according to the measure of the gift of Christ." While there are certain outstanding gifts of what we might call a public character, yet it is blessed to realize that every member of the Body of Christ has something which he may contribute to the blessing of the whole. No matter how feeble, how insignificant, how relatively unknown he may be, he has received something from the risen Lord for the help of all the rest.

Just as there are many members of our physical bodies that are unseen, which function without any outward evidence of their working, and yet are very important in connection with the building of the body and the maintaining of it in health, so every believer has his place to fill in the Body of Christ. If he is not functioning according to the will of God, in some respect he affects the whole body for ill, but if he is functioning according to the will of God he affects the entire Body of Christ for good. These gifts come from the ascended Lord.

In verse 8 we read, "Wherefore He saith, When He ascended up on high, He led captivity captive, and gave gifts unto men." Our blessed Lord chose apostles when He was here on earth, but said that in the regeneration, that is, in the glorious Millennial age, they should sit on thrones judging the twelve tribes of Israel. As the ascended Christ He has given apostles and prophets to His Church, but they are given from heaven. They included the same apostles that He chose on earth, but it was after their enduement with the Holy Spirit at Pentecost, the Spirit that He Himself sent, that they were looked upon as given to the Church.

The passage here is quoted from Psalm 68: "Thou hast ascended on high, Thou hast led captivity captive." Just what is meant by that rather peculiar expression? It is a Hebraism. It is taken over literally from the Hebrew. Psalm 68: 18 reads: "Thou hast ascended on high, Thou hast led captivity captive: Thou hast received gifts for men: yea, for the rebellious also, that the Lord God might dwell among them." In the margin of our Authorized Version we have the suggestion that the expression, "Captivity captive," in Eph. 4, might be rendered, "a multitude of captives." That is an attempt to explain a rather peculiar phrase, but when we realize that this is simply a translation of an expression in the psalm, we have to inquire whether the Hebrew text could be translated, "A multitude of captives." I think any Hebrew scholar would acknowledge that it could not. And that is not the only place where this expression is found.

In Judges 5 you have the same expression. Deborah is praising the Lord for the great victory over Canaan. In verse 12 we read, "Awake, awake, Deborah: awake, utter a song: arise, Barak, and lead thy captivity captive, thou son of Abinoam." What does the expression mean there? It could mean only one thing—"Lead captive him who held you captive." That seems to be the meaning of Ps. 68: 18, and also of this quotation in the Epistle to the Ephesians.

In Isaiah 14 we have a similar expression which would be an adequate interpretation of the term. We read, "And the people shall take them, and bring them to their place: and the house of Israel shall possess them in the land of the Lord for servants and handmaids: and they shall take them captives, whose captives they were; and they shall rule over their oppressors" (Isa. 14: 2). This surely makes the meaning clear. In our present passage the teaching is this, that our blessed Lord in His triumph over death led captive him who had the power of death up to that time, that He might deliver those "who through fear of death were all their lifetime subject to bondage" (Heb. 2: 15). In other words, our mighty enemy, Satan, is now a conquered foe. He has been led captive at the chariot-wheels of Christ, and our Lord has now ascended as Man and taken His place upon the throne of the Majesty in the heavens, and there from His exalted seat in glory He gives these gifts to His Church for its edification and blessing. We are reminded that He who has gone up higher than any other man ever went, once for our redemption went down lower than any other man has gone.

"Now that He ascended, what is it but that He also descended first into the lower parts of the earth? He that descended is the same also that ascended up far above all heavens, that He might fill all things." I wonder if our souls really take in the fact that He is a Man like ourselves, only glorified, sinless, and holy, sitting today upon the throne of God, that a man's heart beats in His breast, and that there are no sorrows that come to His people but what He enters sympathetically, compassionately, into them, and therefore, having "not an high priest which cannot be touched with the feeling of our infirmities, but was in all points tempted like as we are," we may "come boldly unto the throne of grace, that we may obtain mercy, and find grace to help in time of need" (Heb. 4: 15, 16).

"There's a Man in the glory I know very well,
 I have known Him for years, and His goodness can tell;
 One day in His mercy He knocked at my door,
 And asking admittance knocked many times o'er;
 But when I went to Him and stood face to face
 And listened a while to His story of grace,
 How He suffered for sinners and put away sin,
 I heartily, thankfully, welcomed Him in."

And now I have the blessed assurance from the Word of God that that Man sits there at the Father's right hand ever living to make intercession for His needy people as they go through this scene.

Go to Him in the hour of trial, "tell not half the story, but the whole," and be assured that He will listen sympathetically and undertake for you according to the riches of His grace. He always has undertaken for His people in a marvelous way.

"He gave some, apostles; and some, prophets: and some, evangelists; and some, pastors and teachers; for the perfecting of the saints, for the work of the ministry, for the edifying of the Body of Christ." These are the gifts that Christ Himself has given. We have in 1 Cor. 12 special operations of the Holy Spirit which were for the Church in the beginning of its early conflict with heathenism, and in giving its chief testimony to Judaism. But here the gifts are for the edification, for the maintenance of the Church, given by the risen Christ to enable the Church to carry the message to a lost world, and to build up its individual members in the knowledge of Christ. The apostles and prophets laid the foundation. We read in Eph. 2: 20: "And are built upon the foundation of the apostles and prophets, Jesus Christ Himself being the chief corner stone." You do not lay a foundation for a building every few stories, but the foundation is built once for all, and then the superstructure is erected. Long ago, nineteen hundred years ago, the apostles and prophets fulfilled their ministry. We are not looking for new apostles and prophets.

A young Mormon elder came to me at one time and asked, "What church do you belong to?" I knew at once what he had in mind, and so I replied, "I belong to the one true Church that has apostles and prophets in it."

"Oh," he said, "then you must be a latter-day saint."

"No, I am a former-day saint."

"But ours is the only church that has apostles and prophets."

"I do not think so. The Church that I belong to is building upon the foundation of the apostles and prophets, and although they themselves have passed off the scene long ago they are still members of this Church, for it does not exist only on earth. They are part of the host though they have passed the flood and are in the presence of God. They are still members of the Church."

"But we have apostles and prophets in our day."

"But, you see," I said, "the apostles and prophets were to lay the foundation, and if I understand the Word of God aright, this blessed temple of the living God, this wonderful Church He is erecting, has been building for nineteen hundred years, and it is now just about completed, and you do not put a foundation on the roof. It is away down there nineteen hundred stories below, and the temple has been rising upon that foundation all through the years. We are now just putting the finishing touches on the roof. We are gathering in poor sinners, just one and another here and there. They are not coming in large numbers these days, but those that are coming are being builded in upon the roof, and it will not be long until it will be complete and then we will all go to heaven."

And now the other gifts are very manifest to-day. What is the evangelist? He is the bearer of glad tidings. The ministry of the evangelist is particularly to the world outside. If God gifts a man as an evangelist, He fills his heart with fervent love for a lost world, gives him the ability to proclaim the gospel in freshness and power. What a marvelous gift is that of the evangelist! We do not all have it in the way we should like to have it. It is a privilege to try to teach the Word, to seek to build up the saints, but when I think of the mighty men that God has qualified and sent forth as evangelists to win the lost, I covet such a gift. If you are a young preacher and have the evangelistic gift, thank God for it, cherish it, do not despise it. Do not say, "I wish I could teach the Bible like certain men, exhort like some of these wonderful men of God, explain the Scripture in the way that some can." It is very good if God gifts you for that, but I would rather be used of God to win poor sinners to Christ than even to teach and instruct Christians. Someone at one time reproved old Duncan Matheson for preaching the gospel at a great conference of believers, and said, "You kept all those people sitting here for an hour listening to what they already know, when they came to hear a wonderful unfolding of new truth."

"Why," he said, "were there no sinners here today?"

"Oh, there may have been a few."

"Very well, that is all right then; I did not make a mistake because, you know, if people are Christians, they will manage to wiggle awa' to heaven some way if they never learn another thing, but poor sinners will have to be saved or be in hell."

Never forget that. And if you are a poor sinner today, you are Christless, lost, hopeless. Let me impress it upon you. It must be Christ or hell, and to neglect the one is but to choose the other. I wish I could sound that out in a way that dying men would hear, and hearing would believe and flee from the wrath to come. That is the special province of the evangelist. He goes out into the world and wins souls for Christ, and then the Spirit of God brings them into the Church of God.

And then we read that He gave some, pastors. The word means "shepherds." A true pastor is a shepherd who has a heart for the sheep of Christ's flock. When our blessed Lord challenged Peter with the words, "Lovest thou Me more than these?" and after Peter earnestly confessed, "O Lord, Thou knowest all things, Thou knowest that I love Thee," Jesus said, "Feed My sheep, feed My lambs, shepherd My sheep," and in that He constituted Peter a pastor of His flock. What a blessed gift that is! The evangelist finds them as lost sheep wandering in the wilderness and brings them into the flock, and then the pastor seeks to lead them into the green pastures of God's Word, to minister to them when they are sick, to be with them when they are dying, to point them to the cross in the hour when faith may be weak, to enter into their sorrows; and that is what constitutes the work of a real pastor. No theological seminary, no college or university can make a pastor. It is the Holy Spirit of God alone who gives a man a pastor's heart, and fills him with yearning love for the people of God.

And then the next is that of the teacher. What is the difference between the pastor and the teacher? In 1 Corinthians 12:8 we read, "For to one is given by the Spirit the word of wisdom; to another the word of knowledge by the same Spirit." We may say that the pastor has in a peculiar sense the word of wisdom, the teacher the word of knowledge. It is the special province of the teacher to open up the truth of God's Word in a clear, orderly way so that people may grasp it and profit by it, that they may understand the divine plan and thus apply the truth to their own needs, and it is the responsibility of the pastor to press the truth home upon the conscience in the power of the Holy Spirit.

Do you ever remember an experience such as this? Maybe it was a time in your life when you were going through some special trial and perplexity, and you said, "I must find my way down to the place where the people of God are gathered." You entered in with a heavy burden. The meeting went on, and some one stood up to expound the Word of God, and you were edified. He took a certain portion of Scripture and made it clear and beautiful, and it did you good, but as you left the place you said, "Well, it didn't touch my case at all. I have no more light upon my trouble than I had when I came in. I am glad I came, for I was blessed. I shall always understand that portion of Scripture better than I have in the past. It was indeed good to be there." But you went away with the trouble, with the burden, with the perplexity. On another occasion you slipped down again, and this time some one read a portion of Scripture, and as he began to expound it you said, "Why, he seems to know exactly what I am going through. He seems to understand exactly what my trouble is. That is just what I need." And as the Word was unfolded your soul was stirred and your heart blessed, and you went away saying, "Blessed Lord, I thank Thee that Thou hast given such gifts to Thy people; I thank Thee that through the opening up of Thy truth my perplexity has been removed." You were listening to the teacher in the first case, and in the second to the pastor. One had the word of knowledge and the other the word of wisdom. What is wisdom? It is knowledge applied to meeting a distinct and definite case.

Look at verse 12. Why did He give apostles, prophets, evangelists, pastors, and teachers? "For the perfecting of the saints, for the work of the ministry, for the edifying of the Body of Christ." Now, just as you have it punctuated in our Authorized Version, what would you understand the work of these special gifts to be? Would you not take it that their ministry was threefold?—that the Lord had given pastors and teachers for three purposes, for the perfecting of the saints, for the work of the ministry, and for the edifying of the Body of Christ? And to what would that conclusion lead you? That the work of perfecting the saints and the work of the ministry and the edifying of the Body belongs entirely to those who have been set apart in a special way as pastors and teachers. That is the conclusion many have come to, and people are quite content to depend upon the man in the pulpit and say, "Don't we engage him to do the work of the ministry? Isn't he to do the work of edifying the Body of Christ?" But there are no punctuation marks in the original text; they have simply been put there by editors. I am going to take the liberty of removing these commas. Go back to verse 11, "He gave some, apostles; and some, prophets; and some evangelists; and some, pastors, and teachers; for the perfecting of the saints for the work of the ministry for the edifying of the Body of Christ." Do you see any difference? It is not that the pastors and teachers are a kind of close corporation whose business it is to do all these things. But when God gifts a man as a preacher or a teacher he is to exercise that gift for the perfecting, the developing, of the saints in order that *they* might do the work of the ministry and thus edify the Body of Christ. This is an altogether different thing. A dear young fellow came to me and said, "Are any of your sermons copyrighted?"

"No; indeed they are not," I said.

"I am glad to hear it, because I heard you a week ago and went out and preached your sermon at a mission. I wondered whether I had any right to do it."

I said, "If something gripped your soul that you can pass on to somebody else and make it a blessing to them, I thank God for it. If you get a convert, you will be the father and I will be the grandfather."

I read in Moody's life story that years ago he would go on Sunday morning to hear the different preachers of the day, and then in the afternoon and evening he would be out in the missions and on the street corners preaching. He would come back and say to one of these ministers, "Doctor, I preached your sermon five times last week, and won about forty souls," and the preacher would look at him in a queer way, for he had probably never seen a soul saved for weeks or months. The blessed risen Lord gives some the gift of apostles, some prophets, some evangelists, some pastors, and some teachers, but it is in order that all may profit thereby, for it is for the perfecting of the saints for the work of the ministry and for the edifying of the Body of Christ. Do not be content to come to meeting and just be a spiritual sponge. Fill up, and then let the blessed Lord do some squeezing. Give it out to somebody else, and then you will be carrying out the true principle of New Testament ministry.

How long will this go on? "Till we all come in the unity of the faith, and of the knowledge of the Son of God, unto a perfect man, unto the measure of the stature of the fulness of Christ." What does that mean? It means until at last the entire Church will be gathered home to heaven, and Christ will be fully displayed in every one of us. What is the fulness of Christ? We read in chapter 1:23: "Which is His Body, the fulness of Him that filleth all in all." Christ is the Head up there in glory, we are the members of His Body and constitute His completeness as the one new man. When at last we have gone home to heaven, our day of toiling over, and we are in all perfection like Himself, then this kind of ministry will be ended. There will be no room for the pastor, for the teacher, for the evangelist in heaven, for there we will all praise alike the name of our blessed Lord Jesus Christ, and none shall need to teach another for all shall know even as we have been known.

MANIFESTING THE TRUTH IN LOVE

✓ ✓ ✓

"That we henceforth be no more children, tossed to and fro, and carried about with every wind of doctrine, by the sleight of men, and cunning craftiness, whereby they lie in wait to deceive; but speaking the truth in love, may grow up into Him in all things, which is the Head, even Christ: from whom the whole Body fitly joined together and compacted by that which every joint supplieth, according to the effectual working in the measure of every part, maketh increase of the Body unto the edifying of itself in love" (Eph. 4:14-16).

✓ ✓ ✓

I NEVER knew until I became the father of children how much is involved in the words that occur in a well-known hymn,

"No infant's changing pleasure
Is like my wandering mind."

How children's minds jump from one thing to another! How hard it is for them to concentrate! And many of God's children are just the same. Very often when one is trying to open up some line of truth to believers, he is embarrassed by the questions that are asked showing that there is no concentration, no following up of the truth already before them, and as a result people are never truly established. It is in order to save us from this thing that God has set in His Church those who are responsible to instruct and build up His saints, that they should not be like little children tossed to and fro, like leaves carried about by the wind, or, using the figure the apostle has in mind, like little sail-boats on the water, carried hither and thither, blown from their course, and tossed by every changing wind.

It is a blessed thing to see Christians who are builded up by the Spirit of God in accordance with the truth. But so many always seem to be running after some new thing, never seeming to have any discrimination. Let me give you an absurd case. Years ago as I sat in my office in Oakland there came in through the bookroom a man whose very appearance betokened a heretic. He was tall and gaunt, had long flowing hair coming down over his shoulders, and a long unkempt beard. He came up to where I sat writing. I did not like to be interrupted, for I felt that he was going to waste my time with some religious oddity. He said, "I gather, sir, from the books I have seen in the window that you are a truth-seeker, and I thought I would come in and have a chat with you."

"You are mistaken," I said; "I am not a truth-seeker at all."

"Oh, you are not; may I ask why you are not?"

"Why, because, sir, I have found Him who is the Way, the Truth and the Life, and therefore my seeking is at an end. Once I was a truth-seeker, but now I am a truth-finder, for I know Christ."

"Well, but are there not many things that you still need to know?"

"Oh, yes; there are a great many things that I need to know, but I have found the great Teacher, and I am not going around seeking truth any longer. He instructs me through His Word."

"Well, as for me, I am always seeking; I go anywhere and everywhere that I think I can learn more."

"Yes," I said, "I was reading of you in my Bible the other day."

"Of me?"

"Yes."

"What did it say about me?"

"It said, 'Ever learning, but never able to come to the knowledge of the truth.'"

"Why, that has no reference to me," he said.

"Pardon me, but you said that you are always seeking and if a man is always seeking he is never finding. But, you see, those of us who know Christ have found Him and have been found of Him."

Then he began to impart some of his weird gospel to me and said, "But you don't know who I am."

"No," I said; "beyond what is written here I do not know who you are."

"I am one of the 144,000 of whom you read in Revelation."

"What tribe, please?" I asked.

"Well, the Lord knows; I don't," he said.

"Then you will have to excuse me for not taking your word for it and really believing that you are one of the 144,000."

"But have you not heard that the first resurrection has already taken place?" he asked. "I am in my resurrection body."

"Is that it you have with you?"

"Why, yes; this is my resurrection body."

"Oh, I am dreadfully disappointed," I said. "I never thought it would look like that. I thought it was to be something beautiful."

Maybe I was a little discourteous to the poor old gentleman, but he was so indignant he turned and cursed me in the name of the Lord, and tramped out, knocking his shoes against the floor to shake off the dust as a witness against me. "Ever learning, and never able to come to the knowledge of the truth."

That is an extreme case, but what a lot of folks there are like him in some degree, just running from one thing to another and never getting anywhere. The apostle says, "Hold fast the form of sound words," and you get sound words in the Book of God and nowhere else.

"That we henceforth be no more children, tossed to and fro, and carried about with every wind of doctrine, by the sleight of men." That is, men who have selfish purposes to serve, and want to make disciples in order to profit from them. "And cunning craftiness, whereby they lie in wait to deceive." When men come to you with strange and new things, Christian, ask for a "Thus saith the Lord," ask them to give chapter and verse in God's blessed Book for the strange doctrines they bring you. If Christians would only do this, they would not be running after these modern religious fads. Here you have something that has stood the test of nineteen hundred years. It is God's own blessed Word, and you can depend upon it. You can live upon it and as you feed upon the precious truth here revealed you will grow in grace and in the knowledge of our Lord and Saviour, Jesus Christ.

But now, although we want to be very insistent upon a good confession we need to be just as insistent upon a godly life and upon the manifestation of the Spirit of Christ, and so in the next verse we read, "But speaking the truth in love, may grow up into Him in all things, which is the Head, even Christ." It is an important thing to stand for the fundamentals, but as we seek to bear witness to the great fundamental truths, let us never forget that the greatest fundamental of all is love. "Though I have the gift of prophecy, and understand all mysteries, and all knowledge; and though I have all faith, so that I could remove mountains, and have not love, I am nothing. And though I bestow all my goods to feed the poor, and though I give my body to be burned, and have not love, it profiteth me nothing" (1 Cor. 13: 2, 3).

It is a very interesting fact that here in the original text there is only one Greek word for the three English words, "speaking the truth." In the original it is a present participle formed from the word "truth," and if we turn it into literal English we would have to render it in a rather awkward way. We would have to say "truthing." "But truthing in love." Perhaps a better rendering than "speaking the truth in love," and more suited to our ears, would be "manifesting the truth in love." In other words, it is not just the testimony of the lips, declaring that certain things are divine truth, but it is the life manifesting the truth. I have heard people say of certain ones, "Yes, yes; he seems to say things all right, but I do not see much evidence of divine love in his life." And then I have heard people sometimes bear witness of others in this way, "I believe in what Mr. So-and-So says because he lives it out from day to day."

A young man was asked the question, "What have you found to be the best translation of the New Testament?" Without a moment's hesitation he answered, "My mother's." His friend said, "Your mother's! I didn't know she was a scholar. Did she translate the New Testament?" "My mother was not a scholar, she could not read a word of Greek, but she translated the New Testament into her beautiful life, and that made more of an impression on me than anything else I have ever known." That is what you and I are called upon to do, to manifest the truth in our lives. The love of God has been shed abroad in our hearts by the Holy Spirit which was given unto us and now we are to be controlled by that Holy Spirit. We are to manifest the love of God in all our dealings with others. Even,

> "When truth compels us to contend,
> What love with all our strife should blend."

The Christian is never entitled to act in an un-Christlike way, no matter what the provocation. We are ever to be "truthing in love," and as we thus live in the power of the truth of God and are dominated by the love of Christ, we are growing up into Him, daily becoming more like Himself. Are people seeing more of Christ in you from day to day?

I remember years ago a young preacher coming to the city of Toronto, where I was born and where I lived until I was ten years old, and though I was only about eight years old at the time, I recall being taken by my mother to hear this

preacher, for she insisted that I must go and
hear the gospel every Sunday night. She used to
say, "It is far more important that my children
hear the gospel than that they have sleep, or anything else. They must know Christ from child-
hood up." Of course in Canada our gospel meeting used to begin at 6:30 o'clock, and little folk
could attend and still be home and in bed in good
time. Before I was ten years old I got to be
quite a sermon taster, as the Scotch used to say.
I loved to come home and get on a chair and
take off the preachers, trying to give the intona-
tions of their deep Scotch voices or those from the
north of Ireland, for all the preachers I ever heard
in those days had the old country twang. I listened to this young Irish preacher, a fine, tall,
handsome young man. A little group came home
with us after the meeting to spend an hour or so
in singing around the old-fashioned cabinet organ.
Someone asked the question, "How did you like
the young preacher from Ireland?" One replied,
"It did me good to hear the old tongue again. It
was just grand." Another said, "I thought he
had a splendid delivery; you could hear him so
plainly." Another, "He seemed to me to be most
eloquent." Another, "How well he knew his
Bible. He opened up the truth in a beautiful
way." A lady sitting quietly was asked, "And
what did you think of him?" "Well, you know,"
she replied, "there was something about his be-

havior that appealed to me. He seemed the most like Jesus of any preacher I have ever listened to." How one might wish to have that kind of recognition—to be like Him. Some of us, as we try to preach His Word, are made very conscious of the fact that we are so unlike Him. There is so much about us that would never have been seen in Him. Never a night but one has to bow the knee before God and acknowledge it, but as we walk with Him, as we seek to "truth" in love, we grow up into Him, and so we become more like Him as the days go by.

It is a beautiful thing to grow old gracefully, to manifest more of Jesus from day to day. Our blessed Head is the One from whom we draw all our supplies for spiritual upbuilding, and we read, "From whom the whole Body fitly joined together and compacted by that which every joint supplieth, according to the effectual working in the measure of every part, maketh increase of the Body unto the edifying of itself in love." It is just the figure of the human body, and every part, every separate organ, every joint and sinew, every gland, working for the upbuilding of the whole. That is the ideal picture of the Christian Church and of Christian fellowship. Have you ever read "Hebich's Tub?" It tells the story of a quaint Dutch preacher over in the East Indies. Many years ago he was conducting religious services for a group of British army officers. He was characterized by a shrewd, keen humor and pressed the truth home in the most amazing illustrations. He happened to know that there were certain little dissensions among the group, and so on one occasion he took for his text, "That which every joint supplieth," and went on to read, "According to the effectual working in the measure of every part." He looked at his audience, and then with his eyes half-shut he said, "Did you effer see a tob? What iss it that makes a good tob? If you haff a good bottom to it, iss that a tob? No. If you haff a good side, iss that a tob? No. If you haff good hoops around it, iss that a good tob? No. But if you haff good boards for the bottom and fitly choined together, and then the good boards for the sides all fitly choined together, and then the good hoops and all of these things fitly choined together, you haff a tob. And it is the same with the Christian Church. You haff got to haff every believer in his place, and all fitly choined together by the power of the Holy Spirit. You may haff all choined together, but iff there iss a little pebble in between two of the staves, you do not haff a tob that will hold water. Iff the staves haff shrunk and drawn apart, it is useless, and iff I am a Christian and haff some selfishness in me, iff through selfishness or envy I do not haff real Christian fellowship, or iff little things come in, I am useless. Iff the Colonel's lady has some unkind feeling toward the Major's lady and they come to church and join in prayer and in singing hymns and listen to the sermon, yet they are not fitly choined together, and you don't have real Christian fellowship." How many little things there are that come in to hinder and keep believers from functioning as they ought!

"Fitly joined together and compacted by that which every joint supplieth." You have to contribute your share and I have to contribute mine, all for the good of the whole. And then what? "According to the effectual working in the measure of every part, maketh increase of the Body unto the edifying of itself in love." May God give every one of us a deeper sense of our individual responsibility to manifest the truth in love for the blessing of all.

THE WALK OF THE NEW MAN

✓ ✓ ✓

"This I say therefore, and testify in the Lord, that ye henceforth walk not as other Gentiles walk, in the vanity of their mind, having the understanding darkened, being alienated from the life of God through the ignorance that is in them, because of the blindness of their heart; who being past feeling have given themselves over unto lasciviousness, to work all uncleanness with greediness. But ye have not so learned Christ; if so be that ye have heard Him, and have been taught by Him, as the truth is in Jesus: that ye put off concerning the former conversation the old man, which is corrupt according to the deceitful lusts; and be renewed in the spirit of your mind; and that ye put on the new man, which after God is created in righteousness and true holiness" (Eph. 4: 17-24).

✓ ✓ ✓

"THIS I say therefore"—we may well ask, "Wherefore?" In view of all that has come before us in the earlier part of this epistle, in view of the fact that we have been chosen in Christ before the foundation of the world that we should be holy and without blame before Him, in view of the fact that in love He has predestinated us unto the adoption of children by Christ Jesus unto Himself, in view of the fact that we have redemption through His blood, even the forgiveness of sins, according to the riches of His grace, in view of the fact that we have been made members of His Body, of His flesh, and of His bones, and are by the Spirit united to a risen Christ in glory—because of all these things, the apostle says, "I testify in the Lord, that ye henceforth walk not as other Gentiles walk." The Christian is called out from the world. His life is not to be as the lives of those about him. A very common saying is, "When you are in Rome, do as the Romans do," but that does not apply to the Christian. No matter where you find him, he is to walk as a heavenly man, as one whose interests are really in another scene, as a stranger and a pilgrim here. He is called upon to refrain from everything that would in any way tarnish his pilgrim character.

"Walk not as other Gentiles walk, in the vanity of their mind." The word translated "vanity" here does not mean what it does ordinarily. We usually think of it as meaning "pride." But the word here is not pride, the original word rather means something like a mirage, an illusion, that which is imagined but not actually true. Unsaved men have illusions of their own minds, they see mirages of all kinds and imagine them to be real, but they are not. They believe all sorts of theories, scholastic ideas, and such like, and would even bring this blessed Book to the bar of their theories instead of bringing their theories to the test of the Word of God. The Christian ought to be concerned about these things, and not walk in the delusions of the fleshly mind, for these poor Christless men, whatever their talents, whatever their culture, whatever their education, have the understanding darkened, have never been born of God, and are incapable of taking in divine things.

"The natural man understandeth not the things of God." I wish our Christian young people would realize that. I wish the Christian young men and women thronging our colleges (in many instances, unhappily, placed under the instruction of brilliant but unconverted professors, many of whom use their high office as an occasion to seek to undermine faith in the Word of God), could realize that the natural man, no matter what his intellectual qualifications, understands not the things of God; they are foolishness to him because they are spiritually discerned. Without a new life and a new nature there can be no real apprehension of divine things, and so the greatest of this world's sages is but as an ignoramus when it comes to the things of God, until he has been regenerated.

"Having the understanding darkened, being alienated from the life of God through the ignorance that is in them, because of the blindness of their heart." In other words, there is no divine life. Some say there is a divine spark in every man, but that is not true. "He that hath the Son hath life, but he that hath not the Son hath not life." Until Christ is received by faith, until people have accepted Him as their own Saviour and Lord, there is no life whatever except, of course, this material, this natural life. "Being alienated from the life of God through the ignorance that is in them." They are wise as to the things of this world, but utterly ignorant as to the things of God. "Because of the blindness of their heart." The word "blindness" is really "hardness," and yet that does not give the thought sufficiently. It means a heart that is under the influence of an anesthetic. A person may be alive and quivering with pain, but when he is put under the influence of an anesthetic he is not awake to the true condition of things. Men and women have come under the influence of the awful deadening power of sin and their hearts are hardened, they are blinded, and they do not understand the real state of affairs, they do not understand their own condition, the condition of their country or of the world around them. Sin has a terrible, hardening, blinding, deadening, effect upon people. The apostle describes the condition of the Gentile world in his day. Any one who is at all familiar with Greek and Roman literature, the literature of the great poets of the ancients, particularly the Comic poets, knows how very true is the description given here. How characteristic of society, too, in the days in which we live. Is it not true that the same fearful things that the ancients told of without a blush are practised in the world today in public and in secret? But Christians are called out from all this.

Notice the awfully graphic picture of the ancient world and the world today. "Who being past feeling have given themselves over unto lasciviousness, to work all uncleanness with greediness." "Being past feeling"—it might be translated, "Being beyond pain." Do you remember how pained you were the first time you committed some sin against which your conscience rebelled? The hour of temptation came, and you hesitated and said, "Shall I commit this sin or not?" Conscience was roused and you did not see how you could go on and indulge in that evil, unholy thing; but perhaps lured on by godless companions, who mocked at your conscientious scruples, you said, "Oh, I will try anything once," and you took the fatal step, you committed that sin and polluted your soul by it. But you remember the pain that came afterward, you remember as you walked home, or possibly it was in your own home, you could not bear the thought of facing those nearest and dearest to you. Perhaps you were not so much concerned about the fact that the eye of God was upon you as you ought to have been, but you were concerned about what others might think of you. The second time the temptation came, and again you plunged into the sin, more recklessly this time, and afterward the pain was less. And so, on and on and on, and now you continue in that sin, in that evil course, and there is scarcely ever the least evidence of an exercised conscience. We read of people whose conscience is seared as with a hot iron. Here you have the description of an unsaved man going contrary to every divine direction until he is beyond pain. That is what sin does for people. Oh, what a mercy when the Spirit of God comes in and awakens one to see something of the terribleness of sin in the sight of a holy God and leads him at last to Christ, and out of the depths of an anguished heart to cry, "What must I do to be saved? God be propitious to me, the sinner." There had been such crises in the lives of these Ephesians. Many of us have known what this means, and now these words of instruction come to us, as to them, regarding the walk that should characterize us.

We are not to be as we once were and as those still are who, having got beyond pain, have given themselves over to lasciviousness and all kinds of unholy thoughts resulting in unclean works. What a mercy that this is in the past for many of us. Am I speaking to anyone who is still living in these things? Does your heart sometimes cry out with a desire for purity, for holiness, for goodness? Do you sometimes say:

> "Tell me what to do to be pure
> In the sight of all-seeing eyes.
> Tell me, is there no thorough cure,
> No escape from the sins I despise?

    Will the Saviour only pass by,
        Only show me how faulty I've been?
    Will He not attend to my cry?
        May I not this moment be clean?"

Oh, yes; there is cleansing for you. "Come now, and let us reason together, saith the Lord; though your sins be as scarlet they shall be as white as snow; though they be red like crimson, they shall be as wool" (Isa. 1: 18). They tell me that two of our Chicago professors have gotten out a new Bible in which they have turned these two wonderful statements into questions, but I challenge any man who knows a word of Hebrew to look them up and see if they do not stand exactly as written in our Bible. It is the unbelief of the natural heart that would put a question-mark here, where God has made everything so clear. There is heart purity for the sinner, there is a possibility that the dark red stains of sin may all be washed away, for it is written, "The blood of Jesus Christ, God's Son, cleanseth us from all sin," and one thus cleansed should be characterized by an altogether different walk to that which is common to the unsaved.

The apostle goes on to say, "But ye have not so learned Christ; if so be that ye have heard Him, and have been taught by Him, as the truth is in Jesus." I want you to notice particularly the way he uses the divine titles. We know that Jesus is Christ and Christ is Jesus. We do not for one moment consent to the wretched theory that a good many hold today, the one that has been popularized by Mrs. Mary-Baker-Patterson-Glover-Eddy in her false religion in which she tries to draw a distinction between Jesus and Christ. According to that system, Jesus was simply a man, the natural born son of Mary, but Christ was a divine Spirit that came and took possession of Jesus at His baptism in the Jordan. That is an old gnostic heresy condemned by every right-minded Christian. Jesus is the Christ. "Whosoever confesseth that Jesus is the Christ is born of God." But although that is true, this is also true, Jesus was His human name here on earth, He never had that name until He came to earth. Scripture says, "Thou shalt call His name Jesus; for He shall save His people from their sins." But He was Christ from all eternity. In the eighth chapter of Proverbs, wisdom is personified, and we read, "I was set up from everlasting, from the beginning of His way, before His works of old." The Hebrew term, "Set up," is the same word for Messiah, or Anointed. "I was the Anointed, I was Messiah from everlasting, I was the Anointed from the past eternity." Then, when the Spirit of God came upon Him after His baptism in the Jordan, He was the Anointed, the Christ, in a new sense. And when God raised Him from the dead, we read He made that same Jesus to be both Lord and Christ! He is the Anointed now as the risen and glorified One.

And now Paul says, "Ye have not so learned Christ;" and he is thinking of Him as the risen One, Christ sitting at the right hand of God, and we learn of Him as we take time to behold Him. "But we all, with open face beholding as in a glass the glory of the Lord, are changed into the same image from glory to glory, even as by the Spirit of the Lord" (2 Cor. 3:18). "But ye have not so learned Christ; if so be that ye have heard Him, and have been taught by Him, as the truth is in Jesus." What does he mean by that? He means this, that when He trod this earth as the lowly Man, Jesus, in His life He was the manifestation of the truth. That is why He could say, "I am the Way, the Truth and the Life." Suppose I want to know the truth about man, what God's thought about man is, where do I find it? In Adam? Oh, no. In Adam I see a man who listened to his wife, after she listened to the devil, and did what she told him to do, a man without a backbone, a man utterly untrustworthy. Go down all through human history, and every other man is just a reproduction of that first man. But if I want the truth concerning man, I find that it is written, "There is one Mediator between God and men, the Man Christ Jesus," and so we see in Him as Man here on earth all that man should be for God. It is the full standard of humanity as God reveals it in His Word.

If I want to know the truth about God, where

do I find it? Do I go to the universities of this world? No; they do not know anything about God. They cannot tell me anything about Him. But where shall I go? To a lot of modernistic churches, with their unconverted preachers? They do not know anything more about God than unconverted college professors. Well, then, where shall I go? To Creation? Out in the woods? Out playing golf on Sunday? No, you will not find out about God there. You will get some evidences of His power and wisdom, but you will not find anything about His love and holiness there. Where do you learn about Him? In Christ. "He that hath seen Me hath seen the Father." The truth has been made known in Jesus.

Suppose I want to find out about sin, where will I go? To some of our modern, humanistic philosophies, to some of these teachers who talk about behaviorism and actually try to make men and women believe that every tendency within is perfectly lawful and perfectly right? No; not there. But where? In the cross of Jesus. There, as I behold Him, my blessed Saviour, taking the sinner's place, I see what sin deserved. The truth is in Jesus, and Christ in glory points me back to Jesus on earth and says, "If you want to know how you should walk as you go through this world, there is where you will find it." "Christ also suffered for us, leaving us an example, that ye should follow His steps" (1 Pet. 2: 21).

But how will I be able to walk like this? I have an old nature, I once had a corrupt, sinful life, how am I going to walk aright? Here is what Jesus teaches. "That ye put off concerning the former conversation the old man, which is corrupt according to the deceitful lusts; and be renewed in the spirit of your mind; and that ye put on the new man, which after God is created in righteousness and true holiness." What do I mean when I speak of the old man? Some people confound the old man with the old nature. You see, the old man is more than the old nature. The old man is the man of old, what you once were before you were converted. Now you are through with the man of old. If you are a Christian, you are not to live like that man any longer, but you are now to live in accordance with the truth of the new man. And who is the new man? The new man is the man of whom the Apostle Paul speaks in 2 Corinthians 12: "I knew a man in Christ ... of such an one will I glory." A man in Christ— that is the man that I now am through infinite grace. But I am through with the old man, the man after the flesh. I have put him off, his tastes, his appetites, all that he once delighted in, and I am learning the truth as it is in Jesus.

The old man was corrupt according to the deceitful lusts, and in these we once walked in our unconverted days. But now a great change has taken place, we have been born again. That does not mean we have attained perfection. The Apostle Paul said, "Not as though I had already attained, either were already perfect: but I follow after, if that I may apprehend that for which also I am apprehended of Christ Jesus. Brethren, I count not myself to have apprehended: but this one thing I do, forgetting those things which are behind, and reaching forth unto those things which are before, I press toward the mark for the prize of the high calling of God in Christ Jesus."

"And be renewed in the spirit of your mind." A better rendering is, "Being renewed in the spirit of your mind." In what sense am I being renewed in the spirit of my mind? How am I being renewed in my physical strength? As I am careful to eat those foods that are nourishing and that will help me to build a strong body. Then how am I renewed in the spirit of my mind? As I feed upon His Word, as I enjoy communion with Him, enjoy fellowship with His beloved people. In all these ways we are being renewed in the spirit of our minds. You never saw a strong Christian who was not a Bible-loving Christian. You never saw a strong Christian who was not one who delighted in communion with fellow-believers. Where you find people who cannot have anything to do with other Christians, who go about with the "I am holier than thou" attitude, you will never discern much real holiness in their lives.

"Being renewed in the spirit of your mind; and

putting on the new man, which after God is created in righteousness and true holiness." Righteousness is my behavior manward. I am to be righteous in my dealings with my fellow-man. It does not mean that I can be careful about my devotion to Christ and careless in regard to my life among others. A man got up in a meeting one day and said, "I want to tell you that I am standing in Christ on redemption ground." Another man arose and said, "I want to call that man down. He says he is standing in Christ on redemption ground. I do not believe a word of it. He is standing in a pair of shoes he bought from me months ago, and he has not paid for them yet." Righteousness is right dealing between men. The person who professes to be a Christian and is not careful about that which is right, is a disgrace to the name of the Lord Jesus Christ.

Holiness has to do with my attitude toward God. It is of the heart, it is the inward life, holiness of thought, a heart separated to God in accordance with the truth of His holy Word. This is practical Christianity, and this is how you and I are called to manifest the new life, to manifest the fact that we belong to a new creation.

Have I been setting the standard too high? I have not been setting it at all. I have been giving it to you from the Word of God.

Unsaved one, are you saying, "I should like to

reach this standard, but I do not see how I ever could"? You cannot. With all your trying you will never be able to reach it. Come to God as a poor, lost sinner, give up your trying, put your trust in the Lord Jesus Christ, and He will give you a new heart, a new nature, and will enable you to live to His glory.

GRIEVE NOT THE HOLY SPIRIT

✦ ✦ ✦

"Wherefore putting away lying, speak every man truth with his neighbor: for we are members one of another. Be ye angry, and sin not: let not the sun go down upon your wrath: neither give place to the devil. Let him that stole steal no more: but rather let him labor, working with his hands the thing which is good, that he may have to give to him that needeth. Let no corrupt communication proceed out of your mouth, but that which is good to the use of edifying that it may minister grace unto the hearers. And grieve not the Holy Spirit of God, whereby ye are sealed unto the day of redemption. Let all bitterness, and wrath, and anger, and clamor, and evil speaking, be put away from you, with all malice: and be ye kind one to another, tender-hearted, forgiving one another, even as God for Christ's sake hath forgiven you" (Eph. 4: 25-32).

✦ ✦ ✦

THE most important part of this entire section is verse 30, "And grieve not the Holy Spirit of God, whereby ye are sealed unto the day of redemption." The term, "grieve" means "to give pain." Give not pain to the Holy Spirit of God. How may we pain Him? By walking in disobedience to any of the admonitions that are given us in this particular section. We have here the behavior that should characterize a believer. We have seen something of our wonderful privileges, our great blessings in Christ in the heavenlies, and now we are considering that part of the epistle which stresses for us our practical responsibilities.

It is a poor thing to talk of living in the heavenlies if we are walking with the world. It is most inconsistent to glory in our privileges in Christ if we are behaving according to the flesh. And so here the apostle emphasizes the importance of true Christian living. He says, in verse 25, "Wherefore putting away lying, speak every man truth with his neighbor; for we are members one of another." We have seen how the exalted Christ in glory turns our hearts back to consider the blessed example set us by Jesus as He walked through this scene, that we may consider the truth as it is in Jesus. They came to Him on one occasion and said, "Whom makest Thou Thyself?" And He said (using the exact rendering), "Altogether what I say unto you." What a tremendous statement, nothing covered, nothing hidden, no sham, no pretence; He was exactly the same in the presence of God as He was before men. This indeed is truth in life, and you and I who have put our trust in Him are called to put away everything that is false.

The word translated "lying" is simply the Greek word that we have taken over into the English, *pseudo*—"that which is false." We are to put away everything that is merely pretence or sham, and speak every man truth with his neighbor. The Christian is called to be punctilious, to be honest even in little things, not to make bargains that he does not keep. If a business man, he is not to over-state the case when trying to sell something. In Proverbs we read, "It is naught, it is naught, saith the buyer: but when he is gone his way, then he boasteth" (Prov. 20 : 14). Even that is contrary to the Holy Spirit of God. The Christian is called on to be true in everything; true in his behavior, true in his speech.

Notice the motive given, "For we are members one of another." He is thinking especially here, of course, of our relation to fellow-believers, as though he would say, "Why should you attempt ever to deceive a fellow-believer? Why should you ever be false to another child of God? Why should you pretend to something that is not true when dealing with another Christian? Why should you be unfaithful to a member of the same Body to which you yourself belong?" Can you imagine members of our natural bodies being false to one another? What is for the good of one is for the good of all; and so in the Body of Christ, what is for the good of one member is for the good of all, and the Christian is called to see that he never defaults in any way in his dealings with a fellow-Christian.

Then we read in verse 26, "Be ye angry, and sin not: let not the sun go down upon your wrath: neither give place to the devil." This verse has perplexed many people. Some imagine that it is always wrong to be angry. There are circumstances under which it would be very wrong not to be angry. Our blessed Lord though absolutely perfect in His humanity was angry on more than one occasion. He saw the pretentious Pharisees going in and out of the temple of God with a great air of sanctity, and yet He knew some of them held mortgages on widows' homes, and when occasion arose they foreclosed on them and turned them out into the streets because they could not meet their obligations. Our Lord's indignation was aroused, His anger flamed up, and He said, "Woe unto you, scribes and Pharisees, hypocrites; for ye devour widows' houses, and for a pretence make long prayer: therefore ye shall receive the greater damnation" (Matt. 23:14). If my spirit would not be stirred to indignation by anything of the kind today, I am not the sort of Christian I ought to be. If I were to see a great brute of a fellow abusing a little child and were to pass by with that sweet simpering Christian Science smile that says, "Oh, well; everything is lovely; God is good and good is God; all is God and God is all, and there is nothing wrong in the world," and would not be stirred to anger, I would be a cad and not a Christian. There is an anger that is righteous. We read that our Lord Jesus on one occasion "looked round about on them with anger, being grieved for the hardness of their hearts." How, then, am I to be angry and sin not? A Puritan has put it this way, "I am determined so to be angry as not to sin, therefore to be angry at nothing but sin."

You see the moment self comes in, my anger is sinful. You do me a wrong and I flare with anger. That is sin. But you blaspheme the name of my Saviour and if I am not stirred to anger, that is sin. If I am wholly reconciled as I should be, it will arouse my indignation when I hear His name blasphemed, or see the truth dragged in the dust. But so far as I am concerned, I am to suffer all things, I am to endure all things. Men may count me as the offscouring of the earth, they may do the worst they can against me, but if I become angry, I sin, for self is the object there.

Who is there then that is sinless? No one. That is why He says, "Let not the sun go down upon your wrath." If you are stirred to sinful anger, if you flare up, see then that you do not retire to your bed at night before you confess your sin. If you have given vent to indignation before another, see that you confess it to him. Many people have said to me, "I have such a bad temper. I have tried so hard to overcome it, but I get angry and say things that I regret afterwards, and I make up my mind never to do it again, but I am sure to fail." I usually ask this question, "Do you make it a practice, when you have given utterance to angry exclamation, to go to the person before whom you have sinned and confess it?" Sometimes I get this answer, "No, I never cherish anything; I flare up, and then it is all over." Yes, but the memory is not all over. The other person remembers it. If every time you sin through anger you would go immediately to the one sinned against, and confess and ask forgiveness, you would soon get tired of going so often and you would put a check upon yourself. It would not be so easy to fly off the handle. But as long as you can flare up and pay no attention to it, or, while you may confess it to God you do not do so to your brother, you will find the habit growing on you.

This expression, "Be ye angry, and sin not," is a direct quotation from the Septuagint translation of Psalm 4: 14. Our English version reads, "Stand in awe, and sin not: commune with your own heart upon your bed, and be still." The Hebrew word translated, "stand in awe" is a word that means, "tremble," and our translators rendered it, "Stand in awe"—tremble at the presence of God. But that is not necessarily all that it means. The Septuagint made it read, "Be ye angry, and sin not." These words were probably recorded at the time that David was fleeing from Absalom, his own son, and his heart was stirred as he thought of the unfilial character of his son's behavior. That son for whom he had so often prayed was bringing dishonor upon the name of the Lord, and it moved his heart to indignation. But he said, "I am not going to sleep tonight until all that indignation is quieted down —'Stand in awe, and sin not: commune with your own heart upon your bed, and be still.' " Just get quietly into the presence of God and then you will be able to look at things from a right standpoint, and as you think of your own failures, of the many, many times that God in grace has had to forgive you, it will make you very lenient as you think of the failures of others, and instead of getting up on the judgment-seat and judging another believer, it will lead you to self-judgment and that will bring blessing, whereas the other is only harmful to your own spiritual life.

"Let not the sun go down upon your wrath: neither give place to the devil." Why? Because anger cherished becomes malice, and Satan works through a malicious spirit. He seeks to get control of Christians and have them act in malice toward fellow-believers. All this grieves the Holy Spirit of God. These are searching things, and we have to take them each for himself. "The Word of God is quick, and powerful, and sharper than any two-edged sword, piercing even to the dividing asunder of soul and spirit, and of the joints and marrow, and is a discerner of the thoughts and intents of the heart" (Heb. 4:12). Let us not avoid it but face it honestly.

"Let him that stole steal no more: but rather let him labor, working with his hands the thing which is good, that he may have to give to him that needeth." There is many a person who steals who would not like to be called a thief. We have names for stealing that sound much better, for instance, "pilfering," and "purloining." They mean the same thing but do not sound quite as bad as "stealing." But the Spirit of God covers them all in this, "Let him that stole steal no more." Let him that appropriated that to which he had no right, steal no more. The Christian is to be intrinsically honest. You know, it is easy to become slack along these lines. It is easy, if you are working in an office, for instance, to say to yourself, "Oh, well; they don't pay me anything like what I am worth, and therefore there are certain little things about the office I can claim." I knew one young man who had a habit of stealing lead pencils until he had accumulated a gross of them, and then his conscience smote him, and the day came when he had to go back to the boss with the lead pencils and say, "I am a Christian and I am returning these pencils to you." Christians are called upon to be faithful in very small things, things that others may not pay any attention to at all. What a pity that sometimes Christians cannot be trusted. The child of God ought to be one who can be trusted anywhere, one who will be faithful in another man's things just as much as in his own things.

But it is not enough that we refrain from thievery. The Law says, "Thou shalt not steal," but grace comes in and how much higher is the standard set under grace than that under Law! It is not only, "Let him that stole steal no more," but he adds, "But rather let him labor, working with his hands the thing which is good, that he may have to give to him that needeth." I could live up to the righteousness that is in the Law if I refrained from taking what is another's, but I cannot live up to the holiness of grace except as I share with others what God in His kindness gives to me. What a wonderful standard is that of Christianity.

And then in verse 29 we have the care of the tongue. The Psalmist says, "Set a watch, O Lord, before my mouth, keep the door of my lips." And James says, "If any man offend not in word, the same is a perfect man, and able also to bridle the whole body" (James 3:2). I have met some "perfect" people. I knew they were perfect because they told me so; but when I was with them a while and listened to their speech, heard their careless, worldly chatter, noticed how critical of other people they were, heard the unkind, cutting remarks they could make concerning other people, I knew their perfection was all a delusion.

"If we say we have no sin, we deceive ourselves and the truth is not in us." Here the apostle says, "Let no corrupt communication proceed out of your mouth." Corrupt communication comes from the old nature which is corrupt. You see, the new nature produces holy communication; the old, the corrupt nature, produces corrupt communication. "Let no corrupt communication proceed out of your mouth, but that which is good to the use of edifying, that it may minister grace unto the hearers." "Oh," says somebody, "this is where my trouble is. My tongue is always getting into difficulty. I make up my mind never to say anything unkind, and the next instant my tongue seems to be set on a pivot." Very well, when you find that you just must talk and you cannot stop, say, "Now, Lord, this tongue of mine wants to get going; help me to say something good." And then quote some Scripture and speak of the grace of the Lord Jesus Christ, tell that which is good for the building up of your hearers, and you won't go away with regrets and at the close of the day have to get down on your knees and say, "O Lord, forgive me for my careless chatter and un-Christianlike words today." We are not cut out to be dumb, some of us like to talk, but we are to talk about good things, we are to let Christ be the burden of our speech, to present Him to others.

I have known men with whom it was a delight

to spend a little time because I never went from their company without learning more of the Lord Jesus. I am thinking of a friend of mine in whose company I have never been for ten minutes but what he would say to me, "You know, I was thinking of such and such a scripture, and while I was meditating the Spirit gave me such and such a thought." How different it is with others at times. How different it has been many, many times with this tongue of mine. What sorrows it has brought upon me, speaking unadvisedly with the lips. "Let no corrupt communication proceed out of your mouth, but that which is good to the use of edifying (that is, for the building up of those to whom you speak) that it may minister grace unto the hearers."

And now we come to the crucial text—"And grieve not—pain not—the Holy Spirit of God, whereby ye are sealed unto the day of redemption." As we have already seen, the Spirit of God dwells in each believer, a divine Person, a blessed, heavenly Guest, and He is listening to everything you say and is taking note of everything you do. All that is said, all that is done contrary to the holiness of Christ and to the righteousness of God, grieves that blessed indwelling Holy Spirit. Have you ever known what it was to have some one in the house who did not approve of anything you were doing? Perhaps they did not say anything, but you had the sense that they did not like things. That is the way it is with the Spirit of God if a believer is not walking in accordance with the truth.

Do we read, "Grieve not the Holy Spirit of God, lest you should grieve Him away?" No, you are not going to grieve Him away. Jesus said, "I shall send you another Comforter, that He may abide with you forever." When He comes to indwell a believer, He never leaves. David, in the Old Testament dispensation, said, "Take not Thy Holy Spirit from me," but in the glorious dispensation of grace, that prayer is not becoming to our lips, for when He comes to indwell us, He never leaves us until we are presented faultless in the presence of the Lord Jesus Christ. But the point is just this, He does not leave, He dwells within, but is grieved all the time that we are walking in disobedience to the Word. That is why many of us are never very happy; that is why we do not enjoy communion with God, that is why we are not singing songs of victory. You see, as long as the Holy Spirit dwells in me ungrieved He is free to take of the things of Christ and show them unto me, and that fills my heart with gladness. But the moment I begin to grieve Him He stops doing the work He delighted to do, He is not free to open these things to me. He has to occupy me with my own failure and sin until I confess it.

Then, I have the joy of knowing that I am

sealed—how long? "Unto the day of redemption."
What does he mean by that? Is not the day of
redemption the day Christ died on Calvary's
cross? That was when Jesus died to redeem my
soul. But there is the coming day of the redemption of the body when the blessed Lord will return
again to transform these bodies of our humiliation and make them like unto His own glorious
body. It is the redemption referred to in Romans
8:22, 23: "For we know that the whole creation
groaneth and travaileth in pain together until
now. And not only they, but ourselves also, which
have the first-fruits of the Spirit, even we ourselves groan within ourselves, waiting for the
adoption, to wit, the redemption of our body."
We are sealed unto the redemption of our bodies.
When we get that, the old nature will be gone, we
will not have to be on our guard any more against
grieving the Holy Spirit. It is here and now in
this body that we need to watch against this
thing.

He concludes this section by saying, "Let all
bitterness, and wrath, and anger, and clamor, and
evil speaking, be put away from you, with all
malice." I wish that as Christians we would let
the Word of God have its way with us! Is there
any bitterness in your heart against any one on
earth? Do you say, "But you don't know how I
have been tested, how I have been tried, insulted,
offended?" If you had not been offended there

would be no reason for the bitterness at all, but he says, "Let all bitterness, and wrath, and anger, and clamor, and evil speaking, be put away from you, with all—a-l-l—malice." Now, you see, if you do not live up to that, you are not living a real Christian life. This is Christianity in the power of the Holy Ghost. And we are not merely told to put these things away, there must be the positive side.

"Be ye kind one to another, tender-hearted, forgiving one another, even as God for Christ's sake hath forgiven you." To what extent must I forgive? "I have forgiven over and over and over again, and I cannot go on forgiving forever," you say. Wait a minute. What does the apostle say about the extent to which we are to forgive? "Even as God for Christ's sake hath forgiven you." Can you ever get beyond that? Has any one ever wronged you as much as you wronged God? But if you have trusted the Saviour, God in Christ has forgiven you all your trespasses. Now this is the standard for Christians, we are to forgive one another even as God in Christ has forgiven us.

CLEAN CHRISTIANS

✓ ✓ ✓

"Be ye therefore followers of God, as dear children; and walk in love, as Christ also hath loved us, and hath given Himself for us an offering and a sacrifice to God for a sweet-smelling savor. But fornication and all uncleanness, or covetousness, let it not be once named among you, as becometh saints; neither filthiness, nor foolish talking, nor jesting, which are not convenient; but rather giving of thanks. For this ye know, that no whoremonger, nor unclean person, nor covetous man, who is an idolater, hath any inheritance in the kingdom of Christ and of God. Let no man deceive you with vain words: for because of these things cometh the wrath of God upon the children of disobedience. Be not ye therefore partakers with them" (Eph. 5:1-7).

✓ ✓ ✓

THE city in which the church was found to which this letter was addressed, abounded with iniquity of the vilest kind, and it was therefore of great importance that the early Christians should be warned of the danger of following in the ways of those still in their sins, and it is just as necessary today. The human heart is unchanged and with all our veneer of civilization unmentionable vilenesses are practised throughout the length and breadth of our land, enough to cause every Christian heart to shudder and make one feel the importance of living very close to the Lord Jesus Christ that we may be kept from these evil things.

Notice upon what the apostle bases the call to clean living. "Be ye therefore followers of God, as dear children." "Therefore," that is, of course, because of what he has told us in the previous verses. He has told us that God for Christ's sake has forgiven us; which means that God thought enough of us to send His only begotten Son into the world that we might live through Him, that God was as in Christ reconciling the world unto Himself, not imputing men's trespasses unto them; but those trespasses were imputed to Him, the Holy One, when He took our place and bore our shame, endured the judgment due to our sins —because of this, let us walk now in such a way as to manifest the gratitude of our hearts for so great salvation. "Be ye therefore followers of God, as dear children."

The word rendered, "followers," really means "imitators." "Be ye therefore imitators of God." In what sense are we to imitate God? One thinks of a passage in the Old Testament where God said to His people, "Ye shall put out of the camp of Israel every leper"—every one who hath any kind of a vile, infectious disease; not only for the safety of those who were not yet infected, but the singular thing about it was that back in the Law the reason given is this, "Because ye shall be holy, for I the Lord thy God am holy." And as in the legal dispensation all physical uncleanness was looked upon as a thing accursed and not fit for the holy presence of God, so today all uncleanness of the flesh and spirit must be put away if we would walk in fellowship with the Holy One. To imitate Him in holiness of life, to imitate Him in purity of thought, to imitate Him in cleanness of speech as His dear children, children in whom He can delight—this is what we are called upon to do.

You parents know how there are times when your own children, much as you love them, cause you sorrow and grief if they walk in disobedience, if they fall into anything that dishonors the family name, anything that grieves your heart, and so it is with God's children. The least sin indulged in by His children grieves the Holy Spirit. If we would be His dear children, in the sense of children in whom He can delight, we must walk before Him as imitators of God and "walk in love, as Christ also hath loved us, and given Himself for us an offering and a sacrifice to God for a sweetsmelling savor." The reference here, of course, is to the burnt offering. In the burnt offering spoken of in the first chapter of Leviticus we have the offerer coming to God with a sacrifice, not merely because of any sin committed, but because his heart is filled with thanksgiving and he wants to present something to God as an expression of his loving adoration. And so there is one aspect of the work of our Lord Jesus Christ on the cross that rises far above the mere meeting of our need; it has in view the glorifying of God in the scene where He had been so terribly dishonored.

The Lord Jesus said to His disciples on the last night on which He was betrayed as they sat with Him at the table, "That the world may know that I love the Father, and as the Father hath given Me commandment even so I do. Arise, let us go hence." And He went out to die. Why did He endure that death upon the cross? His first object was the glory of the Father. God had been terribly dishonored by the first man and all that had come after him, but here at last was a Man who walked this scene in absolute holiness. He said, "I seek not Mine own will, but the will of the Father which hath sent Me" (John 5:30), and to do the will of God He went to that cross. He went there to settle the sin-question for us, but above everything else it was to show that at least one Man had been found to whom the glory of God meant more than anything else, to whom the will of God meant more than any personal desires that He Himself might have had. And so in Gethsemane's garden we hear Him saying, "Nevertheless not as I will, but as Thou wilt." This is the great Burnt Offering. He offered

Himself without spot *to God* a sacrifice of sweet-smelling savor. But we are not left out. He offered Himself *for us,* a sacrifice of sweet-smelling savor to God for us. And since we have thus been redeemed, what manner of persons ought we to be in all holy conversation and godliness?

It is always with a shock that the sensitive soul turns to the next verse, and is brought up against terms that speak of the vilest corruption of which the human heart is capable. This is given that we may realize that all these things must be judged if we would now walk with Him who has redeemed us to God. And so we read, "But fornication, and all uncleanness (impurity), or covetousness, let it not be once named among you, as becometh saints." The word rendered "covetousness" does not refer here to greed for money. It is, rather, sensual greed. It is that vile, disgusting greed for sensual gratification, the vilest thing of which the human heart is capable. Is it possible that saints of God need to be warned against these things? Yes; because in every believer there is the same corrupt nature that there is in the man or woman of the world. It is true that the saint has received a divine nature and the Holy Spirit of God has come to dwell in him, but, nevertheless, he must always watch against the least activity of that old nature lest he fall into sin through not judging its first motions toward that which is evil.

"Fornication, and all uncleanness" (or sensual greed). These things are in the very air around us. Modern literature is full of them, and the worst of it is that people glory in their vileness. But some say, "Well, our modern writers at least are very frank; they show up sin as it really is." Yes, frank enough in the way they speak of it, disgustingly so, and yet they seem to throw a halo about it as though these unclean things are so natural to human beings that no one need be ashamed of them. And the world is fast getting to the place our Lord Jesus Christ predicted it would just before His second coming. He said, "As it was in the days of Noah, so shall it be also in the days of the Son of Man," and, "As it was in the days of Sodom and Gomorrah so shall it be at the coming of the Son of Man." The days of Noah were days of great corruption and violence. The days of Sodom and Gomorrah were days of unmentionable vileness, and we are living in very similar times. All of our boasted civilization has not changed the tendency of the human heart one iota, and the child of God is to guard against every evil tendency. The first approach to it is always in the mind, and so He warns against impure thoughts. We are not to indulge in thoughts that are impure. We are to guard against lust of every description. Can you think of any greed more dreadful, more vile, more disgusting than that which would lead one to plot the ruin of an innocent young girl's life? It would break the heart of parents who have tried to bring up a precious daughter in the right way, if one came in and sought to turn her away from the path of goodness and purity. Can you think of anything more dreadful than an attempt to break up a happy home by coming between husband and wife, turning one or the other aside from the path of rectitude and right? And yet these things abound everywhere. This is the greed about which the apostle warns us. The pathetic thing is that people look with such indifference upon these things.

Notice what we read in verse 4, "Neither filthiness, nor foolish talking, nor jesting, which are not convenient: but rather giving of thanks." Every word here needs careful consideration. The apostle is not warning us against that bright, happy conversation which leads people sometimes to exchange agreeable thoughts and give vent to lively natural humor. He is not calling us to be long-faced, unhappy people who do not dare to tell anything that provokes an innocent laugh. In fact, I am rather afraid of these people who are so holy that they cannot laugh. A good, hearty laugh is a healthy thing. God meant man to laugh. That is the one thing that distinguishes him from all the other creatures. Until scientists can find a monkey who can laugh, they will never find the missing link! God rejoices over His people and laughs in scorn when men think to thwart His will. The apostle is thinking here about something against which every Christian needs to be on guard. He has warned against these sins, and now he says, "Let it not be once named among you, as becometh saints." It is even defiling to talk about it, even to pass on the news that other people have fallen into those things. If as servants of God we have to do with these things, we find it necessary to get into the presence of God in prayer, for they leave their effect upon the heart and mind.

"Neither filthiness," that is, indecency—do not talk of indecent things. "Nor foolish talking," which really means buffoonery, making a jest, talking like a fool about unclean things. You know people who do that, people who jest of unclean things, people who think it bright, smart, to use words of double meaning, words that bring the blush to the cheek of a beautiful Christian young woman, or even trouble a right-thinking Christian young man. It literally means, "a fool's talk," and the man who talks this way demonstrates that he is a fool. The word "jesting" is really "ribaldry," and is another word that implies in a deeper sense making jest of things that should never be talked about. Christians should be clean, Christians should be like their blessed Lord, clean in thought, in word, and in deed.

In place of these things, what should occupy

the Christian tongue—"Rather giving of thanks."
There is a beautiful play in the Greek language
that does not come out very clearly in the English.
The word translated "jest" and the term "giving
of thanks" begin exactly the same. The Greek
for the one is *eutrapalia,* the Greek for the other
is *eucharistia.* You can see how the apostle was
just balancing the one word against the other.
Not *eutrapalia* but *eucharistia;* that is, not ribaldry but thanksgiving, not vile talk but praising the Lord, not filthy conversation but that
which brings glory to the Lord Jesus Christ. On
one occasion I was attending a conference of
Christians and a number of us were guests at the
home of a very devoted believer. As we gathered
between meetings one day in the beautiful draw-
ing-room, a lady suddenly said, "Well, now, we
will go out and help our hostess get the dinner
ready." Possibly fifteen men were left together.
A man who had just come in remarked, "Since
the ladies have gone out, there is a story I got
hold of today I would like to tell you." Before
any one else had a chance to speak, a friend of
mine said, "Just a minute, brother; there are no
ladies here, but the Holy Ghost is here and is
more sensitive than the most fastidious lady. Is
your story fit for Him?" The man was big
enough to say, "Thank you, Mr. B——, I accept
the reproof. I will never tell such a story again."
Remember, the Holy Spirit of God is grieved if

believers stoop to any of the things mentioned here.

And now the apostle warns us that if any reject such instruction as we have here and live in uncleanness, they simply give evidence that they are not Christians at all. They are children of the devil wearing the livery of Christ. "This ye know, that no whoremonger, nor unclean person, nor covetous man, who is an idolator, hath any inheritance in the kingdom of Christ and of God." Why does he couple idolators with these other things? Because this kind of a beast worships only himself. What does he care if he breaks other people's hearts? What does he care if he wrecks young lives, breaks up homes? He must satisfy his own base cravings. He worships one god; that god is himself. It is absurd for a man like that to profess to be a Christian.

When I think of the stories that those of us who are ministers of Christ have to hear—of the hundreds of broken-hearted young women who have come to me and told the awful story of their betrayal, of the breaking down little by little of their higher ideals and the ruin that has come, I feel the greatest punishment that their betrayers could bear would be to have to listen forever to such stories and know that they were responsible for them. When I have had fathers and mothers come and sit weeping as they have talked of one who was once the joy of their home, the love of their hearts, and tell how she had been lured away into sin, and their hearts were broken and they could no longer find the joy in their child they once did, I have said, "If these betrayers of innocent girls would only have to sit in the confessional and listen to stories of this kind year after year, it would be a fitting punishment." And people like that profess to be Christians! "But," you say, "they are sometimes in the church." More shame to them, coming under the cover of the church and pretending to be what they are not in order to go on in their vile, sinful way! Christians ought to be clean, Christians ought to be pure, because Christians are children of the Holy One, the Holy God.

"Be not ye therefore partakers with them." While one may pray for them, yet there is to be no fellowship with them, no condoning of their vile deeds. They should be made to feel that they are unclean lepers until their sins are confessed and judged, and they have given evidence of being delivered from them. God give us Christians to walk in love, that love which would ever preserve us from working any harm to any one else, that love which would lead us ever to seek the good of others, and never in any sense their hurt, even "As Christ also hath loved us, and hath given Himself for us an offering and a sacrifice to God for a sweetsmelling savor."

You may say, "But what if some have fallen

into just such things; is there no hope?" No hope until the sin is judged, no hope until it is confessed no hope until with earnest desire to be completely delivered from it they turn to Him who is the Holy and the True, and cast themselves in penitence and faith upon His atoning work. Then, trusting Him, they will find that He gives them a new heart and a new life, and makes them lovers of purity and goodness.

THE FRUIT OF THE LIGHT

✓ ✓ ✓

"For ye were sometimes darkness, but now are ye light in the Lord: walk as children of light: for the fruit of the Spirit is in all goodness and righteousness and truth; proving what is acceptable unto the Lord. And have no fellowship with the unfruitful works of darkness, but rather reprove them. For it is a shame even to speak of those things which are done of them in secret. But all things that are reproved are made manifest by the light: for whatsoever doth make manifest is light. Wherefore He saith, Awake thou that sleepest, and arise from the dead, and Christ shall give thee light" (Eph. 5: 8-14).

✓ ✓ ✓

THIS section immediately follows the exhortation to personal purity. We have seen that those who have been redeemed to God by the precious blood of His beloved Son are called to be clean in thought, in word, and in deed. And that message was addressed to a people who were living in an impure and vicious environment such as we know very little of in our day. We may shrink with horror from conditions prevailing about us, but nineteen centuries of gospel testimony have made men very much ashamed of many things which they once did shamelessly. In the days when the apostle wrote, things were practised openly which now go on only in private. If Paul could write to Christians in his day exhorting to that purity which we have seen should characterize them, how much more should you and I today, who confess the name of our Lord Jesus Christ, flee everything that has to do with uncleanness or immorality of any kind.

The clear light of God's holiness is to be our standard. "Ye were sometimes darkness, but now are ye light in the Lord: walk as children of light." Do you notice that he does not say, "Ye were sometimes in the dark," but, "Ye were darkness." Darkness is ignorance of God, and we were once, in our unconverted days, in ignorance of God and therefore said to be "darkness." We did not have the Light of life. Every natural man is in that condition. Job asked the question, "Can a man by searching find out God?" and the answer is in the negative, for all philosophizing or reasoning about divine things ends in confusion because men in their natural state are darkness.

"The natural man understandeth not the things of God because they are foolishness unto him." They are spiritually discerned. We were once in that condition, and when in that darkened state, we walked in darkness, and practised things of which we are now ashamed. But having become children of the light, being born of God, and made light in the Lord, we are to walk as becometh children of the light. You remember what is said of our Lord in the first chapter of John: "In Him was life; and the life was the light of men." Did you ever stop to meditate upon those words? In our Lord Jesus Christ divine life was fully manifested, for He was "that eternal life which was with the Father and was manifested" unto men. Now John says, "The Life was the light of men," or, as he puts it in another place, "That was the true Light which coming into the world casts light on every man" (*Lit. Trans.*). Even if He uttered not a word, His pure and holy life, ever in subjection to the Father, was in itself the condemnation of all sinful men. "The Life was the light." You and I are children of the light, and we possess that same life which our Lord Jesus Christ is. He is the eternal life and He has communicated eternal life to us. That life is now to be manifested as light.

A lady said to me some time ago, mentioning a certain servant of Christ, "Did you ever know Mr. So and So?" "Oh, yes," I said, "I knew him well." "Well," she said, "you know, we had him in our home for a month and his very presence there seemed to change everything for us. Why, there was such godliness about it, piety without long-facedness, holiness without morbidity. Our children simply loved him, and yet there was such intense godliness that soon the little things that they used to do and say carelessly, dropped away. They did not like to say in his presence what they would when he was not there, they did not like to do when he was looking the things that ordinarily they would do with utter indifference. The effect of his presence in our home was simply wonderful and yet he never reproved anybody by word of mouth for anything they did or said, but he manifested the life, and the life was the light." We have known the other kind also. I have had the privilege of having in our home all sorts and conditions of preachers and Christians, and we have had some of them that our children fairly loved and were always glad to welcome because of their Christlikeness and devotedness, and I have had others who have made the boys gnash their teeth when they came up the walk. I can recall now one good man who seemed to think it was his business to run the house when he was there. If a child was a little slow to obey or a bit pert, as children sometimes are, instead of leaving the discipline to his parents, he would exclaim, "That child ought to be spanked!" You can imagine the effect on the children. You can imagine how they loved to hear a man like that preach, how they would want to see him as a visitor in our home! It is not the person who goes around constantly finding fault with other people who accomplishes the best results. He only stirs up the flesh, arouses the enmity of the natural heart to things that are pure and good. But the man who lives Christ, the woman who manifests life eternal in the home, among friends, in the Church, these are the people whose testimonies really count for God. "The Life is the light."

You remember how the Apostle Peter emphasizes that when he addresses wives who have unconverted husbands. He says to them in First Peter 3: 1-4, "Likewise, ye wives, be in subjection to your own husbands: that, if any obey not the Word, they also may without the Word be won by the conversation of the wives; while they behold your chaste conversation coupled with fear. Whose adorning let it not be that outward adorning of plaiting the hair, and of wearing of gold, or of putting on of apparel; but let it be the hidden man of the heart, in that which is not corruptible, even the ornament of a meek and quiet spirit, which is in the sight of God of great price." I wonder if our sisters these days have ever noticed this passage. Here is a woman who has been brought to Christ, and her husband is still in paganism, or in Judaism, as the case may be, and she is deeply interested in his conversion. What is to be her attitude? Constantly nagging and talking and reproving? Oh, no; but her behavior is to be so sweet and Christlike and gracious that as he looks upon her he will say,

"Well, my wife has something now she did not have before. She used to be so ready to speak up and answer back, and now she is so sweet and gracious. I wonder what it is that she now possesses that is so contrary to what characterized her by nature."

"If any obey not the Word...they may without the Word be won." In the first clause it is the Word of God that is meant. In the second instance it means, without speech, without nagging. It might be paraphrased thus: "Likewise, ye wives, be in subjection to your own husbands, that if any obey not the Word of God they also may without nagging be won by the good behavior of the wives." And the same principle applies to every one of us. It is not merely something for our sisters to consider, but those of us who are men are called upon to manifest the truth we profess, not by constant finding fault with people, not by criticizing and trying to set everybody and everything right by word of mouth but by manifesting the life of Christ, the purity of Christ, the love of Christ in our lives. This is to walk as children of the light.

"For the fruit of the light" (in our Authorized Version it is, "The fruit of the Spirit," but in the Revised Version it reads "light") is "in all goodness and righteousness and truth." Here then are the graces that should characterize those who are children of the light. It is not enough to profess to believe on the Lord Jesus Christ, to submit to Christian baptism, to take the communion at the Lord's Table, to be members of some Christian assembly or congregation, but we are required to manifest the fruit of the light in our lives. Where there is life there is fruit. Where there is only a dead profession you will not find fruit, but where people are truly born of God there will be fruit. "By their fruits ye shall know them." "Even a child is known by his doings, whether his work be pure, and whether it be right" (Prov. 20:11). Children who have taken the name of Christ upon them are responsible to produce the fruit of the light, and if they act in a wilful or wayward manner they should immediately go to the blessed Lord and confess it. Their lives should be different from the lives of other children who have not yet accepted Christ. Whether young or old we are to manifest the fruit of the light.

What is this fruit of the light? "For the fruit of the light is in all goodness." The word literally means "benevolence," "kindly consideration for other people." If you are really born of God, you possess a new and divine nature, you will follow the footsteps of the Lord Jesus Christ, and of Him we read, "The Son of Man came not to be ministered unto, but to minister, and to give His life a ransom for many." "He laid down His life for us: and we ought to lay down our lives for the brethren" (1 John 3:16). Have we ever thought of that? "We *ought*." That is a word that speaks of duty. "To lay down our lives for the brethren." That is the opposite of selfishness. The world says, "Number one first." But we are called to be considerate of others first. Some one has well said that heavenly grammar is different from worldly grammar. In ordinary grammar you take the persons: first person, I; second person, you; third person, he or she. But in Christianity it is: first person, he or she; second person, you; and third person, I. In Christianity I come in last, I am not to put myself first. When I am thinking of comforts, I am to think of others first. But how different it is with many of us. We are content if we do a little from time to time for somebody else in wretched circumstances, whereas we are called to live for Christ daily and to manifest the fruit of the light continually, which is in all goodness.

And then in the second place, "The fruit of the light is in all righteousness." Now righteousness is simply doing right. What an amazing exemplification of the unrighteousness of the human heart we have seen within the last few years! Trusted officials in banks, big business men who were looked up to and thought to be absolutely reliable, have in many instances proven to be unrighteous men handling other people's money dishonestly, unfaithful to their trust. What a lot of suicides have followed our bank failures. How fast our penitentiaries are filling up with men who a short while ago were looked upon as perfectly dependable, and yet our modern theologians are still dreaming that human nature is not corrupt, and that "every fall is a fall upward."

A friend of mine riding on the street-car handed the conductor a gospel tract. When the conductor's busy time was over, he walked down the aisle of the car to my friend and said, "You handed me this?"

"Yes."

"Why did you give it to me? I have no interest in these things."

"But that is a gospel message."

"I do not need the gospel. It is for sinners, but I do not believe in sin, and I do not believe that man is a fallen creature."

"That is peculiar," my friend said; "why have you that machine at the door of the car?"

"Oh, that is to count the money."

"But why do they need it for men like you in whom there is no sin?"

Theologians can talk about an improved race and a sinless race and deny the fall of man, but business men know differently. The rule today is, "Do not trust anyone until he proves that he is not a rogue." Christian, be careful about attempting to witness for Christ by word of mouth if you are not manifesting the fruit of the light in

your ways. Be sure that behind your testimony
there is a righteous life.

The third thing, "The fruit of the light is in
truth." Righteousness, as we have seen, has to
do with your actions towards others. Truth has
to do with your own inward sincerity. "Thou
desirest truth in the inward part: and in the hidden part Thou shalt make me to know wisdom"
(Ps. 51: 6). Years ago when I was a young Salvation Army officer, on one occasion our Colonel
came to address us. Quite a group had come in
from all over the State for an officers' council.
I have never forgotten through all these years
the faithful words of the Colonel. He said, "Now,
remember, comrades—men will forgive you if you
are not educated, they will forgive you if your
culture is not up to the highest standards, if you
are not eloquent, if you cannot sing charmingly,
but they will never forgive you if they find out
that you are not sincere, that you are pretending
to be what you are not." When Christ dwells in
us, we will be real, we will be genuine in our dealings with God and with men.

"Proving what is acceptable unto the Lord."
In other words, "Testing what is acceptable unto
the Lord." Not so ready to say, "I think this is
all right; I do not see any harm in that," and
run off to do as we will, but considering first, "I
am a Christian and am indwelt by the Holy Spirit
of God. Is this thing what Christ would have?

Will this bring glory to my blessed Lord? If I say this, if I do that, if I go here, will I really be honoring my Saviour?" In that way we "test what is acceptable unto the Lord."

And then on the other hand, "Have no fellowship with the unfruitful works of darkness, but rather reprove them." As we have already seen, we are really proved by the lives we live. The Christian cannot expect to be kept from contamination of sin and evil if he goes on in fellowship with iniquity; you might as well expect a child to play about in the filth and slime of the streets and not be contaminated, as to expect a Christian to go on in fellowship with wickedness and not be affected by it.

This is one of the scriptures together with many others that have exercised my own conscience through the years and kept me from a great many associations into which I would otherwise naturally have gone. When years ago such questions arose as to whether I would affiliate myself with certain secret societies and lodges of various kinds, the question at once arose, Are they composed of born again people? If I do join them, will it mean fellowship with the unfruitful works of darkness? Will I be walking in the path laid down for me by Christ? For the Lord has said, "Come out from among them, and be ye separate, and touch not the unclean thing; and I will receive you, and will be a Father unto

you, and ye shall be My sons and daughters" (2
Cor. 6: 17, 18). That scripture kept me out of
many things. But I have gained immensely, for
the time I would have spent in some of those
associations I have been permitted to spend with
the people of God or over the Word of God. Do
not be afraid that you will ever lose by obedience
to the Book.

The strength of the Christian is in his separation from the world and his devotion to Christ.

Verses 13 and 14 are intimately linked together. "But all things that are reproved are
made manifest by the light: for whatsoever doth
make manifest is light." He has said, "Have no
fellowship with the unfruitful works of darkness,
but rather reprove them." That he does not mean
mere fault-finding is evident from the words, "All
things that are reproved are made manifest by
the light." That is what is needed. Just turn
on the light and it will show up everything that
is contrary to it. In other words, you live the
pure, holy, Christlike, godly, devoted life, and
that in itself will be reproof enough of the iniquity abounding upon every hand. "All things
that are reproved are made manifest by the light:
for whatsoever doth make manifest is light."
John tells us in his epistle, "God is light, and in
Him is no darkness at all." Light is the very
nature of God, and the moment one comes into
the presence of God he is made manifest as a

sinner, but he sees there in the presence of God the precious blood upon the mercy-seat which tells of the sin question settled and sin put away, and thus he enjoys peace with God through our Lord Jesus Christ. And so he walks in the light unafraid because he is in Christ.

The danger is that one may accept all this in the head only. "Wherefore he said, Awake thou that sleepest, and arise from the dead, and Christ shall shine upon thee" (R. V.). It is not possible to find any one Old Testament scripture that contains these words in their exactness. They are rather a free rendering of Isaiah 60: 1. There the Spirit of the Lord speaking through the prophet says, "Arise, shine; for thy light is come, and the glory of the Lord is risen upon thee." The apostle takes that word "arise" to mean, "wake up out of your sleep," as when you go into the boy's room in the morning and say, "Tom, it is time to arise!" Many who profess to be Christians are like people sleeping in a cemetery, sleeping among the dead with their heads pillowed upon the gravestones! You who are children of the light (this is not a message for the unsaved but for those who are saved and have gone to sleep): "Awake, and arise from the dead, and Christ shall give thee light." "Come out from among them and be ye separate." Show by your life that you are different from the unsaved worldlings about you.

Do you want blessing? Do you want a sense of the light of His face shining upon your life? Do not tolerate any hidden wrong; put it right, make confession. Maybe it is a letter you ought to write, maybe an acknowledgment you ought to make, maybe some money you ought to return. Do you say, "I can't afford it"? But it is not yours, you know. Put things right and then trust God for the rest. Righteousness first, and other things will follow. "Awake, thou that sleepest, and arise from the dead, and Christ shall shine upon thee."

THE FILLING WITH THE HOLY SPIRIT

✓ ✓ ✓

"See then that ye walk circumspectly, not as fools, but as wise, redeeming the time, because the days are evil. Wherefore be ye not unwise, but understanding what the will of the Lord is. And be not drunk with wine, wherein is excess; but be filled with the Spirit; speaking to yourselves in psalms and hymns and spiritual songs, singing and making melody in your heart to the Lord; giving thanks always for all things unto God and the Father in the name of our Lord Jesus Christ; submitting yourselves one to another in the fear of God" (Eph. 5: 15-21).

✓ ✓ ✓

WE are now occupied with the walk of the believer. "See then that ye walk circumspectly, not as fools, but as wise." This is the seventh time that the word "walk" occurs in this epistle. I think it will be profitable to go back and notice the occurrences.

In chapter 2: 2 we have the past tense. If we were to include that, it would mean the eighth time, "Wherein in time past ye *walked* according to the course of this world." This was how we used to live when we belonged to the world. But we who are saved are delivered from that and so we read in verse 10 of the same chapter, "For we are His workmanship, created in Christ Jesus unto good works, which God hath before ordained that we should *walk* in them." We are not saved by good works, but we are to walk in good works after we are saved. In chapter 4:1 we read, "I therefore, the prisoner of the Lord, beseech you that ye *walk* worthy of the vocation wherewith ye are called." Having been called with a heavenly calling, we are now to walk, to behave ourselves, as a heavenly people. Following that, in verse 17 of the same chapter we read, "This I say therefore, and testify in the Lord, that ye henceforth *walk* not as other Gentiles walk, in the vanity of their mind." In our unconverted days we walked in the pride and folly of the human mind at variance with God, but as believers we are not to do this any more, but we are to walk in lowliness and in obedience to the Word of God. Then in chapter 5:2 we are told to, *"Walk* in love, as Christ also hath loved us, and hath given Himself for us an offering and a sacrifice to God for a sweetsmelling savor." In verse 8 we read, "Ye were sometimes darkness, but now are ye light in the Lord: *walk* as children of light." And now in verse 15 the apostle says, "See then that ye *walk* circumspectly, not as fools, but as wise."

Our English word, "circumspectly" means "looking all around," like one who is walking in a very dangerous place. There are pitfalls on this side, quagmires on that side, traps and snares all about. And so this person as he walks is constantly observing where he should next place his feet. That is a circumspect walk, a walk looking all around. Christian, your path leads you through a world of sin, a world of folly, a world where you are exposed to all kinds of temptations and unholy influences. Snares and traps abound for your unwary feet. Therefore, walk circumspectly, be careful where you put down your feet, be careful as to the company you keep, be careful as to your behavior in any company, so that there be that which will bring glory to the Lord Jesus Christ. Walk not as fools, not as simple ones, not as those who are still darkness, but walk as wise men—made wise by the wisdom of God.

"Redeeming the time, because the days are evil." The apostle uses this expression in one of his other letters, and in each instance it literally means, "Buying up the opportunities." Just as people go out bargain hunting and say, "There, if I buy that today, I can get it at a good price, much better than if I have to let it go until another time. It is worth my while to buy these bargains up at this rate." Let the Christian be just as eager, just as earnest, to obtain opportunities to witness for Christ, to serve the blessed Lord, and to be a means of blessing to others with whom he comes in contact. Buying up the opportunities, seeking to use them to the glory of our Lord Jesus, realizing that the days are evil and the time for serving Christ is slipping fast away, and that opportunities once lost will never be found again. Therefore, the importance of buying them up while we have the chance.

"Wherefore, be ye not unwise, but understanding what the will of the Lord is." And mark it, the only way that you and I can be delivered from our own natural foolishness, is by being divinely enlightened. We do not understand what the will of the Lord is excepting as we give ourselves to the careful, thoughtful study of His Word. Years ago I used frequently to stop in the midst of a discourse and ask everyone in my audience who had read the Bible through once to raise his hand. The last time I did that I was so ashamed that I made up my mind never to do it again. I had an audience of five hundred people, all of whom professed to be Christians, and when I put that question to them, only two raised their hands, and I was ashamed to have the devil see it. I was so thankful that there were not a lot of sinners there to see it. They would certainly say, "Those Christians do not value their Bible very much." I am reminded of something that occurred just recently in this city. There was an open religious forum down town. Clarence Darrow was there to represent the Atheists, another to represent Protestantism, another Roman Catholicism, and another, Judaism. The Catholic got up and told why he was a Catholic, and the Protestant got up and told why he was a Protestant, the Jew why he was a Jew, and then Clarence Darrow, the Atheist, got up to speak, and he said, "Gentlemen, I have been very much interested in one thing. I notice neither Protestant, Catholic, nor Jew ever referred to the Bible. Evidently they no longer value that so-called Holy Book as they used to do." And then he went on to declare that he was an Atheist because he had no use for the Book that they never even mentioned. What a pitiable thing that professed Christians should attempt to tell why they were Catholic or Protestant and never once refer to the Bible! Oh, that you and I might be genuine Bible Christians!

A friend of mine used to be designated as a walking Bible, and I thought, What a splendid description! If anybody ever came and said, "Mr. So-and-So, what do you think about such and such a thing?" he would say, "Let us see what God says about it," and out would come his Bible. "Why," the man would say, "I didn't know it was answered in the Book that way." I never knew this friend to say, "I think," but always, "God's Word says so and so." If you and I would be wise with the wisdom that cometh from above, we need to search the Scriptures. I like that little chorus:

> "In my heart, in my heart,
>   Send a great revival;
>   Teach me how to watch and pray,
>   And to read my Bible."

The pitiable thing is that the great majority of Christians, I dare say, are so busy with other things that they have very little time for their Bibles. Although engaged exclusively in Christian service now for forty-five years, I do not dare come into the pulpit, I do not dare undertake my day's work without first going to the Word of God to gather fresh manna from day to day. If sometimes I am so hurried in the morning because of being out very late the night before and oversleeping a little, or an urgent call comes and I rush out thoughtlessly without going to the Book, I find myself saying, "What is the matter with me today? I feel so dried up and half-starved spiritually. I am in no condition to try to minister to other people." And then the answer comes, "Why, you didn't have your spiritual breakfast this morning. You went off without a bit from God's Word," and I have to say, "Lord, forgive me for thinking that anything is more important than time spent with Thyself."

If you are not in the habit of reading your Bible methodically, prayerfully, let me beg of you, let me plead with you, go into the presence of God and confess to Him the sin of thus neglecting His Holy Word. He says, "Search the Scriptures," and if you disobey a command, it is sin. If you have been disobedient go to Him and confess it, and say, "Lord, henceforth teach me to say with Thy servant, 'Neither have I gone back from the commandment of His lips; I have esteemed the words of His mouth more than my necessary food' " (Job 23:12). Give God the first place in your life, give His Word the place it ought to have and then indeed you will understand what the will of the Lord is.

And now the apostle continues, "And be not drunk with wine, wherein is excess; but be filled with the Spirit." You will notice he puts two things in opposition, the one to the other—drunkenness with wine and the filling of the Holy Spirit. Why does he contrast these two things, these two conditions? You see, the man who has been over-imbibing, the man who is drunk with wine, is controlled by a spirit foreign to himself. Men, when they are under the influence of the spirit of alcohol, do and say things that they never would do in their normal condition. They make fools of themselves, they descend to all kinds of ribaldry and nonsense, and people say, excusing them, "Oh, well; you mustn't hold it against him; he is drunk, he is not himself." The apostle says that that condition should never be true of a Christian, but on the other hand the Christian should be dominated and controlled by a Spirit other than himself. He should be controlled by the Holy Spirit of God, and in the power of the Holy Spirit one is enabled to say and to do what he could not say and do in his merely natural condition. And so the filling of the Holy Spirit ought

to be the normal experience of every believer—
"Be not drunk with wine, wherein is excess; but
be filled with the Spirit." The word here is not
really in the past tense but in the present—"Be
habitually filled with the Holy Spirit."

What is the filling with the Holy Spirit? I
think the thought that a great many people have
is that it is some strange, ecstatic, emotional experience that comes to them at a given moment
and then later passes away and has to be repeated
again. But that is not it. This is the normal experience of the Christian life: "They were all
filled with the Holy Ghost, and they spake the
Word of God with boldness" (Acts 4: 31). They
were dominated, they were controlled by the
blessed Holy Spirit of God, and this does not
necessarily result in any special emotional break-
down, but rather preserves one in the path of
orderliness and common sense. In the second
Epistle to Timothy we read, "God hath not given
us the spirit of fear; but of power, and of love,
and of a sound mind." I have been in some
places where people talk a great deal about the
fulness of the Spirit and where I have seen things
that I never would have thought possible a few
years ago outside of an insane asylum, people
rolling upon the floor and raving like maniacs,
and yet calling that the fulness of the Spirit. That
is not the spirit of a sound mind. The man who
is filled with the Holy Spirit does not go off into

some wild, fanatical state, but walks thoughtfully and carefully with God, and his testimony has power with men.

Turn to the Epistle to the Colossians, chapter 3: 16, "Let the word of Christ dwell in you richly in all wisdom; teaching and admonishing one another in psalms and hymns and spiritual songs, singing with grace in your hearts to the Lord." Notice the effect there of the Word of Christ dwelling richly in the soul. Then turn back to Ephesians and read these verses again. Do you observe that you get the exactly the same results in Colossians when the Word of Christ dwells in you richly that you get in Ephesians when you are filled with the Spirit? What then is the inference? There is an old rule in mathematics that "things equal to the same thing are equal to one another." If to be filled with the Word is equal in result to being filled with the Spirit, then it should be clear that the Word-filled Christian is the Spirit-filled Christian. As the Word of Christ dwells in us richly, controls all our ways, as we walk in obedience to the Word, the Spirit of God fills, dominates, and controls us to the glory of the Lord Jesus Christ. Therefore, if you would be filled with the Spirit and you know of anything in your life which is contrary to the Word of God, if you are tolerating anything in your private life which is contrary to the Word of God, if there is anything in your outward asso-

ciations, in your behavior before the world that
is contrary to His Word, go into His presence,
confess your sins, sins of omission, sins of commission, deal with it all before Him, and when
everything has been uncovered and faced in His
presence, dare to believe that He means what He
says when He declares, "If we confess our sins,
He is faithful and just to forgive us our sins, and
to cleanse us from all unrighteousness" (1 John
1:9). And now, seek grace from Him to walk
in obedience to His truth, cry out from the depths
of your heart as the Psalmist did, "Order my
steps in Thy Word" (Ps. 119:133), and as you
walk on in obedience to the Word of God, you
will be filled with the Spirit.

Do not get the idea that you must have some
remarkable outward demonstration, some amazing sign that the Spirit of God has actually taken
possession, but remember that He dwells in every
believer, and as you give Him room, He cleanses
out of you everything that hinders. As you let
Him take full possession you are filled with the
Spirit. What will be the evidence of it? One
will be fulness of joy. The Holy Spirit is a Spirit
of gladness, the Spirit of joy. Now do not misunderstand me, there is a difference between holy
joy and mere natural merriment. Take the life
of our blessed Lord Jesus Christ. Even though
He was the Man of Sorrows and acquainted with
grief, as we read the records in the four Gospels

we cannot help but be impressed with the fact that we are not reading the life of a sad Man but of a glad Man. "At that time Jesus rejoiced in spirit and said, Father, I thank Thee." That is characteristic of the blessed Lord. In spite of all the grief and sorrow that He bore He was joyful. But having said that, let me remind you that in these records you do not see depicted what the world calls a jolly man. His was no mere worldly jollity, no mere worldly merriment, but a deep-rooted gladness that was based upon unbroken communion with the Father, and that is the joy that you and I should possess. The one who is filled with the Spirit will be a glad, joyous believer.

"Speaking to yourselves in psalms and hymns and spiritual songs, singing and making melody in your heart to the Lord." It might be translated, "Speaking to one another." The world considers that a man who talks to himself is a bit queer, but that is not always the case. It is well sometimes for us to sit down and talk to ourselves about things in our lives. What the apostle is saying here is really, "Speaking to one another, to the entire company." How? "In psalms and hymns and spiritual songs." As we meet with one another, greeting each other in a glad, happy way, the praises of the Lord bubble up in our souls. Psalms were the vehicle of expression in the congregation of God in olden times. The book of Psalms was the hymn-book of the congregation of the Lord in ancient times, and there are wonderful expressions there that suit every mood of the human heart. While we do not rise to the height of the Christian's privilege in the book of Psalms yet we can find something to express every state and condition of our souls as we come into the presence of God. A hymn is an ascription of praise addressed directly to the Deity.

"Holy, Holy, Holy! Lord God Almighty!
Early in the morning our songs shall rise to Thee."

How the Christian heart naturally goes out to God in hymns of worship and adoration. No more worldly songs for the Christian. The day is gone, or should be, when he can sing the worldly songs. I always think a Christian has dropped from the high level on which he belongs when I hear him singing such songs, because he has something better, he has spiritual songs, songs that tell of the love of Christ, of what grace hath wrought, that tell of redemption by the precious blood of Jesus. Who would sing the old songs when we have learned the new?

"We will sing of the Shepherd that died,
     That died for the sake of the flock,
His love to the utmost was tried,
     But firmly endured as a rock;
We will sing of such subjects alone,
     None others our tongues shall employ,
Till fully His love becomes known,
     In yonder bright regions of joy."

One reason that the spirituality of the Church is at such a low ebb today is because people are so careless about matters of this kind, so ready to drop down from the high and holy state that should characterize those that are filled with the Spirit of God.

"Singing and making melody in your heart to the Lord." We cannot all make melody on an instrument. Some of us would never be able to produce any melody if dependent upon an instrument, but every believer's heart is like a harp, and as the Spirit of God breathes over the heart-strings, real melody goes up to the ear of God.

And now, the Spirit-filled believer will be a thankful believer. "Giving thanks always for all things unto God and the Father in the name of our Lord Jesus Christ." "Oh, but," you say, "there are some things I cannot give thanks for, there are some things so hard, so difficult to bear, there are some things that lacerate my very soul." Wait a moment. Have you ever undergone a serious physical operation as a result of which you have been delivered from something that was just wearing out your very life? When you had to undergo it, it seemed very hard, but as you look back upon it, can you not give thanks for the surgeon's knife, can you not give thanks for the very sufferings you had to endure because of the blessed after-result? Very well, Christian, some day.

"When we stand with Christ in glory,
Looking o'er life's finished story,"

we shall see as we cannot now just why all the
hard things were permitted, and how God our
Father was seeking to set us free from hindrances
and from encumbrances, by pruning the branches
from which He wished to get fruit for Himself.
In that day we will thank Him for all the sorrow
as well as for all the joy. In faith let us do it
now.

Nothing can come to me but what His love
allows. "All things work together for good," and
so a Spirit-filled believer will be loyal and sub-
missive, not the kind who tosses his head and
says, "I am not going to have anybody dominate
me; I will do what I think and what I like."
That is the old walk of our unconverted days,
that is the old nature, not the new.

"Submitting yourselves one to another in the
fear of *Christ,*" as the better version reads. He
was God manifested in Christ. The Spirit-filled
believer, then, is characterized by these three
things, joyfulness, thankfulness, lowliness. May
God give to each one of us to be filled with the
Spirit.

THE CHRISTIAN FAMILY

✓ ✓ ✓

"Wives, submit yourselves unto your own husbands, as unto the Lord. For the husband is the head of the wife, even as Christ is the Head of the Church: and he is the saviour of the body. Therefore as the Church is subject unto Christ, so let the wives be to their own husbands in everything. Husbands, love your wives, even as Christ also loved the Church, and gave Himself for it; that He might sanctify and cleanse it with the washing of water by the Word; that He might present it to Himself a glorious Church, not having spot, or wrinkle, or any such thing; but that it should be holy and without blemish. So ought men to love their wives as their own bodies. He that loveth his wife loveth himself. For no man ever yet hated his own flesh; but nourisheth and cherisheth it, even as the Lord the Church: for we are members of His Body, of His flesh, and of His bones. For this cause shall a man leave his father and mother, and shall be joined unto his wife, and they two shall be one flesh. This is a great mystery: but I speak concerning Christ and the Church. Nevertheless let everyone of you in particular so love his wife even as himself; and the wife see that she reverence her husband" (Eph. 5: 22-33).

✓ ✓ ✓

YOU will notice how intimately verse 22 is linked with verse 21: "Submitting yourselves one to another in the fear of God." This is a principle of Christian living which applies to believers in every relationship of life, and now

that the apostle turns to consider the Christian
family he shows that it applies there. Did you
ever stop to think what a wonderful institution
the Christian family is? In reading a letter from
a missionary in a heathen land I was struck by
a paragraph which read something like this:

"How we wish that some of our Christian people could come and settle among us, even if not
to engage in missionary work. There are different ways by which one might make his living
among this semi-civilized people. For instance,
we might have a Christian dentist and his wife,
or a Christian worker in leather, a shoemaker,
harness-maker, and his wife and family. It
would mean a great deal to us to have a har-
monious family here, for we can conceive of
nothing that could so commend Christianity to
our people as just to see a Christian family functioning according to the New Testament. It
would be so utterly different from anything our
people have ever known. A Christian husband
loving and honoring his wife, a Christian wife
living in sweet and beautiful subjection and loyalty in her home, Christian children who really
delight in obedience to their parents, parents who
love their children and seek to bring them up in
the nurture and admonition of the Lord." This
is something that is unknown in many heathen
lands. It is Christianity, it is the knowledge of
Christ, that produces the Christian home, and

how jealous we should be of this blessed and delightful institution.

It is a very remarkable thing that in this letter the writer leads us up to the highest heights of divine revelation, to that which thrills our souls, as he speaks of our being predestinated according to the riches of grace to a place that angels have never known, accepted in the Beloved, blessed with all spiritual blessings in heavenly places in Christ. Then in the closing portion he seems to descend to what we might consider very commonplace. He applies this wonderful body of truth to the behavior of a Christian family. It is a poor thing to talk high truth while living on a low level in the home. I am afraid there are those who can repeat very glibly the statements of the first half of the Epistle to the Ephesians and delight in the wondrous privileges that belong to the people of God, who fail wretchedly when it comes to exemplifying the truth in the last half of this epistle in the daily life; and yet that is simply the truth of the first chapters made practical.

"Submitting yourselves one to another in the fear of God." And then immediately you have the exemplification of that in the relationship of the husband to the wife. Look at the verse: "Wives, submit yourselves unto your own husbands, as unto the Lord." If you happen to have the Revised Version, you will see that the words, "submit yourselves" are in italics, and correctly so. That means that they are not found in the best manuscripts. Let us read it exactly as it is in the Greek: "Submitting yourselves one to another in the fear of God, wives unto your own husbands, husbands loving your wives." Do you see? He is not calling upon the wife to take the place of a slave—she often takes that place in pagan lands—but he is calling for mutual loyalty, mutual respect, mutual submission. Pass over the intervening words to verse 25, "Husbands, love your wives, even as Christ also loved the Church, and gave Himself for it." That is how the husbands submit themselves unto the wives, so it is a mutual thing. That which makes the Christian home what it ought to be is this mutual loyalty, the one to the other, the wife to the husband, the husband to the wife. This is a marvelous thing when you think of it.

Here is a beautiful young woman. She has had her own way to a large extent, she has made her own way through the world, perhaps, or she may have come from a home where she has been carefully nurtured and cared for. By-and-by she meets a man, no blood relation of hers whatever, yet somehow or another her heart goes out to him, and she says, "For his sake I would be willing to go to the ends of the world, face all kinds of experience, keep house for him, care for his and my children, take the place of loving sub-

mission." It is a man whom a little while ago
she did not know. Or, here is a man; he has
made his own way, gone on into that period of his
life when the world dubs him a bachelor. He
has made his own money and could say what he
would do with it and with his time. But he
meets a woman to whom his heart goes out and
he says, "For her dear sake I am willing to work
and toil and labor, and if it means to impoverish
myself to care for her, I will gladly do it." That
is the Christian ideal, and when the Spirit of God
dwells in each heart, what a beautiful picture it
becomes of the mutual relation of Christ and the
Church! And you see, it is exactly the same
thing that takes place in the spiritual world.

Here was one going on in his own way utterly
independent of God, but he is brought face to
face with Christ, and his heart says, "For His
sake I resign my own way; I give Him control
of my life; I trust myself to Him; I am willing
for His name's sake to go and do whatever He
would have me do." Christ on His part laid down
His life to purchase the one He loves, and now
delights to lavish blessings upon this one whom
He has made His own. We shall never know the
fulness of this until we get to heaven. He has
designed that every Christian home should exemplify this very thing.

How we ought to challenge our hearts as to
how far our homes harmonize with this blessed

picture that the apostle brings before us here!
Let us examine each verse somewhat carefully.
"Submitting yourselves one·to another in the fear
of God, wives unto your own husbands, as unto
God." Remember, it is only of a Christian family that directions like these could be given. Here
is marriage not only in the flesh but in the Lord.
What a sad thing for the Christian ever to contemplate marriage apart from subjection to the
Lord. "Be ye not unequally yoked together with
unbelievers," is a word that applies here as well
as to many another relationship of life. "For
the husband is the head of the wife, even as
Christ is the Head of the Church: and the saviour
of the body."

Our blessed Lord Jesus Christ as the Head of
the Church undertakes now to provide for the
Church, care for it, minister to it in all its neces-
sities. So the Christian husband is the one, not
to lord it over others in a harsh, arbitrary, mas-
terful way, but to exemplify the gracious care of
the Lord Jesus Christ as the saviour of the body.
And so the Christian husband charges himself
with the support of the wife and the family. He
is ready to toil and labor that they may be kept
in a measure of comfort and ease, and because of
this, as the Church is subject to Christ so should
the wife be to her own husband.

On the part of the husband we read in verse
25, "Husbands, love your wives, even as Christ

also loved the Church and gave Himself for it."
A dear young fellow who had but lately taken to
his heart and home a beautiful bride came to me
in distress one day and said, "Brother Ironside,
I want your help. I am in an awful state. I am
drifting into idolatry."

"What is the trouble?" I asked.

"Well, I am afraid that I am putting my wife
on too high a plane, I am afraid I love her too
much, and I am displeasing the Lord."

"Are you indeed?" I asked. "Do you love her
more than Christ loved the Church?"

"I don't think I do."

"Well, that is the limit, for we read, 'Husbands, love your wives, even as Christ also loved
the Church, and gave Himself for it.'"

You cannot get beyond that. That is a self-denying love, a love that makes one willing even
to lay down his life for another.

You remember that striking story about the
wife of one of Cyrus' generals who was charged
with treachery against the king. She was called
before him and after trial condemned to die. Her
husband, who did not realize what had taken
place, was apprised of it and came hurrying in.
When he heard the sentence condemning his wife
to death, he threw himself prostrate before the
king and said, "O Sire, take my life instead of
hers. Let me die in her place!" Cyrus was so
touched that he said, "Love like that must not be

spoiled by death," and he gave them back to each other and let the wife go free. As they walked happily away the husband said, "Did you notice how kindly the king looked upon us when he gave you a free pardon?" "I had no eyes for the king," she said; "I saw only the man who was willing to die for me." That is the picture that you have here. That should characterize the Christian husband—willing to lay himself out to give of his best, even of life itself, for the blessing of his dear ones.

"Husbands, love your wives even as Christ also loved the Church, and gave Himself for it; that He might sanctify and cleanse it with the washing of water by the Word." It is as though the apostle can scarcely speak on this subject but that it brings before him the One who has won his own heart, and he must tell us more about Him. This blessed Husband, this glorious Head of the Church, this ideal for every Christian husband, gave up His own precious life for the Bride of His heart, the Church, that He might sanctify and cleanse it with the washing of water by the Word. Some imagine that this is a reference to baptism, a kind of sacramental washing, but I take it rather that the words explain themselves. He has found us in our sins, in our uncleanness, unfit for association with Him, the Holy One, but He applied the water of the Word of His truth to us and we were sanctified by the truth and made fit to enter into this communion with Him, the Holy and True One. If my hand becomes defiled, I wash it in water and the defilement disappears. So when my conscience, my heart, my life were all defiled, the blessed Lord by the Holy Spirit applied the truth of His Word to me and I was regenerated by the washing of water, and thus made clean in His sight, and so fitted for union and communion with Him. By-and-by the full regeneration will be seen in glory when He shall present His Bride to Himself, a glorious Church, not having spot occasioned by sin, or wrinkle occasioned by age.

In Revelation 21: 2 we read, "And I John saw the holy city, the New Jerusalem, coming down from God out of heaven, prepared as a bride adorned for her husband." This is the glorious picture of the Church as it will be throughout all the ages to come—"without spot or wrinkle or any such thing." There are some of my brethren who in their hyper-dispensational teaching can read this chapter and deny that the Church is the Bride of the Lamb. They tell us that Israel is the Bride. But the apostle says the Bridegroom is the blessed Lord; the Church, His redeemed spouse, and the two are linked together for eternity. He then applies it to us again, "So ought men to love their wives as their own bodies. He that loveth his wife loveth himself." The two have become one now, and therefore, the

man who would treat his wife unkindly is as one
who would destroy or injure, or cause grief to his
own flesh, and so we may put it contrariwise. We
have heard of wives who are so vixenish in their
tempers that they cause even good and devoted
husbands unspeakable anguish. Both are one flesh,
and need to learn that, "No man ever yet hated
his own flesh; but nourisheth and cherisheth it,
even as the Lord the Church." For so intimate is
our union with Him that, "We are members of
His Body, of His flesh, and of His bones."

If some insist that the Church is the Body but
not the Bride, the very argument that the apostle
uses contradicts them. The Church is both the
Body and the Bride even as a man's wife is both
his body and his bride. And so it was written
in the book of Genesis: "For this cause (because
of this union) shall a man leave his father and
his mother, and shall cleave unto his wife: and
they twain shall be one flesh." What a marvelous
thing it is when two are thus brought together
through divine grace, the Lord having first united
their hearts to Himself and then to each other,
and so they set up a Christian home.

Is your home such as the apostle is here depict-
ing, where husband and wife walk together in
mutual love and subjection, and where Christ is
ever honored? If not, it would be well to inquire
why it is not. Perhaps you would find that the
true root of the trouble is in the neglect of the

family altar. May I turn you to another passage of Scripture? 1 Peter 3:1, "Likewise, ye wives, be in subjection to your own husbands: that, if any obey not the Word, they also may without the Word be won by the conversation of the wives." Here you have a case where there is no spiritual unity in the family—where the husband is not a Christian and the wife is. Look at verse 7, "Likewise, ye husbands, dwell with them according to knowledge, giving honor unto the wife, as unto the weaker vessel, and as being heirs together of the grace of life; that your prayers be not hindered." Here you have the Christian relationship—"that your prayers be not hindered." Notice those words. When a Christian home is the way it ought to be, prayer like fragrant incense will rise unhindered to God the Father from that family altar. But where the home is not as it should be, where husband and wife are not subject to one another, where there is not that delightful relationship, then prayer immediately is hindered. There—may I say?—you get the thermometer that shows what conditions are in the home. What a blessing when husband and wife can happily kneel together and bring their varied problems to the Lord, or together lift their hearts to Him when things are going well. But when there is reserve on the part of either one or the other, you may know there is a storm in the offing, or something has already taken place hindering their fellowship and communion.

If in your home the family altar has not been set up, see to it that not another day goes by until husband and wife read the Word together and kneel together in the presence of God, commending one another and the children to the Lord. You will find it will make a great difference, and day by day anything that would hinder prayer can be judged there at the family altar.

In closing this section, the apostle says, "This is a great mystery." He has spoken again and again of mysteries in this epistle. In chap. 1: 9 he says, "Having made known unto us the mystery of His will." In chapter 3: 3-5 he says, "By revelation He made known unto me the mystery, which in other ages was not made known unto the sons of men, as it is now revealed unto His holy apostles and prophets by the Spirit." And now he says, "This is a great mystery." What is a great mystery? Why, this question of the mutual relationship of husband and wife. This is a great mystery, this indeed sets forth the very mystery that he has been speaking of. "This is a great mystery: but I speak concerning Christ and the Church." There you have it. Christ, the husband; the Church, the wife; Christ, the Head; the Church, the Body. This is the marvelous mystery that was not made known in other ages, but has now been fully revealed in the pages of the New Testament.

Of course we understand that the word "mystery" as used here never means something hard to comprehend. It is not mystery in the sense of being something mysterious and difficult of apprehension. It is rather a sacred secret which the human mind never would have ferreted out, but which awaited divine revelation. In the Old Testament times nobody thought of this wonderful truth, the mystery of Christ and the Church, but it was revealed first to the Apostle Paul and then to others of the New Testament company, and it is the great truth which you and I are called upon to confess and acknowledge in this dispensation of the grace of God.

We are not to be so carried away by the truth back of the marriage relation that we will forget the truth of that relationship between husband and wife. So the apostle drops again from the mystery itself to the commonplace things of life and says, "Nevertheless let every one of you in particular so love his wife even as himself; and the wife see that she reverence her husband." It is such Christian homes as these all over the city, all over the land, that will commend the gospel that is preached from the pulpit. People must see these things lived out in the life, and realize the power of Christ to bind two hearts together and enable them to manifest the mutual relationship of Christ and the Church.

LECTURE XXIII.

THE CHRISTIAN HOUSEHOLD

❧ ❧ ❧

"Children, obey your parents in the Lord: for this is right.
Honor thy father and mother; which is the first commandment with promise; that it may be well with thee, and thou
mayest live long on the earth. And, ye fathers, provoke
not your children to wrath: but bring them up in the nurture and admonition of the Lord. Servants, be obedient to
them that are your masters according to the flesh, with fear
and trembling, in singleness of your heart, as unto Christ;
not with eyeservice, as men-pleasers; but as the servants of
Christ, doing the will of God from the heart; with good will
doing service, as to the Lord, and not to men: knowing that
whatsoever good thing any man doeth, the same shall he
receive of the Lord, whether he be bond or free. And, ye
masters, do the same things unto them, forbearing threatening: knowing that your Master also is in heaven; neither is
there respect of persons with Him" (Eph. 6: 1-9).

❧ ❧ ❧

IN these nine verses we have the conclusion of
that section of the epistle which begins with
verse 22 of the previous chapter. We have
considered the instruction given to Christian
wives and husbands in chapter 5, and have seen
that there is to be mutual love, respect, and loyalty, the wife serving in her particular capacity
to make the Christian home what it ought to be,

and the husband taking the **responsibility to pro-**viding for the family, the acknowledged head of that home seeking to act as in the fear of God— the wife reverencing her husband, the husband loving his wife. Now we come to consider other members of the family, or the same persons in other relationships.

The apostle speaks first to children. Of course, he is speaking directly to those who alone really may be expected to heed the Word of God, to Christian children. This is one way in which children may adorn the doctrine of Christ in these early formative years before they launch out into the world to make a place for themselves and to take part in public service for Christ. This is how they may glorify God and bring honor to the name of the Lord Jesus Christ. "Children, obey your parents in the Lord: for this is right." You see the matter of obedience is put on the common ground of what is correct and proper—"This is right." You profess to be a Christian, young man or woman, boy or girl; you have accepted the Lord Jesus Christ as your Saviour. Well, then, here is the first admonition He lays upon you, "Obey your parents." Why? Because it is the right thing to do. "This is right." In the Epistle to the Colossians, where you have the same admonition, he bases it upon another ground. "Children, obey your parents in all things: for this is well pleasing unto the Lord" (Col. 3: 20).

Do you say sometimes, as some Christian children do say, "I should like to do some big thing for Christ; I should like to feel that my life in a special way is counting for Him?" Well, "this is well pleasing to the Lord." Obedience, the recognition of parental authority and loving subjection is well pleasing to Him. In this our blessed Lord Jesus Christ is our example. We remember that in Luke 2:51 we read, "He went down with them," that is, with His mother, Mary, and Joseph, his foster father, "and came to Nazareth, and was subject unto them." Here you see our blessed Lord Jesus, the eternal Son of God, become flesh, the example for all Christian children. What a wonderful thing! If you are a boy or girl in the home and have trusted the Lord Jesus, you can say, "My Lord was once a child like me. He once occupied the same position in the home that I do and He filled it well. He was obedient, He was subject to His parents in all things." The wonder of it is that He, the Creator of the universe, took that place of subjection, leaving us an example that we should follow His steps. Later on as you grow up and go into life you will have Him as your example in other spheres, but now He is your example in the home. How Christian children ought to take this to heart.

It is a most inconsistent thing for a child to profess to be a Christian, to have his name on the roll of some church, to be in fellowship with an assembly of saints, even partaking of the sacred supper of the Lord, and yet be characterized by wilfulness and waywardness in the home. There is nothing more distressing, there is nothing in some senses more disgusting, than to see a child who takes the place of a Christian outside and behaves and acts as anything but one in the private home circle. Disobedience to parents is one thing about which God's Word speaks most sternly. In Romans 1, where the apostle is describing the iniquities that prevail in the heathen world, you will find it linked with the vilest kinds of sin. In verses 29, 30, we read, "Filled with all unrighteousness, fornication, wickedness, covetousness, maliciousness; full of envy, murder, debate, deceit, malignity; whisperers, backbiters, haters of God, despiteful, proud, boasters, inventors of evil things, disobedient to parents." Notice the place that disobedience to parents has; it is linked with the vilest immoralities, even with the crime of homicide, and the reason for it is that if children are not taught to obey when they are young, if they do not obey their parents in the home, they will not obey God, and will not obey the powers that are ordained of God when they go out into the world. That judge in Gary, Indiana, was right who, when recently executing sentence on some young culprits, said, "I wish it were possible to put the parents of these children in the penitentiary for allowing them to grow up like this." As Christian parents we are responsible to see that our children are obedient. And as Christian children we are responsible to obey our parents.

When we turn to Second Timothy we find that the apostle in chapter 3 is describing the outward evidence of the apostasy in the last days, and he again speaks of disobedience to parents as one of the manifest evils of the times. "This know also, that in the last days perilous times shall come. For men shall be lovers of their own selves, covetous, boasters, proud, blasphemers, disobedient to parents, unthankful, unholy" (2 Tim. 3: 1). In Romans 1 we have the sins that characterized the heathen world when Christianity began; in Second Timothy 3 we have the sins that will characterize Christendom at the very end immediately before the coming of our Lord Jesus Christ, and you have the same sin emphasized in each case.

Then notice, the apostle draws our attention to the fact that the commandment having special reference to obedience to parents is marked out in a peculiar way. In the Law we read, "Honor thy father and thy mother; that thy days may be long upon the land which the Lord thy God giveth thee" (Exod. 20: 21). Read the ten commandments. You see you have four of them with no special promise attached, and then you come to the fifth and you find that God added something.

He added a special promise. It shows the importance that He attaches to obedience to parents.

How important, then, that Christian children
should lay this to heart. Do not be content with
lip service, do not be content with attending Sunday School and attending the church and young
people's meeting, and think that these things constitute Christianity. First learn to show piety at
home. It is in the home circle that your life is
under closest inspection, and it is there you are
called upon to give evidence of a second birth by
obedience to your own parents.

Then in verse 4 the apostle speaks to fathers.
He does not address himself here particularly to
mothers. He says, "Ye fathers, provoke not your
children to wrath." You see, it is we fathers who
are more inclined to become impatient and unduly
harsh and unkind with our children, and yet on
the other hand, let me point out that in Hebrews
11, where the Spirit of God is speaking of Moses,
exactly the same word that is used here and translated "fathers" is used for Moses' parents. "By
faith Moses, when he was born, was hid three
months of his parents." The word "parents"
there is exactly the same Greek word that is
translated "fathers" in Ephesians 6:4. Fathers
and mothers are in this sense addressed together,
and so the admonition comes home to every one
with perhaps peculiar emphasis being placed upon
the fathers.

"Ye fathers, provoke not your children to wrath." As Christian parents, have in mind your children's well-being, do not be needlessly demanding of them, do not lay upon them burdens that are too hard for them to bear, for remember, as the children have the Lord Jesus as their example, you have God Himself as yours.

We read, "Like as a father pitieth his children, so the Lord pitieth them that fear Him," and, "If we call Him Father who without respect of persons judgeth according to every man's work," see that you walk circumspectly before Him. Let your attitude toward your children be in accordance with His attitude toward you, and of Him it is written, "He doth not afflict willingly nor grieve the children of men." How we need to take this home to our hearts. "Ye fathers, provoke not your children to wrath;" but bring them up in the nurture and admonition of the Lord, setting them an example of what a Christian should really be, ministering the Word of God to them, praying with them, and walking before them consistently, in the fear of the Lord.

I remember the bitterness with which a young woman, attending a university, came to me and said, "I am in the greatest spiritual distress, and the saddest thing about it is that I cannot consult my own father, who is a minister of the gospel. But I never remember to have heard him lift his voice in prayer with his family, and I never knew him to gather us about him while he read the Word of God. He kept all of his religion for the pulpit, and we never saw any of his piety in the home." It is in the home we are called first to manifest godliness, to give prayer and the Word of God their proper place. Let the grace of Christ be seen in your life, and though everything else should go, your children will have the memory of godly parentage and pious upbringing. What a sheet-anchor that has been to many young persons launching out in life.

In verse 5, the apostle turns to consider another relationship. He says, "Servants," whether they be in the home or employees outside. At the time the apostle wrote, they were slaves, generally speaking. The word *doulos*, translated here "servants," means slaves, one purchased, but you notice in verse 8 he is thinking not merely of the purchased slaves, "Knowing that whatsoever good thing any man doeth, the same shall he receive of the Lord, whether he be bond or free." And therefore the instruction which of old was given to slaves now applies to all employees. Slaves were purchased with the money of the master, or born into the house and raised up by the master, but today we enter into an agreement, we sell our labor, and in that way enter into a certain relationship which makes us just as responsible to heed the admonition given here. There would never be trouble between capital and labor if the

Word of God were properly revered in this connection, if the instruction given here had proper place in all our hearts and lives. However, it is not expected that unsaved men will heed this admonition, but he is addressing Christian employees. "Servants, be obedient to them that are your masters according to the flesh, with fear and trembling, in singleness of your heart, as unto Christ." That means, of course, the fear of **not rendering** proper service to your employer, **and so** of grieving the Holy Spirit of God.

How this dignifies labor! Whether a man be working at the bench, whether one be engaged in the office, whether the miner be down in the bowels of the earth, or the farmer working on the surface of the earth, each may say to himself, "I serve the Lord Christ." When Carey applied for foreign missionary service, somebody said to him, "What is your business?" They intended it as a slur, for he was not a minister. He said, "My business is serving the Lord, and I make shoes to pay expenses." And so every one engaged in any occupation should be able to say, "My business is serving the Lord, and whatever my occupation, that is to pay my expenses, but I am there to serve Him."

"Not with eyeservice, as men-pleasers." I was looking up that word "eyeservice" and found it to be very interesting. It comes from exactly the same word as that translated "servants" in verse

5, and that is, properly speaking, "a slave." Eye-service, then, would be eye-slavery. Did you ever know any one who was an eye-slave? The man who soldiers at his work until somebody says, "The boss is coming!" The young woman who wastes her employer's time until somebody says, "Look out, there is the manager coming through the office," and she immediately gets busy and the typewriter rattles as it has not done for hours. That is eye-slavery. Do not let there be anything like that with the Christians. "Not with eye-service, as men-pleasers; but as the servants of Christ, doing the will of God from the heart." Does not this dignify labor in a wonderful way? No matter what my employment is, I am to do it as unto God from the heart. It is the place in which He has set me and I am there to labor for Him. This lifts me far above all concern about the failure of an employer to properly recognize my worth. When I know I am working for the Lord and He knows everything, it saves from all such thoughts. "Ye are bought with a price; be not ye the servants of men" (1 Cor. 7: 23). I may have an employer who does not seem to appreciate me at all, who only wants to get all he can out of me and pay as little as possible, but I have sold my labor to him, and therefore I go on and labor earnestly. I say to myself, "Never mind, there is One who does appreciate, and He knows that I am doing this work in an

upright manner and doing it for His glory, and
some day I shall receive of Him." "Oh, yes, yes,"
you say; "that is all very well. Religion is the
opiate of the people." People of Communistic
tendencies say, "You like to preach resignation to
the poor and tell them that no matter how hard
their lot is here it will be right when they get
to heaven, in order to keep them contented here."
Not at all, that is not what the apostle is saying.
"Be not deceived, God is not mocked, for whatsoever a man soweth that shall he also reap." It
is true in this life as well as in the world to come
that the one who honestly serves the Lord Jesus
Christ is rewarded for it. How many a man
can bear testimony to that! One has labored apparently unappreciated for years until suddenly
under the hand of God circumstances change so
that he is recognized and honored and respected
for what he really is. The Lord sees to this even
in this life, and there is a great deal more coming
in the life ahead.

Now he turns to the masters, Christian masters, again we have to say. "And, ye masters, do
the same things unto them, forbearing threatening: knowing that your Master also is in heaven;
neither is there respect of persons with Him."
"The same things"—you expect your employees
to honor you, to recognize their responsibility to
rightly serve you. Very well, now, masters, it is
your responsibility to properly consider the wel-

fare of your employees; you have been trusted with means or have been put in a position where you administer the means of others—see that you do not look upon your employees as mere "hands," and so much labor to be ground from them, just to get the very most out of them and give the very least; but remember that as they are responsible to serve the Lord Christ, so are you, and you are to do it to His glory.

"Forbearing threatening." Nothing of an unkind, cruel, or discourteous character is to be seen in the Christian master, "Knowing that your Master also is in heaven," and that you have to give an account, therefore, for all your dealings with your employees. If you cut down their wages when it is not necessary, if you seek to force them to work under unhealthful and insanitary conditions, God is looking on and jotting everything down in His books of record when He sees that you behave in an unchristianlike way toward those dependent largely upon you because working for you. See how Christianity equalizes everything. Here is the true socialism, not a leveling of all distinctions, but men and women of every class subject to Christ. That puts everything right. "Ye masters, do the same things unto them, forbearing threatening: knowing that your Master also is in heaven; neither is there respect of persons with Him." Your wealth will not avail if you do not handle it correctly, your place of authority will amount to naught if you do not use it for His glory. "There is no respect of persons with Him." He judgeth according to the works of each one.

What salutary instructions we have here! How important that every Christian, whatever his relationship, should act in accordance with this truth. In the beginning of this epistle we have the highest kind of of spiritual revelation. There it is that we learn that we have been raised up together and seated together in heavenly places in Christ. "Very well," says the apostle, "if you are a heavenly man, a heavenly woman, a member of the Body of Christ, now behave on earth as Christ would if He occupied your position in life, whatever your business may be. Let the Spirit of Christ be manifested in you." This is the thing that will commend Christianity to a lost world.

We have had too much talking of high truth coupled with low living. We have had too much delight in wonderful dispensational unfoldings and yet the truth never affecting the feet. "Order my steps in Thy truth," prays the psalmist. Oh, may God grant that whether as husband or wife, child or parent, employee or employer, we may each one who names the name of Christ manifest His grace in every relationship of life.

If today you are unsaved and you have sometimes stumbled over the inconsistency of Christians, let me say that the Word of God takes it for granted that Christians need constant admonishing, but you are invited to come just as you are to Christ, trust Him as your Saviour, receive the divine life by faith, and then live as a Christian should, and show the rest of us what a real Christian ought to be. Do not be foolish enough to stumble over any one's else inconsistency down to the pit of woe. Remember, there is power to make you what you ought to be, and to make you to be a Christian not in word only but in deed and in truth.

THE CHRISTIAN'S CONFLICT

✓ ✓ ✓

"Finally, my brethren, be strong in the Lord, and in the power of His might. Put on the whole armor of God, that ye may be able to stand against the wiles of the devil. For we wrestle not against flesh and blood, but against principalities, against powers, against the rulers of the darkness of this world, against spiritual wickedness in high places" (Eph. 6: 10-12).

✓ ✓ ✓

WE have already tried to point out the correspondences between this New Testament letter and the Old Testament book of Joshua. We have seen that in the book of Joshua we have the Israelites, a redeemed people, entering upon their possession, the land of Canaan. In the Epistle to the Ephesians we have believers, moved upon by the Spirit of God, entering in possession of that which is now their portion in Christ. We are told of our heavenly inheritance, not merely something which is to be ours when we die and leave this world, or when our blessed Lord comes and summons us to be with Himself, but we are told that here and now we have been blessed "with all spiritual blessings in heavenly places in Christ." There is a grand, a wonderful sphere of blessing which God would have us enter into in spirit while we are in this world as to the body.

A great many people are accustomed to think of Canaan as representing only heaven after death, and therefore they think of the river Jordan as always representing death itself. If you will stop and think for a moment, you will realize that there is a sense in which Canaan could scarcely represent the heaven to which we are going in all its fulness, because it was after the people of Israel entered that land that their real conflict began. They found it was already tenanted by hostile nations who immediately rushed to arms to withstand the people of Israel, and who sought to keep them from the enjoyment of that which God had given them. When you and I who are saved are finally called away from this world, we are not going to the other side for conflict, we shall not find ourselves engaged in battle with evil spirits in heaven. But as believers in the Lord Jesus Christ, when we seek here on earth to appropriate the blessings that are already ours in Him, we find at once that there is a host of evil powers seeking to keep us out of the experience of these precious things. Therefore, we can see how Canaan represents primarily our present place of blessing in the heavenlies. The armies of Canaan, disputing Israel's possession, represent what we have here in verse 12, the principalities and powers, the world-rulers of this darkness, who are doing their utmost to keep Christians living on a low, worldly level, and thus failing to enjoy the victory that is theirs by right because of their relationship to the Lord Jesus Christ.

We have considered the Christian home and the Christian household, and reading those precious verses we found ourselves in an atmosphere of peace and blessing such as the unconverted know nothing of. When Paul wrote this letter, there were very few Christian homes in the world, but, thank God, as a result of the proclamation of the truth during nineteen centuries, all over this and other lands may be found homes that answer to what we have here in Ephesians—homes where husband and wife together are seeking to glorify the Lord Jesus Christ, each giving honor to the other, each seeking to fulfil his or her place in the economy of the family, and where the children are growing up in the nurture and admonition of the Lord, where masters and servants alike recognize their responsibility to the great Master in heaven who was once a Servant here on earth.

It is very striking that as we turn from the beautiful description of the Christian household we immediately find ourselves in an altogether different atmosphere. The apostle has barely concluded his admonition to husband and wife, parents and children, masters and servants, before he speaks of warfare and conflict; for we cannot always enjoy the sweetness and quietness of a Christian home. We have to go out into the world, we have to go out into life, there to meet cruel enemies on every hand who seek to disrupt and destroy our Christian experience and endeavor in every possible way to lead us to do or say things that will bring dishonor on the name of our blessed Lord. We go from the home to the battle-field.

We are reminded, as the apostle closes his letter, that we are not yet in heaven, we have not reached the rest that remains for the people of God, and therefore he says, "Finally, my brethren, be strong in the Lord, and in the power of His might." Perhaps it might be rendered, "My brethren, be daily strengthened," for it is in the continuous tense; be constantly receiving strength from the Lord and go forth in the power of His might. It is important to realize that even after we have been converted for many years we have no more power in ourselves to insure victory over the foe than we had when first saved. The excellency of the power is not in us but in God, and therefore the necessity of living in communion with Him. The preacher cannot do his work aright unless in communion with God, the choir cannot sing aright, the workman at his bench or machine cannot do his work aright and bring glory to the name of the Lord Jesus Christ, the young woman at her desk, the man selling goods upon the street, the farmer at the plow, cannot work aright unless in communion with God. We all need His mighty quickening power to enable us to triumph in our respective spheres just as much as any missionary going to a foreign field to carry the gospel to lost men and women. Here is a challenge to everyone of us. We must face it for we cannot overcome in our own strength, therefore the importance of living near to the Lord, being strengthened in the Lord and in the power of His might.

"Put on the whole armor of God, that ye may be able to stand against the wiles of the devil." This is the armor that we have delineated for us piece by piece in the next section of the epistle. But the armor is of God, it is nothing of ourselves, for we have nothing in ourselves whereby we can meet the foe. "Put on the whole armor of God, that ye may be able to stand against the wiles of the devil." It is not only here but in other scriptures as well that the apostle by the Spirit insists upon this. In Romans 13:11 we read, "And that, knowing the time, that now it is high time to awake out of sleep: for now is our salvation nearer than when we believed. The night is far spent, the day is at hand . . . let us walk honestly, as in the day; not in rioting and drunkenness, not in chambering and wantonness, not in strife and envying. But put ye on the Lord Jesus Christ, and make not provision for the flesh, to fulfil the lusts thereof." How many a Christian has forgotten words like these, and forgetting them has found himself absolutely powerless in the hour of temptation, unarmed, exposed to every imagination of a cruel foe. "Put on the whole armor of God."

Then again, in 2 Corinthians 10, the apostle speaks of this same warfare. He tells us that it is not a conflict with the flesh. We are not told to fight the flesh but to reckon ourselves dead to sin in the flesh. Our conflict is with the fallen spirits that dominate this present age of evil. These spirits, of course, cannot indwell believers, but they can do a great deal in the way of alluring believers into by-paths where they bring dishonor to the name of the Lord. In verses 3-5 we read, "For though we walk in the flesh, we do not war against the flesh: for the weapons of our warfare are not carnal, but mighty through God to the pulling down of strongholds. Casting down imaginations [or human reason, for Satan works through the mind, getting men to reason rather than to believe what God has revealed in His Holy Word], and every high thing that exalteth itself against the knowledge of God, and bringing into captivity every thought to the obedience of Christ." Here, then, is our conflict. We are exposed to these evil spirits who are haters of God and of our blessed Saviour and therefore seek to bring dishonor upon the Lord, upon that holy Name whereby we are called, by leading us off into things that grieve the Holy Spirit and bring discredit upon our testimony. How needful then the admonition, "Put on the whole armor of God, that ye may be able to stand against the wiles of the devil."

It would be a very simple thing if the adversary of our souls came to us honestly and said, "Good morning. I am the devil, and I want you to get into something that is going to cause you a lot of misery and wretchedness, and which will dishonor your Saviour; and if you will only listen to me and obey me, I will be able to accomplish this." We would have no difficulty in saying to him, "Get thee behind me, Satan: for thou savorest not the things that be of God, but the things that be of men" (Mark 8:33). But he does not come that way. He is transformed into an angel of light, and he seeks to deceive us. Here we read of the *wiles* of the devil. The word, "wile," is the very one from which we get our English word "method," but it implies a subtle method or craftiness. He is an old campaigner; he has been at the business of deceiving men and women for at least six millenniums, and he knows exactly how to approach every individual soul as he comes with his crafty method. You get an illustration of that in the book of Joshua.

God had told Joshua to cross over Jordan and that he would find there the seven nations of Canaan. They were corrupt and abominable, given to all kinds of vileness and idolatry, and the

Israelites were commanded not to enter into any leagues or marriages with them, but to destroy them utterly. The words were plain, and for a time Joshua and the people carried them out implicitly. But one day there came a strange-looking group of men limping up the highway, dressed in rags. They had worn sandals on their feet, and carried on their arms old sacks which contained moldy bread. Their goat-skin water-bottles were cracked and dried up. Some of Joshua's scouts went out to see them and asked, "Who are you, and what do you want?"

"We would like to see your general," they said.

And so they were led into the presence of Joshua, and he inquired, "Well, what is it you want with us? Where do you come from?"

"From a very far country," they said. "You see these clothes of ours. They were brand-new the day we left home and you can realize that we have come a long way. These sandals were bought from the shoe-dealer the day we left. This bread was brought fresh from the oven, but now it is all moldy. We have come a long distance because we have heard of you and of how God is with you. We would like to make an alliance with you. Let us be friends. We would be very proud to be linked up with you, and we hope that you will be willing to make an alliance with us."

"This is most interesting," said Joshua; "you

say you are from a long way off. How did you hear about us?"

"Oh, the word is going all through the land. We heard of the victory as you entered the land, how Jericho and Ai fell before you. Let us get together and make an alliance."

And we read that the men made a league with them and asked not counsel of the Lord. Thus they were deceived by the wiles of the Gibeonites. A day or two after they had made the league, when there was no chance to break it, they found out that these men came from a nearby village and were anxious to link up with them in order to save their own lives. How the devil has wrought along that line through the years! One of his first attempts to corrupt the Church of God is by getting unconverted people into its fellowship. Today the membership of churches is largely made up of unsaved men and women. When it comes to public service for the Lord, one of the great abominations in the church today is that of unconverted people joining together in a choir to professedly sing the praises of the Lord. Choirmembers who are flirting with the world are just as truly a hindrance to the work of God as the preacher flirting with the world. It is one of the wiles of the devil to try to mix the saved and the unsaved together. Of course there is no blessing when such a condition exists. Oh, to be out and out for God!

We are to stand against the wiles of the devil, recognizing this, that we wrestle not against flesh and blood. We have no quarrel with men, no fight with our fellow-beings, we are not wrestling with flesh and blood but against principalities and powers. These are the principalities of fallen angels who are marshaled under the skull and cross-bones banner of the devil himself. "Against principalities, against powers, against the rulers of the darkness of this world, against spiritual wickedness in high places." It might be translated, "Against the world-rulers of this darkness." Who are the world-rulers of this darkness? They are the great evil powers, evil angels, who are seeking to control the hearts of those in authoritative positions in the world, to hinder men and women from subjecting themselves to the truth of God. Take the last great world conflict. Who were the rulers of the world? "Well," you say, "there was President Wilson, King George of England, Kaiser Wilhelm of Germany, King Victor Emmanuel of Italy." No, they were not the actual rulers of the world; they were simply like the pawns upon the chess-board. The world-rulers were the wicked spirits endeavoring to influence the hearts of men and move them for the destruction of the human race. So malignant is the spirit of these evil beings spoken of here in the Word of God that we are not competent to meet them; we cannot face foes like these and come forth victorious save as we put on the whole armor of God, save as we draw our strength day by day from our blessed Lord Himself, and as we use the sword of the Spirit which is the Word of God.

When we get home to heaven our conflict will be over. But you ask, "Do we not read of conflict there?" In Revelation 12 we read: "Michael and his angels fought against the dragon; and the dragon fought and his angels, and prevailed not; neither was their place found any more in heaven. And the great dragon was cast out, that old serpent, called the Devil, and Satan, which deceiveth the whole world: he was cast out into the earth, and his angels were cast out with him." You see when we go up, he, the mighty foe who throughout the centuries has been the accuser of the people of God, comes down. But our conflict is while we are still in this world. I am afraid a great many Christians never realize this; they never stop to think that day by day Satan and his hosts are doing their very best to keep them from honoring the Lord Jesus, to keep them from prayer, to keep them from the study of the Word, to bring into their lives something that will bring discredit on the Saviour's name, and consequently we see today a largely divided Church simply because believers do not know what our conflict is. "We wrestle not against flesh and blood, but against principalities, against powers, against the rulers of the darkness of this world, against spiritual wickedness in high places."

Note that last expression, "Against spiritual wickedness in high places." It seems as though the translators of our beautiful Authorized Version hardly dared accept what this passage really teaches, although they have put in the margin the rendering that makes it clear. It is, "Against wicked spirits in heavenly places." It is an altogether wrong thought that Satan and his hosts are already confined in hell. Quite the contrary is true; they are still in the heavenly places. That does not mean that they are in the immediate presence of God. In Scripture, we have three heavens: the heaven where the birds fly, the atmosphere; and then the stellar heaven; and beyond all that the heaven of heavens, the third heaven, the immediate presence of God. Satan and his hosts are represented in Scripture as in the lower heavens. The devil is "the prince of the power of the air." And inasmuch as the eyes of the Lord are everywhere, he is pictured as in the very presence of God as the accuser of the brethren. Our conflict is with these wicked spirits.

We may well sing:

> "A charge to keep I have,
> A God to glorify,
> A never-dying soul to save,
> And fit it for the sky."

We have been saved as far as deliverance from the guilt of our sin is concerned, but we are now to be saved practically by conformity to Christ and subjection to the Word of God, that thus we may be fitted in the fullest possible sense for fellowship with Him. May God give us to be on our guard, to remember that we cannot put the sword out of our hand, that we cannot rest upon past victories as long as we are in this scene. "Let him that thinketh he standeth take heed lest he fall." And yet there is no reason for discouragement because, as our faith and trust is centered in Christ, we may know that "greater is He that is in you than he that is in the world."

THE WHOLE ARMOR OF GOD

✓ ✓ ✓

"Wherefore take unto you the whole armor of God, that ye may be able to withstand in the evil day, and having done all, to stand. Stand therefore, having your loins girt about with truth and having on the breastplate of righteousness; and your feet shod with the preparation of the gospel of peace; above all, taking the shield of faith, wherewith ye shall be able to quench all the fiery darts of the wicked. And take the helmet of salvation, and the sword of the Spirit, which is the Word of God: praying always" (Eph. 6: 13-18).

✓ ✓ ✓

AS we have considered the Christian's conflict we have found that it is not with flesh and blood, nor is it with our own carnal nature, for we have not been called upon to fight with that but simply to deny it, to refuse its claims. It is a conflict with the wicked spirits in the heavenlies who would seek to keep us from the blessed enjoyment of our portion in Christ. This they do in many insidious ways as well as by open manifestations of warfare. We are to stand against the wiles of the devil, for in every conceivable manner he will seek to hinder us from making progress in our Christian lives, in our Christian experience, and therefore, we need to be constantly upon the watch and we need to be accoutered with the whole armor of God.

"Wherefore take unto you the whole armor of God." This is something very different from the garments in which we stand before God through grace. Every one of us who have put our trust in the Lord Jesus Christ has been made the righteousness of God in Him, the best robe is his. We stand before God in Christ, but we do not put this on ourselves. God has clothed us. But when it comes to the panoply for conflict, we need to put on each separate piece of armor in order to withstand in the evil days when the hosts of hell are pressing upon our souls and it seems as though we would be borne down and defeated. We are not to turn our backs and flee from the foe. We are not to act on the presumption that "he who fights and runs away may live to fight another day," but we are to face the foe, for there is no armor for the back. If we turn our backs, if we retreat, we but expose ourselves to the fiery darts of the wicked one, but as we face the foe unflinchingly in the power of the finished work of Calvary we shall be able to stand.

"And having done all, to stand." Where and how do we stand? Is it simply by determination of our own, in some goodness of our own? Not at all. But we stand in the perfection of Christ's finished work. The foe cannot harm us there. We meet the foe in the name of Christ, the Victor. We claim victory over him because of the One who has already defeated him on the cross. There Satan bruised the heel of our blessed, divine Redeemer, but his own head was bruised also, and now we are entitled to consider the devil as one already defeated. But, though he knows he is defeated and that his doom is sure, he will do everything he can to harass and distress the Christian as long as he is in this scene. Therefore the need of standing strong in faith, resisting the devil in the power of the cross of Christ.

"Stand therefore, having your loins girt about with truth." That may seem to us Occidentals a somewhat awkward expression. There would be no question in the mind of an Oriental, for he wears long flowing garments in which he is perfectly comfortable when just moving about at leisure; but if going on a journey or engaged in any kind of conflict, he must draw them up about his waist, holding them in by a girdle, so as not to impede his efforts or hinder progress. Just so, you and I as believers are to have our loins girt about with truth. What does he mean? Elsewhere we read, "Gird up therefore the loins of your minds." Just as the Orientals' flowing garments are to be rightly girded that they may not be carried about by the wind, so we are to have the loins of our minds girt about with truth in order that our imaginations may not be "carried about by every wind of doctrine, by the sleight of men, and cunning craftiness, whereby they lie in wait to deceive." We are to gird up, to draw up, the loins of our minds, "bringing every thought into captivity to the obedience of Christ." In other words, our minds are to be controlled by what God has spoken, not by what we think.

I wish Christians would come back to the Book. I am often distressed when people ask me, "What do you think about this, or what do you think about that?" And I have to tell them, "It does not make any difference what I think. My thoughts do not amount to anything. The great question is, What has God said? What is written in the Word?" If the Word does not speak, we have no right to attempt to speak, but where it has given a clear definite declaration, we should be positive and sure in our faith. That is what it is to have the loins of the mind girt about with the truth of God, our thoughts all brought into subjection to His Holy Word. How important that is when you have to face the devil, because he works through wily error, presenting all kinds of false systems and views and evil-speaking in regard to Christ. It is only as our minds are controlled by the Word that we will be able to meet these things. The better you know the Bible, the better fitted you are to meet the assaults of the enemy, and yet some of you have never even read your Bible through once. Have you? You have never gotten beyond the genealogies. You came right up against them and stopped. You never went any farther. You did not know that hidden in those genealogical chapters there are some of the most beautiful little gems you will find anywhere in the Bible. You will miss them if you are not careful.

A friend of mine used to tell of listening to Andrew Bonar many years ago. Dr. Bonar was speaking on heaven and the great reunion of loved ones over there, and in his eloquent way he pictured the believer newly come from earth walking along the golden street and suddenly coming right up against a group of Old Testament sages and prophets. In a moment he recognizes them and says, "Why, this is Ezekiel; isn't it?"

"Yes," says Ezekiel, "I am so glad to meet you."

"And this is Micah and Zechariah and Amos."

And then Andrew Bonar said, "And just imagine Ezekiel saying, 'Oh, you knew about me; did you? How did you like the book I wrote?'

'Book? What book was that?'

'Oh, surely you remember my book! Did you enjoy it?'

'I am sorry to say I never read it.'

"And then Micah would say, 'And what did you think of my book?'

'Let me see; was that in the Old Testament or in the New Testament? It seems to me I remember there was such a book.'

"How would you feel to have to meet these men when you never have read their books?"

Some of you had better get busy. There is far too much time spent in reading novels and in reading the newspapers and too little time given to the Word of God. Good literature is fine, reading the newspaper is all right, but these things should not crowd out time for reading God's Word.

There was an old Scotchman who could neither read nor write. His minister wanted to teach him and so, although he was very busy, he arranged to go to this man's house for an hour every day and teach him. He took the Gospel of John as a text-book, and the old Scot was greatly interested. By-and-by the minister was called away for a time, and when he came back he wanted to see how his pupil was progressing. He went to his home, but the man was not there. The minister asked the wife how her husband was getting along with his reading. "Oh," she said, "he is doing very well."

"Is he able to read now?"

"Yes, he is doing wonderfully."

"Is he able to enjoy the reading of his Bible?"

"Oh," she said, "he has gotten away out of the Bible and into the newspaper long ago."

Remember, the Bible is the only Book that will last for all eternity, and anything you get out of it here you will have for all the ages to come.

And then we are to have on "the breastplate of righteousness." I want you to follow me carefully here, for sometimes I have difficulty in making this verse clear to people. It is a blessed truth that we have been made the righteousness of God in Christ. It is a wonderful thing to know that righteousness is imputed instead of sin to every believer in the Lord Jesus; but that is not the righteousness referred to here. You see, you and I do not put on the righteousness of God. God does that for us. But here is something we are to put on. Turn back to Isaiah 59, the portion that the apostle evidently had in mind. You will see that the righteousness referred to is practical righteousness. "And he saw that there was no man, and wondered that there was no intercessor: therefore His arm brought salvation unto Him; and His righteousness, it sustained Him. For He put on righteousness as a breastplate, and an helmet of salvation upon His head; and He put on the garments of vengeance for clothing and was clad with zeal as a cloke" (Isa. 59: 16, 17). Isaiah speaks here of the Messiah, our blessed Lord. He put on righteousness as a breastplate. That is something different from what was always His in eternity. He came into this world as a Man, and, as a man, was obedient in all things to the will of God. He put on righteousness as a breastplate, and now you and I are called to imitate Him by putting on the breastplate of righteousness.

The breastplate covers the heart of the man, and when we think of the heart we think of the conscience; and mark this, unless you as a Christian keep a good conscience in regard to practical living, you will never be able to defeat your foe. When the devil comes against you and you know there is some hidden sin in your life, you will go down, you will not be able to stand against him. How many a one has failed when Satan made a tremendous assault upon him, and people said, "Wasn't it sad?—such a failure and coming so suddenly." But it was not suddenly, for there had been an undermining going on weeks and months and perhaps years, little unrighteousnesses indulged in here and there, unholy thoughts, wicked things going on that were not dealt with in the presence of God; and when the foe came there was an exposed breast because righteousness had not been put on as the breastplate. Go to deal with the unsaved, and if they know that you do not have on the breastplate of righteousness, your testimony will not amount to very much. You may say to a friend, "I would like you to come to meeting with me," and he may say to you, "I don't know, Jack; but it doesn't seem to have done very much for you." He has been watching you day by day in your work and has seen that you are just as irritable and impatient, that you have just the same meannesses that others have, and he says,"You may talk about good meetings at your church, but I do not see that they have done much for you." You have not the breastplate of righteousness on. If you want to win in this battle, you must practise righteousness. Your life must be clean, there must not be hidden sin, or unholy thinking tolerated, no unrighteousness in your life covered up, if you would have victory in this conflict. That is what the breastplate of righteousness means. Do not talk about being made the righteousness of God in Christ if you are not living righteously, for when God justifies a man He makes him just. He justifies us by faith, but having been justified He now makes us just in our dealings with other people.

Then, some of us need a new pair of shoes. "And your feet shod with the preparation of the gospel of peace." What does that mean? It means walking in accordance with the gospel. You tell men that you have been saved by the grace of God, that you have peace with God. Very well, let your life show it, let your walk be in accordance with that. There is also the suggestion of feet swift to carry the gospel of peace. The latest Spanish translation of this is, "Having your feet shod with a joyful readiness to propagate the gospel of peace." But we are not to go about propagating the gospel of peace by word of mouth unless we are living in the power of it and walking in it ourselves. Otherwise we just bring dishonor upon the name of the Lord Jesus Christ.

And then over all, "Taking the shield of faith, wherewith ye shall be able to quench all the fiery darts of the wicked." The shield covered all the rest of the armor. It is the shield of confidence in God. That is what faith is. It is not "the" faith; it is not *what* you believe, but *how* you believe. It is faith in the sense of confidence, trust—going to meet the foe with your trust not in yourself but in the living God. Here is a preacher who stands up to preach the gospel to an audience, and says, "Well, I have an old sermon here. I have used it seventy-two times already; it is nearly worn out, but I think it will do for this audience. Yes, I think I will use it again. I remember years ago there were eighteen converted when I preached this sermon, and it is still good." The devil hears all that, and he says, "I will show you that you have come up against a greater foe than you realize." The meeting is a poor, wretched failure, and the preacher says, "I do not understand it. I have preached that sermon any number of times. I wonder what the trouble was." It was that the confidence of the preacher was in himself instead of in the living God. I do not care how many times you have preached on a text, if you ever dare to stand up before an audience when you go to preach the Word without getting your message fresh from the living God and going out in confidence in Him instead of in yourself, you will be a failure. I want that lesson to be impressed upon my own heart, that is why I am putting it so strongly to you. "Having the shield of faith, wherewith ye shall be able to quench all the fiery darts of the wicked."

Now there is something for our heads. "And take the helmet of salvation." That is, if I have any doubt as to my own salvation, I will have no real confidence when it comes to facing the foe. Therefore, for a helmet, I take the knowledge of salvation that He has given through His Word.

Then we read, "And the sword of the Spirit, which is the Word of God." Do not make a mistake here; the sword of the Spirit is not the Bible. This Bible is not the sword of the Spirit, it is the armory. There are thousands of swords in here and every one of them is powerful and two-edged. There are two different terms in Greek for "word." There is *"logos,"* which is the term we usually use, but the other word, *"rhema,"* is the one used here. It means, "a saying." "And the sword of the Spirit, which is the saying of God." If the devil comes and you throw the Bible at him, it is not going to drive him away. You might do that, and go down yourself. But when he comes, and you say, "Here is what God says," and you have a definite saying of God to meet the case, you defeat him. Take the example of the blessed Lord in the wilderness. The devil came so cunningly and said, "If Thou be the Son of God, command that these stones be made bread." Jesus answered, "It is written, Man shall not live by bread alone, but by every word that proceedeth out of the mouth of God." He took the sword out of the armory. You need to know your Bible so that you will be able to meet the devil whenever he comes with these suggestions. Then the devil showed Jesus all the kingdoms of the world, and said, "All these things will I give Thee, if Thou wilt fall down and worship me." Out came another sword and the Lord went at the devil with it. He replied, "It is written, Thou shalt worship the Lord thy God, and Him only shalt thou serve." Then the devil tried to use the saying of God himself. He took Jesus up on a pinnacle of the temple and said, "It is written, He shall give His angels charge concerning Thee: and in their hands they shall bear Thee up, lest at any time Thou dash Thy foot against a stone." Think of the effrontery of the devil quoting Scripture, and that to the Lord of life and glory Himself! But he left out the most important part of the verse. It reads, "For He shall give His angels charge over Thee, to keep Thee in all Thy ways. They shall bear Thee up in their hands, lest Thou dash Thy foot against a stone." The Son of God was not falling from the temple in order that men should see Him borne up by angel hands. That was not part of "His ways." The Lord used another "saying" from the Book of God; He said, "It is written again, Thou shalt not tempt the Lord thy God." The sword of the Spirit is the saying of God. Get to know your Bible, and then when the devil comes against you, you will be able to say, "But the Book says thus and so," and you will have the Word for him.

If we want the blessing of God, we must walk in obedience to His blessed Word.

But now after all this, when you have the various parts of the armor in place, there is something that must never be omitted. Bunyan speaks of it as actually a part of the armor. He says, "In addition to all the rest there was a piece called 'all prayer.'" "Praying always with all prayer and supplication in the Spirit." You see, the armored believer is independent of the devil because he is utterly dependent upon God, and prayer is the source of his dependence. But we must consider this more fully in our next chapter.

PRAYER AND SUPPLICATION IN THE HOLY SPIRIT

✦ ✦ ✦

"Praying always with all prayer and supplication in the Spirit, and watching thereunto with all perseverance and supplication for all saints; and for me, that utterance may be given unto me, that I may open my mouth boldly, to make known the mystery of the gospel, for which I am an ambassador in bonds; that therein I may speak boldly, as I ought to speak. But that ye also may know my affairs, and how I do, Tychicus, a beloved brother and faithful minister in the Lord, shall make known to you all things: whom I have sent unto you for the same purpose, that ye might know our affairs, and that he might comfort your hearts. Peace be to the brethren, and love with faith, from God the Father and the Lord Jesus Christ. Grace be with all them that love our Lord Jesus Christ in sincerity. Amen" (Eph. 6: 18-24).

✦ ✦ ✦

WE have been considering the armor of the Christian soldier. We have noticed that he is to put on the breastplate of practical righteousness, that he is to have his feet shod with the preparation of the gospel of peace. In other words, his walk is to be in accordance with the gospel. Then in the third place, he is to have his loins girt about with truth, and, fourth, he is to take the shield of faith, of confidence in God wherewith to quench the fiery darts of the foe. On his head he is to have the helmet of salvation, for no one can go forth with boldness to meet Satan and his cohorts unless he has the assurance of his own salvation through the finished work of Christ. Then he is to have in his hand the sword of the Spirit, which is not merely the Word of God in the sense that the Bible is the Word, but, as we have seen, the "saying" of God. He is to know his Bible so well that he can draw from this blessed armory the particular saying that he needs at a given moment. In addition to this, he is to keep the line of communication between himself and his God clear.

Some of you remember that during the late World War a regiment went into the Argonne Forest and was lost. For days they were out of touch with headquarters and we were reading about the "lost regiment." When at last they were located, their ranks had been sadly decimated. When a Christian in the conflict with Satan gets out of touch with headquarters, it is a terrible thing. The apostle, after indicating the various pieces of armor, says, "Praying always with all prayer and supplication in the Spirit." The trouble with many of us is that we pray only when we get into difficulty, when times are hard and circumstances are going against us. Then we remember the Word, "Call upon Me in the day of trouble: I will deliver thee, and thou

shalt glorify Me" (Ps. 50: 15). But we would be
spared a great many of our troubles if we continued instant in prayer; if, when everything was
going well with us, we were just as faithful about
the hour of prayer as when things were going
against us. "Praying always with all prayer."

God declares in His Word that He will not hear
the prayer of the wicked. It is an abomination
to the Lord, and David says, "If I regard iniquity
in my heart, the Lord will not hear me." But if
I have judged all known sin and have on the
breastplate of righteousness, I am in that attitude,
that position, where I can pray in confidence.
"All prayer" is an approach to God, but note the
added word, "supplication." This suggests definite petition. It is one thing to approach God in
prayer with a heart full of praise and thanksgiving and in a general way commit one's affairs
to Him. It is another thing to come with a very
definite supplication for a particular matter, for
special trouble at a given time. We read, "Be
careful for nothing; but in everything by prayer
and supplication"—there you have the same word
again, it is prayer and petition—"with thanksgiving, let your requests be made known unto
God. And the peace of God, which passeth all
understanding, shall keep your hearts and minds
through Christ Jesus" (Phil. 4: 6, 7). No difficulty that I have to face is too great for God, and
nothing that troubles me is too insignificant for
His care.

Arthur T. Pierson sat with George Mueller one day, and Mr. Mueller was telling him of some of the wonderful things that God had done for the orphanage at Bristol. As he talked he was writing, and Dr. Pierson noticed that he was having difficulty with his pen-point. Right in the midst of the conversation Mr. Mueller seemed to lose sight of his visitor, he bowed his head for a moment or two in prayer, and then began writing again. Mr. Pierson said, "Mr. Mueller, what were you praying about just now?" "Oh," Mr. Mueller said, "perhaps you didn't notice that I was having trouble with this pen-point. I haven't another, and this is an important letter, so I was asking the Lord to help me so that I could write it clearly." "Dear me," said Dr. Pierson, "a man who trusts God for millions of pounds also prays about a scratchy pen-point." Yes, you may go to Him about everything.

Then notice, it is "prayer and supplication in the Spirit." And that may check many of us when it comes to the hour of prayer. Prayer in the Spirit is prayer in accordance with the mind of the indwelling Holy Spirit of God. No unconverted person, of course, can pray in the Spirit, but there are even Christians who are in such a low carnal condition of soul that it is impossible for them to pray in the Spirit. I cannot pray in the Spirit if I am harboring a grudge against my brother. I cannot pray in the Spirit if there is anyone I will not forgive because of some real or fancied wrong done to me. I cannot pray in the Spirit if I have a selfish motive, if I am seeking merely my own glory or comfort. I cannot pray in the Spirit if I have a covetous heart.

You remember the Apostle James says, "Ye ask and receive not, because ye ask amiss, that ye may consume it upon your lusts" (James 4:3). I can pray in the Spirit only as I am walking in the Spirit, as I am living in the Spirit. Then He, the blessed Third Person of the Trinity, who dwells in every believer, will guide my thoughts aright as I come to God in prayer. Very often one goes to God about certain things when in an unspiritual state, only to find out when restored to fellowship that he would be better far without them, and so he no longer asks for them. In the Old Testament we read, "Delight thyself also in the Lord, and He shall give thee the desires of thine heart." If I am really delighting myself in the Lord, I will want only those things which will glorify God, I will not be asking from a selfish viewpoint. I shall want God to do for me that which will magnify Christ in my life and make Him more precious to my soul.

"Praying always with all prayer and supplication in the Spirit, and watching thereunto with all perseverance." "Watch and pray," our Lord Jesus Christ said, "lest ye enter into temptation," and this, of course, only emphasizes what we have seen already. If I would pray aright, I must live aright, and so I am to watch against anything that would come into my life to grieve the Spirit of God and thus hinder real prayer.

Then, observe, the Lord would not have me concerned only with my own affairs. He says, "And supplication for all saints." A brother beloved said to me the other day, "For years my interests have largely been in the work in which I myself was engaged, or in connection with certain institutions in which I had a part, but I find the Lord is drawing me in these days to think of His work everywhere, and of His people in every place." This surely is an evidence of growth in grace. We are so inclined to narrow down our thoughts to our own little circles. We may not pray in the same way as the man who said, "God bless me, and my wife, our son John, and his wife. Us four, and no more," but we do pray most earnestly for those connected intimately with us. We should do this, but in addition let us consider the whole Church of God; let us think of all His beloved people in every place, and bear them up in the arms of our faith and love. If in this way we go to God, we will never lack subjects about which to speak to Him.

Some years ago I was visiting a very devoted company of Christians in a western State. They had some rather peculiar ideas. They came together weekly to study the Bible, and for preaching, and remembering the Lord in observing His Supper, but they had no prayer-meeting. I said to them, "Do you never have a prayer-meeting?"

A brother said, "Oh, no; we have nothing to pray for."

"How is that?" I asked.

"Why, God has blessed us 'with all spiritual blessings in heavenly places in Christ,' so we do not need to pray for spiritual blessings. We do not need to pray for temporal blessings, for we have everything we need. We are well cared for; we have all the land we know how to till. We do not need to pray for money, for we have plenty to keep us going. We do not need to pray for wives, for we are all married. We do not need to pray for children; I have thirteen, and Brother So-and-So has fifteen. We have nothing to pray for, so we just give God thanks."

"My dear brother," I said, "I wish, if for nothing else, you would come together to pray for me."

"We can do that at home," he said. "If we came together to pray we wouldn't have anything to say."

"But what about the word, 'And supplication for all saints?' Suppose you do nothing else but come together to remind one another of the Lord's dear children that you know, and spend an hour telling God about them."

But he did not see it. They seemed to have no idea of what prayer really is. Sometime after that I was in Minneapolis. One day I tumbled over, and when I came to I had a fever of one hundred and four degrees. I was on my back with typhoid fever for six weeks. When at last, a year later, I got out to that same section, they said to me, "When we got word that you were so very sick, we had two prayer-meetings a week to pray for you, and our hearts were greatly burdened, but as soon as we got word that you were well enough to go home again, we stopped." "Why did you stop?" I asked. "When flat on my back, I did not have any trouble with the devil, but when strong and well and I have to go out to face the foe, I need prayer far more." He looked at me in amazement and said, "I never thought of it in that way." The Apostle Paul himself not only exhorted saints to pray for one another, but he said, "And for me, that utterance may be given unto me, that I may open my mouth boldly." I am sure that those of us who stand on public platforms and preach Christ will never know until we get to heaven how much we owe to the prayers of God's hidden ones. It has often come like a benediction when some dear saint, possibly a shut-in, writes to me and says, "My dear brother, daily in prayer I remember you and the work that God has given you to do." How much it means to know that all over this and other lands there

are prayer-helpers who are crying to God, "Keep
that brother from blundering, keep him from sin."
There are temptations on every hand, and how
much the man who stands in the pulpit needs
divine help that he may be kept from anything
that would mar his testimony.

"Pray," says the apostle, "for me, that utterance may be given me, that I may open my mouth
boldly, to make known the mystery of the gospel."
Sometimes God's dear children are far more
ready with criticism of preachers than they are
with prayer for them. They say, "Well, I don't
know; but Mr. ——— doesn't seem to me to have
much power, he doesn't seem to have much gift,
he doesn't seem to make things very clear." And
I often feel like saying, "Do you ever pray for
him that he may have power, that he may have
clarity to so preach the truth that men and women
will believe?"

In Acts 14: 1 we read that the apostles "so
spake that a great multitude believed," which implies that one may so speak that no one will believe. What is needed is not only the word of the
preacher, but that message backed up by the
prayers of the people of God. It is a blessed thing
to know that one is being borne up by the saints
in prayer. Paul valued this, and he was the
greatest of all the apostles in his ministry. I am
sure that at the judgment-seat of Christ, when
our blessed Lord is giving a reward to the Apostle

Paul, He will call up many of the saints of whom we have never heard and have them stand with Paul, for they were his fellow-helpers in his ministry, and He will say, "You held up his hands in prayer, and you must share in the reward."

He speaks of making known "the mystery of the gospel." This does not mean that it is something hard to understand, but it is a divine secret that man would never have guessed if God Himself had not made it known. One reason why I am absolutely certain that the gospel is of God is, that no man left to himself would ever have dreamed of telling us that God became Man to save us from our sins. All human religions take the opposite viewpoint. They try to tell us how man may save himself and eventually obtain a position akin to the Godhead. But not one of them tells us that God became Man to save us from our sins. This is the mystery of the gospel, the divine secret that we are called upon to proclaim to men.

"I am an ambassador in bonds." What a remarkable declaration! The ambassador from the court of St. James comes to Washington and has his many medals and decorations on him, but here the ambassador of the highest court of heaven says, "Do you want to see my decorations?" And he points to his fetters and says, "I am an ambassador in chains." Somebody has well said, "God is not going to look us over for medals and decorations but for scars, to see what we have endured for Christ's sake." He was a suffering, afflicted, jailed ambassador, and he says, "Pray for me, that I may speak boldly, as I ought to speak." And right there in the prison he witnessed for Christ. The very soldiers who were guarding him heard the story of salvation. We read in another of his epistles, "All the saints salute you, chiefly they that are of Caesar's guard." Our Authorized Version says, "Caesar's household," but he is not talking about Caesar's butler and baker and candlestick-maker, but of his soldiers. They probably were heathen when set to guard him, but Christians before they got through with him. He preached the mystery of the gospel to them and their souls were saved. How much of that was in answer to prayer we will never know until the books are opened in that day.

In the next two verses he gives us the only personal word in the epistle in which he names any one else other than himself and the Lord. "But that ye also may know my affairs, and how I do, Tychicus, a beloved brother and faithful minister in the Lord, shall make known to you all things: whom I have sent unto you for the same purpose, that ye might know our affairs, and that he might comfort your hearts." In Acts 20:4 we read of Tychicus. He was an Asian. Ephesus was in Asia, and probably Tychicus was well-known to these brethren, so Paul sent him back in order to give a report as to how things were going with him. Notice the language he uses concerning him, "A beloved brother and faithful minister in the Lord." In Colossians 4:7 he says, "All my state shall Tychicus declare unto you, who is a beloved brother and a faithful minister and fellow-servant in the Lord · Tychicus must have been a very delightful man to meet. It is not often the two things are combined in one man— beloved and faithful. Generally your beloved brother is so gracious and gentle and easy-going that everybody likes him because he does not find fault with anyone, and they say, "Isn't he nice?" It is like the lady who, after she had listened to a Scotch preacher, was asked, "What did you think of the sermon? Wasn't it beautiful?" "Yes, it was beautiful," she said; "but it wouldn't hurt a flea." They like the preacher who does not hurt anybody, who draws beautiful word-pictures, etc., and who never reproves sin. "A good mixer," they call him today. That is the very thing Paul said we were not to be. "Come out from among them, and be ye separate." But as a rule they are the beloved kind. On the other hand, the faithful brother is apt to be so rigid that he gets a little bit legal, and goes around clubbing this one and that one, and saying, "I don't care what people think of me; I am going to be faithful." He is rather disagreeable, you know. You do not like to get too close to men like that. But Tychicus combined in himself the beloved pastor and the faithful exhorter. That is a wonderful combination, too high for most of us to attain to.

And then in verses 23, 24 we have the closing words. You will observe there are no personal salutations in Ephesians. The reason probably was that the Epistle to the Ephesians was a circular letter, intended not only for the saints in Ephesus, but sent around a circle of assemblies until it reached Laodicea. Paul, writing to the Colossians, said, "Read the epistle from Laodicea." Some think of this as a lost letter, but it is undoubtedly this letter to the Ephesians, and on account of its general character there are no personal salutations for individuals in the Ephesian church.

"Peace be to the brethren, and love with faith, from God the Father and the Lord Jesus Christ" —that peace which is the portion of all who have learned to commit everything to the care of our blessed Saviour. "Love," love for all saints, coupled with faith in the Lord Jesus Christ, the gift of God the Father in His blessed Son.

He closes with the characteristic Pauline salutation, "Grace be with all them that love our Lord Jesus Christ." And then he adds a very searching word at the very end, "in sincerity." The marginal translation is "in incorruptness." In other words, those who love our Lord Jesus Christ will manifest it by holy living. It is only thus we show in a practical way that we are one with Him in the heavenly places.